# Fundamentals of Academic Writing

# Fundamentals of Academic Writing

Noushad Husain

SHIPRA

₹ 1600
US$ 64
ISBN: 978-93-88691-88-8

First Published in India in 2021

*Fundamentals of Academic Writing*



Published by:
**SHIPRA PUBLICATIONS**
LG 18-19, Pankaj Central Market
I.P. Ext., Patparganj, Delhi 110092, India
Tel.: +91 11 2223 5152/6152; 96500 28065
E-mail: info@shiprapublication.com
www.shiprapublication.com

Author Gratefully Acknowledges his Indebtedness to

**God**

For His Mercy

Dedicated to

My Wife **Razda Khan** and

My Children **Arsh Husain** & **Areeb Husain**

"WRITING

IS

THE PAINTING

OF

THE VOICE"

– Voltaire

# Preface

Academic writing is an *art*, *science* and *craft*. It is an *art* because academic writing is an expression of you and your thinking. As an academic writer, one needs to find the strategies that work best and develop the writing style that is most effective in conveying one's message to the intended readers. Academic writing is also a *science* in that there are genres, structure and form of academic writing that should be the base of your academic writing. Academic writing can also be described as a *craft*. A craft is a skill or a set of some specific skills developed over time through experience. We cannot expect to be master of academic writing after the completion of one course or reading of one or two books on academic writing or by writing one or two articles or papers for journals or magazines. For mastering over academic writing, it needs practice, experience, reflections and a desire to improve.

Academic writing is different from simple writing as it has some specific rules and follows some skills. It is written in a systematic and scientific manner with a specific style. Students, research scholars and some teachers face various difficulties in the development of their academic writing skills. As an academic writer, we should have the capacity to present our ideas, thoughts and thinking in words.

Academic writing is often highly problematic but potentially a transformational activity. Despite great diversity within and between different academic disciplines, several common themes are associated with the experience of writing in academia. This book aims to identify and explore these common themes to help its readers to become a more effective writers with healthier, more analytical and positive approaches to what it means to be an academic and more particularly what it means to be a writing of academic text.

Quality academic writing is aimed at students, M. Phil. and Ph.D. Scholars and faculty in all the disciplines. Writing is an integral part of the process of research. It also facilitates success in academics. Through academic writing, we have to demonstrate our knowledge and insights whether we are students, research scholars or teachers. When attempts are made to teach writing, the focus seems to be more on getting sentences grammatically correct rather than on presenting knowledge in ways that make reading and comprehension easy. The aim of the present book is to guide students, researchers and teachers to refine their academic writing, so that they do well in their studies, publish in national and international journals and make themselves more useful to society.

We hope that the reflections, strategies, guidance and advice that this book contains will help to make your academic writing effective, pleasurable and satisfying.This book describes the place of academic writing in the broader process of research and creation of scientific knowledge, distinguishes academic writing from other forms of writing, describes the process of composing academic research papers, articles and reports and provides guidelines for appropriately acknowledging the use of others' work in one's academic writing.

This book has been developed for better academic writing in easy and simple language. Figures, structures, samples and tables have been extensively used for better understanding, clarity and the characterization of academic writing as a part of research (knowledge generation process) and science. It also contains a few hypothetical examples of various components of conceptual and empirical papers. I shall be grateful to the readers if they provide their valuable suggestions.

I thank a lot of my indebtedness to 'God for His Mercy' because without the mercy of God, the present work could not have been completed. He gives me direction, knowledge, support and patience to write down the book.

I show my gratitude towards all those thinkers, writers, authors and publishers whose works have been consulted, quoted and abstracted to make the book up-to-date and useful for its users.

With great pleasure, I express my thanks to my family members, specially my son Arsh Husain and Areeb Husain, for their encouragement and support. In the end, I am thankful to Mr. D. Kumar, Shipra Publications for the meticulous processing of the manuscript and publishing this book with accuracy and style.

**Prof. Noushad Husain**

6 June 2021
Bhopal, India

# Contents

# List of Figures

# CHAPTER 1

# Concept and Principles of Academic Writing

## Writing

Writing is a visual representation of speech. Writing is an act of forming letters or characters and artfully putting them together so as to express ideas. Writing is a method of representing language in visual or tactile form. Writing systems use sets of symbols to represent the sounds of speech. Some definitions of Writing are as under:

1. According to Sampon (1985: 26), *"Writing is a system for representing utterances of spoken language by means of permanent visible marks."*
2. Lado (1971) says, *"Writing is a graphic representation of a language and information is conveyed through the written medium by the use of conventional graphemes."*
3. Elbow thinks of *"writing as a kind of 'magic' that can be performed by anyone who is involved in and believes in his tale".*
4. According to Shaughnessey (1977), *"Writing is the record of an idea developing. It is a process whereby an initial idea gets extended and refined. He thinks, toys with an idea and develops it."*
5. According to Emig (1977), *"Writing allows us to have our ideas immediately available for review, reevaluation, a process that can lead us to reconsider and refine our ideas, i.e. to learn what we think by writing. Writing is a thinking process at various stages. Writing is best understood as a set of distinctive thinking processes in which writers orchestrate to organize during the act of composing. Writing is originating and creating a unique verbal constant that is graphically recorded."*
6. According to Flower and Hayes (1081), *"Firstly, writing is an act of discovery. Secondly, it is a goal-directed and purposeful activity. Thirdly, it involves a conscious exploration of the subject matter one is to write about and lastly, writing involves synthesis of complex cognitive operations and it is not a straightforward linear process but a recursive one."*

7. The *Blackwell Encyclopedia of Writings Systems* (1999), *"Writing is a set of visible or tactile signs used to represent units of language in a systematic way, with the purpose of recording messages which can be retrieved by everyone who knows the language in question and the rules by virtue of which its units are encoded in the writing systems"*

### Nature of Writing

Writing is a visual form of communication, either printed in hard-copy or in electronic form. It follows conventions that are mutually understandable by the writer and the reader, even if these conventions change over time or are used with specific meanings in smaller speech communities (e.g., special texting rules used by a group of teenagers). Writing is considered a productive skill because the writer creates new language and does not only interpret existing information.

### Differences in Speaking and Writing

Effective communication on paper is not the same as communicating through speech. Written communication follows different rules of logic, layout, conciseness and clarity which is not expected in speech. By learning these structures and formats, one can write clearly and effectively.

### Sub-skills of Writing

According to Venkateswaran (1995), the sub-skills of writing are:

1. Manipulating the script of a language–forming the shapes of letters, using the spelling system, using punctuation,
2. Expressing information explicitly,
3. Expressing information implicitly through inference and figurative language,
4. Expressing the communicative value of sentences and utterances,
5. Expressing relations within a sentence using elements of sentence structure, modal auxiliaries, intra-sentential connectors,
6. Expressing relations between parts of a text through lexical cohesion devices,
7. Expressing relations between parts of text through grammatical cohesion devices,
8. Using indicators in discourse for introducing an idea, developing an idea, transition to another idea, concluding an idea, emphasising point, explanation of point already made, anticipating an objection,
9. Reducing the text through avoiding irrelevant information.

### *Terms Used in Writing*

The main terms used in writing are:

| | |
|---|---|
| *Content* | ideas (message or content) that the author intends to convey to the audience. |
| *Genre* | type of expressive style a piece of writing has (e.g., poetry, short story, lecture notes). |
| *Lexicon* | vocabulary that is needed to convey the author's intended meaning. |
| *Grammar* | formal aspect of language (e.g., subject-verb-agreement, tense, aspect markers, references). |
| *Pragmatics* | implicit messages a text conveys to the reader; shared expectations for communication by a social group (e.g., ways to greet in a letter, appropriate ways of phrasing ideas) |
| *Orthography* | the way to write letters or symbols of written language, handwriting |
| *Mechanics* | punctuation, spelling (accuracy), capitalisation. |

### *Qualities of Good Writing*

Some important qualities of writing are discussed below:

*Simplicity:* Good writing usually aligns with the saying *'the simple, the better'*. Many people think that good writing means using difficult language and uncommon words and expressions; however, that is not true. A good composition always expresses things in the most direct and simple way. We should always aim for the simplest way to express our ideas.

*Unity:* One should require to state his/her ideas in a meaningful and logical manner so that they seem connected, if so, then his/her writing will be considered. This trait is referred to as the unity or flow of the text. The flow of a good piece of writing is a smooth sail, rather than a road full of bumps.

*Focus:* Another important quality of good writing is *focus. Focus is* not only important for the overall writing, but, it is absolutely crucial to maintain a sense of flow and unity in the writing. A good piece of writing does not bombard its readers with unnecessary information and ideas, but it is entirely focused on the central idea/plot of the writing.

*Authority:* A good piece of writing always incorporates a sense of authority. Ensuring the reader, the writer knows exactly what he is talking about. A composition is good, if the writer seems to be well-informed and credible about the subject that he is discussing. On the other hand, presenting weak or wrong information can make faulty writing and also have adverse effects on the reputation of the writer.

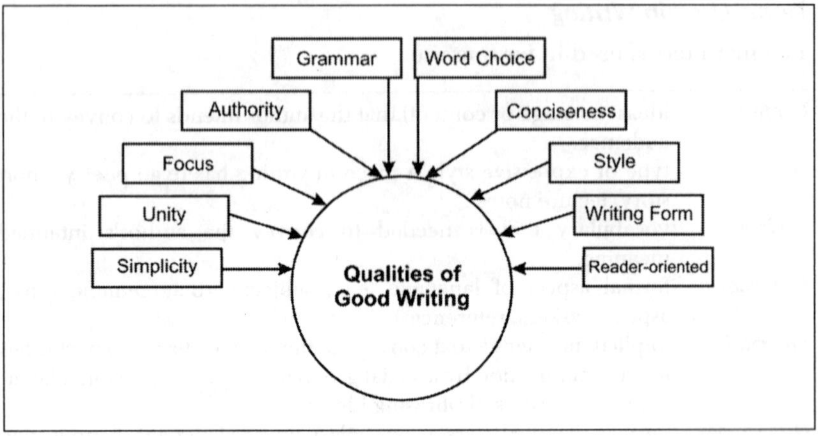


Figure 1.1: Qualities of Good Writing

*Grammar:* A good grammar skill is crucial to craft a good piece of writing. As a writer, you are supposed to follow the grammatical rules of Standard English precisely. Grammatical mistakes, spelling errors, and a weak proofreading are very likely to have a negative impact on your readers. We should pay due attention to the grammatical correctness of our text.

*Word Choice:* As a writer, you should always use words insightfully. English is one of the languages, where there are multiple words for the same idea. A good piece of writing will always incorporate the most suitable and accurate words. Good word choice greatly contributes to the clarity and readability of the text.

*Conciseness:* This is an important quality that distinguishes good writing from bad writing. To be concise means to avoid unnecessary words and fillers because they distract the readers. Sometimes writer may deliberately use unnecessary words, which makes writing difficult to it readers. This is a bad writing practice and should be avoided.

*Style:* Each writer has its unique writing style. That is why your writing style is what makes your writing unique and sets it apart from all the other writers. Your writing style plays a great role in determining whether your writing is good or bad. Writing style basically means the way the writer presents his/her text to the reader. Writer's word choice, voice, and fluency all contribute to his writing style. There are no precise rules to mark a writing style as good or bad; however, as a general guideline, a good writing style is always in line with the writer's opinion, the readers' expectations, and the topic's context.

*Writing Form:* All writing is not the same and there are different forms of writing to which the writer needs to adapt his style and content. A good academic writer is not necessarily a good short story writer; similarly, someone great at blog writing might not do well with technical writing. All the different forms of writing have a varying scope and requirements. In order to produce a good writing, it is writers' job to understand these varying requirements and craft his writing in accordance with them.

*Reader-Oriented:* A good writing is always reader-oriented. Before writing, it is important to know the audience and their needs and expectations from your writing. Whether your writing is to share an opinion, to educate your readers, or to provoke a thought; understanding your audience can greatly aid you in crafting a good composition.

### *Writing Process*

Writing is a process in which a text develops and changes all the way from first ideas to finished text. By revising and rewriting, writers develop both their thinking and their texts during this process. The writing process is often presented graphically in a manner which indicates the linear, but also cyclical nature of writing; as the text develops, writers return to previous stages of the process to make additions and to revise their texts.

The writing process can be divided into several stages. The work that is done before the writing begins, when material is collected and ideas are developed, is often referred to as the pre-writing stage or the invention stage. The actual writing of the text is often divided into stages such as drafting and revising, and the last phase of the writing process (often referred to as the rewriting stage) consists of the stages of editing, proofreading and publishing.

## ACADEMIC WRITING

Academic writing refers to a style of expression that researchers use to define the intellectual boundaries of their disciplines and their specific areas of expertise. It is conducted in several sets of forms and genres, normally in an impersonal and dispassionate tone, targeted for a critical and informed audience, based on closely investigated knowledge, and intended to reinforce or challenge concepts or arguments.

Academic writing does many of the things that personal writing does not: it has its own set of rules and practices. These rules and practices may be organised around a formal order or structure in which to present ideas, in addition to ensuring that ideas are supported by author citations in the literature.

In contrast to personal writing contexts, academic writing is different because it deals with the underlying theories and causes governing processes and practices in everyday life, as well as exploring alternative explanations for these events. Academic writing follows a particular *'tone'* and adheres to traditional conventions of punctuation, grammar, and spelling.

Academic writing is a particular style of formal and expressive writing. It is a third-person and formally-toned writing. It gives clear opinion on topic. In this form of writing, one chooses very formal and precise words. Academic writings are of different types, such as:

- Abstract writing
- Article writing
- Book writing
- Dissertation writing
- Essay writing
- Explication writing
- Report writing
- Research paper writing
- Research writing
- Review writing
- Seminar paper writing
- Term paper writing
- Thesis writing
- Translation

Academic writing is clear, concise, focussed, structured and backed up by evidence. Its purpose is to aid the reader's understanding. It has a formal tone and style, but it is not complex and does not require the use of long sentences and complicated vocabulary.

Each subject discipline will have certain writing conventions, vocabulary and types of discourse that you will become familiar with over the course of your degree.

Academic writing, in a broad sense, is any writing assignment accomplished in an academic setting such as writing books, research paper, conference paper, academic journal and dissertation and thesis. More specifically, it is a writing activity performed to fulfill a requirement of a college, university, conference and publication.

## Meaning of Academic Writing

Based on all the above, we can make the following generalisations about academic writing:

- Academic writing differs from non-academic writing because academic writing engages in theories and causes. The writing itself will likely explore alternative views and explanations of these events.
- Academic writing has its own set of rules and practices which are often set by the institution where you study, or the instructor who invites you to write. It is important that you familiarise yourself with these rules and practices.
- Academic writing is organised, ordered and structured. The organisation, order and structure of the presented ideas are important

as the text is going to be read by an audience who expects to be guided through your text and absolutely does not like reading in-between the lines.

- Academic writing is driven by references to outside sources. Often, the opinion of the author is secondary to those offered by external references and citations. In addition, these references need to support the ideas of the author.
- Academic writing follows a specific writing style reflected in the use of an academic language register. The language of academic writing is about clarity and not about sophistication.

## Definitions

Some definitions of Academic Writing are given below:

1. According to Irvin (2010), *"Academic writing is always a form of evaluation that asks you to demonstrate knowledge and show proficiency with certain disciplinary skills in thinking, interpreting, and presenting."*
2. Murray (2005) defines academic writing as *'the set of conventions used in publishing a paper, or in writing a thesis in a specific discipline'.*
3. Oshima and Hogue (2007) view that "*Academic writing is a kind of formal writing used in high schools and a college classes, which is clearly different from personal and creative writing".*
4. According to *The Oxford Companion to the English Language, "The register of English used by scholars and scientists; an elevated and often complex style associated with concern for accuracy, objectivity, and dispassionate comment."*
5. According to V. Hillard and J. Harris, *"Academic writing names the kind of intellectual prose students are expected to produce as undergraduates: writing that takes a sustained interest in an issue under consideration and gathers much of its evidence from a careful reading of sources."*
6. In view of K. Gocsik, Academic writing is *"writing done by scholars for other scholars".*
7. Academic writing can be defined as a form of expository prose which should be precise, semi-formal, impersonal, and objective.
8. Academic writing refers to a style of expression that researchers use to define the intellectual boundaries of their disciplines and their specific areas of expertise. It is conducted in several sets of forms and genres, normally in an impersonal and dispassionate tone, targeted for a critical and informed audience, based on closely investigated knowledge, and intended to reinforce or challenge concepts or arguments.

9. Academic writing is the process of breaking down ideas and using deductive reasoning, formal voice and third person point-of-view. It is about what you think and what evidence has contributed to that thinking.
10. Any writing that can either be backed up by past research to validate a certain claim or is conducted to explore a particular subject; commonly assigned by universities and colleges.
11. Academic writing can be defined as a form of expository prose which should be precise, semi-formal, impersonal, and objective.
12. Academic writing is the process of breaking down ideas in order to increase one's understanding about a particular thing. It uses deductive reasoning, semi-formal voice, and third person point of view.
13. Academic writing is the systematic processing of a topic which involves recognising the problem content of tasks, demonstrating the relevance of the subject matter of the paper, systematising thoughts, and structuring content clearly and logically, and expressing it convincingly.

In a nutshell, academic writing is a style of written expression with specific intellectual boundaries and area of expertise.

## Purpose of Academic Writing

Writers should be clear why they are writing. The most common reasons for academic writing include:

- to report on a piece of research, the writer has conducted
- to answer a question, the writer has been given or chosen
- to discuss a subject of common interest and give the writer's view
- to synthesise research done by others on a topic.

## General Characteristics of Academic Writing

There are some general characteristics of academic writing that are relevant across all disciplines:

- *Based on analysis:* Academic writing is the process of breaking down ideas in order to increase one's understanding about a particular thing.
- *Use of deductive reasoning:* In academic writing, writer first states the thesis (main idea) early and then follows with supporting examples and details, so as to make complicated ideas easier to understand.

- *Semiformal voice:* This means no slang, colloquialism (common expressions of ordinary speech), contractions of nouns and verbs, etc. are used in academic writing.
- *Third person point-of-view:* Third person points-of-view (e.g., he, she, it, and they as well as their accusative, dative, and possessive forms) should be used. No first and second person points-of-view (e.g., I, you, we) are used in academic writing.

## Characteristics of Academic Writing

The main characteristics of academic writing are discussed below:

*Develop Analytical Skills:* In academic writing, students learn to form an informed opinion by looking at the ideas and works of somebody else. It involves more than just describing their views. Students read the material and then decide on its importance as a literary work to the subject.

Students think about the reason why the study was carried out, and the findings can prove useful, in the future. The research process allows students to cover a range of material on the subject. In turn, students learn how to classify and analyse the information.

*Convey Understanding:* If students struggle with academic writing, it may be difficult for them to explain a complicated subject they have learnt. The scholarly essays that they have to write help them learn how to use the right terminology and style that will make the information easy to understand by others. It also helps students to develop a reasonable flow of thoughts with full-fledged ideas.

*Encourages Critical Thinking:* Critical thinking is a must thing for every student. Writing any essay or dissertation involves critical thinking. It demands a purposeful and reflective analysis to reach any solid conclusion of the argument. Critical thinking is important for every student because it teaches them to scrutinise every argument or the positions that they had been taking for granted their entire life.

*Makes a Good Researcher:* Writing is one of the skills which a lot depends on research skills. The more and better a student researches, the more and better he could write. This is why students should have good research if they want to complete their academic assignments. The only way we can improve our research skills is to write it down, which also increases the importance of writing.

## Key Terms of Academic Writing

The key terms of academic writing are:

*Discourse Community:* A discourse community is a group of people involved in and communicating about a particular topicor issue in a particular field. A discourse community is a group of people who share a set of discourses, understood as basic values and assumptions, and ways of communicating about those goals. Linguist John Swales defined discourse communities as *"groups that have goals or purposes, and use communication to achieve these goals"*.

According to John Swales, a discourse community is defined by six characteristics:

- A discourse community has a broadly agreed set of common public goals.
- A discourse community has mechanisms of intercommunication among their members.
- A discourse community uses its participatory mechanisms primarily to provide information and feedback.
- A discourse community utilises and possesses one or more genres in the communicative furtherance of its aims.
- In addition to owning genres, a discourse community has acquired some specific lexis.
- A discourse community has a threshold level of members with a suitable degree of relevant content and discoursal expertise.

A discourse community is essentially a group of people that shares mutual interests and beliefs. According to Porter, *"It establishes limits and regularities...who may speak, what may be spoken, and how it is to be said; in addition [rules] prescribe what is true and false, what is reasonable and what foolish, and what is meant and what not"*. People are generally involved in a variety of discourse communities within their private, social, and professional lives. Some discourse communities are very formal with well established boundaries, while others may have a looser construction with greater freedom. Additionally, discourse communities have approved channels of communication in which members write or speak through. These channels can be a web page, a journal, a blog, or any medium people use to communicate through. Examples of discourse communities may include but certainly not limited to:

- Medicine
- Law
- Psychology
- Films (Movies)
- General Forums
- Technology
- Sociology
- Philosophy
- Chemistry
- Physics
- Mathematics
- Writing
- Rhetoric and Composition

The concept of discourse community is vital to academic writers across all disciplines because the academic writer's purpose is to influence a discourse community to think differently. The discourse community can except or not to expect any writing. For this reason, the academic writer must follow the constraints set by the discourse community, so his or her ideas earn approval and respect.

*Intertextuality:* Intertextuality is the combining of past writings into original, new pieces of text. The term intertextuality was coined in 1966 by Julia Kristeva. All texts are necessarily related to prior texts through a network of links, writers (often unwittingly) make use of what has previously been written and thus some degree of borrowing is inevitable. This generally occurs within a specific discourse community.

Intertextuality, also referred to as citation, is a defining characteristic of academic writing. The felicitous incorporation of other literature in the field is an important skill because papers are unlikely to be published without reference to relevant theories and previous research. Academic writers can choose from a variety of strategies to integrate other authors' ideas into their text. Paraphrasing is one intertextual strategy alongside direct quotation, summary, and generalisation from multiple sources. In a paraphrase, the writer rephrases a passage from an author's text using their own words and grammatical structures while retaining the original proposition. Keck (2006) defines paraphrases as passages reproducing the source text that contain at least one lexical change, e.g. the insertion of a synonym. Experienced academic writers use paraphrases to minimise the similarities between their texts and the source material and to encode their own assessment of the reproduced statements.

*Types of Intertextuality:* There are two distinct types of intertextuality as defined by Porter: iterability and presupposition.

- *Iterability* is the capability of a text to be reiterated and repeated in various contexts. Iterability is explicitly seen in texts, as opposed to presupposition, which refers to assumptions a text makes.
- *Presupposition* is the process by which implications are made without being specifically stated or explained within text. These assumptions are usually extremely basic thoughts made by a vast majority of the audience; such thoughts may be considered "common sense" or otherwise obvious to anyone who reads the text.

*Examples of Intertextuality Aladdin:* The classic Disney movie *Aladdin* has many distinct examples of intertextuality throughout. For example, one scene depicts the Genie that comes out of Aladdin's lamp being pinched by a crab – the same crab from another popular Disney movie, *The Little*

*Mermaid.* In another scene, the two main characters are flying through the sky on a magic carpet and, for a moment, Zeus's temple from the movie Hercules can be seen in the background. These are examples of intertextuality because they pull from past Disney works and use them to create something new and original.

*Academic Framework:* A frame is the section in an academic paper in which a perspective that has already been accepted by a specific discourse community is presented in order to blatantly explain to the reader the point of view from which the rest of the essay will be analysed. Because of the established framework, the reader will logically understand the progression of the writer's argument because the writer has legitimised his or her claim by citing an accepted theory (framework) and thus the reader will be directed towards a particular conclusion.

Framing is a metaphor for describing the lens, or perspective, from which writers present their arguments. One can think of a frame as metaphorical glasses that are put on in order to see a topic in a new way. For example, if one is trying to analyse a situation from a psychological perspective, one may put on the "glasses" of Sigmund Freud and approach said topic from his "psychoanalytical" point of view. This frame has allowed the writer to see a topic from a particular angle. This means that one may be disregarding the socioeconomic, biological, or other lenses from which one could view a particular topic.

A frame also establishes credibility for the author in a certain field of study, or "discourse community". A discourse community can be composed of medical professionals, historians, or even the individuals that make up the readership of Wikipedia. When establishing a frame, the author is telling the discourse community that he or she is aware of what is current in the discourse and that the paper being presented has something relevant to add. Without a frame, a paper is not grounded in any particular community and thus has no academic relevance, or any legitimate importance to an academic audience. The framing concept that one chooses to use has already been accepted by the community and is thus a part of their intertextual matrix. A well-developed frame is the doorway into an academic conversation that has been going on for quite some time before one's arrival and is "still vigorously in progress" after the new argument has been established.

A paper is not about the frame itself. The purpose of an academic paper is not to rehash the concept used to frame it, but rather to use the frame as a tool (a pair of glasses) to "see" a unique claim as moulded in a certain light. No text stands alone as "the individual writer's work is part of a web, part of a community search for truth and meaning"

(Porter). In essence, a writer does not randomly come up with "new" ideas but writes about already established concepts in novel ways. This is where the frame comes in. Without a frame, an author is simply making a statement; one which has most likely already been made throughout the history of the topic or within the discourse. However, a frame gives you a way to look at your statement, an explanation for phenomena, and therefore questions to ask and research. It is the frame that allows one to establish the argument because it gives a tired topic new life or novelty.

## Features of Academic Writing

The main features of Academic Writing are discussed below:

*Complexity:* Written language is relatively more complex than spoken language. Written language has longer words, it is lexically denser and it has a more varied and specialised vocabulary. It uses more noun-based phrases. Greater use of nouns than verbs helps to construct meanings and make them compact. C. Tribble explains that *"lexically dense, nominalised styles make it possible to give prominence to certain categories of information and construct a distant impersonal relationship with the reader"* (Tribble, 1996: 21). In addition, written language has more subordinate clauses, more passives, more "that/to" complement clauses, more long sequences of prepositional phrases, more attributive adjectives and more passives than spoken language.

The following features are common in academic written texts:

- Noun-based phrases
- Subordinate clauses/embedding
- Complement clauses
- Sequences of prepositional phrases
- Participles
- Lexical density
- Passive words
- Lexical complexity
- Nominalisation
- Attributive adjectives
- Adjectival groups as complements.

*Formality:* Academic writing is relatively formal. In general, this means that the writer should avoid contractions, colloquial words and expressions, tautology, vague words or phrases and everyday similes. In a similar manner, the use of technical, elevated or abstract vocabulary, complex sentence structures and the avoidance of the personal voice (the use of I, you) are also meant by formality. D. Hacker maintains that

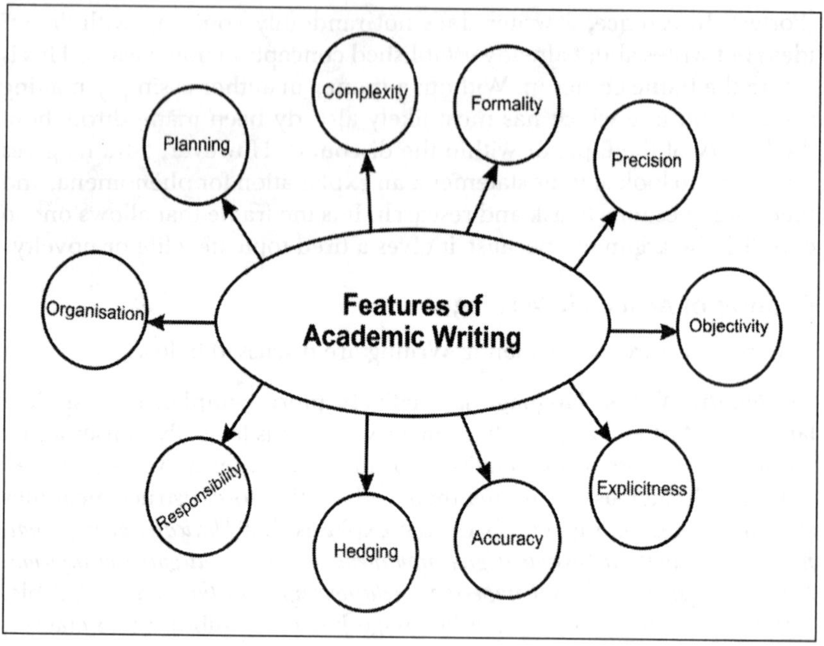


Figure 1.2: Features of Academic Writing

*"formal writing emphasizes the importance of its subject and the exactness of its information. Its tone is dignified, and it maintains a certain distance between writer and audience"* (Hacker, 1998:126).

*Precision:* In academic writing, facts and figures are given precisely. In academic writing, one needs to be precise when he uses information, dates or figures. Do not use "a lot of people", when you can say "50 thousand people".

*Objectivity:* Academic writing is, in general, objective rather than personal. It, therefore, has fewer words that refer to the writer or the reader. This means that the main emphasis should be on the information that the writer seeks to convey and the arguments he or she wants to make rather than the writer himself/herself. For that reason, academic writing tends to use nouns (and adjectives), rather than verbs (and adverbs).

This is related to the basic nature of academic study and academic writing, in particular. Nobody really wants to know what writer *"thinks"* or *"believes"*. They want to know what writer has studied and learned and how this has led him (writer) to express his various conclusions. The thoughts and beliefs should be based on writer's lectures, reading, discussion and research and it is important to make this clear.

Table 1.1: Differences between the Personal and the Objective Writing

| *Personal* | | *Objective* |
|---|---|---|
| personal writing | → | more objective academic writing |
| telling one's own story | → | commenting on, analysing and evaluating someone else's ideas |
| using everyday words | → | subject specific vocabulary |
| information from your own experience | → | using information from a variety of sources |
| personal feelings and views | → | views expressed on the basis of evidence |

*Source: Academic Style, The Open University, 2004, <http://www.open.ac.uk/study-strategies/english/pages/academic_2.asp>*

One of the key steps of academic writing, therefore, is to learn to move from the personal to the objective while writing. Table 1.1 shows how the two varieties of conveying information differ.

*Explicitness:* Academic writing is explicit about the relationships in the text. It is the responsibility of the writer to make it clear to the reader how the various parts of the text are related. These connections can be made explicit by the use of different signalling words.

Academic writing is explicit in several ways:

- It is explicit in its signposting of the organisation of the ideas in the text. As an academic writer, it is his responsibility to make it clear to his reader how various parts of the text are related. These connections can be made explicit by the use of different signalling words.
- It is explicit in its acknowledgment of the sources of the ideas in the text. Academic writer should present the source of the ideas and acknowledge it properly.

*Accuracy:* Academic writing uses vocabulary accurately. Most subjects have words with narrow specific meanings. Linguistics distinguishes clearly between *"phonetics"* and "phonemics". In academic writing you need to be accurate in your use of vocabulary. Do not confuse, for example, *"phonetics"* with *"phonology"*, or *"grammar"* with *"syntax"*. Choose the correct word. You also need to be accurate in your use of grammar.

*Hedging:* In any type of academic writing the writer does, it is necessary to make decisions about his or her stance on a particular subject, or the strength of the claims he or she is making. Different writers prefer to do this in different ways. A technique common in certain kinds of academic writing is known by linguists as a *'hedge'*.

*"Hedging refers to the way in which a writer shows the extent to which he or she wishes to be responsible either for the accuracy of the ideas being put forward or for the ideas themselves"* (Tribble 1996:100). R.R. Jordan (1997:240-243) also claims that a feature of academic writing is the need to be cautious in one's claims or statements and presents the following taxonomy of hedges:

- *Shields*, e.g. all modal verbs expressing possibility; semi-auxiliaries like: to appear, to seem; probability adverbs like: probably, likely.
- *Approximators*, e.g. of quantity, degree, frequency and time viz. approximately, roughly, often.
- *Expressions* such as 'to our knowledge', etc. which express the author's personal doubt and direct involvement.
- *Emotionally-charged intensifiers*, such as: extremely interesting, particularly encouraging.
- *Compound hedges*, i.e. the juxtaposition of several hedges, e. g. It may suggest that..., It seems reasonable to assume..., We might possibly be wrong (though it is not likely), etc.

It is often believed that academic writing, particularly scientific writing, is factual, simply to convey facts and information. However, it is now recognised that an important feature of academic writing is the concept of cautious language, often called "hedging" or "vague language".

Table 1.2: Language used in Hedging

| *Sl. No.* | *Language Used* | *Examples* |
|---|---|---|
| 1. | Introductory verbs | Seem, tend, look like, appear to be, think, believe, doubt, be sure, indicate, suggest |
| 2. | Certain lexical verbs | Believe, assume, suggest |
| 3. | Certain modal verbs | Will, must, would, may, might, could |
| 4. | Adverbs of frequency | Often, sometimes, usually |
| 5. | Modal adverbs | Certainly, definitely, clearly, probably, possibly, perhaps, conceivably |
| 6. | Modal adjectives | Certain, definite, clear, probable, possible |
| 7. | Modal nouns | Assumption, possibility, probability |
| 8. | That clauses | It could be the case that.<br>It might be suggested that.<br>There is every hope that. |
| 9. | To-clause + adjective | It may be possible to obtain.<br>It is important to develop.<br>It is useful to study. |

In other words, it is necessary to make decisions about your stance on a particular subject, or the strength of the claims you are making. Different subjects prefer to do this in different ways.

*Responsibility:* In academic writing, you are responsible for demonstrating an understanding of the source text. You must also be responsible for, and must be able to provide evidence and justification for, any claims you make. This is done by 'paraphrasing' and 'summarising' what you read and acknowledging the source of this information or ideas by a system of 'citation'.

*Organisation:* Academic writing is well organised. It flows easily from one section to the next in a logical fashion. A good place to start is the genre of your text. Once you have decided on the genre, the structure is easily determined. Academic writers write many different kinds of texts. Depending on the subject, these could be essays, laboratory reports, case-studies, book reviews, reflective diaries, posters, research proposals, and so on and are normally referred to as genre families or genres.

Genres are defined by their purpose, their audience and their structure. The following genres are common in higher education:

- Essays
- Reports
- Case studies
- Research proposals
- Book reviews
- Brief research reports
- Literature reviews
- Reflective writing
- Introductions
- Research methods
- Research results
- Research discussions
- Writing conclusions
- Research abstracts
- Research dissertations and theses

*Planning:* Academic writing is well planned. It usually takes place after research and evaluation, according to a specific purpose and plan.

The following procedure is typical when writing an extended essay or assignment:

Table 1.3: Tasks Used in Academic Writing

| *Sl. No.* | *Task* |
|---|---|
| 1. | ▶ Read the question or brief and understand what you are required to do.<br>▶ Think about the subject, the purpose and the audience. |
| 2. | ▶ Think about what you know about the subject.<br>▶ Write it down in some way. |
| 3. | ▶ Go to the library or internet and find relevant books, articles or websites. |

*(Table 1.3 Contd.)*

*(Table 1.3 Contd.)*

| *Sl. No.* | *Task* |
|---|---|
| 4. | ▶ Find the books on your reading list – if you have one – and study them. |
| 5. | ▶ Make notes on these books and articles.<br>▶ Record full details of the materials you use. |
| 6. | ▶ Organise your piece of work. |
| 7. | ▶ Type or write your first draft. |
| 8. | ▶ Discuss your first draft informally with friends, other members of your class and your lecturer if possible. |
| 9. | ▶ Revise your first draft, bearing in mind any comments that were made in your discussions.<br>▶ Go back to Point 2. if necessary<br>▶ Produce your second draft. |
| 10. | ▶ Proofread your draft. |
| 11. | ▶ Produce a final typed version. |
| 12. | ▶ Check everything. |

## Principles of Academic Writing

The principles of academic writing are:

*Clear Purpose:* The goal of academic writing is to answer the question, the writer posed as his topic. Writer's question gives him a purpose. The most common purposes in academic writing are to persuade, analyse/synthesise, and inform.

*Persuasive Purpose:* In persuasive academic writing, the purpose is to get your readers to adopt your answer to the question. So, you will choose one answer to your question, support your answer using reason and evidence, and try to change the readers' point of view about the topic. Persuasive writing assignments include argumentative and position papers.

*Analytical Purpose:* In analytical academic writing, the purpose is to explain and evaluate possible answers to your question, choosing the best answer(s) based on your own criteria. Analytical assignments often investigate causes, examine effects, evaluate effectiveness, assess ways to solve problems, find the relationships between various ideas, or analyse other people's arguments. The "synthesis" part of the purpose comes in when you put together all the parts and come up with your own answer to the question. Examples of these assignments include analysis papers and critical analyses.

*Informative Purpose:* In informative academic writing, the purpose is to explain possible answers to your question, giving the readers new

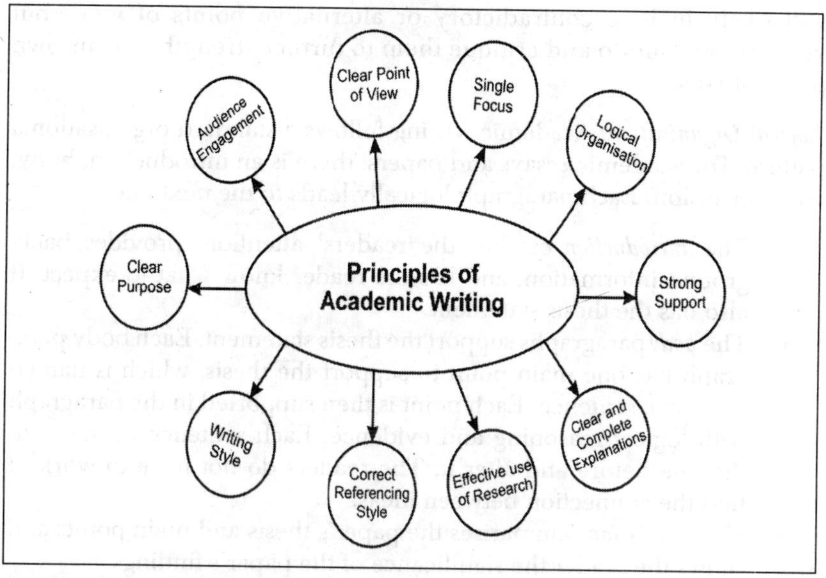


Figure 1.3: Principles of Academic Writing

information about your topic. This differs from an analytical topic in that you do not push your viewpoint on the readers, but rather try to enlarge the readers' view.

*Audience Engagement:* As with all writing, academic writing is directed to a specific audience in mind. Unless your teacher says otherwise, consider your audience to be fellow students with the same level of knowledge as yourself. As students in the field, they are interested in your topic, but perhaps not so interested in reading a paper. So, you will have to engage them with your ideas and catch their interest with your writing style. Imagine that they are also skeptical, so that you must use the appropriate reasoning and evidence to convince them of your ideas.

*Clear Point of View:* Academic writing, even that with an informative purpose, is not just a list of facts or summaries of sources. Although you will present other people's ideas and research, the goal of your paper is to show what you think about these things. Your paper will have and support your own original idea about the topic. This is called the thesis statement, and it is your answer to the question.

*Single Focus:* Every paragraph (even every sentence) in your paper will support your thesis statement. There will be no unnecessary, irrelevant, unimportant, or contradictory information (Your paper will likely include contradictory or alternative points of view, but you will respond to and critique them to further strengthen your own point of view).

*Logical Organisation:* Academic writing follows a standard organisational pattern. For academic essays and papers, there is an introduction, body, and conclusion. Each paragraph logically leads to the next one.

- The *introduction* catches the readers' attention, provides background information, and lets the reader know what to expect. It also has the thesis statement.
- The *body* paragraphs support the thesis statement. Each body paragraph has one main point to support the thesis, which is named in a topic sentence. Each point is then supported in the paragraph with logical reasoning and evidence. Each sentence connects to the one before and after it. The readers do not have to work to find the connection between ideas.
- The *conclusion* summarises the paper's thesis and main points and shows the reader the significance of the paper's findings.

*Strong Support:* Each body paragraph will have sufficient and relevant support for the topic sentence and thesis statement. This support will consist of facts, examples, description, personal experience, and expert opinions and quotations.

*Clear and Complete Explanations:* This is very important! As the writer, you need to do all the work for the reader. The reader should not have to think hard to understand your ideas, logic, or organisation. English readers expect everything to be done for them; your thoughts and thought processes should be clearly and completely explained.

*Effective Use of Research:* The paper should refer to a variety of current, high-quality, professional and academic sources. You will use your research to support your own ideas; therefore, it must be integrated into your writing and not presented separately. That means that source material will be introduced, analysed, explained, and then cited. Research and APA Style Guide 2010 covers this topic in depth.

*Correct Referencing Style:* All academic papers should follow the correct referencing style e.g. APA, MLA, Chicago regarding in-text citations, the reference list, and format.

*Writing Style:* Because this is your work, you should use your own words whenever possible. Do not try to write like a boring, overly formal scholarly article. Use the natural conversational style that you would use in the classroom. Your writing should be clear, concise, and easy to read. It is also very important that there are no grammar, spelling, punctuation, or vocabulary mistakes in academic writing. Errors convey to the reader that you do not care.

## Structure of Academic Writing

*Introduction:* The introduction (opening paragraph) basically accomplishes two goals:

1. Gains the reader's attention
2. Identifies the focus, or thesis, that is developed in the main part (body) of the essay.

There are several ways to draw the reader's attention to the subject:

- Open with a series of questions about the topic.
- Present startling or unusual facts or figures.
- Define an important, subject related term.
- Quote a well known person or literary work.

*Body:* Developmental paragraphs (body paragraphs) are the heart of an essay.

- They must clearly and logically support the thesis.
- They must be arranged in the best possible way, e.g. chronologically, order of importance, etc.

The paragraphs should flow smoothly from one to the next, e.g. the first sentence in each new paragraph serves as an effective link to the preceding paragraph. In addition, minor supporting ideas are linked together within the paragraphs in a smooth manner.

*Conclusion:* The conclusion is the summary paragraph. It should accomplish the following:

- Remind the reader of the paper's thesis by paraphrasing it.
- Tie together all of the important points in the essay by way of a summary and draw a final conclusion for the reader.

## Stages of the Academic Writing

Writing usually takes place in steps or stages. There are five stages or steps in the writing process. (1) Getting ideas or Prewriting: free writing, brainstorming, questioning, clustering and Venn diagram, (2) Writing: making brief outline and drafting, (3) Revising, (4) Editing, (5) Proof Reading, and (6) Publishing.

1. *Prewriting*

Prewriting covers all the thinking and planning you do for a writing assignment. It includes thinking about the assignment, identifying a topic, collecting details, and creating a writing plan.

Prewriting is the first stage of the writing process. Prewriting, as its name suggests, is something you do before you write a paragraph or essay or other written work. The purpose of the prewriting stage is to find a topic for writing, to collect ideas and information, and to do research if necessary. There are many different types of prewriting that help writers generate ideas. The different types of prewriting that we will explore here are: free writing, brainstorming, clustering, questioning, and Venn diagram.

Figure 1.4: Stages of the Academic Writing

*Freewriting:* Freewriting is when someone writes freely what comes to mind in sentences or phrases, without worrying about grammar, punctuation or making sense. Free writing is also a very useful technique. Here you just write down whatever comes into your mind about the topic. Continue writing for sometime without stopping to worry about grammar or spellings, etc.

*Brainstorming:* Brainstorming or listing is when you freely write down all ideas in the order which they occur to you. For ideas jot down points or ideas and their details as they come to your mind. Just write them down without putting them in any special order. Try to accumulate as many details as you can think of. This is one strategy of beginning an essay.

*Questioning:* When you prewrite with the questioning technique, you are trying to find out the How? Who? What? Where? When? and Why? about your topic.

*Clustering:* Clustering, or mind mapping is a "visual of outlining", putting the main topic in the center of paper and lining it with any new ideas associated. You can also group sub-ideas around this new idea. This strategy allows you to collect ideas effectively and, particularly, understand the logic contained between ideas.

Here you begin by writing your subject or topic in the centre of a blank sheet of paper. Then as ideas come into your mind you put them down in boxes or circles around the subject or topic. You will now see a sample of clustering.

*Venn diagram:* A Venn diagram is used to help visualise the similarities and differences between two subjects. Venn diagrams are very useful when brainstorming a compare and contrast essay.

2. *Writing*

Writing the first draft means getting your ideas on paper. A first draft is your first look at your writing and your first chance to see how well things are coming together. This stage involves mainly two activities, namely making brief outline and drafting.

*Making Brief Outline:* Prepare a rough outline. This is going to be the backbone or skeleton on which the rest of the writing will be built. It shows at a glance the point of the paragraph and the support for that point. It will help you to see if you need to do more writing to clarify your main point or its support. Example of an outline is as follows:

Biography of a celebrated man

- Friends and enemies
- school fellows – pranks, conversations
- offices held, distinguished figures
- relatives – accounts of his acts of humanity and virtues.

*Drafting:* Drafting is the second stage of the writing process. At this stage, the writer should write a complete first draft using his or her notes from prewriting as a guide. The purpose in drafting is to have a complete draft, not a perfect one, so writers are encouraged to ignore spelling or grammar mistakes and write quickly.

3. *Revising*

Revising refers to changing and improving your first draft. It is your opportunity to think about what you have written and then add, cut, or change it as needed. Your goal is to make all of your ideas clear and complete.

Revising is the third stage of the writing process. In fact, to revise means literally to "re-see" or "re-look" at your writing. When you revise, you look at the parts of your essay and make sure that each part works together to make a coherent whole. Similarly, feedback from others can help you identify those parts of the essay that work well – and those that do not. Revising often includes adding, cutting, moving, or changing information in order to make the ideas clearer, more accurate, more interesting, or more convincing.

Revising means that you rewrite, build upon what has been written to make it better. It is at this stage that you get rid of unnecessary material, improve on what you are going to retain. A typical revision means writing on two or more drafts. Here you insert details left out, put in transition words which would make smoother reading. If you are working on a word processor take out a hard copy so that you can see your entire document at one time.

4. *Editing*
Editing is checking your revised writing line by line for errors. Also proofread for errors after writing the final copy of your writing. Editing is the fourth stage of the writing process. In this stage, you check your text to make sure that there are no errors in grammar, punctuation, and spelling.

5. *Proof Reading*
This is the final stage in the writing process. It means checking carefully for spelling, grammar, punctuation and other errors. Use your dictionary for this purpose. Proof reading is often hard work and students want to avoid proofing. If proofing is done carefully, it will ensure that your written work looks as good as possible.

6. *Publishing*
Publishing refers to sharing the final copy of your writing. Publishing comes in many different forms depending on the purpose and audience for your writing.

This is the last stage of the writing process. In this stage, you share the essay you have written with the readers you determined in the pre-writing stage. The purpose of publishing is to share and celebrate your finished products. When writers publish their writing, they produce a clean, neat final draft that is free of errors.

## Heterogeneity of Academic Writing

On looking more closely at examples of academic writing across disciplines, it becomes quite clear that each discipline has its own special norms

Table 1.4: A Continuum of Academic Knowledge (taken from Hyland 2009: 63)

| *Sciences* | *Social Sciences and Humanities* |
| --- | --- |
| *HARDER* ⟺ | *SOFTER* |
| Empirical and objective | Explicitly interpretative |
| Linear growth of knowledge | Dispersed knowledge |
| Experimental methods | Discursive argument |
| Quantitative | Qualitative |
| More concentrated readership | More varied audience |
| Highly structured genres | More fluid discourses |

and customs when it comes to text and information structure. To some extent, this is true also for grammatical and lexical aspects. No doubt, the aforementioned norms stem from a long, historical process in which disciplines follow ontological and epistemological traditions and ideals.

## Academic Disciplines and Disciplinary Domains

Hyland (2009: 62-63) argues that the dividing line in the history of science and scholarship has run between natural sciences and technology on the one side, and humanities and social sciences on the other.

Hyland's schematic distinction between the more comprehensive disciplinary domains, as he calls them, offers a general, and perhaps predominantly general view, but a view which at the same time is problematic. To say that some disciplines belong to a more hard or soft domain obscures the fact that a subject within a discipline can have one foot in each camp.

Hyland emphasises the fact that the distinction should be seen as a continuum rather than a one-dimensional scale. If nothing else, the continuum serves as a background to understanding the existing variation and heterogeneity in an academic community.

## Variation in Preferred Genres and Text Types

Various disciplines and their subjects are more or less strongly linked to the different knowledge criteria presented in the table above. This also has repercussions on the writing in these disciplines. If there is variation in the way knowledge is constructed, we can also expect to see a variation in how this knowledge is reported in writing.

One clear example of this variation can be seen in the preference for different text types that disciplines and subjects exercise. Indeed, students of mechanical engineering, for example, will differ from students of comparative literature, political science and biochemistry, in the types of academic texts they are normally required to write.

Table 1.5: Favoured Text Genres in Different Disciplines
(Taken from Coffin et al. 2003: 46)

| *Sciences* | *Social Sciences* | *Humanities/Arts* | *Applied Fields* |
|---|---|---|---|
| *Examples:* | *Examples:* | *Examples:* | *Examples:* |
| Physics, Geology, Biology, Chemistry | Sociology, Politics, Economics, Media studies, Psychology | English, History, Languages, Classics, Fine arts, Religion | Business, Health and Social welfare, Music, Engineering |
| *Typical Genres:* | *Typical Genres:* | *Typical Genres:* | *Typical Genres:* |
| Lab reports, Project proposals and reports, Fieldwork notes, Essays, Theses | Essays, Project reports, Fieldwork notes, Theses | Essays, Projects, Critical analyses, Translations | Essays, Case studies, Theses, Project reports |

The following example comes from Coffin et al. (2003), showing what genres and text types are favoured in different disciplines, covering both undergraduate and postgraduate programmes.

Similarly, in a survey carried out in the UK, Nesi and Gardner (2006) investigated what text types and genres were used as university assignments. The survey shows that a large variety of text types were used across disciplines, for example essay, report, laboratory report, book review, case study, and marketing proposal.

According to Nesiand Gardner (2006) common text types in certain disciplines are as follows:

Table 1.6: Text Types in Different Disciplines

| *Text Types* | *Discipline* |
|---|---|
| Essay | Anthropology, Archaeology, Biology, Computing, Economics, Engineering, English, Food Sciences, Health, History, Hospitality and Tourism, Law, Mathematics, Medicine, Philosophy, Psychology, Publishing, Theatre Studies |
| Report | Computing, Food Sciences, Hospitality and Tourism, Law, Psychology |
| Laboratory report | Archaeology, Biology, Physics |
| Project report | Biology, Economics, Engineering, Mathematics, Sociology |

*(Table 1.6 Contd.)*

*(Table 1.6 Contd.)*

| *Text Types* | *Discipline* |
|---|---|
| Research project | Biology, Mathematics, Theatre Studies |
| Dissertation | Anthropology, Archaeology, Biology, Computing, Law, Medicine, Publishing, Sociology, Theatre Studies |
| Group project | Archaeology, Engineering, Health, Physics, Publishing |
| Poster | Anthropology, Biology, Engineering, Mathematics, Physics, Psychology |
| Book review | History, Psychology |
| Website evaluation | Medicine, Theatre Studies |
| Problem sheets | Biosciences, Economics, Food Sciences, Hospitality and Tourism, Mathematics |
| Case studies | Health, Publishing |
| Case notes, draft appeal to House of Lords, Advice Notes to a client, Submissions in preparation for a case, Moots, Problem Question (judgement) | Law |
| Field study | Sociology |
| Patient case report | Medicine |
| Letter from publisher to author | Publishing |
| Reflective writing/journal/blog | Engineering, English, Hospitality and Tourism, Philosophy, Medicine, Theatre Studies |
| Critical evaluation (of own production or practical task) | Anthropology, English, Computing, Theatre Studies |
| Marketing proposal/plan | Engineering, Publishing |
| Narrative fiction | Sociology (several modules) |
| Press Release, Fact Sheet, Technical Abstract, Persuasive Writing | Physics (communicating science module) |
| Letter of advice to friend written from 1830s perspective; Maths in Action project (lay audience) | Mathematics |

## Writing in Different Academic Disciplines

Academic writing conventions vary substantially according to discipline, i.e., whether one is working in the humanities, the social or natural sciences, or business. Academic writing in an academic institution setting can generally be divided into three main categories or genres. Writing in the humanities, writing in the sciences, and writing in business. Each genre has its own specific requirements in terms of style, content and format.

*Writing in the Humanities:* Academic writing in the humanities explores questions that deal with human values. The ultimate goal in writing in the humanities is to explain or understand the human experience–to use writing as a tool to reflect upon life. The *"humanities,"* as a discipline, includes not only literature, but also philosophy, ethics, performing arts, fine arts, history, and aspects of anthropology, cultural studies, foreign languages, and linguistics. In the humanities, you might be asked to analyse a poem, a performance or play, a painting, a film, or even a musical work.

*Writing in the Sciences:* Science writing includes writing in two main categories–natural sciences and social sciences. In each genre, the writing focuses on informing readers of new discoveries and assisting them in discovering truth through facts and firm, detailed data. Research-based writing in the sciences typically uses a formal tone, employs a third person voice, and avoids personal references and needless adjectives. Depending on the assignment, you might also write an analytical, explanatory, or persuasive paper in any of these fields for a popular or professional audience.

*Writing in the Natural Sciences:* Natural sciences include physical sciences such as biology, chemistry, engineering, geology and physics. This type of writing is generally concise and includes genres such as lab reports and reviews of scientific literature.

*Writing in the Social Sciences:* The social sciences, on the other hand, focus on human behaviour and societies. They involve documenting actual events as they happen. Categories of social science include psychology, anthropology, political science, sociology, education, and economics.

*Writing in Business:* Business writing often means explaining a situation, event, or change in order to compel the reader toward a very specific action. Format is key to a well-written business document because its structure needs to allow the reader to quickly find particular sections and a contact person who can answer further questions. Writing in business can include memos, cover letters, resumes, project reports, proposals, thank-you letters, emails, and business plans. While adherence to conventional grammar, spelling, and punctuation is important in every discipline, business writing places the greatest emphasis on mechanics.

## Check List for Academic Writing

Here are some useful questions to ask yourself about your writing:

1. Does your writing deal with the topic that was set?
2. Does it answer the question/deal with the brief that was set?

3. Is the correct genre? i.e. is it a report or an essay or a review?
4. Does it cover all the main aspects and in sufficient depth?
5. Is the content accurate and relevant?
6. Is everything relevant to the topic?
7. Is the material logically arranged?
8. Have you used paragraphs well?
9. Is each main point well supported by data, examples and argument?
10. Is there a clear distinction between your ideas and those of other authors?
11. Is your voice clear throughout?
12. Have you acknowledged all the sources you have used?
13. Is the length of the text right for its purpose?
14. Have you considered your audience?
15. Is it written in a suitable style?
16. Is the grammar, punctuation and spelling acceptable?
17. Is it neat and legibly written?
18. Is it on time?

# CHAPTER 2

# Genres in Academic Writing

R.R. Jordan considers that in academic writing the *"primary focus should be on academic discourse genres and the range and nature of academic writing tasks, aimed at helping to socialise the student into the academic context" (Jordan, 1997).* While explaining genres, R.R. Jordan quotes Swales: *"A genre is a recognized communicative event with a shared public purpose and with aims mutually understood by the participants in that event. ... In addition to purpose, exemplars of a genre exhibit various patterns of similarity in terms of structure, style, content and intended audience" (ibid: 230).*

When we study, we read different types of texts e.g. textbooks, reference works, scholarly and popular articles, essays, conference papers, official reports, theses etc. In other words, the texts we read belong to different genres.

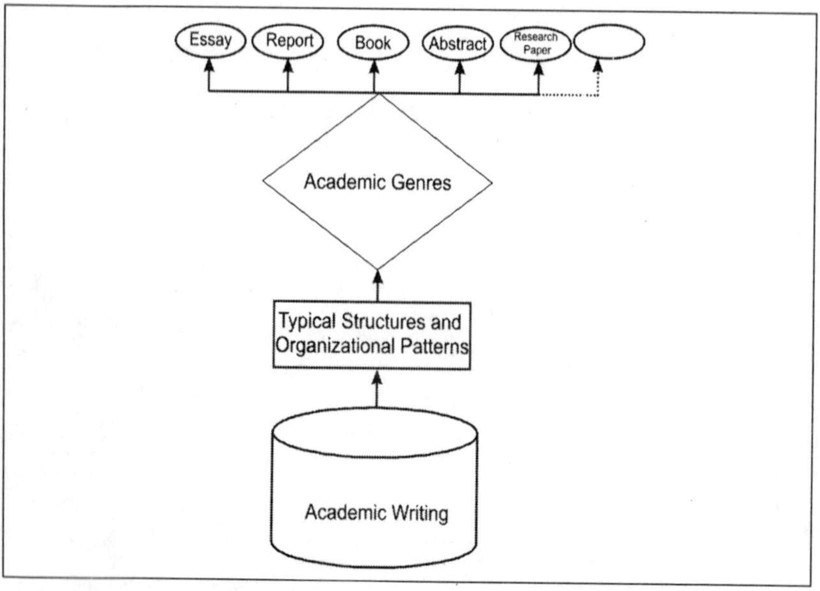


Figure 2.1: Diagrammatical View of Academic Genres

## Definition of Genre

Genre is the organization and classification of writing. Genre is the organization of literature into categories based on the type of writing the piece exemplifies through its content, form, or style. According to Hyland (2007), the term genre is used as a means of *"grouping texts together, representing how writers typically use language to respond to recurring situations"*. Broadly speaking, the term genre refers to a classification scheme for texts.

Generally, the word "genre" means a category or type of thing. In writing, a genre is a category defined by style, intended audience, content, and purpose. Each genre has certain expectations. Each "genre" (type of document) involves specific features that set it apart from other genres. Therefore, writers must understand the format and writing style expected of them.

## Academic Genres

Academic writing can be divided into different text types. Normally these are referred to as genres and could be formulated from a small selection of different kind of texts. The term genre is here used as a means *of "grouping texts together, representing how writers typically use language to respond to recurring situations"*.

## Definitions of Academic Genres

The term 'genre' refers to the typical structure and organisational patterns of a text, its intended audience and its purpose.

## Function of Genre

Genre is important in order to be able to organize writings based on their form, content and style. The genres of academic writing include essays, research papers, book review, textual analysis, literature reviews, project reports, proposals and dissertations/thesis.

## Purpose of Academic Genre

The purpose of a particular genre might be to:

- Present and explain information
- Persuade the audience to accept a new argument
- Describe a process.

## Types of Genres

Each "genre" (type of document) involves specific features that set it apart from other genres. Therefore, writers must understand the format and writing style expected of them. A number of widely used academic genres are:

Table 2.1: Types of Genres

| | | | | |
|---|---|---|---|---|
| Abstract | Annotated Bibliography | Article Reviews | Blog | Book Reviews |
| Case Report | Case Studies | Critique | Data Paper | Document Analysis |
| Encyclopaedia Article | Essays | Field Report | Grant Proposals | Laboratory Report |
| Letters | Literature Review | Manifesto | Policy Memo | Position Paper |
| Posters | Reports | Research Article | Research Notes | Research Proposal |
| Review Article | Scholarly Article | Supplemental Articles | Textbooks | Thesis |

## Abstract

Many research publications require an abstract, which is a brief synopsis of the text outlining its major points. As Samuel Johnson (1755) defined the term, an abstract is *"a smaller quantity containing the virtue or power of a greater"* (quoted in Oxford English Dictionary). In terms of importance, abstracts tend to possess a prominent position among academic genres, as stated by Lorés (2004): *"They [abstracts] constitute the gateway that leads readers to take up an article, journals to select contributions, or organisers of conferences to accept or reject papers"*.

An abstract summarises the major aspects of the entire paper in a prescribed sequence that includes:

- the overall purpose of the study and the research problem(s) you investigated;
- the basic design of the study;
- major findings or trends found as a result of your analysis; and,
- a brief summary of your interpretations and conclusions.

In research writing, there are different formats for abstract writing. The information below is therefore of a general kind; students will need to check with their supervisors if their department has specific guidelines for abstract writing.

The length of the abstract will be decided by the supervisor, publisher, etc. Generally, though, the word count for abstracts for research articles is 100-200 words.

The function of the abstract is to inform prospective readers of the content and argument of the text, but also to attract readers to read the whole text. Vintzileos & Ananth (2010) describe the abstract as "the 'mirror' of the full manuscript" and that it is the part of an article that is most widely read.

*Types of Abstract*

Types of abstracts are discussed below:

*Critical Abstract:* A critical abstract provides, in addition to describing main findings and information, a judgement or comment about the study's validity, reliability, or completeness. The researcher evaluates the paper and often compares it with other works on the same subject. Critical abstracts are generally 400-500 words in length due to the additional interpretive commentary.

*Descriptive Abstract:* A descriptive abstract indicates the type of information found in the work. It makes no judgements about the work, nor does it provide results or conclusions of the research. It does incorporate key words found in the text and may include the purpose, methods, and scope of the research. Essentially, the descriptive abstract only describes the work being summarised. Descriptive abstracts are usually very short, 100 words or less.

*Informative Abstract:* The majority of abstracts are informative. An informative abstract includes the information that can be found in a descriptive abstract (purpose, methods, scope) but it also includes the results and conclusions of the research and the recommendations of the author. The length varies according to discipline, but an informative abstract is usually no more than 300 words in length.

*Highlight Abstract:* A highlight abstract is specifically written to attract the reader's attention to the study. No pretence is made of there being either a balanced or complete picture of the paper and, in fact, incomplete and leading remarks may be used to spark the reader's interest. In that a highlight abstract cannot stand independent of its associated article, it is not a true abstract and, therefore, rarely used in academic writing.

*Article Abstract:* Abstracts usually accompany research articles–in many journals the abstract is published as part of the article, between the title and the proper text. Abstract services and journal providers publish abstracts, which serve to inform prospective readers about the contents of the article.

*Conference Abstract:* Another kind of abstract is the one that is submitted to conference CFPs (Call for Papers). Researchers wishing to present a paper at a conference send an abstract outlining their proposed paper. A call for papers is sent out well in advance of the actual conference. Because of the long-term planning that is necessary for conference participants, conference abstracts are sometimes written before the papers they describe have been written. Therefore, they cannot always show the same level of specificity as will be found in article abstracts.

### *Structure/Format of Abstract*

Graetz (1985) claims that the most common structure for abstracts is *Problem–Method–Results–Conclusions,* i.e. four parts. Many abstracts indeed more or less follow the *IMRaD* (Introduction, Methods, Results, and Discussion) structure, consisting of an introduction to the topic, a section on method and results, and finally a concluding part that discusses the findings presented in the article.

In a study of research abstracts within the field of applied linguistics, Santos (1996) identified a pattern consisting of five "moves". These moves constitute the transitions between the different stages of the abstract, each fulfilling a "communicative purpose" (Santos, p. 485).

In brief, the pattern that Santos identified looks like this:

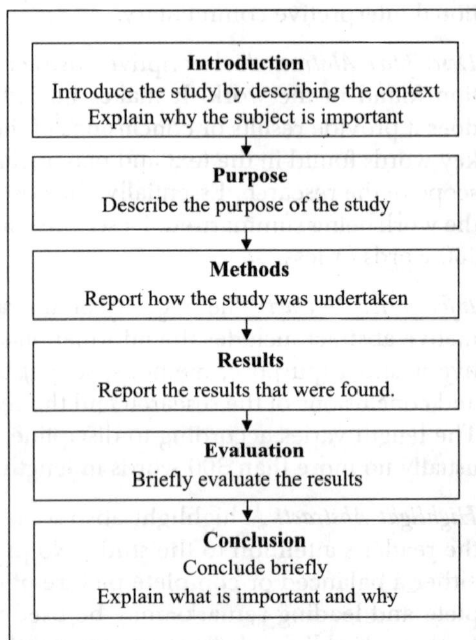


Figure 2.2: Structure of Abstract

Situating the research
Presenting the research

- Describing the methodology
- Summarising the results
- Discussing the research

## Annotated Bibliography

A bibliography is an alphabetical list, by author, of the sources (books, journals, websites, etc.) you have used to research and write your assignment. A bibliography usually includes information such as the author, title, publisher and date. An annotation is a concise summary and/or evaluation of the value or relevance of each source. An annotated bibliography combines these two elements and provides bibliographic information plus a summary and/or evaluation of each of the sources you have used. An annotated bibliography may be one part of a larger assessment item.

An annotated bibliography is a bibliography that gives a summary of each of the entries. The purpose of annotations is to provide the reader with a summary and an evaluation of each source. Each summary should be a concise exposition of the source's central idea(s) and give the reader a general idea of the source's content.

### *Why do we write Annotated Bibliographies?*

You may be asked to write an annotated bibliography for several reasons:

- to provide a review of the literature on your subject
- to demonstrate the quality and depth of your reading.
- to show the scope of sources or research available, e.g. journals, books, websites.
- to inform the reader of the relevance, accuracy and quality of sources that may be of interest.
- to explore and organise sources for further research.

*Murray, S. (2009). The library: An illustrated history (ALA ed.). Chicago, IL: Skyhorse Publishing.*

Murray's book offers an in-depth look at the history of libraries since ancient times. Hein corporates beautiful illustrations, quotations, and descriptions of numerous libraries worldwide. This book states the history of the evolution of the book from era to era. It also serves as a primary source of information for research in library history. This is a good book that should be of interest to book lovers and librarians.

Figure 2.3: Sample Entry of an APA Style Annotated Bibliography

*How to write an Annotated Bibliography?*

There are two main sections to each annotated bibliography entry:

1. the bibliographical information (the reference).
2. the explanatory paragraphs (the annotation).

*Components of Annotated Bibliographies*

The following are the main components of an annotated bibliography. It is important to note that not all fields shown below must be used at once in an annotated bibliography. The fields may vary depending on the type of annotated bibliography and special instructions from the instructor, in case the bibliography is part of a school assignment.

- *Full bibliographic citation:* An annotated bibliography must contain the necessary and complete bibliographical information i.e. (author, title, publisher and date, etc.).
- *Author's background:* You should provide the name, authority, experience, or qualifications of the author.
- *Purpose of the work:* You should provide the reasons why the author wrote the work.
- *Scope of the work:* You should state the breadth or depth of coverage and topics or sub-topics covered.
- *Main argument:* State the main informative points of the paper.
- *Audience:* For whom was it written (general public, subject specialists, student).
- *Methodology:* What methodology and research methods did the work employ?
- *Viewpoint:* What is the author's perspective or approach (school of thought, etc.)? Do you detect an unacknowledged bias, or find any undefended assumptions?
- *Sources:* Does the author cite other sources, and if so, what types? Is it based on the author's own research? Is it personal opinion?
- *Reliability of the source:* How reliable is the work?
- *Conclusion:* What does the author conclude about the work? Is the conclusion justified by the work?
- *Features:* Any significant extras, e.g. visual aids (charts, maps, etc.), reprints of source documents, an annotated bibliography?
- *Strengths and Weaknesses:* What are the strengths and weaknesses of the work?
- *Comparison:* How does the source relate to other works done by other writers on the topic: does it agree or disagree with another

author or a particular school of thought; are there other works which would support or dispute it?

- *Your Voice/Personal Conclusion:* Provide your point of view of the work or your reaction to the source based on other available works, prior knowledge of the subject matter or knowledge pools done by other researchers.

## Article Review

The review article can be seen as a special case of the research article. Its purpose can vary and its format is generally less rigid than the proper research article. Furthermore, it is not uncommon to find alternative genre names used, such as review, review essay, report article, survey article and state-of-the-art survey. In addition, a related concept is meta-analysis, where researchers pool together a large number of studies in the attempt to statistically re-analyse and integrate the results.

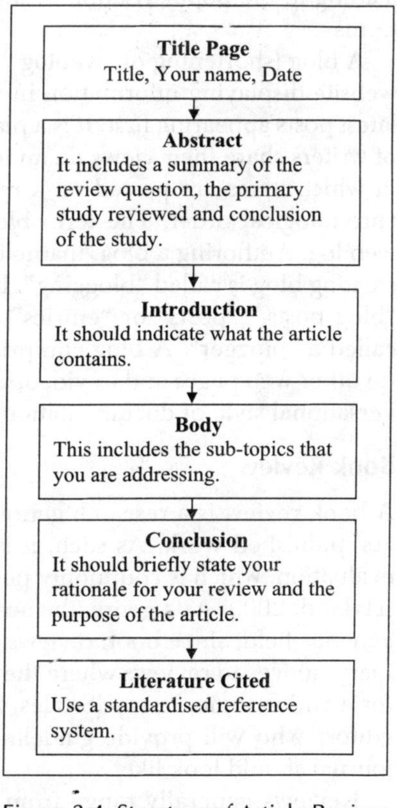


Figure 2.4: Structure of Article Review

## Blog

As academia becomes ever more integrated into the digital environment, researchers will increasingly benefit from the ability to write for different formats. Academic blogs, in particular, have grown to become one of the mainstays for analysis, commentary and the exchange of ideas in many fields of study.

In the first instance, it is important to keep in mind that academic blogs can be diverse in terms of their purpose, style and audience. When writing for (or reading) a blog, these factors should inform the approach that you take. Generally speaking, however, academic blogs are defined by relatively short written contributions and an open audience which can range from academics to practitioners to interested members of the public.

The term "weblog" was coined by Jorn Barger on 17 December 1997. The short form, "blog", was coined by Peter Merholz, who jokingly broke the word weblog into the phrase we blog in the sidebar of his blog Peterme.com in April or May 1999. Shortly thereafter, Evan Williams at Pyra Labs used "blog" as both a noun and verb ("to blog", meaning "to edit one's weblog or to post to one's weblog") and devised the term "blogger" in connection with Pyra Labs' Blogger product, leading to the popularisation of the terms.

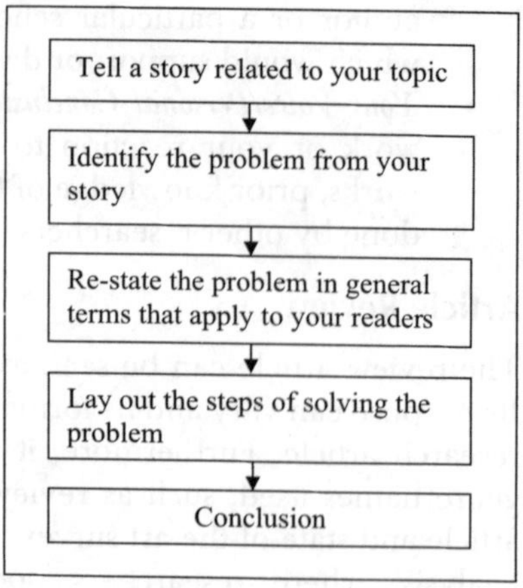

Figure 2.5: Template for Blog Posts

A blog (shortening of "weblog") is an online journal or informational website displaying information in the reverse chronological order, with latest posts appearing first. It is a platform where a writer or even a group of writers share their views on an individual subject. 'A blog is a website in which items are posted on a regular basis and displayed in reverse chronological order. The term blog is a shortened form of weblog or web log. Authoring a blog, maintaining a blog or adding an article to an existing blog is called "blogging". Individual articles on a blog are called "blog posts," "posts" or "entries". A person who posts these entries is called a "blogger". A blog comprises text, hypertext, images, and links (to other web pages and to video, audio and other files). Blogs use a conversational style of documentation.

## Book Review

A book review is a research genre where scholars evaluate other scholars' published work. As such, it is an editorially commissioned public evaluation, which is commonly published in journals in most disciplines (Hyland, 2009).As a genre, the academic book review is a fairly heterogeneous field, since book reviews can be anything between short, summary notices to reviews where the chosen book is used as a springboard for a wide-ranging essay (Swales, 2004). Scientific journals have review editors who will provide guidelines for what a review for a particular journal should look like.

Reviews generally range from 500-1000 words, but may be longer or shorter depending on the length and complexity of the book being reviewed, the overall purpose of the review, and whether the review is a comparative analysis examining two or more books that focus on the same topic.

There are two general approaches to reviewing a book:

- *Descriptive review:* It presents the content and structure of a book as objectively as possible, describing essential information about a book's purpose and authority.
- *Critical review:* It describes and evaluates the book in relation to accepted literary and historical standards and supports this evaluation with evidence from the text and, in most cases, in contrast to and in comparison with the research of others. It should include a statement about what the author has tried to do, evaluates how well [in your opinion] the author has succeeded in meeting the objectives of the study, and presents evidence to support this assessment.

**Introduction**

Introduction will usually include:

- overall impression of the book
- a statement about the author
- a statement on the purpose of the book
- a statement of the significance of the work
- a comment about the relationship between this work and others by the same author, the same subject and the same genre

↓

**Body Paragraph**

The body of review develops the points the reviewer wants to make:

- greater detail on the author's thesis and a summary of the main points
- evaluation of strengths, weaknesses, contribution or bias
- the evidence that is the basis of writer's critique

↓

**Conclusion**

The conclusion (last paragraph) includes:

- reviewer's final assessment
- restatement of overall impression
- (re)statement of reviewer's recommendation

Figure 2.6: Structure of Book Review

## Case Report

In medicines (Medical Report), a case report is a detailed report of the symptoms, signs, diagnosis, treatment, and follow-up of an individual patient. Case reports may contain a demographic profile of the patient, but usually describe an unusual or novel occurrence. Some case reports also contain a literature review of other reported cases. Case reports are professional narratives that provide feedback on clinical practice guidelines and offer a framework for early signals of effectiveness, adverse events, and cost. They can be shared for medical, scientific, or educational purposes.

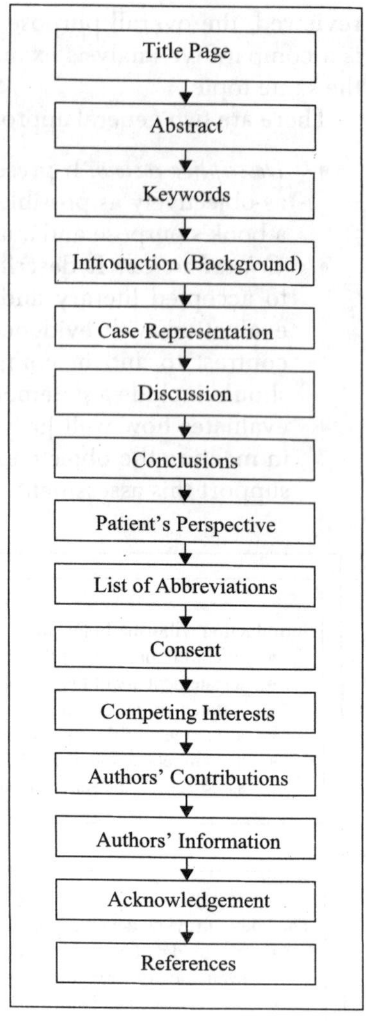


Figure 2.7: Structure of Case Report

## Case Studies

Case studies may be found in any discipline, though they are most common in disciplines such as business, sociology and law. They are primarily descriptive. The term case study refers to both a method of analysis and a specific research design for examining a problem, both of which are used in most circumstances to generalise across populations. A case study research paper examines a person, place, event, phenomenon, or other type of subject of analysis in order to extrapolate key themes and results that help predict future trends, illuminate previously hidden issues that can be applied to practice, and/or provide a means for understanding an important research problem with greater clarity. A case study paper usually examines a single subject of analysis, but case study papers can also be designed as a comparative investigation that shows relationships between two or among more than two subjects. The methods used to study a case can rest within a quantitative, qualitative, or mixed-method investigative paradigm.

**Introduction**

Introduction should serve as a roadmap for your readers to ascertain the scope and purpose of your study. A good introduction answers these four questions:

- What was I studying?
- Why was this topic important to investigate?
- What did we know about this topic before I did this study? How will this study advance new knowledge or new ways of understanding?

↓

**Literature Review**

This includes synthesising studies that helps the case study.

↓

**Method**

In this section, you should explain the strategy to carry out the case study.

↓

**Discussion**

The objectives of your discussion section should include the following:

- Reiterate the research problem/state the major findings
- Explain the meaning of the findings and why they are important
- Relate the findings to similar studies
- Consider alternative explanations of the findings
- Acknowledge the study's limitations
- Suggest areas for further research

↓

**Conclusion**

Summarise your conclusion in clear, simple language; emphasise how the findings from your case study differ from or support prior research and why.

Figure 2.8: Structure of Case Study

## Critique

A critique is a genre of academic writing that briefly summarises and critically evaluates a work or concept. A critique is a written examination and judgement of a situation or of a person's work or ideas.

Critiques can be used to carefully analyse a variety of works such as:

- *Creative works:* novels, exhibits, film, images, poetry
- *Research:* monographs, journal articles, systematic reviews, theories
- *Media:* news reports, feature articles

Like an essay, a critique uses a formal, academic writing style and has a clear structure, that is, an introduction, body and conclusion. However, the body of a critique includes a summary of the work and a detailed evaluation. The purpose of an evaluation is to gauge the usefulness or impact of a work in a particular field.

*Why do we write critiques?*

Writing a critique on a work helps us to develop:

- knowledge of the work's subject area or related works.
- an understanding of the work's purpose, intended audience, development of argument, structure of evidence or creative style.
- recognition of the strengths and weaknesses of the work.

*How to write a critique*

- Before you start writing, it is important to have a thorough understanding of the work that will be critiqued.
- Study the work under discussion.
- Make notes on key parts of the work.
- Develop an understanding of the main argument or purpose being expressed in the work.
- Consider how the work relates to a broader issue or context.

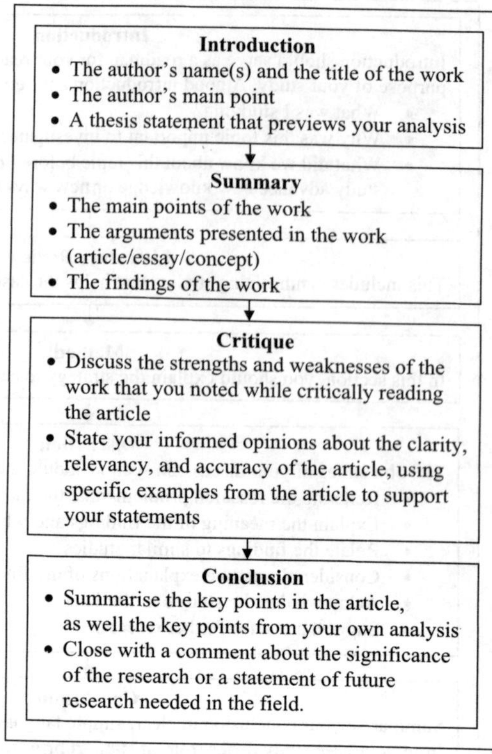


Figure 2.9: Structure of Critique

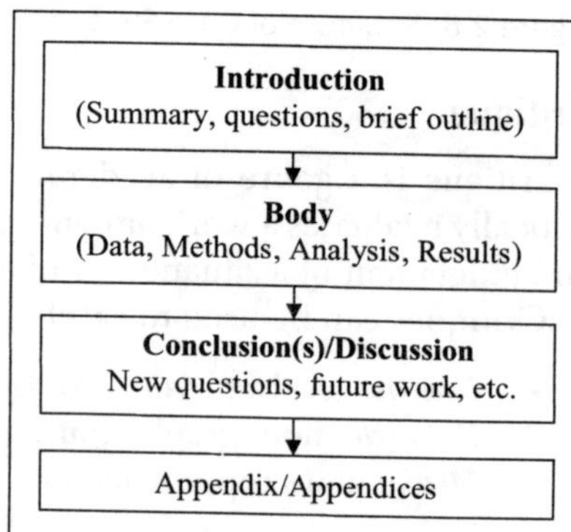


Figure 2.10: Structure of a Data Paper

## Data Papers

Data Papers are articles dedicated to describe datasets. This type of article is becoming popular and journals exclusively dedicated to them have been established, e.g. *Scientific Data* and *Earth System Science Data.*

## Document Analysis

Document analysis is a form of qualitative research in which documents are interpreted by the researcher to give voice and meaning around an assessment topic. Analysing documents incorporates coding content into themes similar to how focus group or interview transcripts are analysed. A rubric can also be used to grade or score a document.

### *Types of Documents*

There are three primary types of documents:

*Public Records:* The official, ongoing records of an organisation's activities. Examples include student transcripts, mission statements, annual reports, policy manuals, student handbooks, strategic plans, and syllabi.

*Personal Documents:* First-person accounts of an individual's actions, experiences, and beliefs. Examples include calendars, e-mails, scrapbooks, blogs, Facebook posts, duty logs, incident reports, reflections/journals, and newspapers.

*Physical Evidence:* Physical objects found within the study setting (often called artifacts). Examples include flyers, posters, agendas, handbooks, and training materials.

### *Process of Document Analysis*

Before actual document analysis takes place, the researcher must go through a detailed planning process in order to ensure reliable results. O'Leary outlines an 8-step planning process that should take place not just in document analysis, but all textual analysis (2014):

1. Create a list of texts to explore (e.g., population, samples, respondents, participants).
2. Consider how texts will be accessed with attention to linguistic or cultural barriers.
3. Acknowledge and address biases.
4. Develop appropriate skills for research.
5. Consider strategies for ensuring credibility.
6. Know the data one is searching for.
7. Consider ethical issues (e.g., confidential documents).
8. Have a backup plan.

## Encyclopaedia Article

The purpose of an encyclopaedia article is to present established knowledge neutrally, concisely and clearly. The target audience is usually general readers, as well as specialists, although there are also scholarly encyclopaedias that require the reader to have specialist knowledge. Encyclopaedia articles are not generally intended to persuade the reader by way of reasoned argument, and they do not clarify or instruct as a textbook would. Encyclopaedia articles are intended primarily to be informative and descriptive. They provide information, define words and concepts and describe relevant circumstances.

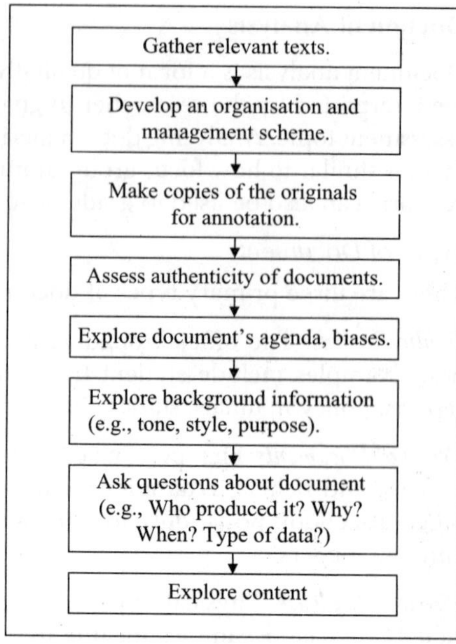


Figure 2.11: Structure of Document Analysis

## Essays

The term *'essay'* is used in a wide sense and can refer to anything from a brief paper to a long degree essay. Student essays vary in length and formality, but they usually contain three sections: Introduction, Main body, Conclusion. They usually need to include citation of sources. Essays help teachers to see what students have learnt and how deeply. Try to read examples of student essays in your discipline to become more familiar with what is expected of you.

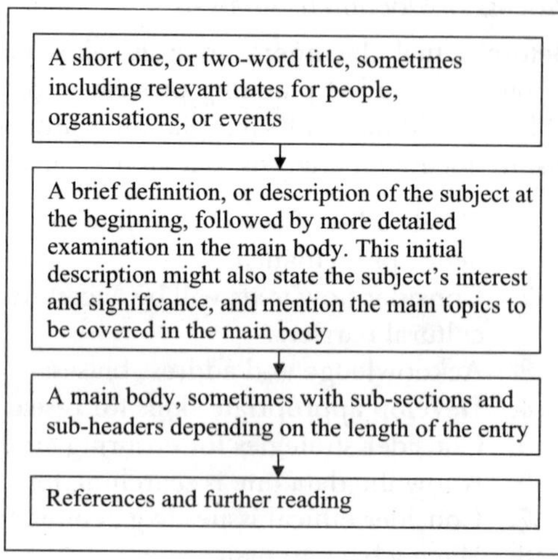


Figure 2.12: Structure of Encyclopaedia Article

### *Basic Structure of Essay*

Essay writing is the most effective way to communicate your ideas and answer the question. All essays should include the following structure:

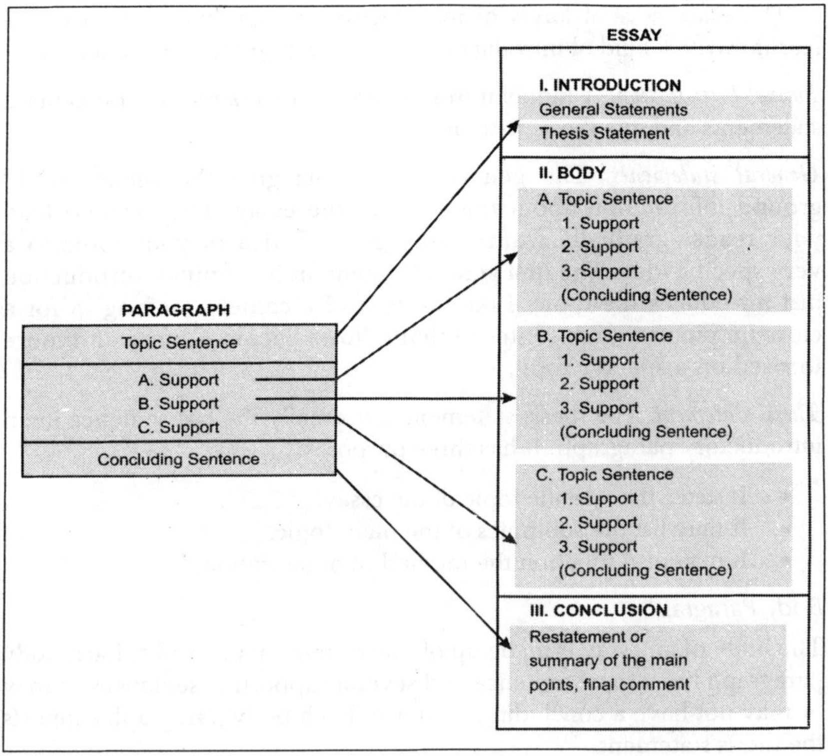


Figure 2.13: The Basic Five-part Essay Structure

- An essay introduction stimulates the reader's interest and tells what the essay is about. The last sentence of an introduction is the thesis statement. Like the topic sentence of a paragraph, a thesis statement names the specific topic of the essay.
- The body consists of one or more paragraphs. Each paragraph develops a subdivision of the topic.
- The conclusion, like the concluding sentence in a paragraph, is a summary or review of the main points discussed in the body.

### *Introductory Paragraph*

The introductory paragraph, or introduction, is the first paragraph of an essay. It has two functions:

- It attracts the reader's interest, and
- It introduces the topic of the essay.

There are several kinds of introductory paragraphs. Now, we will learnto write a kind of introduction known as a *"funnel"* introduction.

*Funnel Introduction:* A funnel introduction has two parts: several general statements and one thesis statement.

*General statements:* The general statements give the reader background information about the topic of the essay. They should lead your reader gradually from a very general idea of your topic to a very specific idea. The first general statement in a funnel introduction just introduces the topic. Like the lens of a camera moving in for a close-up picture, each sentence that follows becomes more and more focused on a specific topic.

*Thesis statement:* The thesis statement is normally the last sentence in an introductory paragraph. It has three purposes:

- It states the specific topic of the essay.
- It may list the subtopics of the main topic.
- It may also mention the method of organisation.

### Body Paragraphs

The body of an essay is made up of one or more paragraphs. Each body paragraph has a topic sentence and several supporting sentences. It may or may not have a concluding sentence. Each body paragraph supports the thesis statement.

### Concluding Paragraph

The concluding paragraph is the last paragraph of an essay. It has three purposes:

- It signals the end of the essay.
- It reminds the reader of your main points.
- It leaves the reader with your final thoughts on the topic.

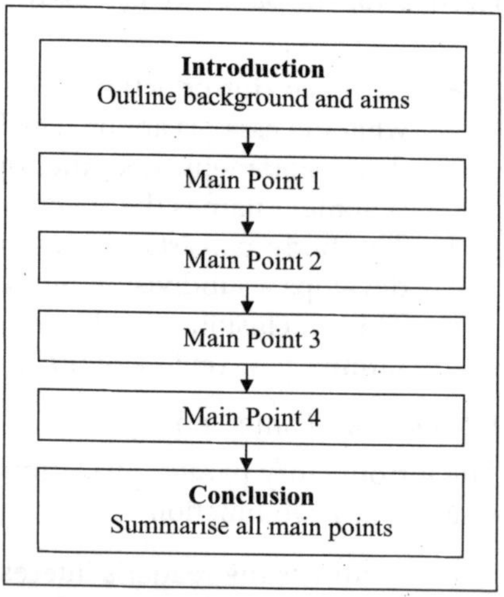


Figure 2.14: Structure of Linear Essay

### Types of Structures of Essay

Following are the main types of structures of essay:

*Linear Essay:* A linear structure goes from one point to the next

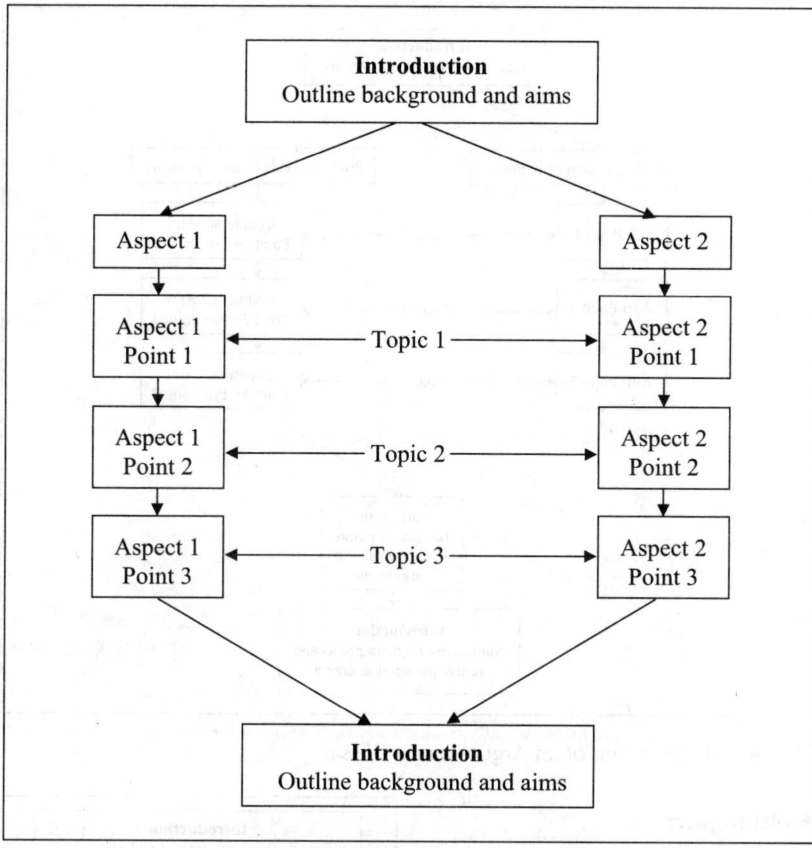


Figure 2.15: Structure of a Two-sided Essay

in a chosen sequence. You could group ideas in order of importance of topic or chronologically.

*Two-sided Essays:* If you are asked to compare, contrast or differentiate two items, use a two-sided approach. However, this structure can be limited. It suggests equality between the two but does not allow for weighing more in favour of one side of the argument.

*Argumentative Essays:* When you argue you lead towards your own opinion or conclusion. The balance of the two-sides will weigh in favour of your argument.

*SPSE (Situation Problem Solutions Evaluation) Essays:* Use this approach when you are asked to look at a problem and suggest solutions to it.

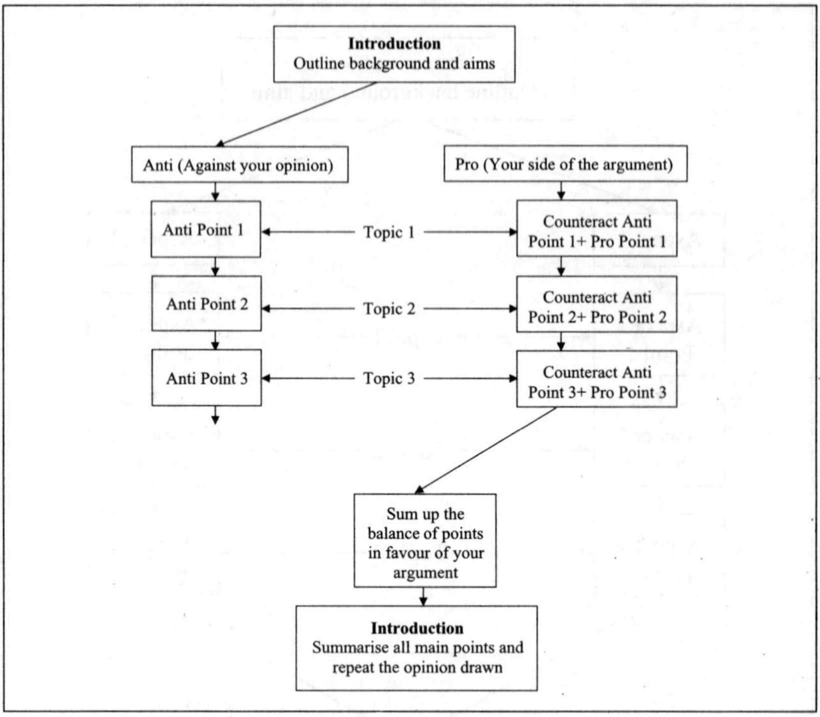


Figure 2.16: Structure of an Argumentative Essay

## Field Report

The purpose of a field report in the social sciences is to describe the observation of people, places, and/or events and to analyse that observation data in order to identify and categorise common themes in relation to the research problem underpinning the study.

## Grant Proposals

Grant proposals, i.e., texts written by researchers requesting funding for research projects, can be seen as a genre of its own.

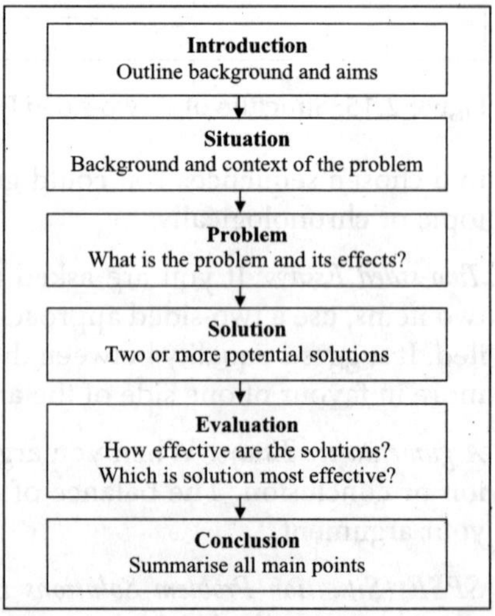


Figure 2.17: Structure of an SPSE Essay

**Introduction**

The introduction should describe:

- the research problem,
- the specific objectives of research,
- the important theories or concepts underpinning the field study,
- the nature of the organisation or setting where you are conducting the observation,
- what type of observations you have conducted,
- what your focus was, when you observed, and
- the methods you used for collecting the data.

↓

**Description of Activities**

A helpful approach to systematically describing the varying aspects of an observed situation is to answer the "Five W's of Investigative Reporting." These are:
*What*—describe what you observed.
*Where*—provide background information about the setting of your observation and, if necessary, note important material objects that are present that help contextualise the observation.
*When*—record factual data about the day and the beginning and ending time of each observation.
*Who*—note background and demographic information about the individuals being observed e.g., age, gender, ethnicity, and/or any other variables relevant to your study.
*Why*—why were you doing this? Describe the reasons for selecting particular si observe.

↓

**Interpretation and Analysis**

Place the analysis and interpretations of your field observations within the larger context of the theories and issues you described in the introduction.

↓

**Conclusion and Recommendations**

The conclusion should briefly recap the entire study, reiterating the importance or significance of your observations.

↓

**Appendix**

Place information that is not essential to explaining your findings, but that supports your analysis, that validates your conclusions, or that contextualises a related point that helps the reader understand the overall report.

↓

**References**

List all sources that you consulted and obtained information from while writing your field report.

Figure 2.18: Structure of Field Report

Naturally, there is variation in the structure of a grant proposal since funding agencies and bodies have different requirements for what information must be included. However, in terms of prototypical parts of a grant proposal, Swales (1990: 186) suggests the following:

## Laboratory Report

Laboratory report is an important part of all laboratory courses and it explains what you did in experiment, what you learnt, and what the results meant. Laboratory report should demonstrate that the writer understands the concepts behind the data. It identifies the reasons and the ways differences have occurred and explains their influence upon the experiment. Finally, lab report shows that a person who conducted the experiment has a full comprehension of the principles the experiment was designed to examine. A key element in such paper writing is careful organisation of ideas and their coherent expression.

Laboratory reports are written to describe and analyse a laboratory experiment that explores a scientific concept. A laboratory report provides a formal record of an experiment. The discussion of objectives, procedures, and results should be specific enough that interested readers could replicate the experiment.

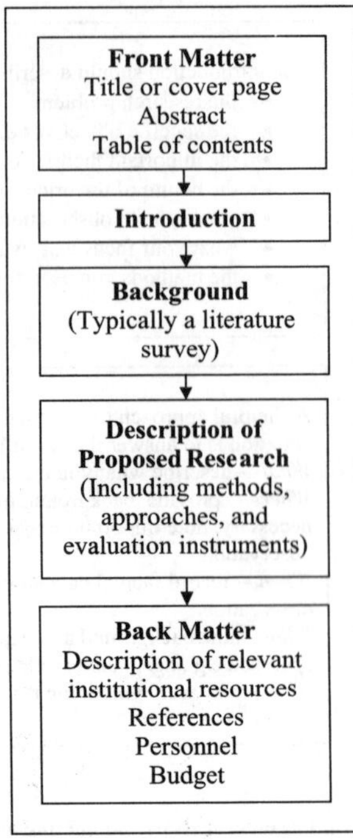


Figure 2.19: Structure of Grant Proposal

They are typically assigned to enable you to:

- Conduct scientific research.
- Formulate a hypothesis(es) about a particular stimulus, event, and/or behaviour.
- Review relevant literature to justify your hypothesis.
- Allow someone to replicate your study by providing precise details.
- Apply statistics to test your hypothesis.
- Explore theoretical explanations.
- Evaluate research objectively and methodically.
- Communicate concisely and precisely.

Although most laboratory reports will include the following sections, some experiments will require a different format. Tailor your report so that it adequately explicates your specific experiment.

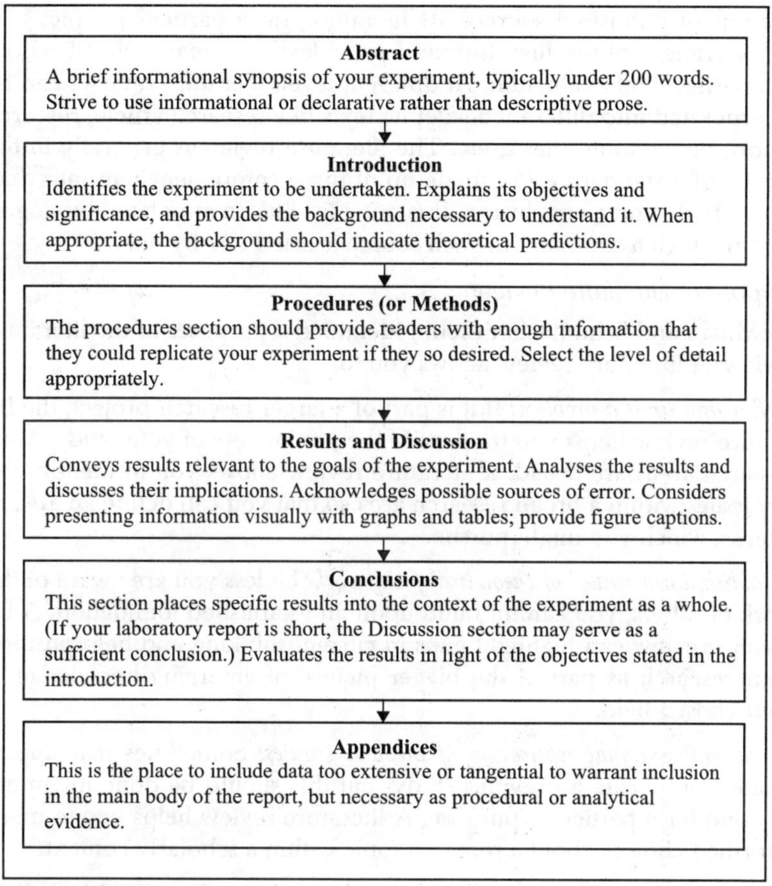


Figure 2.20: Format of Laboratory Report

## Letters

Letters (also called *communications*, and not to be confused with *letters to the editor*) are short descriptions of important current research findings that are usually fast-tracked for immediate publication because they are considered urgent.

## Literature Review

A literature review is a critical survey of the academic publications and research on a particular topic. A literature review is often, but not always, part of a larger research project. A literature review is a critical analysis of published sources, or literature, on a particular topic. It is an assessment of the literature and provides a summary, classification, comparison and evaluation. At different level, literature reviews can be incorporated into different academic texts like research article, research report, dissertation, thesis, etc. The literature review is generally in the format of a standard essay made up of three components: an introduction, a body and a conclusion. It is not a list like an annotated bibliography in which a summary of each source is listed one by one.

### *Purpose of Literature Review*

McMillan and Schumacher (2000) identified 5 purposes of the literature review. A literature review allows you to:

*Define and limit a problem:* If it is part of a larger research project, the literature review helps you to identify the parameters of your study. Most research areas are broad: a literature review allows you to identify the key issues within a broad research area so that you can define an area of interest which you might pursue.

*Establish a conceptual or theoretical framework:* Unless you are aware of the work of others, you cannot build upon an established foundation. A literature review can highlight gaps in current thinking and help position your research as part of the bigger picture of emerging knowledge in your chosen field.

*Avoid unintentional replication of previous studies:* Sometimes it is appropriate to replicate a previous study, but this should be done intentionally and for a particular purpose. A literature review helps you to make informed choices about a research topic within a scholarly context.

*Select methods and measures:* The success or failure of previous investigations can provide useful material for you when you are designing your own research methodology. You can assess what has worked before (or not worked) in previous contexts and why. You may be alerted to new methodologies and procedures.

*Relate findings to previous knowledge and suggest areas for further research:* The findings of your own research need to be related back to earlier studies. This places your work and can point to areas that need further investigation. Your thesis is much more a coherent whole if your discussion section draws on and contrasts with your literature review.

### *Why do we write Literature Reviews?*

One may be asked to write a literature review in order to demonstrate your understanding of the literature on a particular topic. You show your understanding by analysing and then synthesising the information to:

- Determine what has already been written on a topic
- Provide an overview of key concepts
- Identify major relationships or patterns
- Identify strengths and weaknesses
- Identify any gaps in the research
- Identify any conflicting evidence
- Provide a solid background to a research paper's investigation.

### Types of Literature Reviews

Types of literature reviews are discussed below:

*Argumentative Review:* This form examines literature selectively in order to support or refute an argument, deeply embedded assumption, or philosophical problem already established in the literature.

*Integrative Review:* The body of literature includes all studies that address related or identical hypotheses or research problems. A well-done integrative review meets the same standards as primary research in regard to clarity, rigour, and replication. This is the most common form of review in the social sciences.

*Historical Review:* Historical literature reviews focus on examining research throughout a period of time, often starting with the first time an issue, concept, theory, phenomenon emerged in the literature, then tracing its evolution within the scholarship of a discipline.

*Methodological Review:* A review does not always focus on what someone said (findings), but how they came about saying what they say (method of analysis). Reviewing methods of analysis provides a framework of understanding at different levels (i.e. those of theory, substantive fields, research approaches, and data collection and analysis techniques), how researchers draw upon a wide variety of knowledge ranging from the conceptual level to practical documents for use in fieldwork in the areas of ontological and epistemological consideration, quantitative and qualitative integration, sampling, interviewing, data collection, and data analysis.

*Systematic Review:* This form consists of an overview of existing evidence pertinent to a clearly formulated research question, which uses pre-specified and standardised methods to identify and critically appraise relevant research, and to collect, report, and analyse data from the studies that are included in the review.

*Theoretical Review:* The purpose of this form is to examine the corpus of theory that has accumulated in regard to an issue, concept, theory, phenomenon.

*How to Write a Literature Review*

1. *Determine your Purpose:* Work out what you need to address in the literature review. What are you being asked to do in your literature review? What are you searching in the literature to discover? Check your assignment question and your criteria sheet to know what to focus on.
2. *Do an Extensive Search of the Literature:* Find out what has been written on the topic.
   - ➢ What kind of literature?: Select appropriate source material. Use a variety of academic or scholarly sources that are relevant, current and authoritative. An extensive review of relevant material will include – books, journal articles, reports, government documents, conference proceedings and web resources. The Library would be the best place to search for your sources.
   - ➢ How many resources?: The number of sources that you will be required to review will depend on what the literature review is for and how advanced you are in your studies. It could be from five sources at first year undergraduate level to more than fifty for a thesis. Your lecturer will advise you on these details.
3. *Note the Bibliographical Details of Your Sources:* Keep a note of the publication title, date, authors' names, page numbers and publishers. These details will save you time later.
4. *Read the Literature:* Critically read each source, look for the arguments presented rather than for facts. Take notes as you read and start to organise your review around themes and ideas. Consider using a table, matrix or concept map to identify how the different sources relate to each other.
5. *Analyse the Literature You have Found:* In order for your writing to reflect strong critical analysis, you need to evaluate the sources. For each source you are reviewing ask yourself these questions:
   - ➢ What are the key terms and concepts?
   - ➢ How relevant is this article to my specific topic?
   - ➢ What are the major relationships, trends and patterns?
   - ➢ How has the author structured the arguments?
   - ➢ How authoritative and credible is this source?
   - ➢ What are the differences and similarities between the sources?
   - ➢ Are there any gaps in the literature that require further study?
6. *Write the Review:* Start by writing your thesis statement. This is an important introductory sentence that will tell your reader what the topic is and the overall perspective or argument you will be presenting.

Like essays, a literature review must have an introduction, a body and a conclusion.

*Structure of a Literature Review*

*Introduction:* Your introduction should give an outline of:

- why you are writing a review, and why the topic is important
- the scope of the review – what aspects of the topic will be discussed
- the criteria used for your literature selection (e.g. type of sources used, date range)
- the organisational pattern of the review.

*Body Paragraphs:* Each body paragraph should deal with a different theme that is relevant to your topic. You will need to synthesise several of your reviewed readings into each paragraph, so that there is a clear connection between the various sources. You will need to critically analyse each source for how they contribute to the themes you are researching.

The body could include paragraphs on:

- historical background
- methodologies
- previous studies on the topic
- mainstream versus alternative viewpoints
- principal questions being asked
- general conclusions that are being drawn.

*Conclusion:* Your conclusion should give a summary of:

- the main agreements and disagreements in the literature
- any gaps or areas for further research
- your overall perspective on the topic.

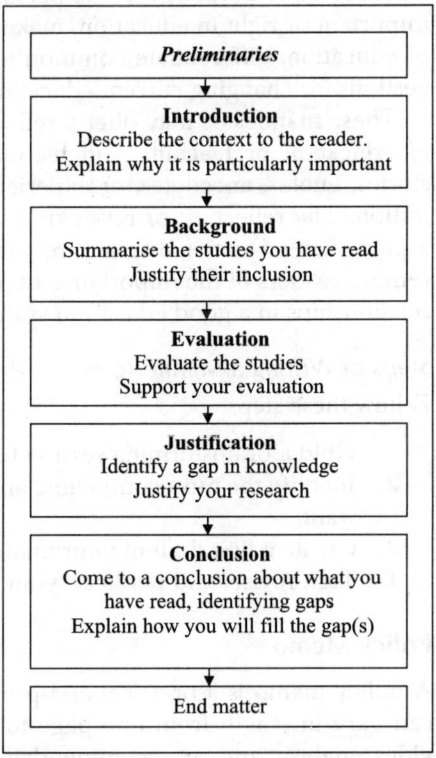

Figure 2.21: Structure of Literature Review

## Manifesto

A manifesto is a published declaration of the intentions, motives, or views of the issuer, be it an individual, group, political party or government. A manifesto is a statement of ideals and intentions. One of the most famous examples is *"The Communist Manifesto"* by Karl Marx and Friedrich Engels.

A manifesto is a statement where you can share your:

- Intentions (what you intend to do)
- Opinions (what you believe, your stance on a particular topic)
- Vision (the type of world that you dream about and wish to create).

Educational manifestos are documents proposing a change or changes to a current education system. They can be written by governing bodies, organisations, or individuals involved in education as parents, student, administrators, or other stakeholders. The writer or writers are positioned as a minority group, with manifestos aimed at a majority group. Educational manifestos include personal or group beliefs about what is important or right in education, make statements about the current state of education, differentiate common terms in education, and make suggestions for changing current education systems.

These manifestos may offer a reflection or rethinking of some aspect of education or teaching and learning. These may include personal stories, quotes, anecdotes, or experiences in the classroom or administration. The reflection or rethinking serves to illustrate how or why an aspect of an educational system requires change. These reflections often remind readers of the importance of positive, consistent teacher-student relationships in a good education system.

### *Steps of Writing a Manifesto*

Follow these steps:

1. Hold a brainstorming session to identify what you truly want.
2. Identify the most compelling and desired aspects of the future you want.
3. Create a first draft of your manifesto or inspirational statement.
4. Test, revise, and publicise your manifesto.

## Policy Memo

A policy memo is a practical and professionally written document that can vary in length from one page to over one hundred pages. It provides analysis and/or recommendations directed to a predetermined audience regarding a specific situation or topic. A well-written policy memo reflects attention to the research problem. It is well organized and structured in a clear and concise style that assumes the reader possesses limited knowledge of, as well as little time to conduct research about, the issue of concern. There is no thesis statement or overall theoretical framework underpinning the document; the focus is on describing one or more specific policy recommendations and their supporting action items.

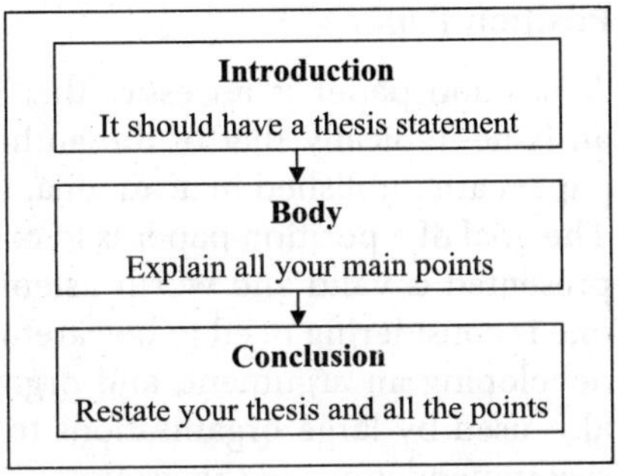


Figure 2.22: Structure of Literature Review

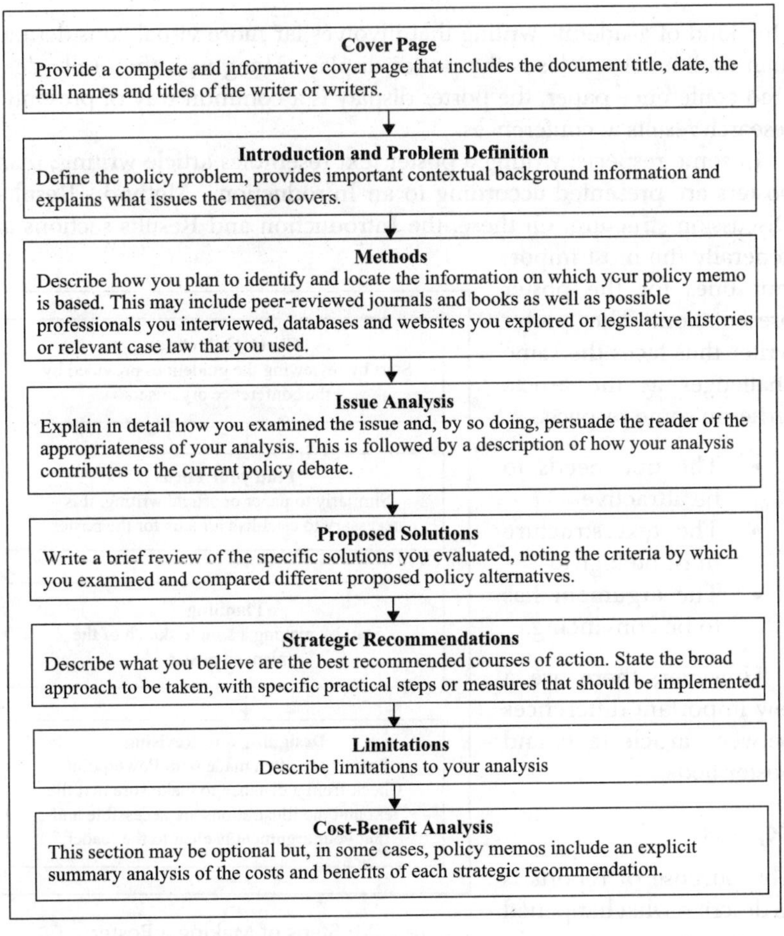


Figure 2.23: Structure of Policy Memo

## Position Paper

A position paper is an essay that presents an arguable opinion about an issue–typically that of the author or some specified entity. Position papers are published in academia, in politics, in law and other domains. The goal of a position paper is to convince the audience that the opinion presented is valid and worth listening to. Ideas for position papers that one is considering need to be carefully examined when choosing a topic, developing an argument, and organising the paper.Position papers are also used by large organisations to make public the official beliefs and recommendations of the group.

## Posters

One kind of academic writing that involves far more visual consideration than traditional articles is the poster display. Along with the orally delivered conference paper, the poster display is a common way of presenting research results at conferences.

In some respects, writing a poster text resembles article writing; many posters are presented according to an Introduction - Method - Results - Discussion structure. Of these, the Introduction and Results sections are generally the most important ones for the poster presentation. The poster writer thus faces the same challenges as the article writer in some respects:

- The title needs to be attractive
- The text structure must be logical
- The argument has to be convincing.

However, there are a few important differences between article texts and poster texts.

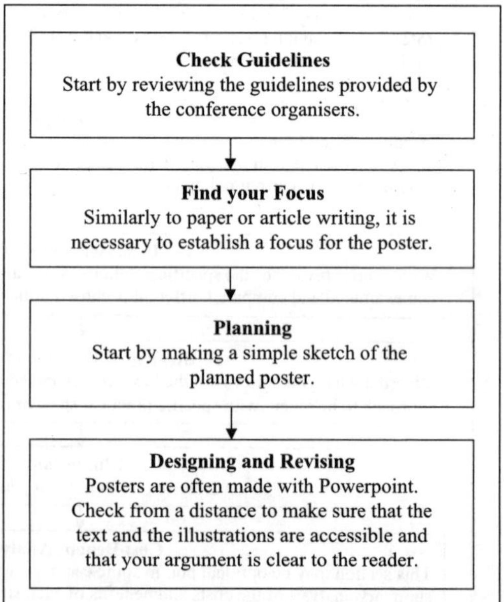


Figure 2.24: Steps of Making a Poster

## Reports

The purpose of reports is to describe what happened (e.g. in a piece of research) and discuss and evaluate its importance. Reports are found in different disciplines, such as science, social science, law and medicine. They typically include some or all of the following:

- Context/Overview (Title, Contents etc.)
- Introduction
- Methodology/Description of the event (e.g. piece of research)
- Findings/Main points
- Discussion/Evaluation
- Conclusion.

Many newspapers and magazines regularly include short reports of current research that may be of interest to the educated reader. For a brief research report, you will probably include the following stages:

- *Short summary:* This summarises the main points of the research. It will include the names of the researchers, where they work and where the main report is published.
- *General background:* This puts the research in the wider context by giving brief details of the subject and the state of present research.
- *Purpose:* This explains the purpose of the investigation, and explains why it was carried out.
- *Procedure:* This explains how the research was carried out. It gives details of who the subjects were, how the data was gathered and any special equipment that was used.
- *Results:* This gives details of any new information that came from an analysis of the data. What was found?

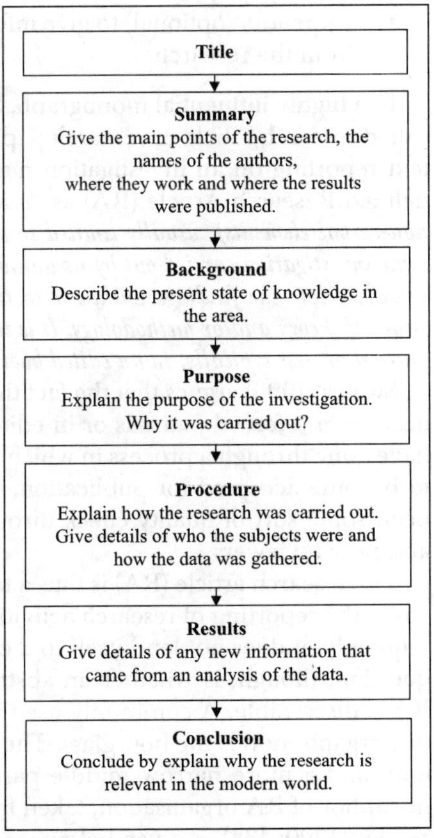


Figure 2.25: Structure of Report

- *Conclusions:* The report concludes by relating the findings to the wider context and explains why the research is relevant today.

## Research Article (RA)

Research articles are written mainly for a specialist audience–researchers, academics and postgraduate students. They usually contain the following:

- Introduction to the research
- Literature review
- Background to the research and method
- Results or main findings
- Discussion, including authors' interpretation of the results
- Recommendations: ideas for future research
- Conclusion
- Bibliography
- Appendix (optional) to give information such as tables of raw data from the research.

In a highly influential monograph, Swales (1990) introduces the genre called research article or research paper. The research article is a written text reporting on an investigation made by a researcher. Swales (1990) defined Research Article (RA) as *"a written text (although often containing non-verbal elements), usually limited to a few thousand words, that reports on some investigation carried out by its author or authors. In addition, the RA will usually relate the findings within it to those of others, and may also examine issues of theory and/or methodology. It is to appear or has appeared in a research journal or, less typically, in an edited book-length collection of papers."*

Swales (1990) argues that the fact that most RAs are intended for publication in refereed journals or in edited book volumes means that they have gone through a process in which they have been shaped in an effort to become accepted for publication. In turn, this means that there has been some sort of quality check through the scrutiny of journal editors and peer reviewers.

The research article (RA) is thus a fairly broad term since it is taken to cover the reporting of research activities in several disciplines, and, consequently, it does not lend itself to a clear-cut, uniform description. The question, though, is whether an abstracted, overall organisation of the RA is discernible. A commonly used metaphor when trying to describe this organisation is the hourglass. The hourglass has a wide top and bottom, and a more narrow middle part. An illustration of the hourglass metaphor of RA organisation, taken from Hill et al. (1982), appearing in Swales (1990: 134), is given below.

The idea behind the hour-glass model is that a transition is made between the general field of study, to the particular study reported in the article, and then another transition at the end of the article, where a move is made from the findings in the particular study to implications for the general field.

## Research Notes

They are short descriptions of current research findings that are considered less urgent or important than *Letters.*

## Research Proposal

A research proposal is a document proposing a research project, generally in the sciences or academia, and generally constitutes a request for sponsor ship of that research. Proposals are evaluated on the cost and potential impact of the proposed research, and on the soundness of the proposed plan for carrying it out.

A research proposal is a concise and coherent summary of a proposed research. It sets out the central issues or questions that the researcher or investigator intends to address. It outlines the general area of study within which research falls, referring to the current state of knowledge

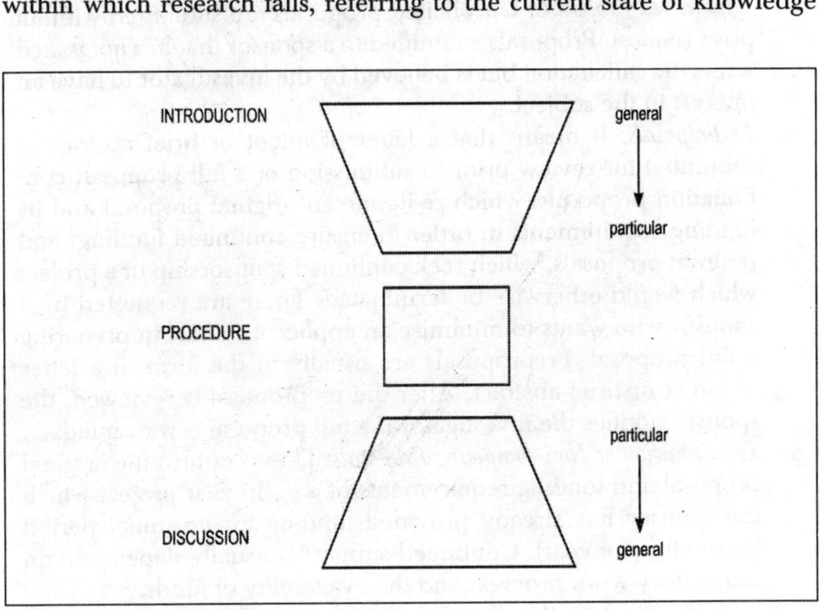


Figure 2.26: The Hour-Glass Model of Article Structure
(Taken from Hill et al. 1982 (Appearing in Swales, 1990: 134))

and any recent debates on the topic. It also demonstrates the originality of the proposed research.

Research proposals generally address several key points given below:

- How much time and expense will be required for the research?
- What prior research has been done on the topic?
- How the results of the research will be evaluated?
- How the research will benefit the sponsoring organisation and other parties?

*Types of Research Proposals*

Five types of Research proposals are given below:

1. *Solicited Proposals:* Solicited proposals are submitted in response to a request with specified requirements, such as a request for proposal. Proposals submitted in response to a specific call issued by a sponsor. Such solicitations, typically called Request for Proposals (RFP), or Request for Quotations (RFQ), usually have specific requirements for format and technical content, and may specify certain award terms and conditions. Broad Agency Announcements (BAAs) are not considered formal solicitations.
2. *Unsolicited Proposals:* Unsolicited proposals are submitted without prior request. Proposals submitted to a sponsor that has not issued a specific solicitation but is believed by the investigator to have an interest in the subject.
3. *Preproposals:* It means that a letter of intent or brief abstract is submitted for review prior to submission of a full proposal; continuation proposals, which re-iterate an original proposal and its funding requirements in order to ensure continued funding; and renewal proposals, which seek continued sponsorship of a project which would otherwise be terminated. These are requested by a sponsor who wants to minimise an applicant's effort in preparing a full proposal. Preproposals are usually in the form of a letter of intent or brief abstract. After the preproposal is reviewed, the sponsor notifies the investigator if a full proposal is warranted.
4. *Continuation or Non-competing Proposals:* These confirm the original proposal and funding requirements of a multi-year project which the sponsor has already provided funding for an initial period (normally one year). Continued support is usually dependent on satisfactory work progress and the availability of funds.
5. *Renewal or Competing Proposals:* Proposals which request continued support for an existing project that is about to end. These requests– from the sponsor's viewpoint– generally have the same status as an unsolicited proposal.

*Parts of a Research Proposal*

Academic research proposals are generally written as part of the initial requirements of writing a thesis, research paper, or dissertation. They generally follow the same format as a research paper, with an introduction, a literature review, a discussion of research methodology and goals, and a conclusion. This basic structure may vary between projects and between fields, each of which may have its own requirements.

The main parts of a research proposal are given below:

*Title:* The first part of a research proposal is the title. A good title should reflect the content, problems and/or the main variable(s) of the study. It has to be brief, concise and clear. It should give an idea as to what the whole problem is about–a description, a comparison, a relation or an evaluation of a certain phenomenon or topic.

*Abstract:* It is a brief summary of approximately 300 words. It should include the main research question, the rationale for the study, the hypothesis (if any) and the method. Descriptions of the method may include the design, procedures, the sample and any instruments that will be used.

*Introduction:* Spell out the peculiarity of the situation or research problem you are interested in investigating. This introduction should build up into focus the main question or the research problem at hand, i.e., how the research problem came about. The introduction should also tell us about the research gap that the study wants to fill up. The Introduction also includes the review of literature and conceptual framework, if needed. A brief summary of the findings of pertinent previous studies on the problem, and the status of current research; and the additional knowledge needed to which the project is expected to contribute. This review should be done to put together materials for the formulation of a conceptual framework, which is best illustrated by a diagram which shows the relationships of all the study variables.

*Problem/Objectives:* Research objectives are the goals to be achieved by conducting the research. They may be stated as *'general'* and *'specific'*.

- *General objective:* The general objective of the research is what is to be accomplished by the research project, for example, to determine whether or not a new vaccine should be incorporated in a public health programme.
- *Specific objectives:* The specific objectives relate to the specific research questions the investigator wants to answer through the proposed study and may be presented as primary and secondary objectives, for example, primary: To determine the degree of protection that is attributable to the new vaccine in a study

population by comparing the vaccinated and unvaccinated groups.
Secondary: To study the cost-effectiveness of this programme.

A good research problem/objective has the following characteristics:

- It should be specific
- It should be relevant to the times
- It should be practical
- It should fill a research gap.

*Variables:* During the planning stage, it is necessary to identify the key variables of the study and their method of measurement and unit of measurement must be clearly indicated. Four types of variables are important in research:

- *Independent variables:* variables that are manipulated or treated in a study in order to see what effect differences in them will have on those variables proposed as being dependent on them. The different synonyms for the term *'independent variable'* which are used in literature are: cause, input, predisposing factor, risk factor, determinant, antecedent, characteristic and attribute.
- *Dependent variables:* variables in which changes are results of the level or amount of the independent variable or variables. Synonyms of dependent variables are: effect, outcome, consequence, result, condition, disease.
- *Confounding or intervening variables:* Variables those should be studied because they may influence or 'mix' the effect of the independent variables. For instance, in a study of the effect of measles (independent variable) on child mortality (dependent variable), the nutritional status of the child may play an intervening (confounding) role.
- *Background variables:* Variables those are so often of relevance in investigations of groups or populations that they should be considered for possible inclusion in the study, for example, sex, age, ethnic origin, education, marital status, social status, etc.

The objective of research is usually to determine the effect of changes in one or more independent variables on one or more dependent variables.

*Questions and/or Hypotheses:* A research question poses a relationship between two or more variables but phrases the relationship as a question; a hypothesis represents a declarative statement of the relations between two or more variables. If you as a researcher know enough to make prediction concerning what you are studying, then the hypothesis may be formulated. A hypothesis can be defined as a tentative prediction or explanation of the relationship between two or more variables. In other words, the hypothesis translates the problem statement into a precise, unambiguous prediction of expected outcomes. Hypotheses are not meant to be haphazard guesses, but should reflect the depth of knowledge, imagination and experience of the investigator. In the process of formulating the hypotheses, all variables relevant to the study must be identified.

*Significance of the Research/Study:* This section presents the reasons for doing the work–such as the needs the project will fill and why the work should be done now. It could also deal with defining the contributions which the research findings can give to its end users–people, agency, region or even nation who are going to make use of the research findings.

The proposal should demonstrate the originality of your intended research. You should therefore explain why your research is important (for example, by explaining how your research builds on and adds to the current state of knowledge in the field or by setting out reasons why it is timely to research your proposed topic).

*Methodology:* The method section is very important because it tells your research Committee how you plan to tackle your research problem. The proposed plans and methods should correspond to the objectives of the research study. The research methodology must include the following:

- *Research Design:* It must be appropriate to the requirements of the research problem.
- *Research subjects/Respondents/participants:* The respondents of the study are identified in this section. They are the subjects of the survey or interview or participants of the focus group discussion. Depending on the type of your study, the following questions should be answered:
  1. What are the criteria for inclusion or selection?
  2. What are the criteria for exclusion?
  3. What is the sampling procedure you will use so as to ensure representativeness and reliability of the sample and to minimise sampling errors?
  4. Will there be use of controls in your study?–What are the criteria for discontinuation?
- *Sample size:* The proposal should provide information and justification (basis on which the sample size is calculated) about sample size in the methodology section.

- *Interventions:* If an intervention is introduced, a description must be given of the devices.
- *Research setting:* The research setting includes all the pertinent facets of the study, such as the population to be studied (sampling frame), the place and time of study.
- *Instrumentation:* Instruments are the tools by which the data are collected. The research instruments used for data collection will be presented here. The components of the questionnaire, interview schedule, focus group discussion, guide, etc. would be made explicit. For validated questionnaires/interview schedules, reference to published work should be given and the instrument appended to the proposal.
- *Collection of data:* A short description of the protocol of data collection.
- *Data analysis:* The description should include the design of the analysis form, plans for processing and coding the data and the choice of the statistical method to be applied to each data.
- *Monitoring, supervision and quality control:* Detailed statement about the all logistical issues to satisfy the requirements of Good Clinical Practices (GCP), protocol procedures, responsibilities of each member of the research team, training of study investigators, steps taken to assure quality control (laboratory procedures, equipment calibration, etc.)
- *Gantt chart:* A Gantt chart is an overview of tasks/proposed activities and a time frame for the same. You put weeks, days or months at one side, and the tasks at the other. You draw fat lines to indicate the period the task will be performed to give a timeline for your research study
- *Significance of the study:* Indicate how your research will refine, revise or extend existing knowledge in the area under investigation. How will it benefit the concerned stakeholders? What could be the larger implications of your research study?
- *Dissemination of the study results:* How do you propose to share the findings of your study with professional peers, practitioners, participants and the funding agency?
- *Budget:* A proposal budget with item-wise/activity-wise breakdown and justification for the same. Indicate how the study will be financed.
- *References:* The proposal should end with relevant references on the subject. For web based search include the date of access for the cited website, for example: add the sentence "accessed on June 10, 2008".

- *Appendices:* Include the appropriate appendices in the proposal. For example: Interview protocols, sample of informed consent forms, cover letters sent to appropriate stakeholders, official letters for permission to conduct research. Regarding original scales or questionnaires, if the instrument is copyrighted then permission in writing to reproduce the instrument from the copyright holder or proof of purchase of the instrument must be submitted.

## Review Articles

Review articles do not cover original research but rather accumulate the results of many different *articles* on a particular topic into a coherent narrative about the state of the art in that field. Review articles provide information about the topic and also provide journal references to the original research. Reviews may be entirely narrative, or may provide quantitative summary estimates resulting from the application of meta-analytical methods.

## Scholarly Article

The purpose of a scholarly article is to present new knowledge or to provide new perspectives on an academic or scientific problem or object. The target audience is other scholars. A scholarly article is primarily argumentative. It claims that something is true or probably true and presents arguments to support the claim. Hence, a scholarly article has to present thorough and consistent reasoning. The reasoning must be properly substantiated, through references to empirical data or other research. Authors of scholarly articles should use acknowledged research methods, and also explain them.

## Supplemental Articles

They contain a large volume of tabular data that is the result of current research and may be dozens or hundreds of pages with mostly numerical data. Some journals now only publish this data electronically on the Internet. Supplemental information also contains other voluminous material not appropriate for the main body of the article, like descriptions of routine procedures, derivations of equations, source code, non-essential data, spectra or other such miscellaneous information.

## Textbooks

A textbook is meant to communicate established knowledge to students of a given subject. It provides a general introduction to the subject as well as relevant problems, concepts and theories. A textbook presents knowledge and explains how it has been used, and can be used. It

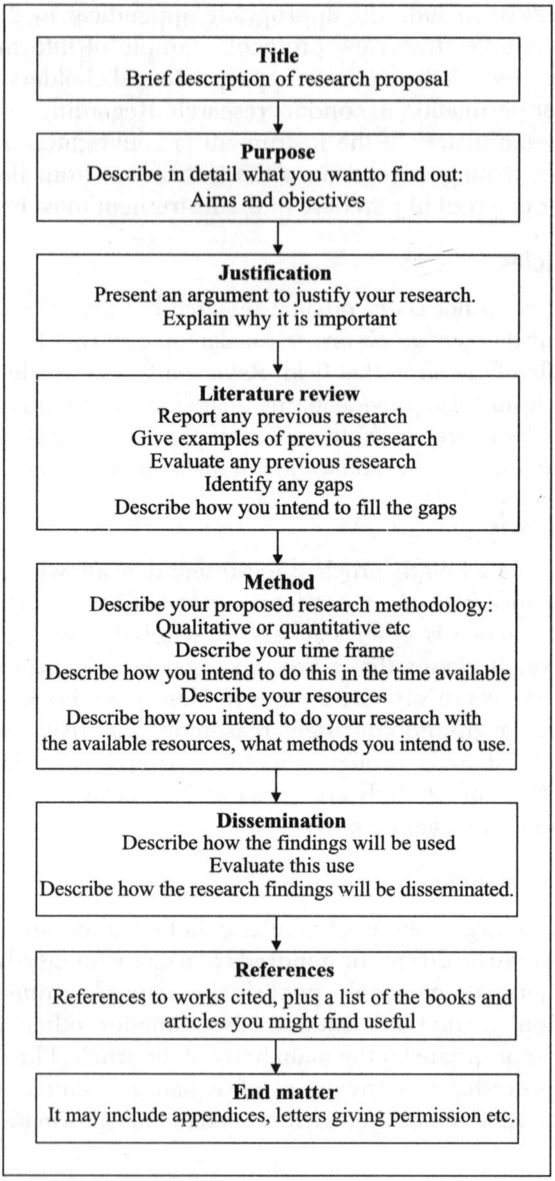


Figure 2.27: Structure of Research Proposal

informs and instructs. Even though a textbook can include discussion and argumentation, its primary objective is not to argue for or against particular positions, but to present the existing views within the subject.

Textbooks are specifically designed to help the learner. For example, they might have summaries or review quizzes. Textbooks vary in style, tone and level depending on their audience. They are a good place to start when learning about a new topic.

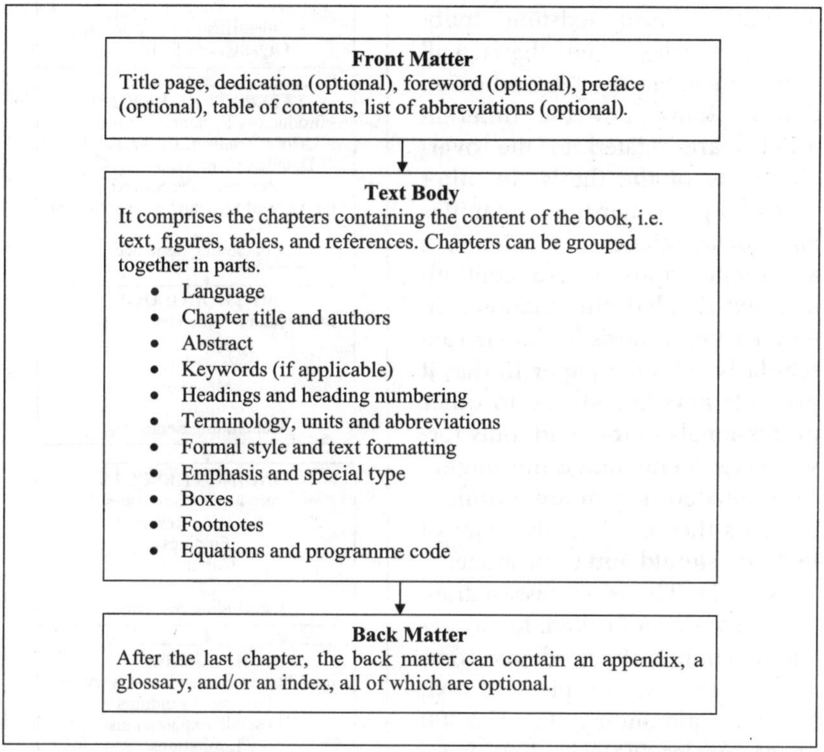


Figure 2.28: Structure of Textbook

The academic textbook is somewhat of a blurred genre. It is the dominant genre of formal education, and its main communicative purpose, according to Bhatia (1998), is to *"make accessible established knowledge in a particular discipline to those readers who are being initiated into a specific disciplinary culture"*. Thus, a textbook is generally seen as a written text that introduces newcomers to a specific discipline.

According to Bhatia (2004), *"Textbooks [...] disseminate discipline-based knowledge and, at the same time, display a somewhat unequal writer-reader relationship, with the writer as the specialist and the reader as the non-initiated apprentice in the discipline, or the writer as the transmitter and the reader as the recipient of established knowledge."*

## Thesis

A thesis is a major piece of scholarly work. In some fields (especially medicine and the natural sciences), theses are frequently assembled from existing (published) articles. The thesis will then include an introduction that explains how the different articles are related to the overall theme of the thesis. In other fields (in particular the humanities and social sciences), most theses are monographs, i.e., a continuous text divided into chapters. In either case, a thesis is similar to a scholarly research paper in that it presents new knowledge to other professionals in the field, puts forward arguments, and is thoroughly substantiated. If you are writing a master's thesis, this is the type of text you should aim to produce.

A Ph.D. Thesis, or dissertation, as it is sometimes called, has a special function in the academic community. This written piece of text, typically amounting to 150-300 pages (Swales, 2004: p. 102), functions as a kind of scholarly qualifying piece of work, through which the author is admitted into the society of academics seen as sharing some sort of common ground in terms of expert knowledge, skills, critical thinking, rigour, and scientific values.

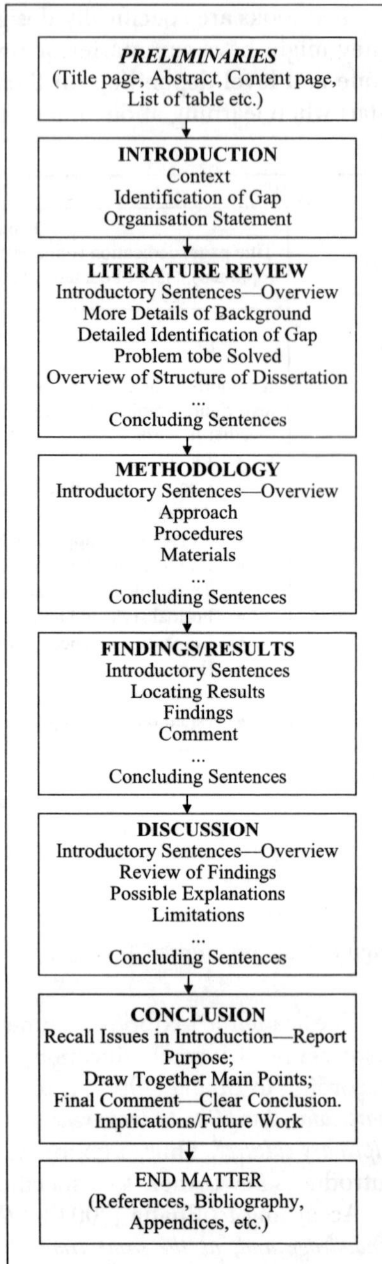


Figure 2.29: Structure of Thesis

### *Types of Ph.D. Theses*

Strictly speaking, there are two main types of Ph.D. theses: the monograph format and the article-compilation format. The monograph, which can be seen as the more traditional type, is written as a coherent, synoptic text, whereas the article compilation thesis (sometimes called multiple-manuscript thesis or anthology) features a series of published/ publishable papers compiled into a coherent whole, often with designated introductory and concluding chapters (Swales, 2004).

In terms of their spread and use, the article-compilation format is predominantly adopted in the hard sciences and engineering, but it does also occur in some disciplines in the social sciences and humanities. The monograph format is arguably the most commonly used in the soft sciences. On the whole, though, there is a lot of variation when it comes to the preferred format in different disciplines.

### *Types of Thesis Structures*

When it comes to the structure of a Ph.D. thesis, there is naturally a great deal of variation going on across different disciplines, but one format is at least at the face of it expected to traditionally dominate: a blown-up version of the IMRD format often used in research articles.

However, as has been pointed out by Swales (2004), the above traditional structure is perhaps not the most widely used. He argues, for example, that one problem with the traditional structure is that it might be problematic to have only a single chapter dealing with results. This, he continues, "produces an unwieldy and out-of-balance monster chapter in the middle of the text" (p. 108).

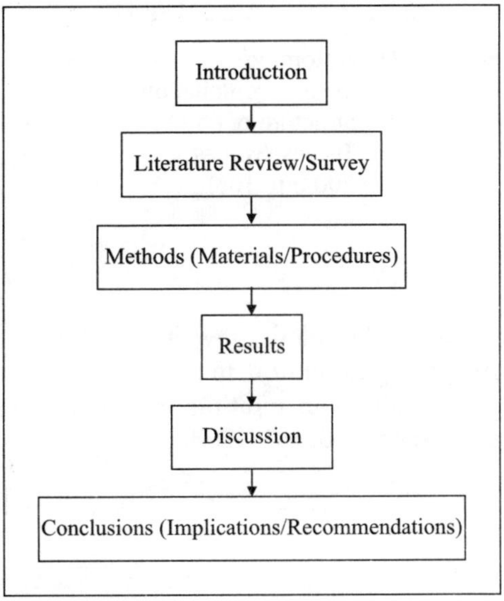


Figure 2.30: Traditional Structure of Ph.D. Theses (Swales, 2004: p. 107)

An alternative structure for a Ph.D. thesis is similar to the article-compilation format mentioned earlier. This format is seemingly more popular in science and engineering disciplines. Click on the link below to see an example of this thesis format.

A third structure, allegedly mostly used in the humanities and social sciences, but also found

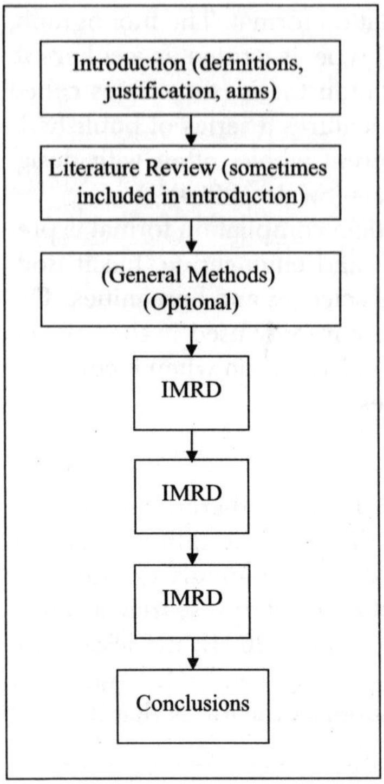


Figure 2.31: A Complex (Article-compilation) Structure of Ph.D. Theses (Swales, 2004: p. 108)

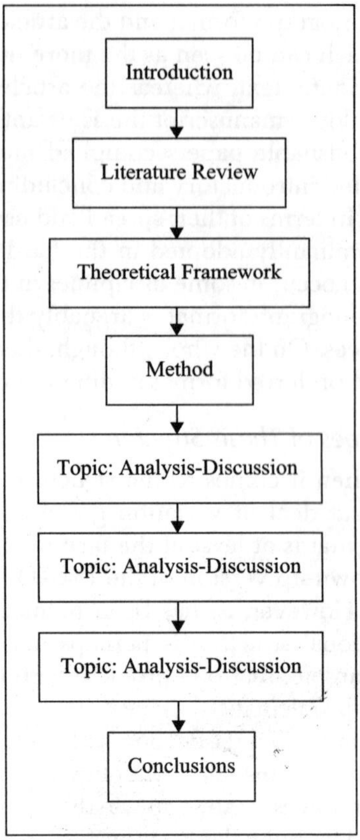


Figure 2.32: Overview of the Topic Specific Structure of the Ph.D. Theses (Swales, 2004: p. 109)

in other disciplines (Swales, 2004), is called the topic-based thesis. According to Bunton, in these types of theses authors "report and discuss their analyses in multiple chapters (ranging from three to seven) with topic-specific titles" (1998, p. 110).

# CHAPTER 3

# Structure of Academic Texts

Structure refers to the order of ideas. The progression of your writing should feel smooth with similar points linked together. Structuring your work is a key aspect of good academic writing ensuring that related sections are linked together and that the ideas and arguments progress in a logical and orderly manner. Writing that is unstructured may link unrelated points, have an illogical or confused argument and lack a real focus. Repetition of points or linking unrelated ideas together can often signify limited preparation and thought.

Structure is an important feature of academic writing. A well-structured text enables the reader to follow the argument and navigate the text. In academic writing, a clear structure and a logical flow are imperative to a cohesive text. Furthermore, in many university assignments the correct use of structure is part of the final assessment. Most academic texts follow established structures.

The structure of academic writing depends on the type of assignment. Two common structures used in academic writing are the three-part essay structure and the IMRaD structure.

## Three-Part Essay Structure

The three-part essay structure is a basic structure that consists of *introduction, body* and *conclusion.* The introduction and the conclusion should be shorter than the body of the text. For shorter essays, one or two paragraphs for each of these sections can be appropriate. For longer texts or theses, they may be several pages long.

### *Introduction*

Your introduction should include the following points (be aware that not all points may be relevant for your project):

- Introduce your topic
- Place your topic in a context
- Provide background information
- Point out the aim of the text

- Describe how you will fulfill the aim
- Provide a thesis statement or research question
- Suggest what your findings are
- Explain why your topic is interesting, necessary or important
- Give the reader a guide to the text
- Catch your reader's interest

The statements you make in the introduction are to be developed in the body of the text and returned to in the conclusion. You may write the introduction at the beginning or at the end of the writing process. If you write it early in the process it can serve as a guide to your own writing but be aware that you most likely will have to go back to it and edit it as the writing progresses.

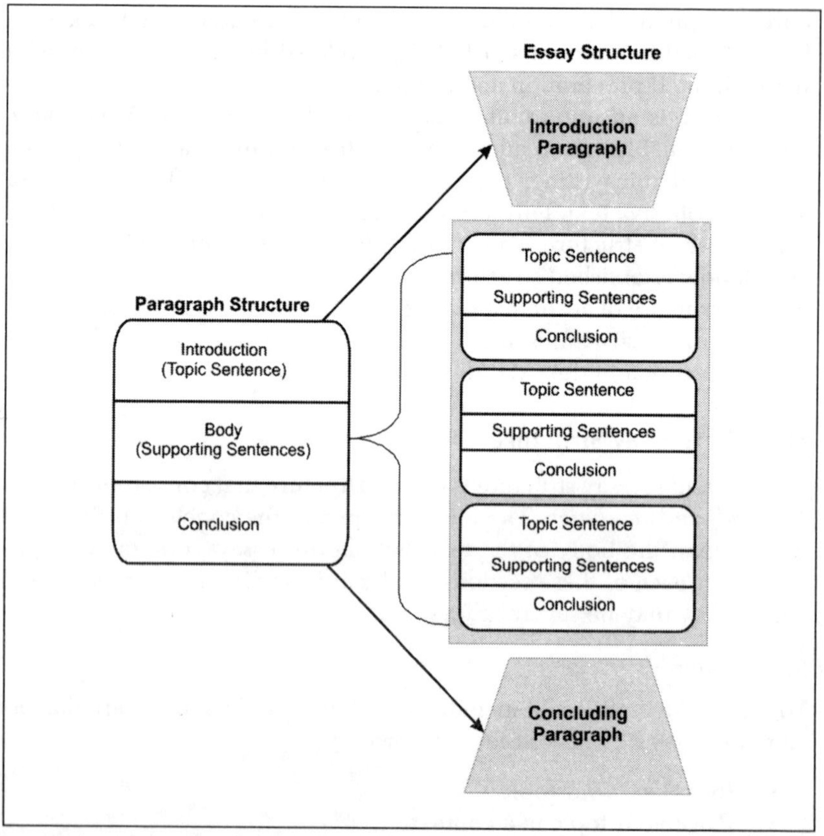


Figure 3.1: The Three Part Essay Structure

*Body*

This is the main section of your text and it should also be the longest. Depending on the length of the text, the body may be divided into subsections. If your text is divided into subsections, remember to briefly introduce each section. For longer works you may also need to conclude sections. The body of the text is where you as a writer and researcher are the most active. It is the most substantial part of the text; this is where the research or findings are presented, discussed and analysed. This is also where you present your arguments that support your thesis or answer your question. The structure and contents of this main part may differ depending on your discipline.

*Conclusion*

In the conclusion you should return to the thesis or problem that you presented in the introduction. But be careful to not merely repeat what you wrote in the introduction; instead, show your reader how what you have written sheds new light on the problem presented at the beginning. For longer works a brief summary of your findings may be in place, but this should not be necessary for shorter texts. Be careful that your conclusion is not just a repetition of what you have already written. In your conclusion, you may also evaluate and explain whether or not you have reached the aim or solved the problem presented in the introduction, and how. No new material should be introduced in the conclusion, but it is quite common to suggest topics for further studies.

## IMRAD Structure

The IMRAD or IMRAD (often pronounced "im-rad") format is a scientific writing structure that includes four or five major sections: introduction (I); research methods (M); results (R); analysis (a); and discussion (D). The IMRAD format is the most commonly used format in scientific article and journal writing and is used widely across most scientific and research fields.

### *When to Use the IMRAD Structure?*

If you are writing a paper where you are conducting objective research in order to answer a specific question, the IMRAD format will most likely serve your purposes best. The IMRAD format is especially useful if you are conducting primary research (such as experimentation, questionnaires, focus groups, observations, interviews, and so forth), but it can be applied even if you only conduct secondary research (which is research you gather from reading sources like books, magazines, journal articles, and so forth.)

The goal of using the IMRAD format is to present facts objectively, demonstrating a genuine interest and care in developing new understanding about a topic; when using this format, you do not explicitly state an argument or opinion, but rather, you rely on collected data and previously researched information in order to make a claim.

While there are nuances and adjustments that would be made to the following document types, the IMRAD format is the foundational structure of many research-driven documents:

- Grants
- Proposals
- Recommendation reports
- Plans (such as an integrated marketing plan or project management plan)

### *Sections of the IMRAD Structure*

The sections of IMRAD structure are discussed below:

#### *Introduction*

In the first section of your paper, make a case for your new research. Explain to your reader why you chose to research this topic, problem, or issue, and why such research is needed. Explain any "gaps" in the current research on this topic, and explain how your research contributes to closing that gap.

The introduction leads the reader from a general subject area to a particular topic of inquiry. It establishes the scope, context, and significance of the research being conducted by summarising current understanding and background information about the topic, stating the purpose of the work in the form of the research problem supported by a hypothesis or a set of questions, explaining briefly the methodological approach used to examine the research problem, highlighting the potential outcomes your study can reveal, and outlining the remaining structure and organisation of the paper.

The introduction states the research problem or the question(s) you intend to address through research. Your introduction would typically include some variation of the following:

- Statement of the topic you are about to address
- Current state of the field of understanding (often, we call this a literature review and it may even merit having its own section)
- Problem or gap in knowledge (what do we not know yet or need to know? what does the field still need to understand? what has

been left out of previous research? is this a new issue that needs some direction?)

- Forecast statement that explains, very briefly, what the rest of the paper will entail, including a possible quick explanation of the type of research that needs to be conducted

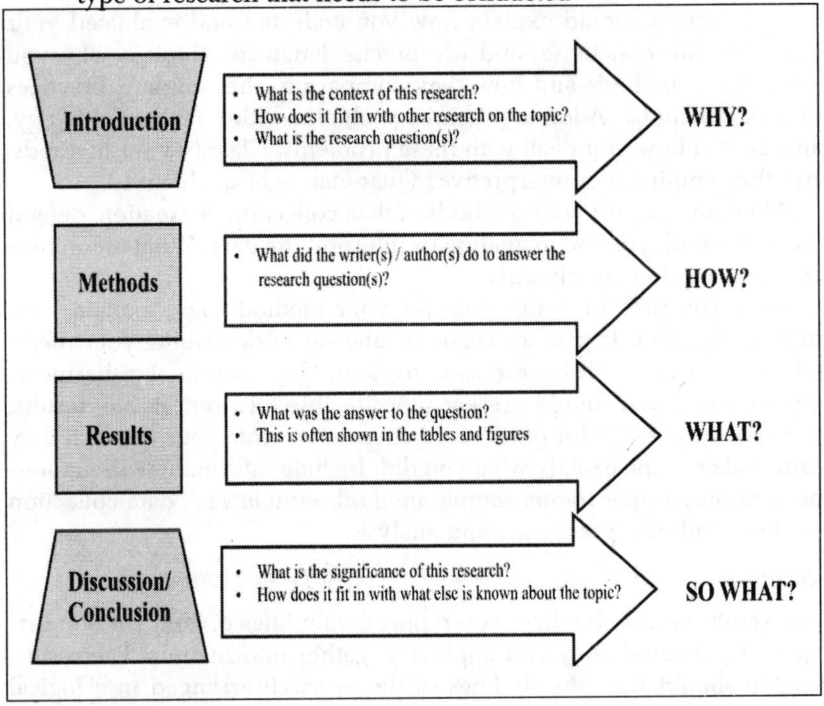


Figure 3.2: The IMRAD Structure of Academic Text

*Method*

The methods section describes actions to be taken to investigate a research problem and the rationale for the application of specific procedures or techniques used to identify, select, process, and analyse information applied to understanding the problem, thereby, allowing the reader to critically evaluate a study's overall validity and reliability. The methodology section of a research paper answers two main questions:

- How was the data collected or generated?
- And, how was it analysed? The writing should be direct and precise and always written in the past tense.

In this section, you describe how you have conducted your study. This is where you present your material and your research as well as any previous research and background material. You describe what method or methods you have used and how you have come up with your results. You may also explain why you have chosen a particular method.

This section should explain how you collected and evaluated your data. Use the past tense, and use precise language. Explain why you chose your methods and how they compare to the standard practices in your discipline. Address potential problems with your methodology, and discuss how you dealt with these problems. Classify your methods. Are they empirical or interpretive? Quantitative or qualitative?

After you support your methods of data collection or creation, defend the framework you use to analyse or interpret the data. What theoretical assumptions do you rely on?

After you provide a rationale for your methodology, explain your process in detail. If you are vague or unclear in describing your methods, your reader will have reason to doubt your results. Furthermore, scientific research should present reproducible (i.e., repeatable) results. It will be impossible for other researchers to recreate your results if they cannot determine exactly what you did. Include information about your population, sample frame, sample method, sample size, data-collection method, and data processing and analysis.

### *Results*

The results section is where you report the findings of your study based upon the methodology you applied to gather information. The results section should state the findings of the research arranged in a logical sequence without bias or interpretation. A section describing results is particularly necessary if your paper includes data generated from your own research.

### *Analysis*

The analysis section details what you and others may learn from the data. While some researchers like to combine this section with the Discussion section, many writers and researchers find it useful to analyse the data separately. In the analysis section, spend time connecting the dots for the reader. What do the interviews say about the way employers think about their employees? What do the observations say about how employees respond to workplace criticism? Can any connections be made between the two research types? It is important in the Analysis section that you do not draw conclusions that the research findings do not suggest. Always stick to what the research says.

### *Discussion*

The purpose of the discussion is to interpret and describe the significance of your findings in light of what was already known about the research problem being investigated and to explain any new understanding or insights that emerged as a result of your study of the problem. The discussion will always connect to the introduction by way of the research questions or hypotheses you posed and the literature you reviewed, but the discussion does not simply repeat or rearrange the first parts of your paper; the discussion clearly explains how your study advanced the reader's understanding of the research problem from where you left them at the end of your review of prior research.

The discussion is the section where you as a writer are the most active and it should be the most substantial section of the entire paper. You should interpret, analyse and discuss your results as well as compare and contrast them to previous research. In this chapter, you discuss the results of your study/project.

At this stage, the following points are discussed by the researcher or author:

- Is it possible to generalise?
- Make comparisons with other studies
- Are there alternative explanations?
- What are the strong and weak aspects of the paper?
- What are the practical implications?
- Is more research needed?
- Make recommendations (to be applied in practice).

Sometimes papers that use the IMRAD structure will have a separate conclusion and sometimes the conclusion will be merged with the discussion. Be sure to check with your instructor what is expected of you.

*For your conclusion:* What answer(s) have you found to your research question? If you have a hypothesis, has it been strengthened, weakened or falsified? Do not introduce issues here that have not been mentioned earlier. If the results of your study do not allow you to draw any conclusions, you can end with a summing up.

# CHAPTER 4
# Forms of Writing

There are several forms of writing like descriptive writing, creative writing, technical writing, expository writing, narrative writing, persuasive writing, argumentative writing, autobiographical writing, and biographical writing and so on. Initially, students begin with descriptive writing and gradually proceed to more complex forms like narrative, expository or autobiographical.

## Descriptive Writing

Descriptive writing focuses on communicating the details of a character, event, or place.

### *Meaning of Descriptive Writing*

It is the clear description of people, places, objects, or events using appropriate details. An effective description will contain sufficient and varied elaboration of details to communicate a sense of the subject being described. Details used are usually sensory and selected to describe what the writer sees, hears, smells, touches, and tastes. Descriptive writing uses a lot of flowery adjectives and adverbs to describe what is going on or how something appears. This form of writing includes using descriptive phrases and figurative language. This includes, but is not limited to metaphors, similes, onomatopoeia, alliteration, personification and hyperbole. The writing is used often to create a feeling or visual experience. Words that are strong to the senses are often used, as well. The reader should be able to imagine how to see, hear, feel, touch, and smell what the author is describing.

Students are often given descriptive writing tasks. It is necessary for students to understand and identify descriptive topics and decide what content to include in their body of writing, which details should be included and which to be omitted.

## Example of Descriptive Writing

An example of descriptive writing is given below:

"A grand exhibition was held in the town. The first impression on entering the ground was of walking in some fairyland. The vast space was decorated with so many colourful lights. The stalls were like small shops and they had all the needful items. All types of amusements could be seen there. The children were enjoying the ride on merry-go-round, the giant wheel, railway train and others. The excitement and joy could be seen easily."

In the above sample, the writer wants to describe his visit to the exhibition. It is a descriptive style of writing.

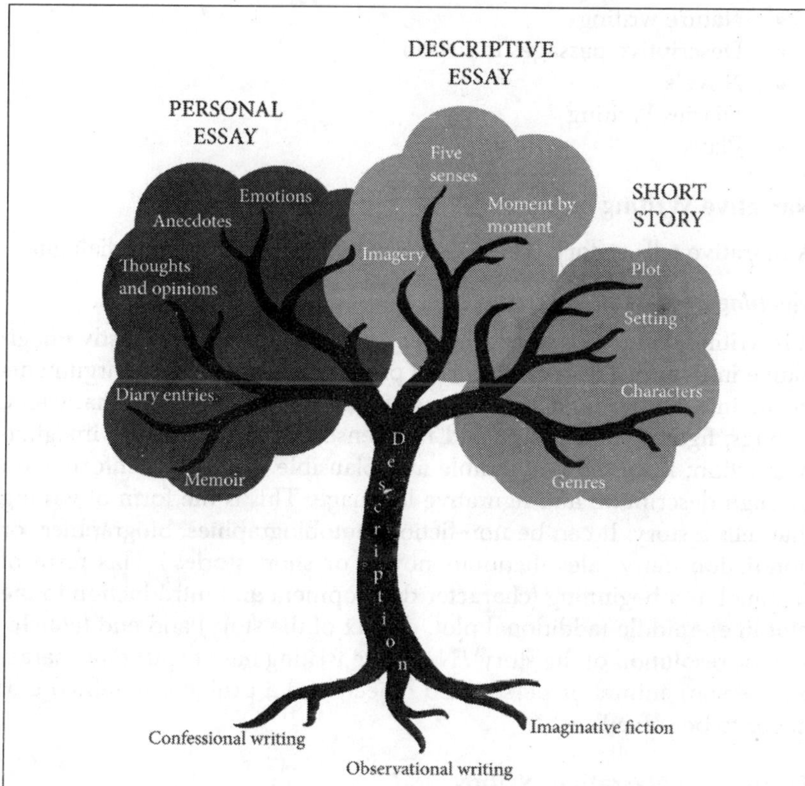


Figure 4.1: Types of Descriptive Essay

### *Highlights/Key Points of Descriptive Writing*

- It is often poetic in nature
- It describes places, people, events, situations, or locations in a highly-detailed manner

- The author visualises what he or she sees, hears, tastes, smells, and feels
- It uses figures of speech
- The writer makes the readers feel, hear, and visualise the situation the way he wants.

### *Areas of Usage/When to Use Descriptive Writing*

- Poetry
- Journal writing
- Nature writing
- Descriptive passages in fiction
- Novels
- Diaries Writing
- Plays

## Narrative Writing

A narrative tells a story. There will usually be characters and dialogue.

### *Meaning of Narrative Writing*

It is writing that tells a story whether true or fictional. It is mostly imaginative in nature. The intention is to present ideas, issues and arguments in an imaginative and credible way through description, characters, settings, figurative language and five senses. While a work of imaginative fiction; it should be credible and plausible. It conveys information through description and figurative language. This is the form of writing that tells a story. It can be non-fiction (autobiographies, biographies) or non-fiction (fairy tales, fictitious novels or short stories.) This form of writing has a beginning (character development and introduction to the plot line), middle (additional plot, climax of the story) and end (conclusion or resolution of the story). Narrative writing has at least one character (person, animal or personified object) and a problem (conflict) that needs to be solved.

## Example of Narrative Writing

An example of narrative writing is given below:

> "It was a hot, sunny day. I finally visited Disneyland. It was a dreamland. I always wanted to visit there. Being there it was like dream come true experience. On entering, the very first thing that I said, "Oh wow! What a wonderful place!" People were walking and enjoying their time with all the Disney characters. Children over there were so happy and excited. I think it is a must visit place for everyone."

Here the writer is sharing his or her personal experience and emotions. It is a narrative style of writing.

### *Highlights/Key Points of Narrative Writing*

- A person tells a story or event.
- Has definite and logical beginnings, intervals, and endings.
- Often has a situation like actions, motivational events, and disputes or conflicts with their eventual solutions.
- The inclusion of dialogues
- Use of metaphor, imaginative language, and figure of speech
- Addition of emotional words
- Have a beginning, intervals, and endings.

### *Areas of Usage/When to Use Narrative Writing*

- Novels
- Short stories
- Novellas
- Poetry
- Autobiographies or biographies
- Anecdotes
- Oral histories
- Fairy Tales
- Screen scripts
- Play
- Legends
- Songs.

## Expository Writing

Expository writing explains or informs. It talks about a subject without giving opinions.

### *Meaning of Expository Writing*

It is writing that explains or gives information. It explains all sides of an argument or issue. It provides a balanced discussion of different views and presents the pros and cons of an issue so that the readers can make up their minds. Compare-Contrast essays show similarities or differences between two subjects. This form of writing exists to give facts. It does not require the plot line of narrative writing, nor the character development. This form of writing is most frequently found in news stories, articles, and reports. The information in expository writing develops the main idea and provides additional details to support this evidence, including facts or quotations. As in all writing, it should have an introduction, body and conclusion that support the main idea.

## Example of Expository Writing

An example of expository writing is given below:

> "The elephant is the largest and the strongest of all living animals. It has thick legs, small tail, little eyes, large ears, long white tusk, and a long nose which is its trunk. Elephants are found in India and in Africa. They live in herds in jungles. The elephant is a very intelligent animal and has great strength. Elephants can carry heavy loads. They live their lives entirely on leaves of trees, grass, and roots."

The above sample tries to provide information about elephants. This is an expository style of writing.

### *Highlights/Key Points of Expository Writing*

- Usually explains something in a process.
- Is often equipped with facts and figures.
- Is usually in a logical order and sequence.
- Organised in a logical order and in proper sequence.
- It explains the subject.

### *Areas of Usage/When to Use Expository Writing:*

- Textbook writing
- Business writing
- Scientific Writing
- Technical writing
- Recipes Writing
- Research Papers
- Encyclopaedias
- Essays
- Reports
- News stories (not including opinion or editorial pieces)
- How-to articles.

## Persuasive/Argumentative Writing

Persuasive writing tries to bring other people around to your point of view.

### *Meaning of Persuasive/Argumentative Writing*

It presents the writer's opinion and tries to convince the reader to agree. The purpose is to argue and convince that author's viewpoint is correct and to influence others to agree with viewpoint. It sets out to argue and prove a case. It aims to convince targeted audience of the validity of a viewpoint on an issue by presenting logical argument. It presents ideas that follow in logical progression. It also anticipates and answers possible objections or opposing arguments. It presents well researched evidence to support the case. In persuasive writing, the author is trying to get the reader to believe in what he or she is writing. Political speeches and speeches given by lawyers in the courtroom are persuasive writing, as are reviews of movies or books and opinion articles in the newspaper. Persuasive writing includes a main idea, introduction, body and conclusion. The main idea encompasses what the author wants the reader to believe, and the remaining information supports that central idea. Good persuasive writing includes facts and strong arguments to make the author's opinion sound logical.

## Example of Persuasive/Argumentative Writing

An example of persuasive/argumentative writing is given below:

> "Our store has the lowest prices and the best collection of footwear in the entire town. Visit us today for a great experience."

In the above example, the writer is trying to convince the reader for the trial as used in an advertisement. This is the persuasive style of writing.

### *Highlights/Key Points of Persuasive/Argumentative Writing*

- Persuasive writing is equipped with reasons, arguments, and justifications.
- In persuasive writing, the author takes a stand and asks you to agree with his or her point of view.
- It often asks for readers to do something about the situation (this is called a call-to-action).
- It asks the readers to do something for the situation
- It has reasons, arguments, and justification.

### *Areas of Usage/When to Use Persuasive/Argumentative Writing*

- Opinion and editorial newspaper pieces
- Reviews (of books, music, movie, restaurants, etc.)
- Letter of recommendation
- Cover letters
- Speeches
- Editorial Pieces
- Letters of Complaints
- Newspaper Opinion
- Review
- Critical Analysis
- Business Idea
- Advertisements or Commercials

## Creative Writing

Creative writing is any composition i.e. fiction, poetry or non-fiction that expresses ideas in an imaginative and unusual manner. Creative texts may be descriptive, narrative or expository, based on personal experiences or popular topics. Any kind of writing that involves an imaginative portrayal of ideas can be called creative writing. Creative writing can technically be considered any writing of original composition. The purpose of creative writing is to both entertain and share human experience. Writers attempt to get at a truth about humanity through poetics and storytelling.

### *Definitions of Creative writing*

Creative Writing can be defined as,

1. A form of writing that expresses writer's feelings, emotions, experiences, ideas, or thoughts obtained at a conscious or subconscious level. It is more driven by the writer's need to "express", and is generally articulated in the most unique, inventive, and poetic way.
2. Creative writing is considered to be any writing, fiction, poetry, or non-fiction that goes outside the bounds of normal professional, journalistic, academic, and technical forms of literature.
3. Creative writing is anything where the purpose is to express thoughts, feelings and emotions rather than to simply convey information.
4. Creative writing is writing that expresses the writer's thoughts and feelings in an imaginative, often unique, and poetic way.

### *Creative Genres*

Genre is a word often used to describe categories or types of written text. Some of the more familiar genres of creative writing are:

- poetry of all kinds
- short stories
- novels including westerns, romances, science fiction, detective stories, mysteries, fantasy, etc.
- stage play scripts
- film and television screenplays
- lyrics
- magazine articles
- newspaper feature stories
- essays

- biographies
- advertisements
- card greetings
- books or articles on science, history, etc.
- Plays
- Fiction (novels, novellas, and short stories)
- Songs
- Speeches
- Memoirs.

### *Techniques Used in Creative Writing*

The following techniques are used in creative writing:

- Character development
- Plot development
- Vivid setting
- Underlying theme
- Point of view
- Dialogue
- Anecdotes
- Metaphors and similes
- Figures of speech
- Imaginative language
- Emotional appeal
- Heavy description.

### *Types of Creative Writing*

Creative writing usually includes descriptive, expository, narrative and argumentative texts.

*Descriptive Text:* In a descriptive text, a writer gives his or her readers pictures to see, sounds to hear, and things to taste, feel and smell.

*Expository Text:* Expository writing defines, explains or describes how something is done or how something happens.

*Narrative Text:* A narrative describes an event chronologically, usually with a beginning, middle and end.

*Argument Text:* An argument is intended to convince others of something or to persuade them to do something.

### *Importance of Creative Writing to Students*

1. Creative writing sharpens students' ability to express their thoughts clearly.

2. It encourages students to think beyond the ordinary and to use their imagination to express their ideas in their own way.
3. Learning about creative writing also makes students familiar with literary terms and mechanisms such as sound patterns or metaphors.
4. It can help students to improve their command over the resources of language e.g. vocabulary, sentence patterns and metaphorical expressions when composing their own creative work.
5. Creative writing helps develop critical thinking skills, as students learn to question and to "think outside the box". The ability to evaluate a piece of literary work improves students' problem-solving abilities too.

### *Approaches to Teaching Creative Writing to Students*

The teaching of creative writing basically focuses on students' self-expression. It is taught by taking students through a series of steps that demonstrate the process of writing.

1. As a first step, students are introduced to a range of fictional and non-fictional texts, with their attention being drawn to the distinctive structural and linguistic features of each text.
2. They are also sensitised to the purpose, audience and context for which specific texts are written.
3. The students are then given practice in the use of linkers, connectives and other semantic markers that are used to connect and present ideas logically in a text. Typical semantic markers in narrative texts are words such as because, although, when, where, since and so on; they perform various functions in the text, such as showing time relationships, cause and effect relationships, conditions, sequence of events and so on.
4. The students are then gradually taught to dramatise events by:
   - establishing a landscape or context,
   - developing dialogues,
   - establishing characters using descriptions of appearance, mannerisms, etc., and
   - developing an appropriate vocabulary (e.g., formal versus informal words and phrases, colloquial terms, terms of endearment).
5. Lastly, students are helped to express more complex and layered meanings in stories that:
   - combine outside events with personal experiences,
   - dramatise inner feelings, and
   - contain reflections and commentary.

## Reflective Writing

Reflective writing is evidence of reflective thinking. In an academic context, reflective thinking usually involves:

- Looking back at something (often an event, i.e. something that happened, but it could also be an idea or object).
- Analysing the event or idea (thinking in depth and from different perspectives, and trying to explain, often with reference to a model or theory from your subject).
- Thinking carefully about what the event or idea means for you and your ongoing progress as a learner and/or practising professional.

Reflective writing is thus more personal than other kinds of academic writing. We all think reflectively in everyday life, of course, but perhaps not to the same depth as that expected in good reflective writing at university level. Writing a piece of reflection is different to more traditional forms of academic writing in that it is more subjective. That is, rather than being purely objective, it reveals and reviews personal bias and feelings. Reflective writing is a method for discovering things about yourself and your area of interest.

Writing reflectively requires writer to draw on his/her experiences, perceptions, values, beliefs and assumptions to explore a particular issue or problem. Reflection is a process through which the kinds of things you are pondering on in your mind are transferred and worked through as you write. It does not provide specific answers or make claims or recommendations about the rights and wrongs of something. Neither does it provide a simple remedy to a specific problem.

To think and write reflectively you have to:

- Experience something
- Think about what happened
- Learn from the experience
- Apply what you have learned.

### *What is Reflective Practice?*

Reflective practice is about using your imagination to untangle through writing what is going on around you so that you can more fully understand what is happening. By imagining other possibilities and ways of thinking you are more able to forecast/predict human behaviour and determine a more appropriate response. Reflective practice allows us to imagine and see our professional relationships with others within a framework of possible role models so that we can get closer to understanding a given situation.

### *Why Reflective Practice?*

Reflective practice in its various forms is a way for you to discover and evaluate what you are learning and demonstrates to your lecturers/tutors how you are actively engaged in your study. Learning to reflect helps you to consolidate what you are learning and develops your thinking and writing skills.

## Example of Basic Reflective Writing

An example of basic reflective writing is given below:

> "Specific tasks were shared out amongst members of my team. Initially, however, the tasks were not seen as equally difficult by all team members. Cooperation between group members was at risk because of this perception of unfairness. Social interdependence theory recognises a type of group interaction called 'positive interdependence', meaning cooperation (Johnson & Johnson, 2008), and many studies have demonstrated that "cooperative tasks can promote and improve learning" (Maughan & Webb, 2010). Ultimately, our group achieved a successful outcome, but to improve the process, we perhaps needed a chairperson to help encourage cooperation when tasks were being shared out. In future group work, on the course and at work, I would probably suggest this."

### *Levels of Reflective Writing*

Hatton and Smith (1995) identify three levels of reflective writing:

- *Descriptive writing about events:* Descriptive writing will describe events in ordinary language.
- *Dialogic reflection:* Dialogic reflection steps back from events to explore your own role in events and actions.
- *Critical reflection:* Critical reflection is more analytical and shows an awareness of the connections between actions and events and other knowledge. You should aim for this level of reflection in your writing.

### *Characteristics of Reflective Writing*

1. Reflective practice demands that you engage with struggle–the struggle to untie your own inner biases as a method for interpreting the events you are writing about.

2. It pushes us to dig deeper into asking open-ended questions that can lead to seeing the complexity and multifaceted nature of reality–where one's discoveries rarely lead to just one answer but rather to a whole range of possibilities.
3. Writing oneself into knowing is concerned with learning how things work and evolve through the process of untangling what appear to be conflicting occurrences.
4. Writing your thoughts down allows you to make comparisons between your reality and the reality of others; it creates a border crossing through which you can imagine multiple layers of reality.
5. Reflective writing allows you to discover not only new facets about yourself and how you are positioned in a particular situation but it also reveals how you have been shaped or changed by your experience.
6. It also offers you the opportunity to develop your writing skills – a necessity for your life as both student and eventual professional.
7. It is about developing a writing practice that allows you to explore your own life experiences, thoughts, feelings, values and assumptions through stories and open-ended questions to generate meaning and understanding.
8. Writing in this way helps you to untangle and consolidate your thoughts and to recognise and make sense of what you are learning.
9. It can assist you in clarifying particular areas in your study or life where your thinking or understanding is unclear and/or still weak.
10. Reflective writing creates a portrait of our human experiences so that we can learn from them. In the process of developing your reflection skills you draw on your own life experiences as a writing vehicle for deepening your awareness and understanding of your world reality in relation to other people.
11. Being reflective means being aware of the unknown–appreciating that life is a mystery and that not all things are knowable.
12. Reflective practice creates a safer place for uncertainty in our lives.

## Difference between Reflective Writing and Academic Writing

Some of the common differences between reflective and academic writing are outlined below:

Difference between Reflective Writing and Academic Writing

| *Sl. No.* | *Reflective Writing* | *Academic Writing* |
|---|---|---|
| 1. | It is a personal or subjective account. | It is an impersonal/objective account. |
| 2. | It might not clearly define the content. | It has very specific content. |
| 3. | It is written in first person. | It usually does not include first person. |
| 4. | It considers writers' personal views and looks at issues from multiple perspectives (includes non-experts). | It may consider others' views (experts in the field). |
| 5. | Contemplates. | Argues and justifies. |
| 6. | It finds solutions to problems. | It compares and contrasts. |
| 7. | It stays open to perplexity. | It attempts to smooth out perplexity. |
| 8. | It aims to explore the process of writers' learning. | It aims to represent what writers' have learnt. |
| 9. | It is frequently written over a period of time. | It is usually written for a specific assignment. |
| 10. | Can have a messy structure and appear disorganised. | Has a clear structure with introduction, body and conclusion. |
| 11. | Based on your own experiences | Based on the literature you've read |
| 12. | Written in the first person to comment on practice (I found this experience…) but tends to use 3rd person to comment on research/theory | Written in the third person (It could be argued that this experience…) |

### How to Think and Write Reflectively

There are several models of reflective practice which help you to structure your reflective thinking and reflective writing.

#### Kolb's Learning Cycle

Kolb's Learning Cycle (1984) has four elements of a loop which you can start at any point, though normally you start with an experience:

The four elements of Kolb's Learning Cycle are given below:

- Experience: doing it
- Observations and reflections: reviewing and reflecting on the experience
- Development of ideas: learning from the experience
- Testing ideas in practice: planning, trying out what you have learned

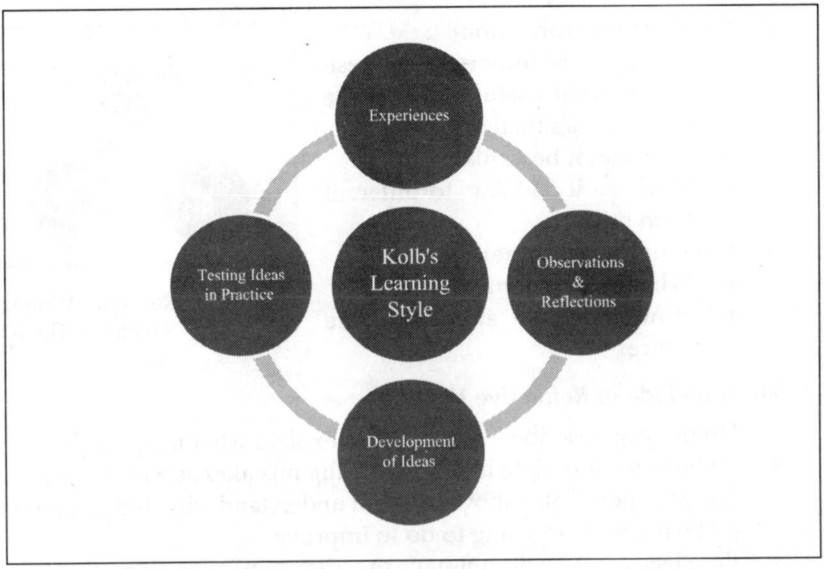


Figure 4.2: Kolb's Learning Cycle

*Schön Model*

Schön (1983) presented the concept of 'reflection in action' and 'reflection on action':

| *Reflection in action* | *Reflection on action* |
|---|---|
| • Experiencing<br>• Thinking on your feet<br>• Thinking about what to do next<br>• Acting straight away | • Thinking about something that has happened<br>• Thinking what you would do differently next time<br>• Taking your time |

Schön's theory is that there are two types of reflection, one during and one after an activity or event.

***How to Write Reflectively***

Creating a piece of reflective writing is different from other academic writing as it is more personal and you are writing about your experiences.

When you write reflectively, use the three Ws:

1. What? (description)
   - What happened?
   - Who was involved?

2. So what? (interpretation)
    - What is most important/interesting/relevant/useful aspect of the event/idea/situation?
    - How can it be explained?
    - How is it similar to/different from others?
3. What next? (outcome)
    - What have I learned?
    - How can it be applied in the future?

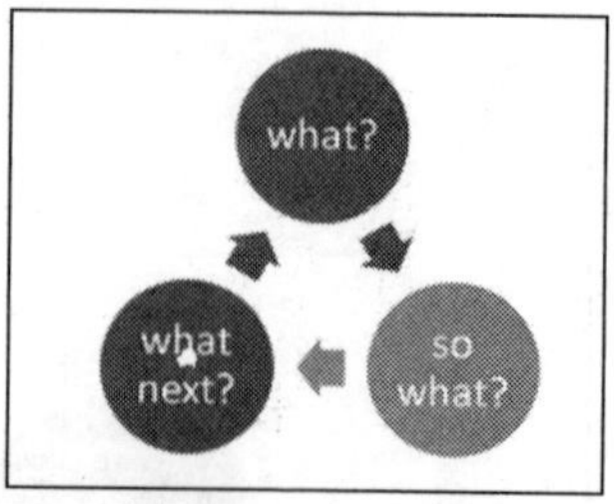


Figure 4.3: Reflective Writing Structure—Three Ws

### *What to Include in Reflective Writing*

- Do not just describe – explore and explain what happened.
- Be honest – it is ok to admit to making mistakes as well as success. But you should also show how you understand why things happen and what you are going to do to improve.
- Be selective – you do not have to write about everything that happened, just key events or ideas.
- Look to the future – reflect on what happened in the past and how it will have an impact on future ideas or activities.

## Connection of Personal Experience to Specific Content in Reflective Writing

In reflective writing, it is common to connect personal experience to specific content. Reflective writing involves:

- Your understanding of theories connected to personal experiences
- How you have changed as a result of reflecting on your learning or practice

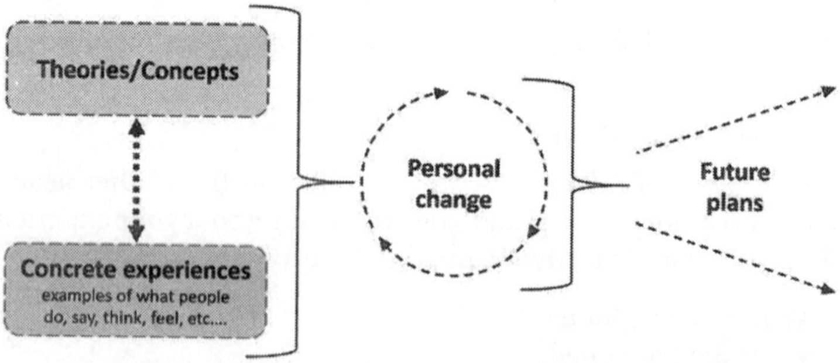


Figure 4.4: Connecting Personal Experience to Specific Content

- What your future plans are
- Connecting personal experience to specific content involves:
- Identifying theories or parts of theories from research
- Matching theory to concrete experiences, such as examples of what people do, say, think, feel, etc...
- Using language to make clear links from theory to experience (and vice versa)

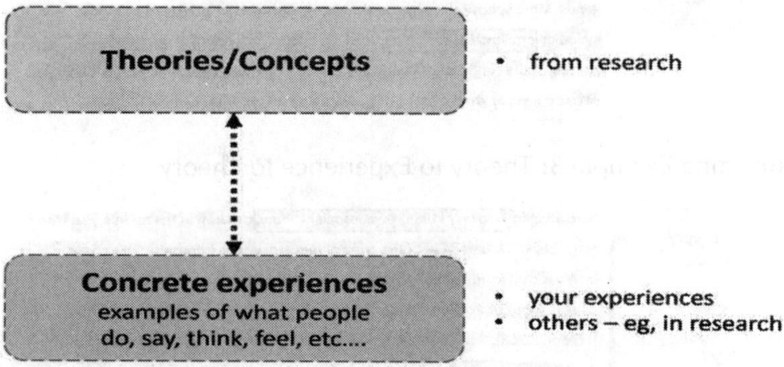


Figure 4.5: How to Connect Personal Experience to Specific Content

Your ability to relate and match experiences to theory shows deep understanding of content. The concrete details of personal experiences may be your own or experiences recorded in research.

Connecting Example 1: Theory to Experience

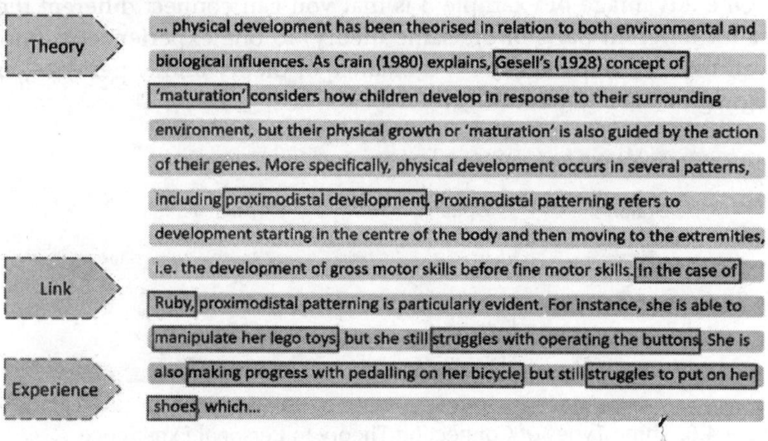

Connecting Example 2: Experience to Theory

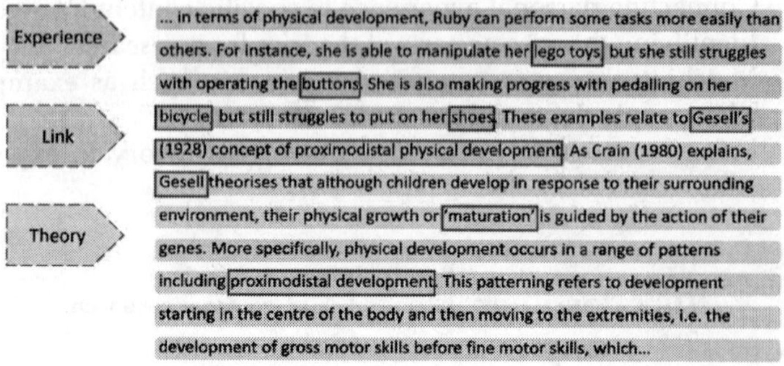


Connecting Example 3: Theory to Experience to Theory

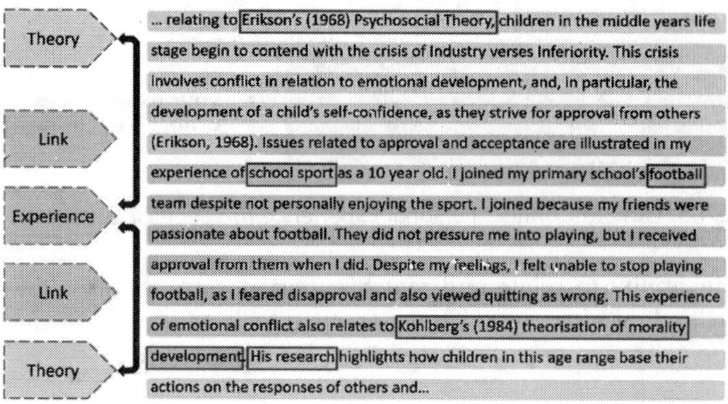


One advantage of example 3 is that you can connect different theories (or different parts of the same theory) to one experience/example. In all three examples, there is a balance of theory and experience, and language is used to make clear links.

Summary of Ways to Connect Theory and Experience

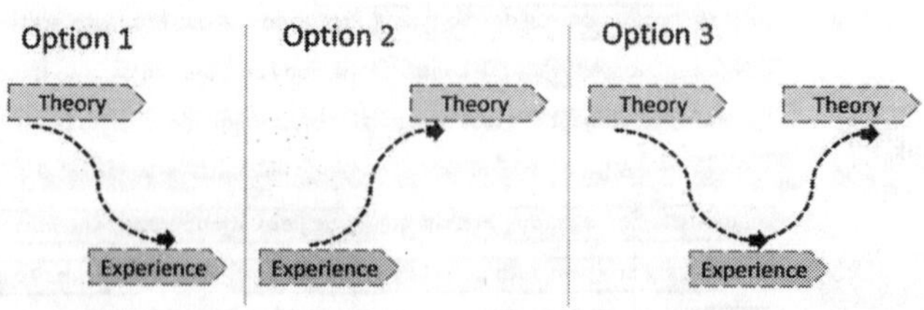


Figure 4.6: Three Types of Connecting Theory to Personal Experience

### *Language for Linking Theory and Experience*

In reflective writing, we can link theory to experience in two different types given below:

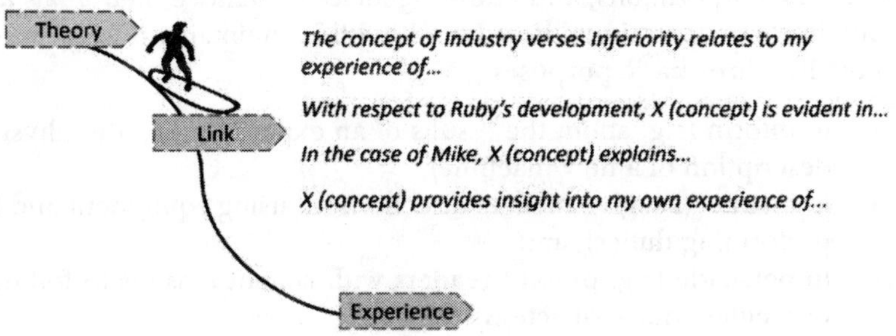


Figure 4.7: Linking Theory to Personal Experience

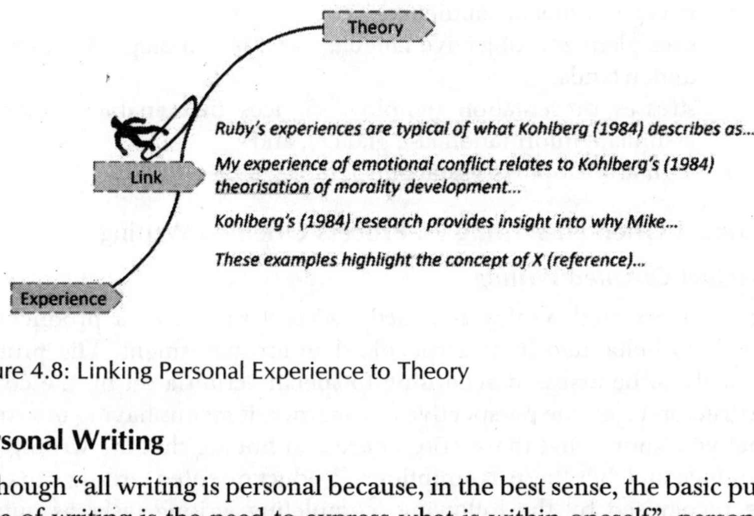


Figure 4.8: Linking Personal Experience to Theory

## Personal Writing

Although "all writing is personal because, in the best sense, the basic purpose of writing is the need to express what is within oneself", personal writing as a kind of writing differs from academic writing in the degree of formality, language complexity, objectivity, etc. and in the purpose. What makes personal writing unique is "the authority taken by the writer to be seen as an expert. Personal writing includes letters to friends and relatives, diaries or journals that people write just for themselves, and even personal e-mail. Personal writing, on the other hand, introduces a wide range of opportunities to practise academic writing and leads to positive attitudes towards writing in general.

## Technical Writing

Technical writing holds on to formal style. Technical writing is the practical writing that people do as part of their jobs. Technical writing enables businesses, corporations, and public agencies to achieve their goals and maintain their operations. Riordan (1993:6-7) maintains that technical writing has three basic purposes:

- to inform (e.g. about the results of an experiment or the physical description of a new machine),
- to instruct (i.e. give readers directions for using equipment and for performing duties), and
- to persuade (e.g. present readers with cogent reasons to follow a particular course of action).

*Characteristics of Technical Writing:* Riordan ascribes four characteristics of technical writing. Technical writing:

- engages a specific audience,
- uses plain and objective language and terminology the audience understands,
- stresses presentation (employs devices that enable readers to assimilate information at a glance), and
- regularly employs visual aids (graphs, tables, drawings).

## Product Oriented Writing vs. Process Oriented Writing

### *Product Oriented Writing*

Product oriented writing is exactly what it says it is: a product that needs to behanded in at a specific date for assessment. The product is likely to be assessed according to specific criteria set by the course instructor. From the perspective of a learner, it means having to assume that you know what these criteria are and hoping that the writing you produce matches these assumptions. Product oriented writing can often be recognised by the following: completing writing tasks as quickly and as painlessly as possible for a maximum score; leaving the writing assignment to the last minute; lack of time for revision and reviewing before handing in the text; and little or no feedback on the final assessed product. Thus, product oriented writing leaves a student with the impression that the grade received on the product is a reflection of what the student has learned or knows about the subject and not so much about whether the written task was dealt with correctly, or incorrectly (the final grade might be a result of poor writing, rather than a lack of subject knowledge).

***Process Oriented Writing***

In comparison to product writing, process writing is basically completing many sub-products, at different stages, for the same final product. In other words, writing has many different stages, and every stage is represented by different processes, all of which contribute to a developed written product. A final written product, as we see published, has undergone many different processes, starting from a stage which is defined as a pre-writing stage, followed by a writing stage, and completed with apost-writing stage.

## Difference between Process Oriented Writing and Product Oriented Writing

V. Steele describes two popular, yet very different approaches, viz. the process approach and the product approach, and presents a number of differences between them. The differences between the process writing and the product writing are tabulated below:

Differences between Process Writing and Product Writing

| *Process Oriented Writing* | *Product Oriented Writing* |
|---|---|
| • text as a resource for comparison<br>• ideas as starting point<br>• more than one draft<br>• more global, focus on purpose, theme, text type, i.e., reader is emphasised.<br>• collaborative<br>• emphasis on creative process | • imitate model text<br>• organisation of ideas more important than ideas themselves<br>• one draft<br>• features highlighted including controlled practice of those features<br>• individual<br>• emphasis on end product |

*Source:* V. Steele, *Product and Process Writing: A Comparison,* http://www.teaching english.org.uk/think/write/approaches.shtml

## Print Writing vs. Web Writing

Web writing and print writing are similar, yet are also very different skills. Both forms of writing should be engaging and useful to the reader, but there is a big difference between readers who are browsing the web for news and other content, and those who settle down with a physical book or magazine. According to Kilian (2001), *"When you write for a Web site, you're not just slapping a poster up on a new kind of wall. The Web is a very different medium from print on paper, and it requires a different kind of writing."*

## Print Writing

When you write a print piece, the responsibility is on you to grab the reader's attention from whatever was on his/her mind to begin with and turn it your brochure, report, magazine article, letter, or book etc. Unless you provide a compelling reason to notice your print piece, your readers will not find it.

Figure 4.9: Difference between Print Writing and Web Writing

## Web Writing

Writing for the Web or Web-based Writing is the most developed form of writing. There are certain important things. Keep in mind that you are writing for the screen, not for the pages. Web-Based Writing is not an alien domain of communication; it is an integral part of the communication phenomenon. It has to be very considerate for the reader as there is no enforcement on the user to stay on the page.

Internet users want to quickly assess your web page to decide whether to keep reading. They often do not want to read every word on your page. When writing for the web, you must make your content easy to skim and scan, so users can quickly find points of interest. This will keep them on your page reading longer. Your visitors form an opinion of your webpage within milli-seconds. If they do not get a good first impression, they will exit without a second glance – probably never to return.

To write well for the web, you need to understand what today's Internet users want and expect. Users want web content that:

- is easy to skim & scan
- is written in a style that is direct, concise and factual

- is focused around their needs (not yours)
- has credibility and inspires trust

## Difference between Print Writing and Web Writing

The four important differences between print writing and web writing are discussed below:

*Structure:* While print readers tend to follow a more structured reading pattern, starting with the introduction and moving on to the main body and conclusion of an article, research shows that 79% of web users scan rather than read word for word.

Eye tracking studies have also shown that when reading print, a person's eyes move from left to right. But, on the web, people's eyes start at the centre of the page and move to the right. This means is that web content needs to be structured quite differently; text should be broken up into shorter paragraphs, and subheadings, bullet points and numbered lists should be used to make the text more visually appealing and easier to scan.

Writing for the web is generally designed to be scanned with the eyes instead of read deeply. Web articles tend to be shorter overall, with shorter sentences in shorter paragraphs, and greater use of both numbered lists and bullet points.

Another factor to consider is that while print readers are generally prepared to spend more time reading a single article, web users often do not have time to read through a whole article, and would rather have the most important points laid out from the beginning so that they know whether or not they will want to keep reading.

*Length:* Research shows that reading on a computer screen can slow readers down by up to 30%, and web users also experience visual fatigue more quickly. With this in mind, web content is often shorter than printed content. If you have a lot of information about a particular topic that you want to share, you should consider splitting it up into two articles or even a series of them.

There is a bit more of a challenge to writing online than print, because even though there is more space, you need to condense your information to get your point across.

Writing for print has its drawbacks too, such as having only a limited amount of space. But, print can be a little more in-depth, which helps with long news stories.

In addition to word count, print writers must be aware of space limitations. For instance, if a magazine commissions a two-page, 1000 word article, the writer must not only make sure that they stick to the word count, but also that their content will fit on those two pages. So bullet points and subheadings are used less frequently in printed publications than online.

*Headlines:* In print, headlines tend to be shorter and are often accompanied by a photo and/or subheading that provides context. More important headlines are often also bigger, so readers are naturally drawn to those stories first.

On the web, headlines are generally longer because they must be able to catch a reader's attention and convey the point of a story without the help of photos, subheadings or larger fonts. They also need to sum up the article's content accurately and use the right keywords and phrases so that it becomes more "searchable" online.

*Links:* In short, web content has links, while print content does not. The opportunity to add links in web content provides writers with the valuable opportunity to include calls to action everywhere. The author can think whether they want readers to sign up to an offer, subscribe to a newsletter, download a fact sheet, contact the organisation or anything else, and they can build these actions into the story lead, picture captions, footnotes and more.

This difference makes online writing easier in some ways, because rather than going into great detail about something that provides context or adds value to your story, you can simply make a brief mention of it and then include the link, allowing the readers to decide for themselves how much detail they want or need.

## Principles of Web Writing

The principles of web writing are discussed below:

### *Understand how users read on the web*

Users read differently on the web – unlike when they are reading a book from cover to cover. On the web, users do not read word for word. They skim content, trying to get a quick impression of what it is about. They scan for the bits they are interested in and ignore the rest. You need to understand how users read on the web, and then write content in a style that makes it easy for them.

### *Write content that is easy to skim and scan*

- Be direct
- Start with your conclusion – this is called the Inverted Pyramid Style
- Limit each paragraph to one key concept
- Use meaningful headings

- Use bullet points and numbered lists
- Include summaries or overviews

### *Keep your wording short and simple*

Be brief and concise. Write clearly and simply. If you are writing for an expert audience explain your terms. Give your users links to simple background information, so that the most casual visitor can work out what you are talking about.

### *Know your audience*

Who are you are writing for? What are their needs? What will they come to your web page to find or achieve? What is their level of expertise? Build a profile of your various audience groups. Focus your content around your users' needs and tasks, not around yourself or your organization).

### *Engage your user*

Imagine who your user will be, and keep that imagined person in mind as you write for him or her. Talk directly to your user. Provide interaction.

### *Build trust*

- Be factual and accurate. Where appropriate, prove the verity of your information with links to trusted websites or by quoting trusted authorities.
- Include only content which conforms to the purpose of your website.
- Protect privacy and respect copyright.
- Keep your content up to date.
- Publish your contact details. Provide users with a sense of knowing who is behind the website.
- Spell-check your content. Invite people to report errors, and then fix them.

### *Test then refine your content*

First test it yourself – review each web page while imagining how it reads to a new user. Then test it on users to learn what works and what causes difficulties. Test your content on different audience groups with different levels of knowledge. Test web page performance in all common browsers. Test, refine, test, refine, test … (You get the idea).

### *Help people (and search engines) find your content*

Organize your content so that your website is easy to navigate. Use hyperlinks to articles on your own website and to other helpful sites. Do keyword research to determine what keywords people are likely to use to find your content. Sprinkle your content with those keyword phrases, paying particular attention to your article title, headings and your leading paragraph. Provide alternate text descriptions for your images (Google loves knowing what images mean).

#### *Create the right tone, look and feel*

When you create web pages, your aim should be a unified tone, look and feel throughout your site. Aim for the right tone to suit your audience group and your subject matter. Keep the tone of your website unrelentingly positive. Use multi-media cautiously – it should enhance the page, not distract the user. Develop an appropriate identifying brand if you do not already have one, and include it on every page and communication. Color, images and the 'tone' of your conversation with the user all help to create a psychological impact on your users, and help to communicate a subtle message about who you are.

#### *Be generous with your expert knowledge*

Users value expert knowledge. It can be a draw-card for visitors to your website and it helps to build credibility because it establishes you as an authority on your subject. Do not give your expert knowledge all at once. Organize it into digestible pieces. Give a summary first, and then let your users drill down for more details.

### Features of Good Web Writing

Good web writing:

- is like a conversation. Think of your content as a focused conversation started by a busy person. When users come with questions, you provide answers. When users come to do a task, you help them. But, because you are not there in person, you have to build your side of the conversation into the site.
- answers people's questions. If you think of the web as a conversation, you will realize that much content is meant to answer people's questions. You do not want pages of FAQs. You do want to think about what people come wanting to know and how to give them that information as concisely and clearly as possible.
- lets people grab and go. Breaking information into pieces for different users, topics, and needs help patrons grab just want they need and go on to look up their next question, do their next task, make a decision, or whatever comes next.
- Web writing is more informal than other formats. You should aim for a voice that is clear, credible, trustworthy, and welcoming.

- Focus on essential messages. Most people come to the web for information, not for a complete document. They don't want the user manual; they want instructions for the task they are doing. They want usable, manageable pieces.
- Give each page a clear and descriptive title. If your page is frequently linked from another place, the page title should match the text link as closely as possible. They should also clearly describe the subject of the page.
- Do not waste space welcoming people to the page. There is no need, and most users ignore any welcome text as filler.
- Write information, not documents. Ask if your web page is too long, and whether it should be broken down into separate, linked pages.
- Your first paragraph is the most important one. It should be brief, clear, and to the point in order to engage the user. One-sentence paragraphs are encouraged.
- Put important information and tasks first. Follow the top-to-bottom hierarchy, saving less important information for last.

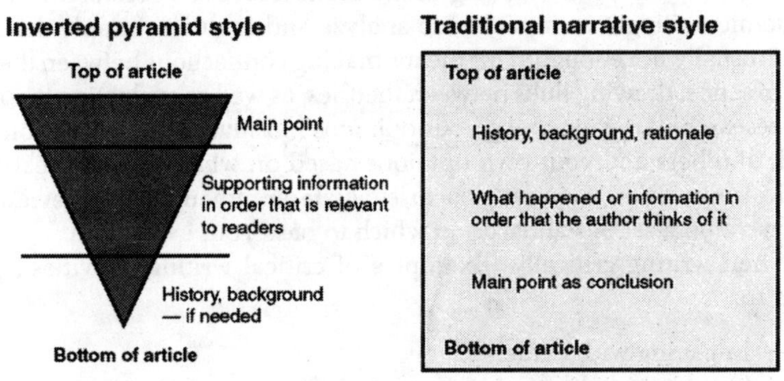


Figure 4.10: Difference between Inverted Pyramid Style and Traditional Narrative Style of Writing

- Web users trying to grab and go prefer inverted pyramid style to traditional narrative style (Redish, 2007)
- Use short paragraphs. Large blocks of text look like walls to the user. Research has shown that short, concise paragraphs and bulleted lists work best for web use.
- Just say it. Phrase things in simple, straight forward language, using familiar words and avoiding jargon.

## Critical Writing

In academic writing you will develop an argument or point of view. This will be supported by concrete evidence, in other words reasons, examples, and information from sources. The writing you produce in this way will need to be 'critical writing'.

As a writer you can engage with your topic in two different ways. If you adopt a descriptive writing approach, you are providing information about the topic or subject you are writing about. On the other hand, critical writing is needed to provide all the background information for your research; you also need to include come critical (or analytical) writing to make sure that you show additional skills. Critical writing is not necessarily writing about the topic in a negative way; it is simply making sure that you have considered all sides of the argument. For example, in your reading you are likely to discover different authors with different views. It is your job as a critical writer to consider all of these views in your essay to show your awareness of all the issues associated with your topic.

## Activities of Critical Writing

Writing critically means writing at the highest levels. Therefore, in most academic writing it is important to analyze and evaluate. Simple description is usually not enough. This means making connections between theory and practice, drawing links between theories, as well as evaluating theories and research. It means giving your opinions (positive and negative) on the work of others and your own opinions based on what you have learned. Critical evaluation requires you to evaluate arguments, weigh evidence and develop a set of standards on which to base your evaluation.

When writing critically (Examples of critical writing activities), you need to:

- Engaging with evidence;
- Open minded and objective inquiry;
- Presenting reasons to dispute a particular finding;
- Providing an alternative approach;
- Recognizing the limitations of evidence: either your evidence or the evidence provided by others;
- Thinking around a specific problem;
- Applying caution and humility when challenging established positions;
- Analyze and categorize theories and research;
- Evaluate theories and research;
- Compare and contrast theories and research;

- Select from theories and research;
- Synthesize from theories and research;
- Make logical connections between theory and practice;
- Give opinions (positive and negative);
- Provide evidence for these opinions;
- Indicate gaps in theories and research;
- Weigh evidence and come to conclusions;

***Definition***

Writing which evaluates and analyses more than one source in order to develop an argument.

***Features of Critical Writing***

The most characteristic features of critical writing are:

- a clear and confident refusal to accept the conclusions of other writers without evaluating the arguments and evidence that they provide;
- a balanced presentation of reasons why the conclusions of other writers may be accepted or may need to be treated with caution;
- a clear presentation of your own evidence and argument, leading to your conclusion; and
- a recognition of the limitations in your own evidence, argument, and conclusion.

## Academic vs Non-academic Writing

There is a distinct difference between academic writing and non-academic writing in their format, audience, purpose, and tone. While academic writing is formal and objective in tone, non-academic writing is personal and subjective in nature.

*Academic Writing*

Academic writing has been explained in details in Chapter-1.

*Non-Academic Writing*

Non-academic writing may be considered that writing which is personal, emotional, impressionistic, or subjective in nature. Such writing is often found in personal journal entries, reader response writing, memoirs, any kind of autobiographical writing, and letters, e-mails, and text messages. Non-academic writing is any other mode of writing that is not directly intended for an academic or scholarly audience. Non-academic writing can be more informal in tone, and may even rely more heavily on emotional appeal or the opinions of the author.

***Purpose of Non-Academic Writing***

- The purpose of non-academic writing may be to entertain its audience or to persuade the reader.
- Non-academic writing is written for a lay audience, to appeal to people who are not experts in the field in question.

## Examples of Non-Academic Writing

- Personal Opinions
- Letters to editors
- Memos
- Magazine Articles
- Writing for Newspapers
- Digital Media.

Difference between Academic Writing and Non-academic Writing

| *Characteristics* | *Academic Writing* | *Non-academic Writing* |
|---|---|---|
| Definition | Academic writing is a formal and impersonal style of writing that is intended for a scholarly or academic audience. | Non-academic writing is an informal and often subjective style of writing that aims the mass public. |
| Audience | Academic. | Mass public. |
| Purpose | Inform the readers with solid evidence. | Inform, entertain or persuade the readers. |
| Style | Formal and impersonal. | Personal, impressionistic, emotional or subjective. |
| Structure | Standard structure. | No rigid structure. |
| Language | Formal language, avoids colloquialisms. | Informal and casual language, may contain colloquialisms. |
| Citations and References | Contain citations and references. | Often does not contain citations and references. |
| Examples | Research papers, dissertations, scholarly articles. | Newspaper and magazine articles, memoirs, letters, digital media, etc. |

# CHAPTER 5

# Writing an Academic Essay

The word essay derives from the French infinitive *essayer*, "to try" or "to attempt". In English essay first meant "a trial" or "an attempt", and this is still an alternative meaning. The Frenchman Michel de Montaigne (1533–1592) was the first author to describe his work as essays; he used the term to characterise these as "attempts" to put his thoughts into writing, and his essays grew out of his common placing.

## What is an Essay?

An essay is a piece of writing which represents the ideas, emotions or arguments of the author. An essay is an extended piece of writing that presents and supports a thesis or proposition. When you write an essay, you are making a case for the validity of a particular point of view, analysis, interpretation, or set of facts or procedures. An essay is a short form of literary composition based on a single subject matter, and often gives the personal opinion of the author.

In simple words, we can define it as a scholarly work in writing that provides the author's personal argument. Writing an academic essay means fashioning a coherent set of ideas into an argument. Because essays are essentially linear, they offer one idea at a time and they must present their ideas in the order that makes most sense to a reader. Successfully structuring an essay means attending to a reader's logic.

An essay is a form of writing in paragraph form that uses informal language, although it can be written formally. Essays may be written in first-person point of view (I, ours, mine), but third-person (people, he, she) is preferable in most academic essays. Essays do not require research as most academic reports and papers do; however, they should cite any literary works that are used within the paper.

## Definitions of Essay

1. A famous English essayist, Aldous Huxley defines essays as, *"a literary device for saying almost everything about almost anything."*

2. The Oxford Dictionary describes it as *"a short piece of writing on a particular subject"*.
3. An essay is a short piece of writing on one particular subject written by a student.
4. An essay is a short piece of writing on one particular subject that is written by a writer for publication.
5. An essay is a short literary composition on a particular theme or subject, usually in prose and generally analytic, speculative, or interpretative.
6. An essay is a short piece of writing that expresses information as well as the writer's opinion.

## Why to Write Essay

Essay writing has important skills development and educational functions. It allows you to practise and develop transferable skills that are valuable to you not only while you are a student but also when you are a teacher and have to write in a professional role.

These transferable skills include:

- reading and note-making,
- critical thinking and analysis,
- organising ideas,
- arguing a case
- communicating effectively with a reader.
- It encourages you to *develop* a formal, *disciplined* approach to writing that communicates clearly and with authority.
- It gives you a focus for *exploring* and *consolidating* what you are learning.
- It allows you to develop and *organize your thinking* about key concepts and issues in the course you are studying.

## Answering Questions: Parts of an Essay

It is helpful to think of the different essay sections as answering a series of questions your reader might ask when encountering your thesis. These questions are:

- *"What?"* The first question to anticipate from a reader is "what": What evidence shows that the phenomenon described by your thesis is true? To answer the question, you must examine your evidence, thus demonstrating the truth of your claim.
- *"How?"* A reader will also want to know whether the claims of the thesis are true in all cases. The corresponding question is "how": How does the thesis stand up to the challenge of a counterargument?

- *Why?* "Your reader will also want to know what's at stake in your claim: Why does your interpretation of a phenomenon matter to anyone beside you? This question addresses the larger implications of your thesis. It allows your readers to understand your essay within a larger context.

## Structure of Essay

Writing an academic essay means fashioning a coherent set of ideas into an argument. Because essays are essentially linear, they offer one idea at a time and they must present their ideas in the order that makes most sense to a reader. Successfully structuring an essay means attending to a reader's logic. The focus of such an essay predicts its structure. It dictates the information readers need to know and the order in which they need to receive it. Thus, your essay's structure is necessarily unique to the main claim you are making. An essay usually takes the following structured format:

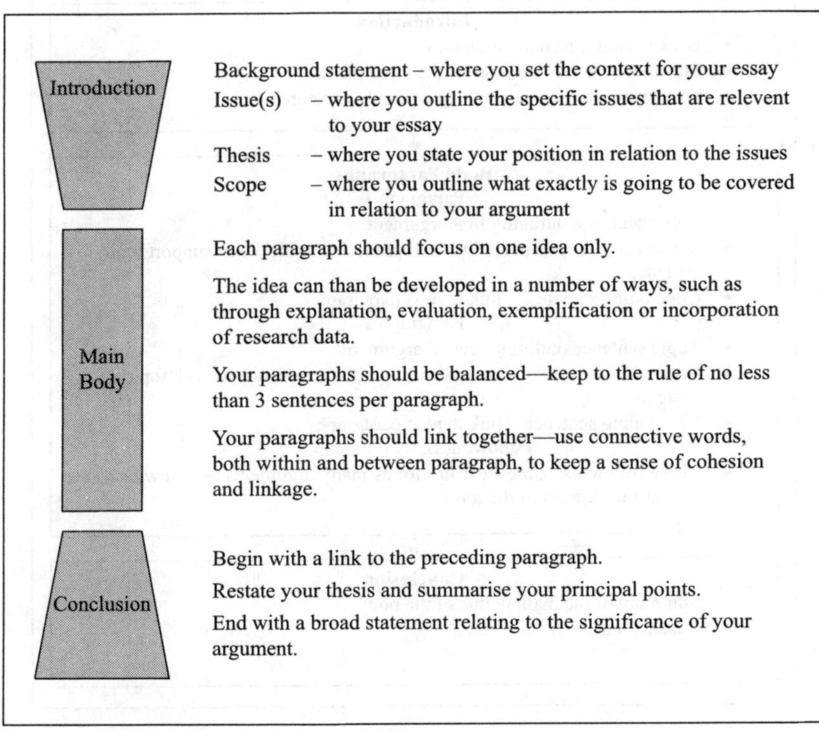


Figure 5.1: Structure of Essay

*Introduction:* The function of the introduction is simply to introduce the subject, to explain how you understand the question, and describe briefly how you intend to deal with it.

*Main Body–A Development of the Issues:* Essays are generally a blend of researched evidence (e.g. from additional reading) and comment.

*Conclusion:* At the end of an essay you should include a short conclusion, the purpose of which is to sum up or draw a conclusion from your argument or comparison of viewpoints.

## Types of Essay

Each subject has specific requirements for the essays to be written. Some subjects need longer essays, while others need shorter ones, such as a five-paragraph essay. There are many types of essay, but they all have the common objective of presenting and defending a topic and a stance to the reader. Some types of essays are discussed below:

**Introduction**

- Background information on topic
- Statement of your position on the topic (thesis)
- Overview of arguments to be presented (structure)

↓

**Body Paragraphs**

Paragraph 1

- Topic sentence outlining first argument
- Sentences giving explanations and providing evidence to support topic sentence
- Concluding sentence – link to next paragraph

Paragraph 2

- Topic sentence outlining second argument
- Sentences giving explanations and providing evidence to back topic sentence
- Concluding sentence – link to next paragraph

Following Body Paragraphs

- These follow the same structure for as many arguments as you wish to put forward in support of the topic.

↓

**Conclusion**

- Summary of the main points of the body
- Restatement of the position

Figure 5.2: Structure of Argumentative Essay

### *Outline of an Argumentative Essay*

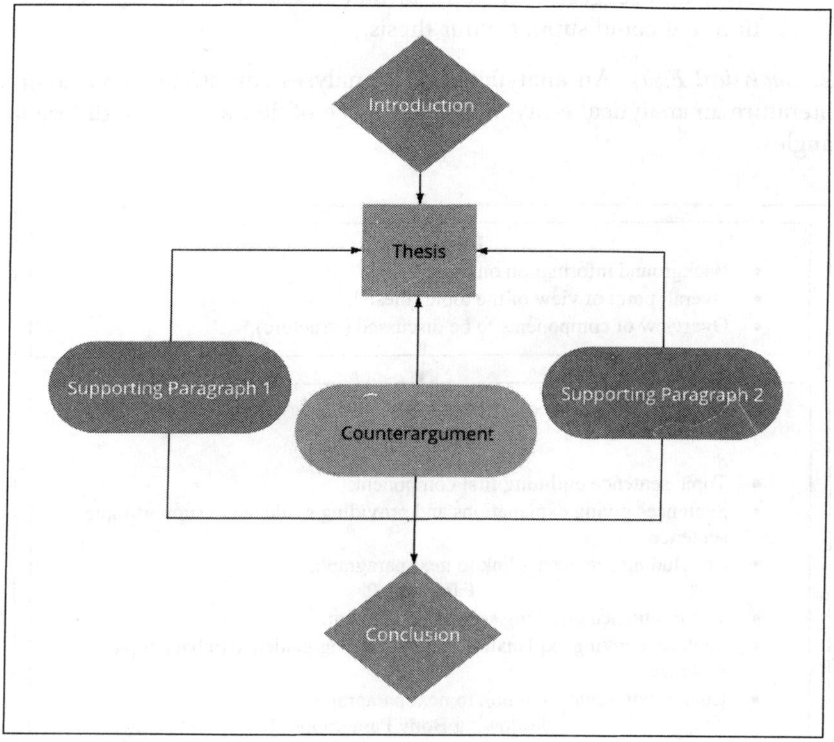


Figure 5.3: Outline of an Argumentative Essay

1. *Argumentative Essay:* An argumentative essay is meant to present arguments in the favour of something. It has an additional fourth body paragraph that is meant to present opposite arguments.

- *Introduction:* Give some background on your topic so the reader knows what you are going to talk about. Try to address some of these questions in your introduction: why is this topic important? How does it affect me? What can be done about it? The introduction should also include your thesis statement where you take a side on the issue.
- *Supporting Paragraph 1:* Present a main argument that supports your thesis.
- *Supporting Paragraph 2:* Present a second argument to support your thesis.
- *Counterargument:* Present the counterargument.

- *Conclusion:* Summarise the main points made in the body of the essay and suggest next steps, further research or possible legislation that could support your thesis.

2. *Analytical Essay:* An analytical essay analyses something, such as in literature an analytical essay analyses a piece of literature from different angles.

**Introduction**

- Background information on topic.
- Overall point of view of the topic (thesis).
- Overview of components to be discussed (structure).

↓

**Body Paragraphs**

Paragraph 1

- Topic sentence outlining first component.
- Sentences giving explanations and providing evidence to support topic sentence.
- Concluding sentence – link to next paragraph.

Paragraph 2

- Topic sentence outlining second component.
- Sentences giving explanations and providing evidence to back topic sentence.
- Concluding sentence – link to next paragraph.

Following Body Paragraphs

- These follow the same structure for as many components as you need to outline.

↓

**Conclusion**

- Summary of the main points of the body.
- Restatement of the main point of view.
- Justification/evaluation (if required by task).

Figure 5.4: Structure of Analytical Essay

3. *Comparison and Contrast Essay:* A comparison and contrast essay makes either a comparison, a contrast, or both between two different or similar things.

4. *Cause and Effect Essay:* A cause and effect essay makes readers understand the cause of things, and their effects on other things.

**Introduction**

- Brief background information on topic
- Outline of two (or more) things being compared or contrasted
- Purpose for making the comparison / contrast
- Overview of the specific points to be compared / contrasted.

↓

**Body Paragraphs**

Paragraph 1

- Topic sentence outlining first similarity or difference
- Sentences giving explanations and providing evidence to support topic sentence
- Concluding sentence – link to next paragraph

Paragraph 2

- Topic sentence outlining second similarity or difference
- Sentences giving explanations and providing evidence to back topic sentence
- Concluding sentence – link to next paragraph

Following Body Paragraphs

- These follow the same structure for as many items or aspects as you need to compare/contrast.

↓

**Conclusion**

- Restatement of the main purpose for the comparison / contrast
- Summary of the main similarities and differences
- Recommendation about suitability of compared items for purpose (if requirement of assessment task)
- Overall conclusion.

Figure 5.5: Structure of Comparative and Contrast Essay

## Outline of Cause and Effect Essay

- *Introduction paragraph:* here you introduce your topic and state your thesis.
- *Supporting paragraph 1:* here you discuss one idea that supports your thesis
- *Supporting paragraph 2:* here you discuss a second idea that supports your thesis.
- *Antithesis paragraph:* here you entertain the opposing side's argument (ex: if you chose global warming, you might write about how some deny its existence).
- *Conclusion:* here you may restate your thesis and present any ideas or thoughts for future research on this topic.

**Introduction**

- Background information on situation under discussion
- Description of the situation
- Overview of the causes or effects to be outlined.

↓

**Body Paragraphs**

Paragraph 1

- Topic sentence outlining first cause or effect
- Sentences giving explanations and providing evidence to support the topic sentence
- Concluding sentence – linking to next paragraph

Paragraph 2

- Topic sentence outlining second cause or effect
- Sentences giving explanations and providing evidence to back topic sentence
- Concluding sentence – linking to next paragraph

Following Body Paragraphs

- These follow the same structure for as many causes or effects as you need to outline.

↓

**Conclusion**

- Summary of the main points of the body
- Conclusion, prediction or recommendation.

Figure 5.6: Cause and Effect Essay

5. *Critical Essay:* A critical essay is written on literary pieces to evaluate them on the basis of their merits or demerits.

6. *Descriptive Essay:* A descriptive essay describes something to make readers feel, smell, see, taste, or hear what is described.

7. *Definition Essay:* As the name suggests, a definition type of essay defines different things, ideas, and perceptions. Definition essay is meant to describe a complex term that has significant background and historical origin and be a relatable term.

8. *Expository Essay:* The term *'expository'* comes from the word *'exposition'*. According to the exposition essay definition this is *'a type of writing meant to explain, inform, or describe'*. An expository essay is a structured academic paper investigating an idea. It consists of looking at evidence, expanding on an idea, and presenting the concept in simple language.

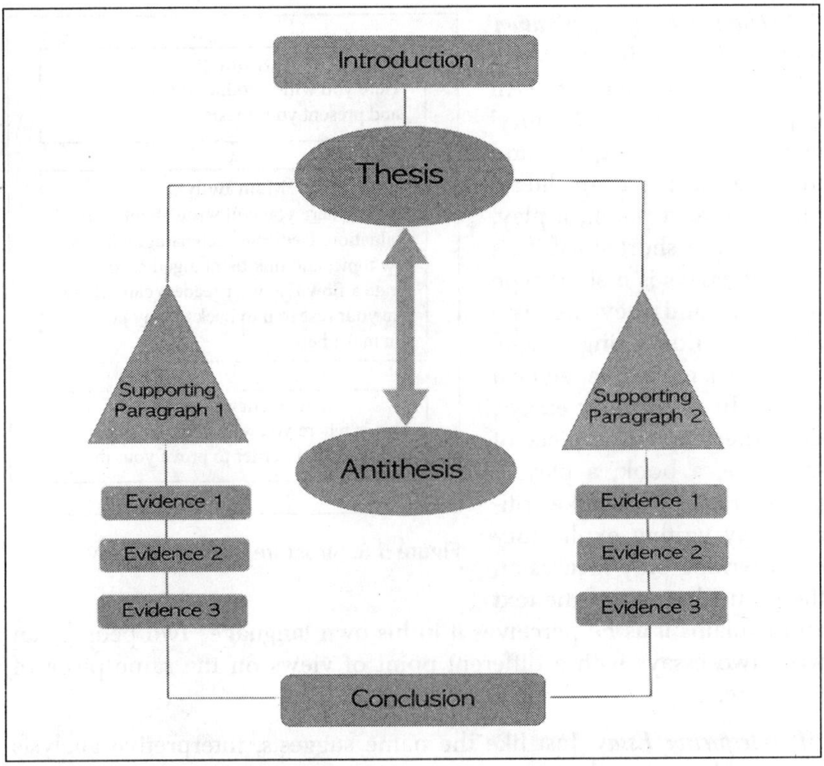


Figure 5.7: Outline of Cause and Effect Essay

An expository essay exposes thing in detail to make readers understand without any complications.

## Outline of Expository Essay

- Introduction: *Here* you introduce your topic in an interesting way by telling a compelling story, citing a shocking statistic or a quote that eloquently sums up the main theme of your paper. The introduction will also include your thesis statement.
- Example paragraph 1: *Here* you give your first example of your thesis.
- Example paragraph 2: Your second example of your thesis.
- Example paragraph 3: Your third example of your thesis.
- Conclusion: Here the reader find conclusion that drives the significance of your topic and, if relevant, suggests further research or discussions that should be conducted.

9. *Explicatory Essay: 'Explication'* means to explain the work of an item of literature. An explication or 'explicatory' essay is used to explain and interpret a piece of literature such as a poem, a play, a novel or a short story. This type of essays is a short type of essays and they are usually written on a single page. They are similar to analytical essays. In explicatory essays, the writer explains a piece of literature, a book, a play, a poem or a novel. Unlike critical essay writing explicatory essay writing only focuses on the particular part of the text and explains it as he perceives it in his own language. Two people can write two essays with a different point of views on the same piece of literature.

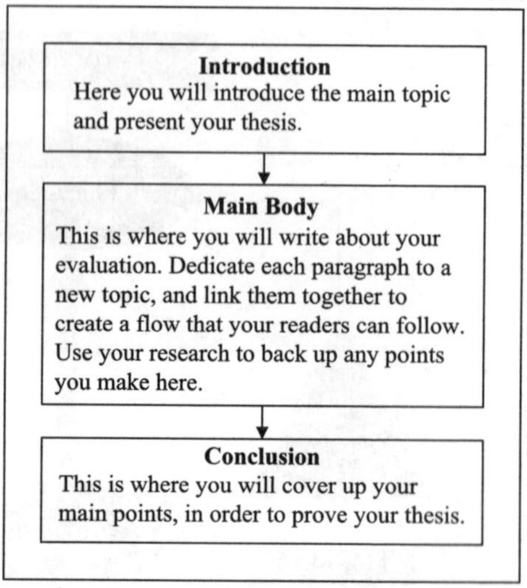


Figure 5.8: Structure of Critical Essay

10. *Interpretive Essay:* Just like the name suggests, interpretive analysis essays asks writer to interpret or critically analyse a subject (such as a work of art or, a person, or event) into its constituent parts, and offer a meaning or alternative meaning of each of the components. An interpretive or critical analysis is a common type of research papers in the arts, literature, and the other humanities.

11. *Narrative Essay:* A narrative essay is a narration like a short story. A narrative essay shows your creativity, character, and ability to tell a compelling story.

12. *Problem and Solution Essay:* In essay writing, problem-solution

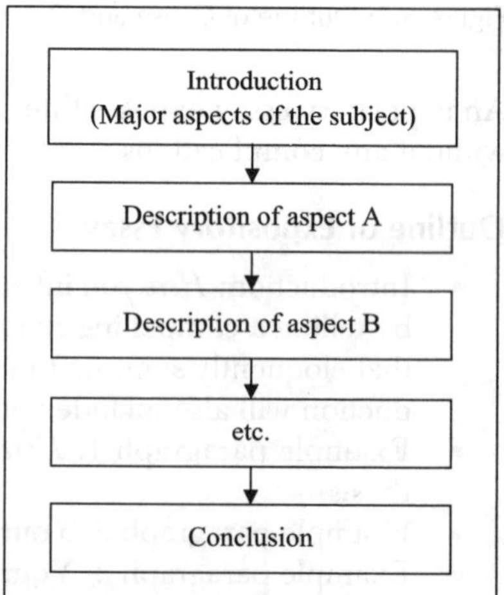


Figure 5.9: Structure of Descriptive Essay

format is a method for analysing and writing about a topic by identifying a problem and proposing one or more solutions. A problem-solution essay is a type of argument. "This sort of essay involves argumentation in that the writer seeks to convince the reader to take a particular course of action. In explaining the problem, it may also need to persuade the reader concerning specific causes."

13. *Persuasive Essay:* A persuasive essay is meant to convince the target audience to do something or not do something. A persuasive essay is one where you choose a position and support it with evidence throughout the body of the essay. A persuasive essay has to be about a topic that you could strongly argue either for or against something.

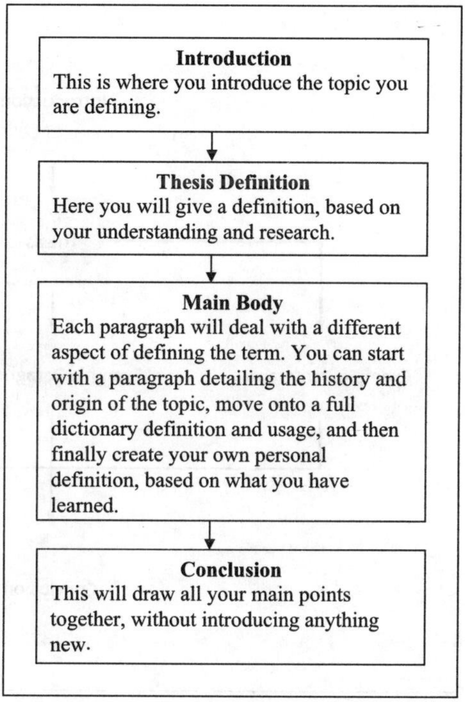


Figure 5.10: Structure of Definition Essay

Outline of Persuasive Essay

An outline for a persuasive essay should look like this:

- Introduction: Introduce your topic with an anecdote, a strong quote by a relevant figure, a shocking statistic or other opening that wows the reader. The story should be leading up to your thesis statement which is where you state your position and is the last sentence of the introduction.
- Supporting paragraph: Introduce evidence to support your thesis.
- Supporting paragraph: More evidence to support your thesis.
- Antithesis paragraph: Entertain the other side of the argument and explain why you still choose the side you choose.
- Conclusion: Suggest further research or questioned that haven't been discussed yet that could lead to an improved understanding of the topic.

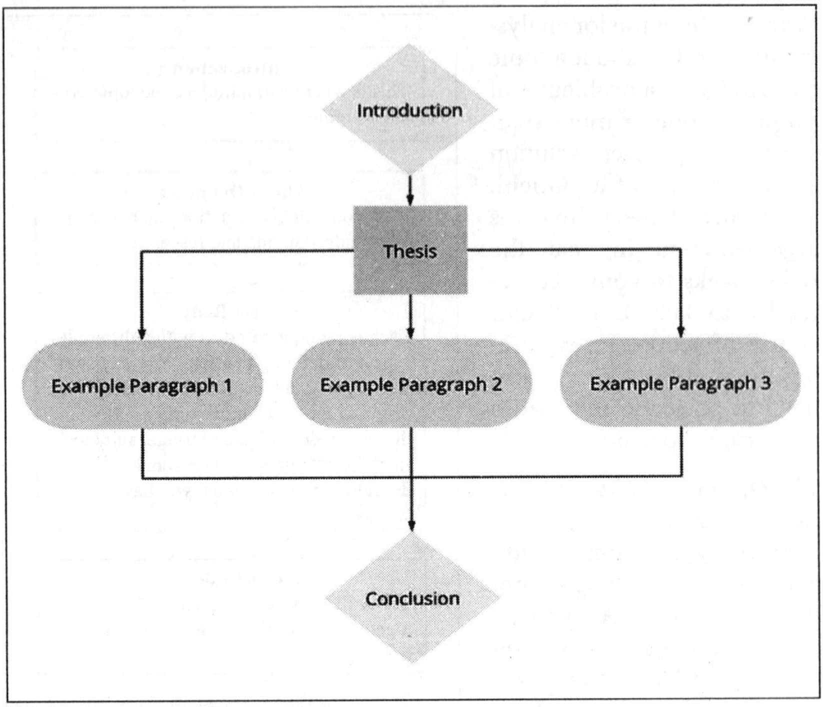


Figure 5.11: Outline of Expository Essay

14. *Process Essay:* A process essay outlines a process of making or breaking or doing something that readers understand fully and are able to do it after reading it.

15. *Rhetorical Analysis Essay:* A rhetorical analysis essay evaluates a speech or a piece of rhetoric on the basis of rhetorical strategies and devices used in it.

16. *Synthesis Essay:* A synthesis essay means to synthesise different ideas to make a judgement about their merit and demerits. There are two types of synthesis essay:

- Explanatory Synthesis Essay: In this type of essay, the writer is intended to assist readers in getting a better understanding of a topic. Writers are required to make an explanation when they refer to segments from a source.
- Argument Synthesis Essay: In this type of essay, the objective of writer is to present your own opinion on what is stated in the sources.

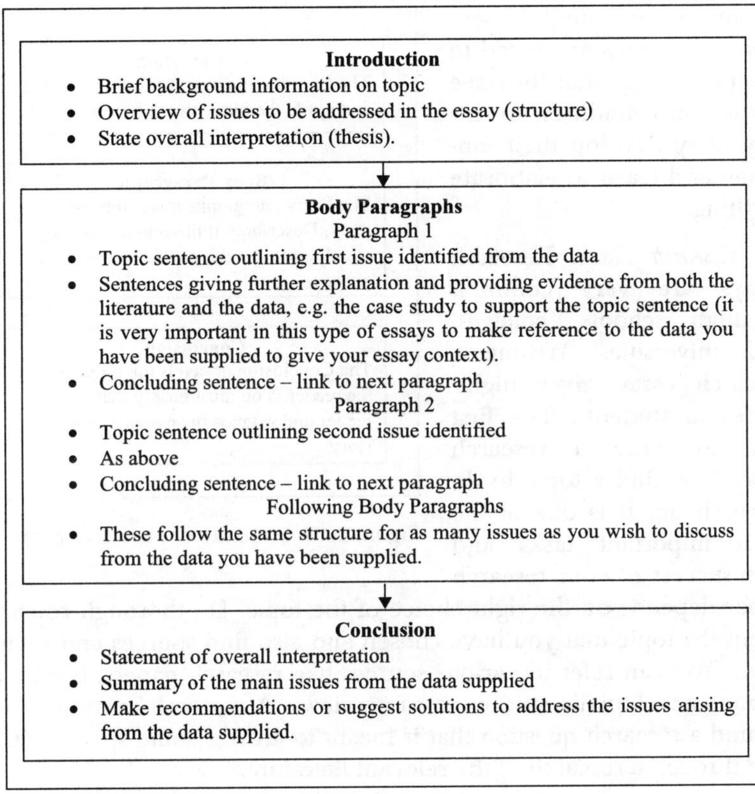


Figure 5.12: Structure of Interpretive Essay

17. *Review Essay:* A review essay is written about books, novels, poems, and movies. A writer should watch or read the work that he/she is going to write about thoroughly. While writing a review essay a writer should provide information about the writer, director and producers and also mention if it is a sequel of any prior work. A writer should write about the plot and character of the stories and also give his/her reviews about how well they have been developed throughout the story. There is no harm to mention anything that you did not like about the work. In review essays, a writer can also give his/her opinion about the work.

18. *Simple Essay:* A simple essay is the most common type of essay. This type of essays is given to students to write on in the beginning years of primary school. This type of essays does not have any particular structure. The purpose of writing such an essay is to teach students

to make meaningful sentences. Students are asked to describe things that they see in their surroundings. In this way, they develop their language and learn to elaborate on things.

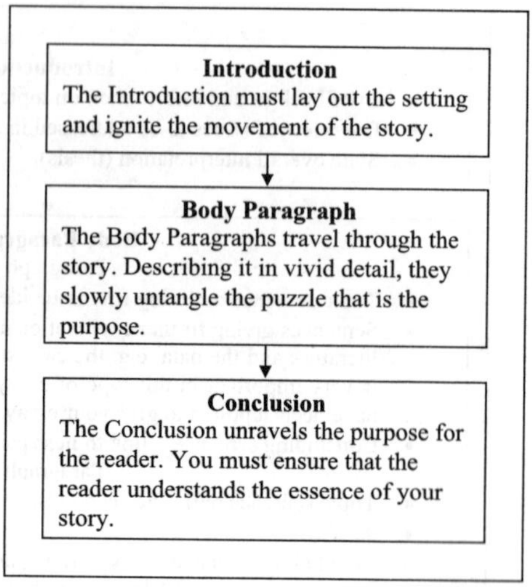


Figure 5.13: Structure of Narrative Essay

19. *Research Essay:* Research essays are very common in high schools, colleges, and universities. Writing a research essay gives nightmares to students. The first step to write a research essay is to find a topic to do research on. It is one of the most important tasks and 90% success of your research paper depends on the right choice of the topic. Do thorough research about the topic that you have chosen and also find sources and review them. You can refer to various sources like research papers, books, an online encyclopedia, and expert interviews. A research essay revolves around a research question that is meant to answer some specific question through a research of the relevant literature.

## Format of an Essay

*The five-paragraph essay* is a format of essay having five paragraphs: one *introductory paragraph*, three *body paragraphs* with support and development, and one *concluding paragraph*. Because of this structure, it is also known as a *'hamburger essay'*, *'one three one'*, or a *'three-tier essay'*. An argumentative essay, however, has an additional paragraph which presents *counter argument* or *opposing arguments* in the same sequence. However, at the end of this paragraph, both the arguments are weighed in the favour of stronger arguments presented earlier in three body paragraphs.

The format of an argumentative essay is given below:

### *Hook*

An essay hook is the first one or two sentences of your essay. It serves as an introduction and works to grab the reader's attention. The first couple of sentences will help your reader decide whether they want to continue reading your essay or not. A hook is an opening statement

**Introduction**

- Background information about the problem
- Description of the problem and why it is serious
- Overview of the solutions to be outlined.

**Body Paragraphs**

Paragraph 1

- Topic sentence outlining first solution
- Explanation of the positive and negative aspects of the solution
- Evidence to support explanations
- Concluding sentence

Paragraph 2

- Topic sentence outlining second solution
- Explanation of the positive and negative aspects of the solution
- Evidence to support explanation
- Concluding sentence

Following Body Paragraphs

- These follow the same structure for as many solutions as you need to discuss.

**Conclusion**

- Summary of the problem and overview of the solutions
- Evaluation of solutions and recommendation of best option.

Figure 5.14: Structure of Problem and Solution Essay

(which is usually the first sentence) in an essay that attempts to grab the reader's attention so that they want to read on. It can be done by using a few different types of hooks, which are a question, quote, statistic, or anecdote. Be mindful that the hook has to be related to the overall topic of the paper.

*Types of Hooks*

Here are a few examples of each type of hook.

- *Question Hook:* A question hook is when you ask the reader something that they can visualise and try to think of in their own minds. Then, the writer answers the question.

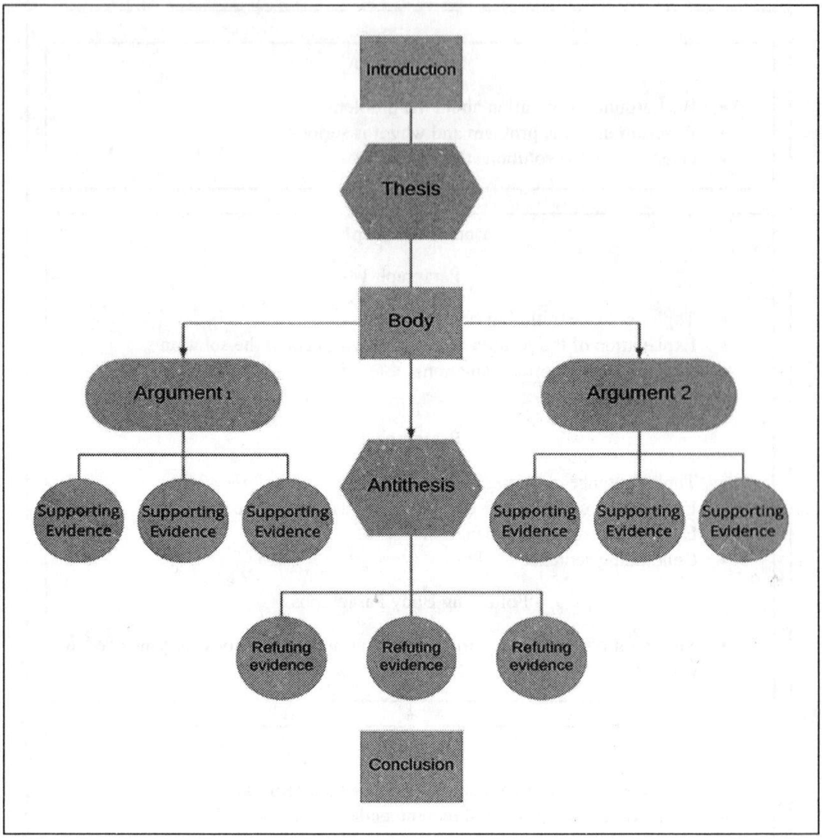


Figure 5.15: Outline of Persuasive Essay

- *Quotation Hook:* A quotation hook is when a quote is used and explained that has relevance to the topic at hand. Make sure this quote comes from a credible source. Also, talk about the quote's meaning afterwards to ensure that the reader is not confused.
- *Fact/Statistic Hook:* A statistic hook can be used for more informational pieces of writing. The writer uses a quote from a source that relates to the main idea of the paper, but the quote must have some type of statistics, such as numbers, decimals, and/or percentages. The meaning and relationship of the quote to the paper needs to be explained afterwards just in case the reader does not quite understand
- *Anecdotal Hook:* When a writer uses a short story to relate to the topic and gain the reader's attention, they are using an anecdote.

This story can be a short, personal story or one that is a figment of your imagination. Make sure that it relates to the main idea of the paper. Show the relevance that it has to the topic of the paper.

- *Strong Statement/Declaration Hook:* A strong statement hook is a sentence that makes an assertive claim about your topic. It connects to the thesis statement and shows the importance of your essay or paper.

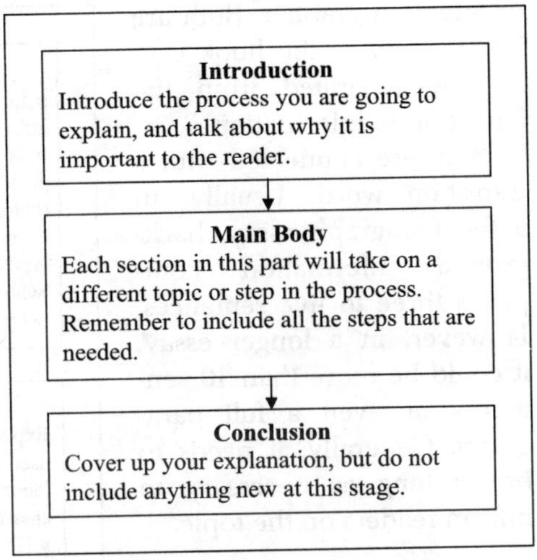


Figure 5.16: Structure of Process Essay

- *Metaphor/Simile Hook:* The metaphor/simile hook engages your readers because it makes them think about a topic in a different way. Your audience wonders what you mean and how you compare a topic to something that seems unconnected. A metaphor is a figure of speech that directly compares one thing to another, but these two things seem unrelated. An example of a metaphor is: *Her boyfriend is a rat.* The boyfriend is not really a rat, but he behaves like one.
- *Story Hook:* This is a hook where you begin with a short story or episode that relates to your topic. Readers love stories, especially a well-written story that is memorable. The key to a great story hook is making sure the story directly connects to your essay or paper topic. Your story can be personal or someone else's story.
- *The Description Hook:* This is a hook where a vivid description of a scene draws your readers into your writing. A good description hook will make your reader want to know what comes next in your writing. It is most popular in narrative essays, but you can use a description hook with any type of writing.

### Background Information

As the name suggests, background information means all information that a reader requires to increase his awareness of the topic an essay is going to explain. Background information is placed shortly after the hook or attention grabber. Both are intertwined, as the hook cannot be separated from the background information.

Both are connected with a transition word. Usually, in a five-paragraph essay, background information comprises three to five sentences. However, in a longer essay, it could be more than 10 sentences or even a full paragraph. Generally, it needs to be as long as necessary to inform readers on the topic.

### *Types of Background Information*

There are as many types of background information as there are types of essay, some of which are as follows:

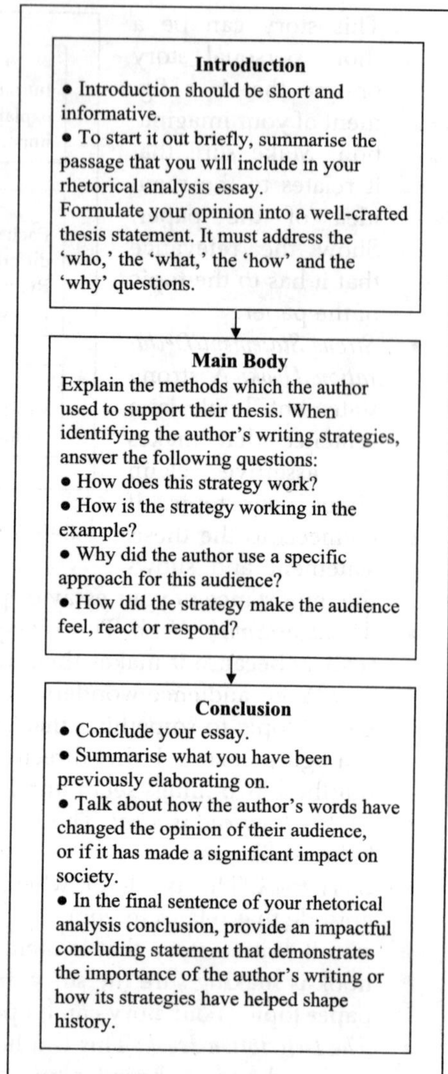


Figure 5.17: Structure of Rhetorical Analysis Essay

- *Description Type:* Description type of background information often describes the topic through sensory description involving all five senses: sense of touch, sense of smell, sense of sight, sense of hearing, and sense of taste. Words are used to make the reader experience any of these or all.
- *Process Type:* In a process type of background information, a writer provides an introduction to the topic, telling readers what process will be used to achieve a goal, or complete a task.
- *Definition Type:* In a definition type of background information, readers become aware of the definition of the topic, as well as how

it differs from other such similar terms and words.

- *Classification/Division Type:* In a classification/division type of background information, readers are informed about the topic, how it is classified and divided, and what further derivations it could have. These are further explained in body paragraphs.
- *Argumentative Type:* In an argumentative type of background information, readers are informed about the topic, the arguments being made in support of the question about the topic, and opposing arguments.
- *Persuasive Type:* A persuasive type of background information attempts to persuade the reader, by giving information about a question.

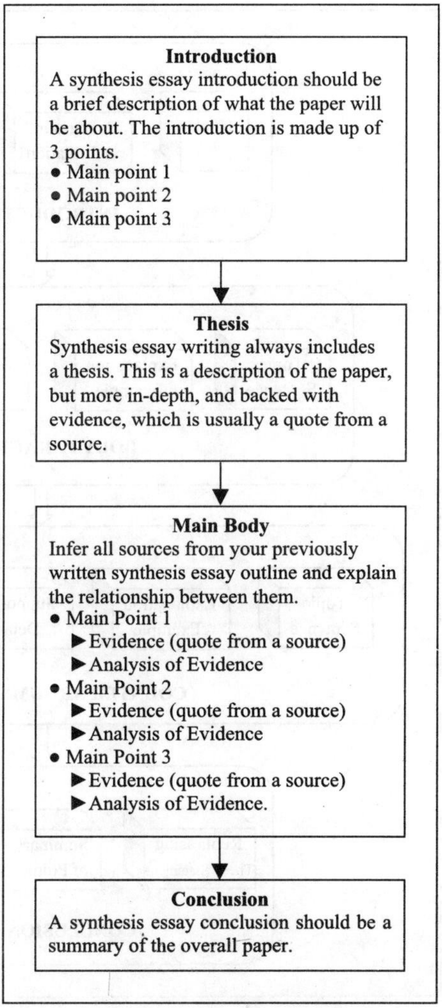


Figure 5.18: Structure of Synthesis Essay

### *Thesis Statement*

A thesis statement is a statement that occurs at the end of the introduction, after the background information on the topic. The thesis statement is connected with the background information through a transition, which could be a full sentence, or a simple transition word, such as therefore, because, but, etc.

The thesis statement is called the "heart of the essay". The idea of an essay without a thesis statement is akin to a body without its heart. It is also called the *"central point"* or the *"core"* of an essay. It is comprised of evidences that the writer uses to elaborate on his topic further. Each of these evidences is then elaborated and discussed in the body paragraphs. If there are three body paragraphs, the thesis statement must have three evidences,

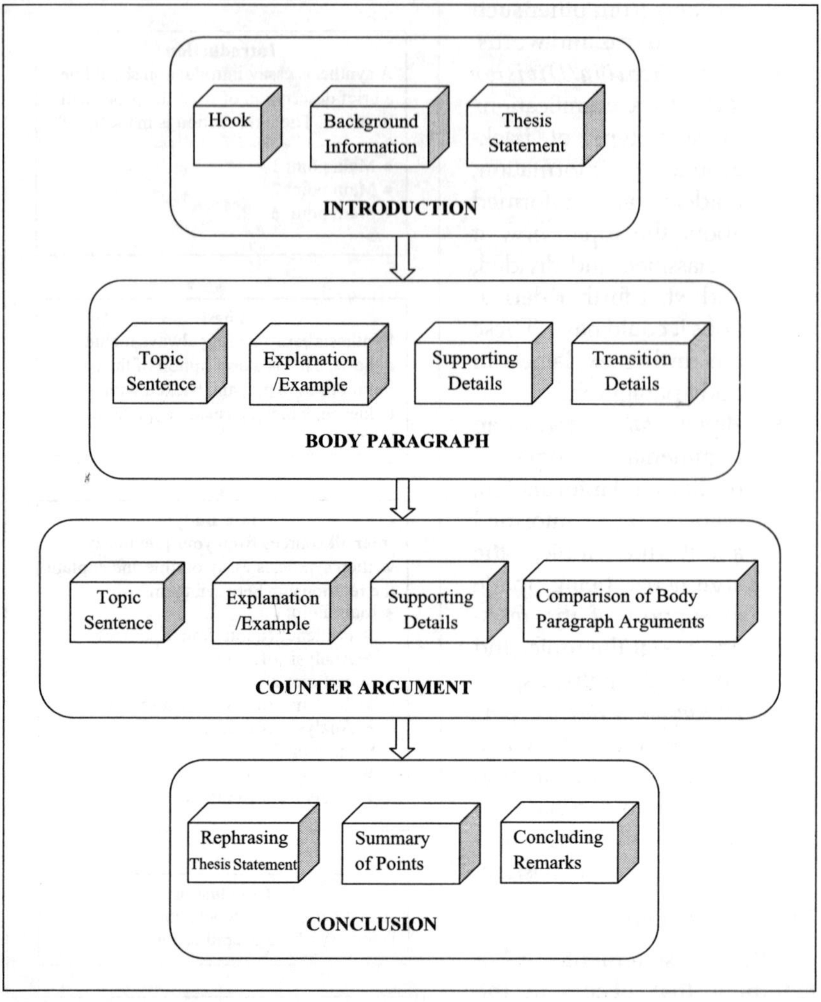


Figure 5.19: Format of Five-paragraph Essay

and should it have more than three body paragraphs, may be additional evidences. In argumentative essays, three evidences support the topic, while the fourth evidence is against it. The same is the case of persuasive essays. This applies to five-paragraph essays, but in case of a longer essay, the thesis statement could make use of more than one sentence.

*Qualities of a Good Thesis Statement*

- It must have evidences.
- It should be interesting.

- It should be limited.
- It should be manageable.
- It should be researchable.

*Difference between a Thesis Statement and Topic*

It must be kept in mind that a thesis statement is not a topic, but a brief explanation of the topic in a way that sets the direction of the essay. It predicts the path the essay will take, and tells readers how the essay is going to be organised, and what each part contains. The topic, however, is a general idea of the essay. It is a specific topic, which has been organised by the thesis statement. The thesis statement in turn elaborates evidences to support to the topic.

### Sentence

Etymologically, the term sentence has its origin in a Latin word '*sententia*' which translates as '*feeling*' or '*opinion*'. In language, a sentence is the largest grammatically independent unit, having a subject and a verb, and expressing a complete thought or an idea.

In English, a sentence starts with a capital letter, and ends with a punctuation mark, such as a period, an exclamation mark, or a question mark. It could be a very simple sentence, with only a subject and a predicate; or a complex one with a group of clauses, phrases, or words, which form a syntactic unit, expressing a wish, a question, an emotion, a command, an assertion, a performance or an action.

*Types of Sentence*

Depending upon the structure and functions, a sentence is of different types. These include:

- *Declarative Sentence:* Declarative sentence uses a simple statement instead of an exclamation, a question, or a command. In this type of sentence, the subject comes before the verb, and a period comes at the end. It is one of the most commonly used sentences in various forms of writing. It can be a positive or negative statement in different shapes. For example, *"We have meat stored in the refrigerator because it is very hot outside"*, is a simple declarative sentence.
- *Interrogative Sentence:* This type of a sentence uses an interrogation or a question. Hence, it ends with an interrogation mark. This sentence uses inversion, which is a reversal of the word order, where subject comes after the verb. For instance, *"Have you taken your breakfast this morning?"*
- *Imperative Sentence:* An imperative sentence gives instructions or advice, or expresses a command or request. It starts with the basic

form of a verb and ends with an exclamation mark or a period such as, "Give me liberty or give me death!"

- *Exclamatory Sentence:* In an exclamatory sentence, the main clause expresses strong emotions or feelings, with an exclamation mark, also referred to as an *"exclamation point,"* at the end. These sentences mostly appear in dialogues, being less common in academic writing. For example, *"Whoa, it's alive! It's alive!"*

### Transition

Transitions are words and phrases that provide a connection between ideas, sentences, and paragraphs. Transitions help to make a piece of writing flow better. They can turn disconnected pieces of ideas into a unified whole and prevent a reader from getting lost in the storyline.

Since the goal of a writer is to convey information clearly and concisely, transitions help achieve that aim by providing a logical connection between one or more sections of a piece of writing. Transitions usually work best when used to link one paragraph to the next and are usually found at the beginning of the paragraph, although they can be used anywhere when needed.

#### Common Locations of Transitions

- *Between Sections:* In longer pieces of writing, transitional paragraphs summarise the information for readers, and specify the relevance of the information in the sections to come.
- *Between Paragraphs:* Transitions form a relationship between paragraphs by connecting them with phrases, words, or sentences that can be placed at the end of the first paragraph, the start of the second paragraph, or in both places.
- *Within Paragraphs:* These help the reader anticipate what is to come by serving as cues. Within paragraphs, transitions are usually short phrases or single words.

### Thesis

A thesis is a statement in a non-fiction or a fiction work that a writer intends to support and prove. One can find examples of thesis statement at the beginning of literary pieces. These thesis statements are of utmost importance, as they provide clear indicators as to which direction the writer will follow in their work.

#### Importance of a Thesis Statement

In writing an essay, a thesis statement determines the worth of the essay by its capacity to stay focused on its thesis statement. For instance, if a writer fails to clearly mention or define a solid thesis statement in his or her essay, it will be difficult for readers to track the issue the writer plans to discuss and explain. Suppose a writer wants to write an essay on how to make a perfect fruit salad, the quality of his or her writing will exceedingly improve if he or she lets the readers know the subject matter at the start of the essay, for example:

> "In this essay, I will tell you how to make the perfect fruit salad. Not only will it be tasty, but also healthy for your body."

### *Concluding Remarks*

A concluding remark is the last sentence of the conclusion in an essay. It is called a concluding remark because it sums up the entire purpose of the essay in a single sentence. As the name suggests, this remark wraps up the entire essay with a period at the end. However, sometimes there could be a question mark or an exclamation mark instead of a period, depending upon the type of remark.

#### *Types of Concluding Remarks*

A concluding remark depends upon the type of the essay, or upon the purpose of the writer of the essay. It could be of several types such as:

- *A Recommendation Remark:* A recommendation remark presents a recommendation that the author makes. It is somewhat like a suggestion, but it is mandatory, while a suggestion is not.
- *A Suggestion Remark:* A suggestion remark comes when the essay ends with a suggestion. Such remarks often have the auxiliary verb 'should' or in case of something compulsory or essential, it uses *'must'* or *'ought to'*. For example, an essay about pollution could end on a suggestive note of, "People should not throw away plastic shopping bags in the open."
- *A Reflective Remark:* A reflective remark could make the readers think about several themes, lessons, or insights having emerged out of the essay. For example, *"People sometimes wish to take charge of their destinies to make their lives a success."*
- *A Futuristic Remark:* A futuristic remark predicts what might happen in the future. It is often placed at the end of an essay when something imaginary is presented in it, or some potential solution to a problem is posed.
- *A Quizzical Remark:* A quizzical remark is not a question or a rhetorical question, but it still poses some question such as, *"It is now up to the people to respond to such traumas."*
- *A Rhetorical Question:* As the name suggests, it is a question writer leave for the audience to reflect upon and respond.

- *An Explanatory Remark:* An explanatory remark is something that gives further explanation or just says that something is obvious.

### *Proof-reading and Editing of Essay*

Editing focuses on the big picture elements such as overall structure, appropriate paragraphing and whether the question has been answered. Proofreading has a micro-focus on the details of your essay, such as formatting, grammar and punctuation.

Here are some things to consider when doing proofreading and editing:

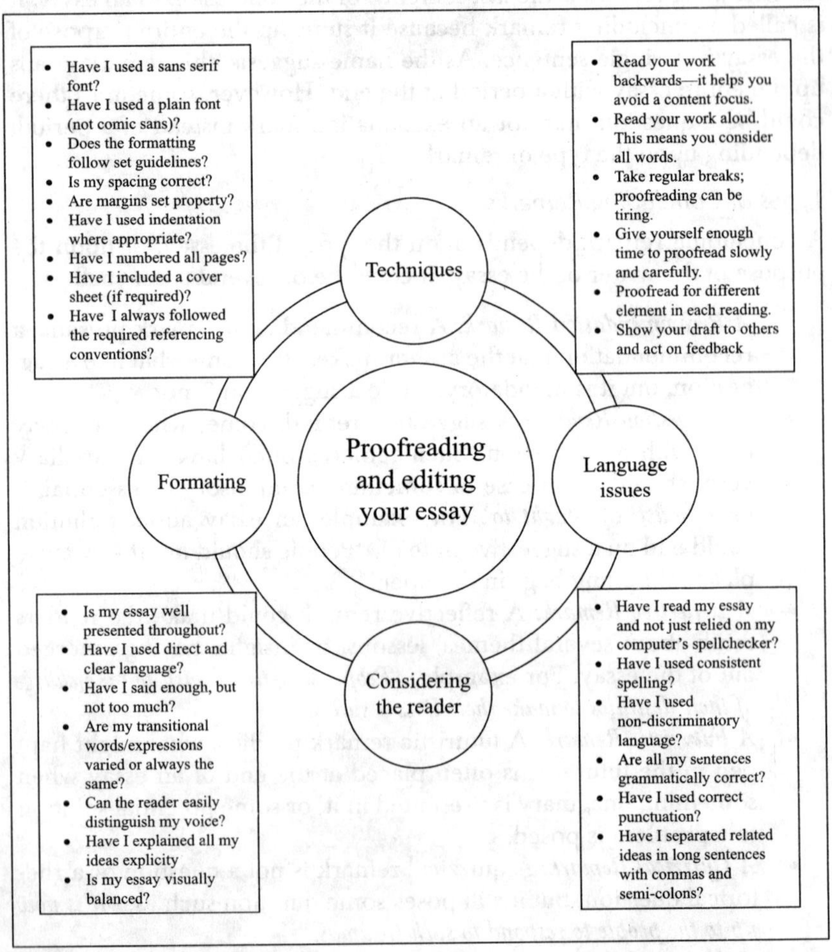


Figure 5.20: Proofreading and Editing of Essay

# CHAPTER 6

# Introduction and Conclusion

Introductions and conclusions are important components of any essay. They work to bookend the argument made in the body paragraphs by first explaining what points will be made (in the introduction) and then summarizing what points were made (in the conclusion).

## INTRODUCTION

An introduction is typically the first paragraph of the paper. The goal of introduction is to let the readers know what he or she can expect from the paper. When writing an introduction to an academic essay, it is useful to remember the main purpose of the introduction. In general, the introduction will introduce the topic to the reader by stating what the topic is and giving some general background information. This will help the reader to understand what you are writing about and show why the topic is important. The introduction should also give the overall plan of the essay.

### Purpose of Introduction

The purpose of an introduction is to tell the reader how the writer will answer question; it sets the scene for the essay. A good introduction:

- introduces the topic of the essay;
- gives a general background of the topic;
- indicates the overall plan of the essay;
- shows the reader how the writer is going to answer the question;
- shows that the writer understands the issues and their implications;
- may include a definition of the topic or key terms (only if needed);
- indicates the structure of the answer and makes clear the main areas that the writer is going to write about;
- shows evidence that the writer has carried out some research by making a reference to key sources;
- only includes totally relevant details;
- is concise: 5% of the word count (e.g.100 words of a 2000 words essay);

### Functions of an Introduction

An introduction:

- captures your audience's attention
- gives background on your topic
- develops interest in your topic
- guides your reader to your thesis.

### Structure of the Introduction

Although essays vary in length and content, most essays will have the same overall structure, including the introduction. The structure is related to the purpose mentioned above. The introduction to an essay should have the following two parts:

- general statements (to introduce the topic and give the background);
- a thesis statement (to show the structure).

*General Statements:* The general statements will introduce the topic of the essay and give background information. The background information for a short essay will generally just be one or two sentences. The general statements should become more and more specific as the introduction progresses, leading the reader into the essay (some writers talk about "attracting the readers' attention", though for an academic essay, this is less important). For longer essays, the general statements could include one or more definitions, or could classify the topic, and may cover more than one paragraph.

*Thesis Statement:* The thesis statement is the most important part of the introduction. It gives the reader clear information about the content of the essay, which will help them to understand the essay more easily. The thesis states the specific topic, and often lists the main (controlling) ideas that will be discussed in the main body. It may also indicate how the essay will be organised, e.g. in chronological order, order of importance, advantages/disadvantages, cause/effect. It is usually at the end of the introduction and is usually (but not always) one sentence long.

In short, the thesis statement:

- states the specific topic of the essay;
- often lists the main (controlling) ideas of the essay;
- may indicate the method of organization of the essay;
- is usually at the end of the introduction;
- is usually one sentence.

## Writing an Introduction

When writing an introduction, you should typically use a *'general to specific'* structure. That is, introduce the particular problem or topic the essay will address in a general sense to provide context, before narrowing down to your particular position and line of argument.

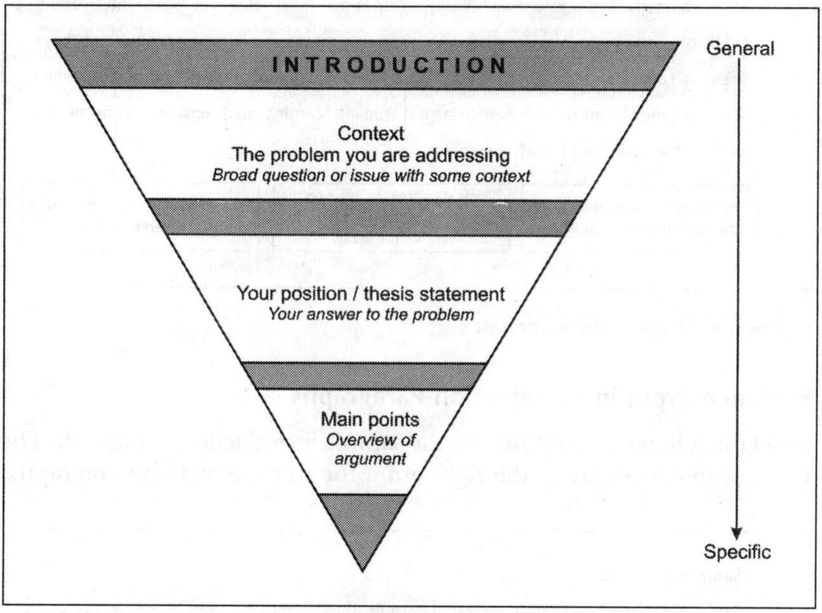


Figure 6.1: A Model/Pattern for Introduction Paragraphs

## Stages of an Introduction

The introduction is usually 'funnel shaped'. The following are the three steps of writing an introduction:

1. *Define the general topic:* It begins with the broadest topic (sentence 1).
2. *Narrow the topic to the essay question topic/thesis statement:* Then, it narrows to the thesis statement or the part of the topic that will be specifically addressed in the essay (sentence 2).
3. *State what you intend to do in the essay:* The last sentence of the paragraph usually outlines the main points that will be covered in the essay (sentence 3).

**Sample question:**

Discuss why assignment essays are common assessment tasks in undergraduate tertiary coursework, and evaluate the effectiveness of assignment as an avenue for learning.

**Introductory paragparh:**

Assignment essays are developed from set questions that give students a period of time to research a topic and produce their answer with references to their sources of information. While there are some disadvantages with using assignment essays as assessment tool, there are sound educational purposes underpinning this practice. This essay examines the reasons why assignment essays are beneficial for student learning and considers some of the problems with this meyhod of assessment.

| Background statement about the general topic of the essay. | Thesis statement to focus on the specific argument to be dealt within the essay. | Outline statement to signal what will be covered in the essay. |
|---|---|---|

Figure 6.2: Stages of Introduction

## Sentence Types in Introduction Paragraphs

Read the following question and the sample introduction paragraph. The types of sentences are in the right order for an introduction paragraph.

**Sample question:**

Some students who enroll in University studies have difficulties with their writing skills. Discuss the reasons for this problem and criticaly assess the effectiveness of University intervention writing programs.

**Introductory paragparh:**

Assignment essays are frequently used as assessment tasks to involve students in research academic reading and formal essay writing. Because poor writing skills can affect studens' success in tertiary education, it is important that writing problems are understood so that university assistance programs are adequate. This essay will identify and examine the main causes underpinning student difficulties with academic writing and consider evidence to evaluate whether programs delivered in universities address this problem.

| Background statement | Thesis statement | Outline statement |
|---|---|---|

Figure 6.3: Sentence Types in Introduction Paragraphs

## Checklist for Introduction

Below is a checklist for an essay introduction. Use it to check your own writing or get a peer (another student) to help you.

Table 6.1: Checklist for Introduction

| *Item* | *OK?* | *Comment* |
|---|---|---|
| The essay begins with general statements, which introduce the topic | | |
| The introduction ends with a thesis statement | | |
| The thesis shows the main ideas of the essay | | |
| The thesis shows how the essay will be organised (e.g. chronological, compare/contrast, advantages/disadvantages) | | |

# CONCLUSION

A conclusion works to remind the readers of the main points of the paper and summarises what writer wants his reader to *"take away"* from his discussion.

## Purpose of Conclusion

The conclusion offers a last chance to convince the reader of the writer's point of view. A good conclusion should:

- be more than just a summary of your essay
- be a good end to your piece of work
- state your main conclusion based on the evidence you have presented, but do so without repeating exactly the same language as your essay
- link back to your title and introduction. Demonstrate you have answered the question and clearly stated your point of view.

## Functions of Conclusion

*Structure of Conclusion:* The concluding paragraph consists of the following two parts:

- a summary of the main points;
- your final comment on the subject.

Summary: It is important, at the end of the essay, to summarise the main points. If your thesis statement is detailed enough, then your summary can just be a restatement of your thesis using different words.

The summary should include all the main points of the essay and should begin with a suitable transition signal. You should not add any new information at this point.

*Final Comment:* Once the essay is finished and the writer has given a summary, there should be some kind of final comment about the topic. This should be related to the ideas in the main body. Your final comment might:

- offer solutions to any problems mentioned in the body;
- offer recommendations for future action;
- give suggestions for future research.

## Writing a Conclusion

When writing a conclusion, a *'specific to general'* structure is usually recommended. This is opposite to the introduction. Begin by re-stating or re-emphasising your position on the topic, and then summarise your line of argument and key points. Finish off by commenting on the significance of the issue, making a prediction about the future of the issue, or a recommendation to deal with the problem at hand.

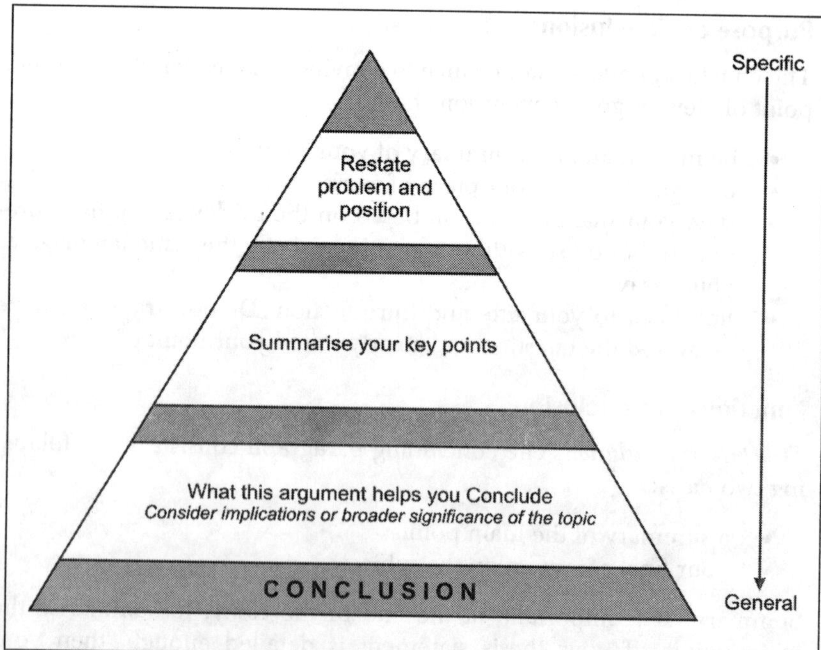


Figure 6.4: A Model/Pattern for Conclusion Paragraphs

## Stages of Conclusion

The conclusion is usually opposite of the 'funnel shaped'. The following are the three steps of writing an introduction:

*Restatement of the main premise:* It begins with the narrowest topic (sentence 1).

*Summary of key points in essay:*Then widens to the summary of key points of the argument in the essay (sentence 2).

Broad statement (evaluate, forecast future, make recommendations): The last sentence of the paragraph usually makes a broad statement that may be a reflection about the essay's argument (sentence 3).

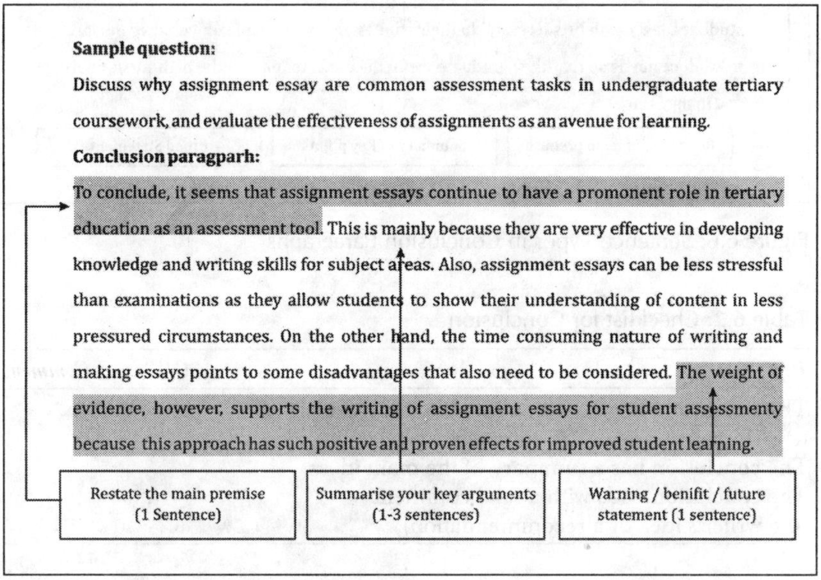


Figure 6.5: Stages of Conclusion

## Sentence Types in Conclusion Paragraphs

Read the following question and the sample conclusion paragraph. The types of sentences are in the right order for a conclusion paragraph.

## Checklist for Conclusion

Below is a checklist for an essay conclusion. Use it to check your own writing, or get a peer (another student) to help you.

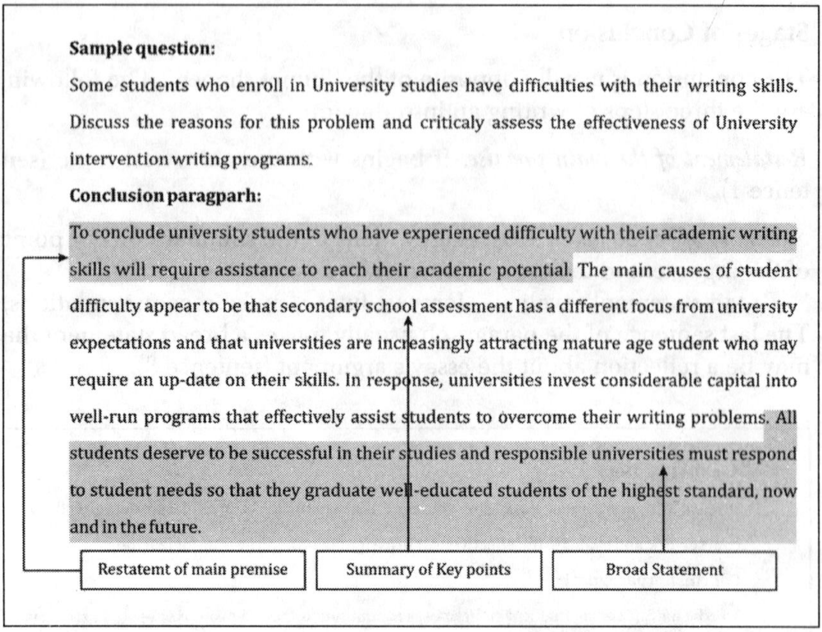


Figure 6.6: Sentence Types in Conclusion Paragraphs

Table 6.2: Checklist for Conclusion

| *Item* | *OK?* | *Comment* |
|---|---|---|
| The conclusion begins with a suitable transition signal (e.g. 'In conclusion...', 'To summarise...', 'In sum...') | | |
| The conclusion has a summary of the main ideas | | |
| The conclusion ends with a final comment (the writer's idea or a recommendation). | | |

# CHAPTER 7

# Citation and Referencing

In academic writing, whenever we take about someone else's ideas, opinions or findings, etc., we have to use citation and referencing. We cannot mention another's ideas as our own. Using someone else's ideas and not including reference or citation is considered an academic theft, which is known as plagiarism. Citation is mentioning the source of the idea in the text itself whereas reference is a list of sources given at the end of the work. This is the main difference between citation and reference.

Providing references and citations is an important and essential part of any type of academic writing. The main purpose is to acknowledge the original source of ideas and work that is not the author's own and to direct the readers to the original sources of information. Whenever we use sources such as books, journals, research papers, web sites, e-resources and others in the writings, one must give credit to the original author by properly citing the sources.

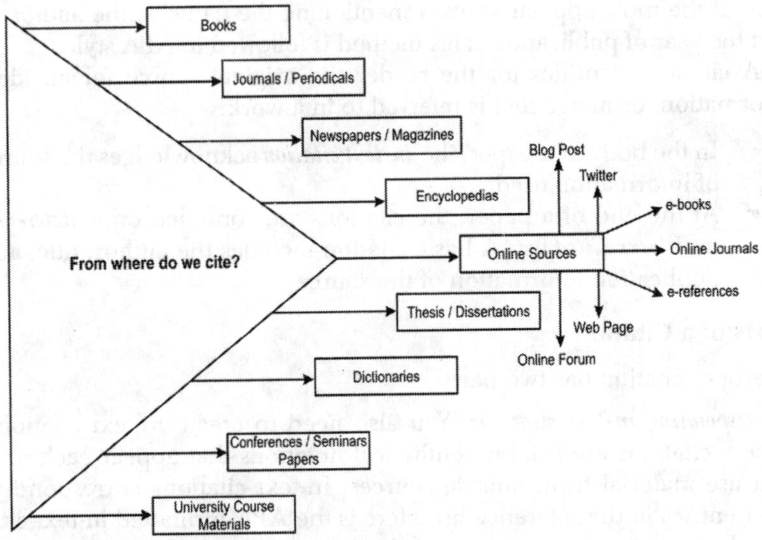


Figure 7.1: Sources of Citation

# CITATION

## What is Citing?

You must refer to all sources you quote or paraphrase within your document, and this is known as citing. You should always briefly cite the sources you use in your work within the text of your paper as this will refer your reader to your reference list or bibliography where you will provide the extended details of the source. If you use the words of another author, you must always use quotation marks to indicate that these words are not your own and you must acknowledge the source, including the page number in your brief in-text citation.

## What is a Citation?

A citation is a reference to a source of information. A citation typically includes enough identifying information, such as the author, title, publisher information, date of publication, database retrieved from, etc. for a reader to be able to locate a copy of the item. A citation indicates the source of your information. It tells the readers from where you took the ideas and information. This is done in the text itself. There are different ways of adding citation to your work.

Figure 7.2: Process of Citing

One of the most popular ways is mentioning the name of the author (s) and the year of publication. This method is followed in APA style.

A citation identifies for the reader the original source for an idea, information, or image that is referred to in a work.

- In the body of a paper, the *in-text citation* acknowledges the source of information used.
- At the end of a paper, the citations are compiled on a *References* or *Works Cited* list. A basic citation includes the author, title, and publication information of the source.

## Parts of a Citation

A proper citation has two parts:

*Corresponding in-text citations:* You also need to create in-text citations. In-text citations are brief parenthetical notations that appear each time you use material from outside sources. In-text citations correspond to their entries in the reference list. Here is the APA-formatted in-text citation that corresponds to the example above:
(Foisy, 2010).

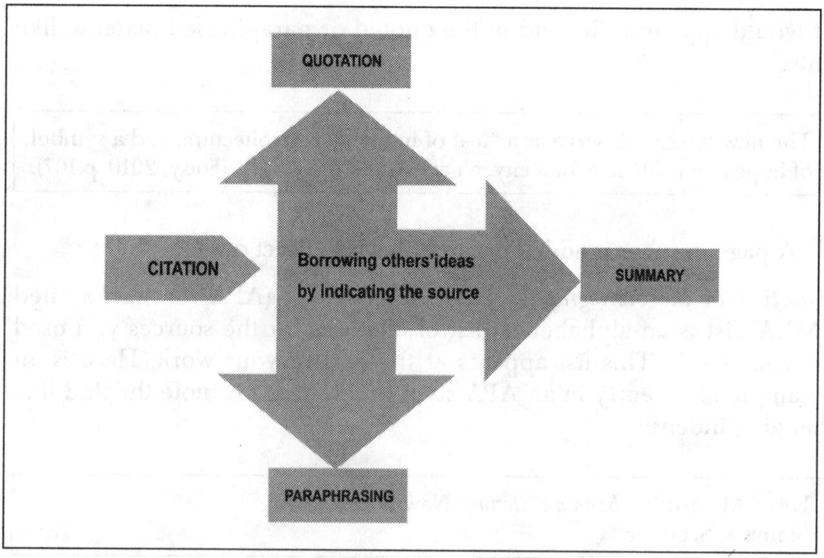


Figure 7.3: Diagrammatical Concept of Citation

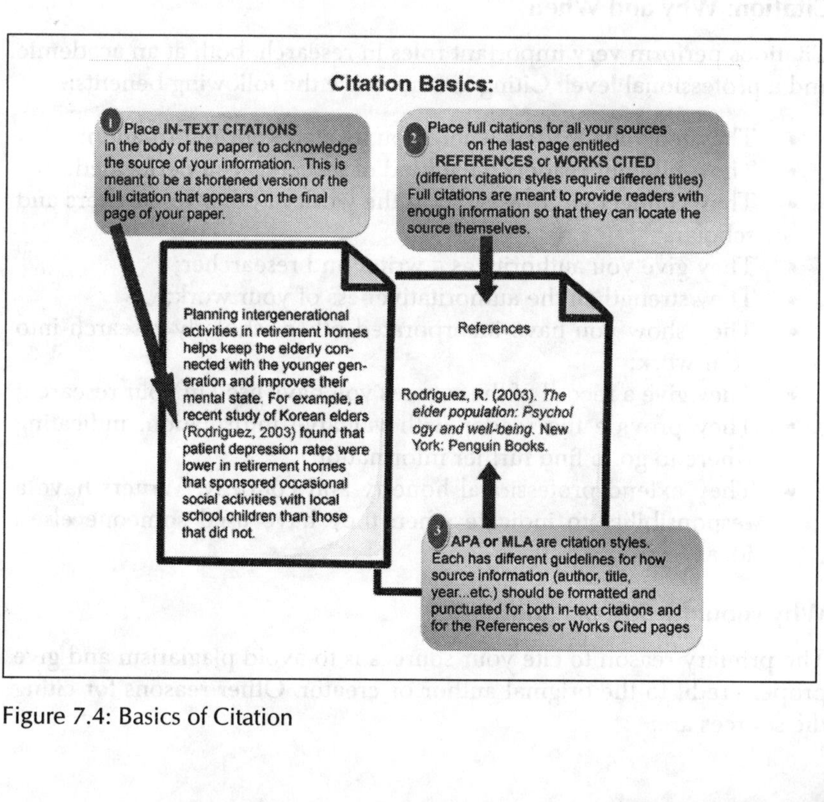


Figure 7.4: Basics of Citation

It would appear at the end of the quoted or paraphrased material like this:

> The new tower will serve as a "feat of innovative architecture, and a symbol of hope and resilience for a city, a nation, and the world" (Foisy, 2010, p.107).

A page number is added because this is a direct quote.

*Citation in the bibliography:* The reference list (APA) or works cited (MLA) list is an alphabetical list of citations for the sources you used in your work. This list appears at the end of your work. Here is an example of an entry in an APA style References list (note the 2nd line hanging indent):

> Foisy, M. (2010). *Urban architecture.* New York, NY:
> Simon & Schuster.

## Citation: Why and When

Citations perform very important roles in research, both at an academic and a professional level. Citing sources have the following benefits:

- They tell your readers where you located your information;
- They tell your readers what kind of research you performed;
- They connect your research to the work of other researchers and scholars;
- They give you authority as a writer and researcher;
- They strengthen the authoritativeness of your work;
- They show you have incorporated other scholarly research into your work;
- They give a record of the sources you have used in your research;
- They provide the reader with valuable information, indicating where to go to find further information;
- They extend professional honesty and courtesy. Writers have a responsibility to indicate when they have used someone else's ideas or words.

## Why should I Cite my Sources?

The primary reason to cite your sources is to avoid plagiarism and give proper credit to the original author or creator. Other reasons for citing the sources are:

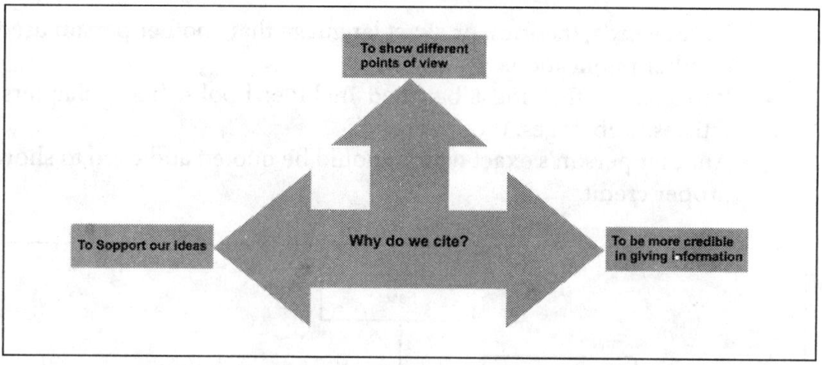


Figure 7.5: Reasons to Citation

- It is the the right thing to do (giving credit to the person or organisation who had the idea);
- It shows that you have read and understood what others think about your topic (you have consulted with experts);
- It helps you avoid plagiarism;
- It helps people find the sources you used in case they want to read more about your topic;
- It demonstrates the accuracy and reliability of your information;
- It shows the amount of research you have done;
- It strengthens your work by lending outside support to your ideas.

## When should I Cite?

You should use citations whenever you quote, paraphrase, or summarise someone else's work.

- *Quotations* are exact duplicates of other people's words.
- *Paraphrases* are other people's ideas rewritten in your own words. They are usually about the same length as the original material.
- *Summaries* are other people's ideas that you have shortened to highlight the main ideas. They are always shorter than the original material.

You should cite your sources whenever you write ideas that are not your original ideas.

## What to Cite

You must cite:

- Facts, figures, ideas, or other information that is not common knowledge

- Ideas, words, theories, or exact language that another person used in other publications
- Publications that must be cited include: books, book chapters, articles, web pages, theses, etc.
- Another person's exact words should be quoted and cited to show proper credit.

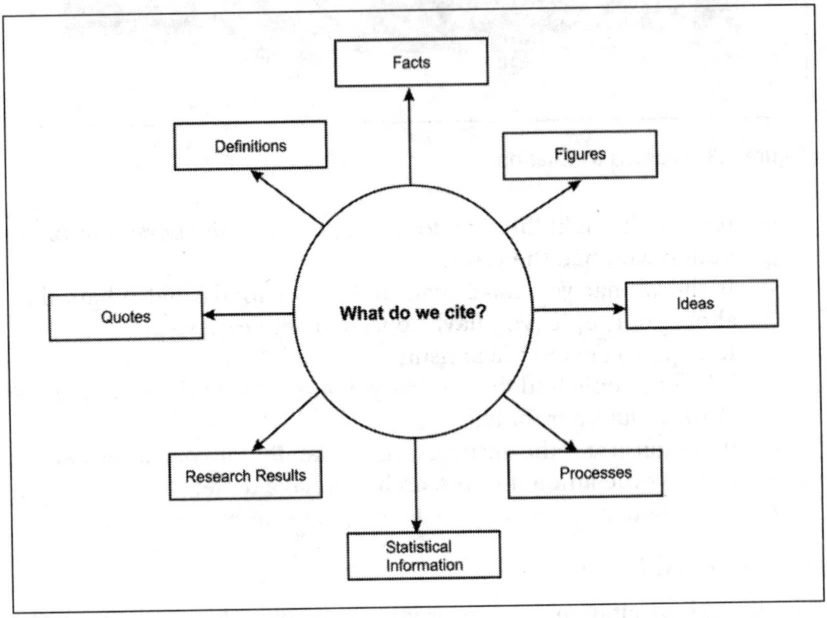


Figure 7.6: Content of Citation

## Are there Situations When I Do Not Have to Cite?

Sometimes, you do not have to create citations for:

- Common knowledge (example: George H.W. Bush was the 41st president of the United States)
- Famous quotes ("That's one small step for man; one giant leap for mankind").

## REFERENCE

### What is a Reference?

Reference is the list of sources given at the end of the work. The information of all the works indicated in citations is given in the reference list.

It provides more details about your sources. For example, it provides information such as the author/s name, the name of the book, journal, etc., publication year, page number, publisher, etc. If the information was taken from a website, the reference usually contains a link to the site as well as the date the information was retrieved. As with citations, there are different styles of referencing.

## What is Referencing?

Referencing is a method used to acknowledge when ideas, information, data, examples, images and words from others' work are included in academic writing.

## Why is Referencing Used in Academic Writing?

There are five main reasons why referencing is used in academic writing. Referencing is used to:

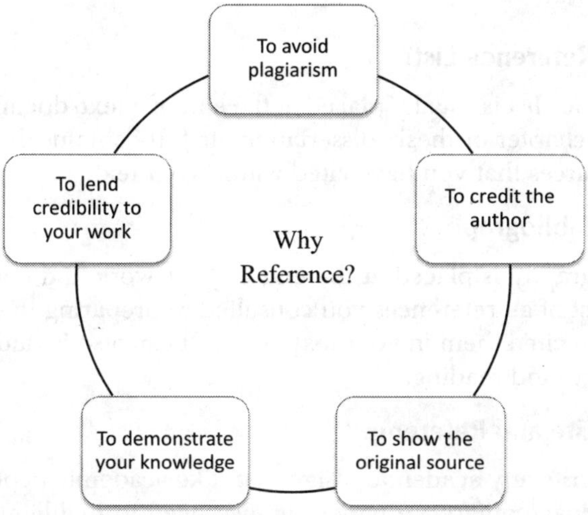


Figure 7.7: Why we need Reference

1. adhere to copyright laws
2. acknowledge the use of other's work
3. recognise the efforts of those who have already produced work on the topic
4. add credibility to the writing by providing verifiable evidence
5. offer a collegial gesture to the reader (e.g. being generous by sharing resources you have found about the topic).

## Elements of a Reference

All references provide the same types of information:

- *Who.* Who is responsible for writing the source? Author, editor, translator.
- *When.* When was the source published or produced? Date. Sometimes just year; sometimes month and year; sometimes day, month, and year.
- *What.* What is the name of the source? Book, article, or journal title; series title; subtitle; etc.
- *Where.* Who produced the source and where are they located? Publisher, publisher location, website URL or DOI, etc. Is the source from a specific location? Book chapter, edition, journal volume and issue number, etc.
- Some citation and reference styles want to know the source's format, such as print or web, as well as when you accessed the material.

## What is a Reference List?

The Reference list is usually placed at the end of a text/document (paper or essay or chapter or thesis/dissertation etc.). It contains the list of citations for sources that you have cited within your text.

## What is a Bibliography?

The Bibliography is placed at the end of your work and comprises the complete list of all references you consulted in preparing the document, whether you cited them in your text or not. It can also include titles useful as background reading.

## Why We Cite and Reference?

When we write any academic assignment like academic paper, research paper, seminar/conference paper etc., we need to highlight our use of other author's ideas and words so that we:

- give the original author credit for their own ideas and work
- validate our arguments
- enable the reader to follow up on the original work if they wish to
- enable the reader to see how dated the information might be
- prove that we have read around the subject
- avoid plagiarism.

## Citations

Citations or In-text citations are similar to references but occur in the body of the text with direct quotes and paraphrases to identify the author/publication for the material you have used. Citations are used

- To show which reference supports a particular statement.
- For direct quotes – when you repeat a passage from a text (or speech, video, etc.) in your assignment without changing any words.
- When you paraphrase – this is when you use your own words to restate the meaning of a text in your assignment.
- One of the most important things to remember is that every citation should also have a corresponding entry in your reference list.

## In-text Citation

APA (American Psychological Association) Style uses the ***author-date*** method for in-text citations. This means that when you cite a source, you should always provide both the author's *last name* and the ***publication year*** for the source. If you are quoting from a source, then you also provide the *page number(s)* of the section you are quoting.

There are two ways you will use other people's words in your work.

- *Quotations:* using the author's exact words
- *Paraphrases and Summaries:* using the author's ideas in your own words

Here are the rules for providing in-text citations in both of these situations.

### *Quotations*

*Rule:* Introduce the quotation with a signal phrase that includes the *author's last name* followed by the *date of publication* in parentheses. Put the page number (preceded by "p.") in parentheses at the end of the quotation.

Example: As Davis (1978) reported, "If the existence of a signing ape was unsettling for linguists, it was also startling news for animal behaviorists" (p. 26).

*Rule:* When the *author's name* does not appear in the signal phrase, place the *author's name*, the date, and the *page number* in parentheses at the end of the quotation. Use commas between items in the parentheses.

Example: "If the existence of a signing ape was unsettling for linguists, it was also startling news for animal behaviorists" (Davis, 1978, p. 26).

*Rule:* When the quotation is *more than 40 words in text*, do not use quotation marks, but indent the quote into its own block of text.

Example: Students having a hard time finding databases is not a new phenomenon. At the University of Washington, they have problems too.

> With the addition of so many new databases to the campus online system, many students were having difficulty locating the database they needed. At the same time, the role of Session Manager had evolved. The increased importance of the Session Manager as a selection tool made it a part of the navigation process itself. (Eliasen, McKinstry, Fraser, & Babbitt, 1997, p. 510)

*Rule:* When *quoting material that has a citation within it*, keep the original citation. (That embedded citation does not need to be included in your reference list.)

Example: "In the United States, the American Cancer Society (2007) estimated that about 1 million cases of NMSC and 59,940 cases of melanoma would be diagnosed in 2007, with melanoma resulting in 8,110 deaths" (Miller et al., 2009, p. 209).

Exception: When citing from an e-book, there may or may not be page numbers. If an e-book has page numbers, include them in the in-text citation. If an e-book *does not have page numbers*, there are a few options to describe the location of the text being quoted.

- Provide the *paragraph number.* Some e-books list paragraph numbers in the margins; otherwise, you can count paragraphs from the beginning of the e-book.
- Provide the *heading* for the section along with the *paragraph number* within that section. (Examples of headings could be chapter titles or sub-chapter titles, section headings, etc.)
- Provide an *abbreviated heading* (such as the first few words) in quotation marks if the full heading is too long to cite in full.

Example:
"'Oh, you can't help that,' said the Cat: 'we're all mad here. I'm mad. You're mad'" (Carroll, 2009, p. 76)
[from Carroll, L. (2009). *Alice's Adventures in Wonderland.* Retrieved from https://www.gutenberg.org/files/28885/28885-h/28885-h.htm]

Example:
"'Oh, you can't help that,' said the Cat: 'we're all mad here. I'm mad. You're mad'" (Carroll, 2014, Pig and Pepper, para. 61)
[from Caroll, L. (2014). *Alice's Adventures in Wonderland.* Retrieved from https://www.gutenberg.org/files/11/11-h/11-h.htm]

*Paraphrases and Summaries*
*Rule:* Work by one author, no quotation marks required.

Example 1: According to Davis (1978), when they learned of an ape's ability to use sign language, both linguists and animal behaviorists were taken by surprise.

Example 2: When they learned of an ape's ability to use sign language, both linguists and animal behaviorists were taken by surprise (Davis, 1978).

*Rule:* When paraphrasing information from a work that is not originally from the source you have, use the phrase "as cited in" at the end. Follow with the author(s) of the source you have, the publication date, and the page number. Provide the information for the source you have in your reference list.

Example: In their e-mail correspondence, Smith and Jones expressed their surprise about an ape's ability to use sign language (as cited in Davis, 1978).

## Rules of In-text Citing as per APA Style

Insert an in-text citation when your work has been influenced by someone else's work, for example:

- when you directly quote someone else's work or
- when you paraphrase someone else's work.

1. The in-text citation consists of author surname(s)/family name(s), in the order that they appear on the actual publication, followed by the year of publication of the source that you are citing.
   - For direct quotes, make sure to include page or paragraph number, e.g. (Weston, 1988, p. 45). Page numbers are not normally included when paraphrasing but may be included if desired.
2. The in-text citation is placed immediately after the information being cited.
3. If your citation is at the end of a sentence, ensure the full stop is placed after the reference.
4. If quoting or citing a source which has been cited within another document, mention the original source together with the secondary reference details; for example: (Smith, 2008, as cited in Jones, 2010). In this case, only the secondary reference (i.e. Jones, 2010) should be included in the reference list.

5. In-text citations are usually included in the word count of your document.
6. For citations in brackets with two authors the '&' symbol is used. If the author citation forms part of your sentence the word 'and' must be used, e.g. (Brown & Black, 2010) OR "Brown and Black (2010) indicate that..."
7. If you wish to quote or paraphrase an author and want to emphasise the author, then your citation becomes 'author prominent'. The citation will look something like this:
   - Jones (2012) has concluded that...
8. If you wish to emphasise the information you have paraphrased or quoted from an author, then your citation becomes 'information prominent'. The citation will look something like this:
   - ... as evidenced from a recent Australian study (Jones, 2012).

Examples:

*One Author*

| | |
|---|---|
| Rule | Surname of author, no initials or suffixes such as Jr. The year of publication is also included |
| Citation examples | ... This was seen in an Australian study (Conger, 1979).<br>OR<br>Conger (1979) has argued that...<br>OR<br>In 1979, Conger conducted a study which showed that... |

*Two Authors*

| | |
|---|---|
| Rule | Cite both surnames every time the reference occurs in the text |
| Citation examples | ...(Davidson & Harrington, 2002)<br>OR<br>Davidson and Harrington (2002)... |

*Three to Five Authors*

| | |
|---|---|
| Rule | Cite all surnames and publication year the first time, thereafter only the first surname followed by et al. Note: There is a full-stop (.) after al (see below). |
| Citation examples | The first time cited: ...(Brown, Soo, & Jones, 1990).<br>Brown, Soo, and Jones (1990)...<br>thereafter:<br>...(Brown et al., 1990).<br>Brown et al. (1990)... |

### *Six or More Authors*

| | |
|---|---|
| Rule | Cite only the surname of the first author followed by et al. and the year from the first citation. Note: There is a full-stop (.) after al (see below). Include all authors, up to seven, in the reference list. Please see instruction for eight or more authors on the introductory page of this guide. |
| Citation examples | .... (Girad-Perregaux et al., 2003).<br>Girad-Perregaux et al. (2003)... |

### *Different Authors: Same Surname*

| | |
|---|---|
| Rule | Add the initials of the author's first or given name/s to their surname to distinguish them. |
| Citation examples | P. R. Smith (1923) to distinguish from S. Smith (1945) ...<br>(S. A. Brown & Jones, 1961) to distinguish from (W. O. Brown & Smith, 1985). |

### *Multiple Authors: Ambiguous Citations*

| | |
|---|---|
| Rule | If a multiple (3+) author citation abbreviated with et al. looks the same as another in text citation similarly shortened, add enough surnames to make a distinction, followed by a comma and et al. |
| Citation examples | ...(Brown, Shimamura, et al., 1998) to distinguish from (Brown, Taylor, et al., 1998). |

### *Multiple Works: by Same Author*

| | |
|---|---|
| Rule | When cited together give the author's surname once followed by the years of each publication, which are separated by a comma. |
| Citation examples | ... (Stairs, 1992, 1993).<br>Stairs (1992, 1993)... |

### *Multiple Works: by Same Author and Same Year*

| | |
|---|---|
| Rule | If there is more than one reference by an author in the same year, suffixes (a, b, c, etc.) are added to the year. Allocation of the suffixes is determined by the order of the references in the reference list, not by the order in which they are cited. Suffixes are also included in the reference list, and these references are listed alphabetically by title. If cited together, list by suffix as shown below. |
| Citation examples | Stairs (1992b) ... later in the text ... (Stairs, 1992a).<br>...(Stairs, 1992a, 1992b). |

*If the Author is Identified as 'Anonymous'*

| | |
|---|---|
| Rule | Use Anonymous in place of the author's surname. |
| Citation examples | ... (Anonymous, 1997) |

*Unknown Author*

| | |
|---|---|
| Rule | Give the first few words of the title. If the title is from an article or a chapter use double quotation marks. If the title is from a periodical, book brochure or report then use italics. |
| Citation examples | ...the worst election loss in the party's history ("This is the end," 1968). |

*Corporate or Group of Authors*

| | |
|---|---|
| Rule | If organization is recognized by abbreviation, cite the first time as follows: |
| Citation examples | ... (Australian Institute of Health and Welfare [AIHW], 2005)<br>Note: [AIHW] is in square brackets for the initial in-text citation and thereafter as<br>... (AIHW, 2005).<br>However, if abbreviation not widely known, give the name in full every time:<br>... (Australian Research Council, 1996) |

*Multiple References*

| | |
|---|---|
| Rule | List the citations in alphabetical order and separate with semicolons |
| Citation examples | ... (Burst, 1995; Nguyen, 1976; Turner & Hooch, 1982). |

*Citing Specific Parts of a Source*

| | |
|---|---|
| Rule | For a direct quote the page number(s) must be given. Indicate page, chapter, figure, table, etc., as specifically as possible. Use accepted abbreviations, i.e. p. for page, para. for paragraph. |
| Citation examples | As one writer put it "the darkest days were still ahead" (Weston, 1988, p. 45).<br>Weston (1988) argued that "the darkest days were still ahead" (p. 45).<br>This theory was put forward by Smith (2005, chap.7).3 |

*Quote from an Electronic Source*

| | |
|---|---|
| Rule | Where page numbers are not provided, use paragraph numbers. |
| Citation examples | ... (Chang, 2001, para. 2) |

*Personal Communications*

| | |
|---|---|
| Rule | These include private letters, e-mail, and conversations. As personal communications are not accessible to others, they are not included in the reference list.<br>However, an in-text citation is required. |
| Citation examples | ... (R. Smith, personal communication, January 28, 2002).<br>R. Smith (personal communication, January 28, 2002) ... |

*Citation of a Secondary Source: (i.e. a source referred to in another publication)*

| | |
|---|---|
| Rule | Note: APA 6th specifies that secondary citations should ONLY be used where the original is unavailable (for example, out-of-print). Wherever possible, read and cite the original source.<br>If the original source is not available, ONLY include the details of the source you actually read. In the example below, the original source would be Farrow (1968), which you saw cited in a paper by Ward and Decan (1988). |
| Citation examples | ... (Farrow, 1968, as cited in Ward & Decan, 1988).<br>Farrow (1968, as cited in Ward & Decan, 1988) ...<br>Ward and Decan (1988) cited Farrow (1968) as finding... |

*Citing Legislation or Legal Cases*

The way you cite legislation or legal cases depends on whether you read the actual legislation or read about it in another source. If it is the latter, the legislation/case should be treated as a secondary source.

| | |
|---|---|
| Rule–Legislation | The title of the legislation and the year (jurisdiction).<br>Note: include the jurisdiction the first time the act is cited. The jurisdiction can be dropped with subsequent citations |
| Citation examples | The Medical Treatment Act 1988 (Vic) states......<br>by virtue of s. 25.1 of the Aged Care Act 1997 (Cth) ....<br>..."A restrictive intervention may only be used on a person..." (Mental Health Act 2014 (Vic), s. 105)<br>as a secondary source<br>.... Occupational Health and Safety Act 2004 (Vic) (as cited in Creighton & Rozen, 2007) |

| | |
|---|---|
| Rule - Cases | The title of the case (year). Note: Include the year with the first citation. The year can be dropped in subsequent citations. |
| Citation examples | According to the case of Rogers v Whitaker (1992) ....<br>as a secondary source<br>..... Chappel v Hart (1988) (as cited in Forrester & Griffiths, 2010) |

## Difference between a Citation and a Reference

In the citation, the author acknowledges the source of a specific part of the text in the research paper, article or assignment. In citation, the author cites or refers to the source in the text to represent that the information is derived from an external source and to mention that source, in brief. Basically, it is an abbreviated reference, which you can find in the main body of the article or assignment, addressing the source of a quote, image, video, paraphrase, chart, table, etc. Due to this very reason, it is also called as "in-text citation", which includes a set of parenthesis.

On the other hand, in referencing an entire list of sources which have been referred and backs the argument of the author is provided at the end of the document or article. It is just a form of credit which the author gives to the person's whose ideas has been borrowed in the work. Reference can be understood as the list of items which you have read and considered in your piece of work. While providing references, the author actually tells its readers about what kind of source he/she has used in the document.

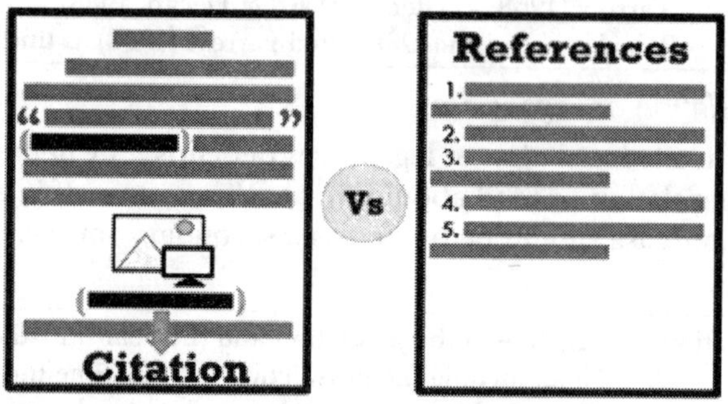


Figure 7.8: Difference between Citation and Reference

Table 7.1: Difference between Citation and Reference

| *Basis for Comparison* | *Citation* | *Reference* |
|---|---|---|
| Meaning | Citation is a way of disclosing within the main body, that the quote, image, chart, statistics, etc. are taken from an outside source. | Reference is a list which contains all the sources which have been sought or cited while writing the article or assignment. |
| Use | It informs the readers, the basic source of information. | It informs the reader, the complete source of information. |

| *Basis for Comparison* | *Citation* | *Reference* |
|---|---|---|
| Purpose | To indicate the source of the material taken. | To support or criticize an argument or point. |
| Placement | Presented in the bracket. | Presented as endnote or end of the document. |
| Information | It contains information like publication year and last name of the author. | It contains information like publication date, title of book/journal, author's name, page number. |

Basically, reference and citation are provided to give the user or reader, the source of facts, images, statistics, charts, tables and diagrams, which are a part of the article or assignment. It may also be used when you are talking about a theory, method or model, discovered by or linked to a specific person or writer. With the help of these two, the author shows acknowledgement to those scholars, whose work or ideas has been used in the article or assignment.

## Referencing Styles

A referencing style is a set of rules which outline how to include references in your writing. These rules help us to communicate clearly and to make sure the work of other people is acknowledged appropriately. There are many different referencing styles. You will need to check which style your subject or school requires you to use.

One of the most important parts of referencing is understanding your referencing style, and how to use it. Each referencing style has specific formatting details, which you need to follow closely, so that your writing and referencing is easier to understand.

### *Parts of Referencing Styles*

There are two parts to most referencing styles: the citations within the text and the reference list at the end of your work.

#### *In-text Citations*

In-text citations provide brief information about the sources you have used so that readers can locate the resource in your list of references. They acknowledge when you have used the words or ideas of someone else and support your work with evidence. You need to include citations for direct quotations (when you are using someone's exact words) and when you paraphrase their ideas into your own words. Each referencing style uses a different format for in-text citations, so make sure you check your referencing style guide for more details.

A common in-text citation method for many referencing styles uses the authors' family names and the date of publication. Another common method is to use a numbered style. In-text citations may also require you to provide a page number to direct people to the specific location of the information.

### *Reference Lists*

Most referencing styles require you to provide a reference list or bibliography. A reference list provides the full details of the sources you have cited in the text of your work. A bibliography is similar to a reference list, but it includes all sources you have used to create your work, not just the ones you have cited in the text.

It is important to check the style guide to find out how to format your reference list correctly. Each referencing style has specific requirements for what information is included in a reference, as well as punctuation and layout. The details you need for each reference will depend on what type of resource you have. For example, journal articles and books require slightly different information.

## Types of Citing Referencing Styles

There are a number of different reference and citation styles available. Styles are basically well-established practices and conventions. Depending on the discipline in which one is working and also the widely used style in the respective discipline, one can decide to select and use a particular style.

The following are the different types of referencing styles:

*AAA Style (American Anthropological Association):* The American Anthropological Association (AAA) Documentation Style is close to the Chicago Manual of Style (CMS). It is the citation style used by many anthropologists, and it is the style used in all AAA journals.

*ACS (American Chemical Society):* It is widely used in chemistry and related disciplines. The ACS manual gives instructions for numbered referencing and also for in-text referencing.

*AGLC (Australian Guide to Legal Citation):* This is now the standard Australian guide for referencing in Law. It is a footnote style and includes detailed provisions for referencing statutes, case reports and other legal materials.

*AIP Style (American Institute of Physics):* The American Institute of Physics (AIP) has a Style Manual which specifies how to format documents for submission to an AIP journal. AIP is the format commonly used in the field of physics. AIP is a numbered style with references numbered in the order of appearance in the article and listed in that order at the end of the article.

*AMA (American Medical Association):* This style is numbered footnote style widely used in medicine, especially in journals published by the American Medical Association.

*AMJ (Academy of Management style):* The "Academy of Management style" is an author-date style for citing and referencing information in assignments and publications.

*APA (American Psychological Association):* This is the standard style used in Psychology, but it is also widely used in other disciplines, especially in the Social Sciences. It is an author-date style.

*APSA Style (American Political Science Association):* It is the citation style used by many political science scholars, and it is the style used in all APSA journals.

*Chicago Style:* University of Chicago Press has created and maintains the Chicago Style. It is the citation style preferred by historians but is also often used in other arts and humanities subjects.

*CMS (Chicago Manual of Style):* The Chicago Manual of Style is the most widely consulted of all style manuals. It includes provisions for footnote referencing and author-date referencing.

*CSE (Council of Science Editors):* It was first issued in 1960 by the Council of Biology Editors (CBE) and is still sometimes referred to as the CBE manual. It is widely used in the life sciences, and its provisions are applicable to other scientific disciplines also.

*Harvard Style:* Harvard is a generic term for any style which contains author-date references in the text of the document, such as (Smith 1999). There will also be a list of references at the end of the document, arranged by authors' names and year of publication. There is no official manual of the Harvard style: it is just a generic term for the many styles which follow that format.

*IEEE (Institute of Electrical and Electronics Engineers):* The IEEE is the major professional body and publisher in the fields of electrical engineering and computer science. Their style manual is widely used in those disciplines. It uses a numbered reference list.

*MLA (Modern Language Association of America):* The MLA style is widely used in the fields of modern literature and linguistics. Works are cited in the text with brief parenthetical citations keyed to the list of works cited.

*Turabian Style:* Turabian style is widely used in humanity and social science subjects. It offers the option of using an author-date system with notes and parenthetical references. Bibliography items are listed alphabetically at the end of the research paper.

*Vancouver:* Vancouver is a generic term for a style of referencing widely used in the health sciences, using a numbered reference list.

## Faculty-wise/Subject-wise List of Citing and Referencing Styles

*Art, Design and Architecture*

| *Department* | *Recommended Style* |
|---|---|
| Architecture | Chicago 16th edition |
| Fine Arts | Turabian footnote – bibliography |
| Design | Turabian author – date |

*Arts*

| *School/Centre* | *Department* | *Recommended Style* |
|---|---|---|
| Centre for Ancient Cultures | Ancient Cultures | Citing and Referencing for Archaeology and Ancient History (Guide) |
| Centre for Theatre and Performance | Theatre and Performance studies | MLA |
| Languages, Literatures Cultures and Linguistics | Literary studies | Use any footnote/endnote style consistently |
| Languages, Literatures Cultures and Linguistics | Linguistics | APA style |
| Media, Film and Journalism | Communication and media studies | Use any footnote/endnote style consistently |
| Media, Film and Journalism | Film and Screen studies | MLA |
| School of Music | Music | Sir Zelman Cowen School of Music Referencing Guide |
| Geography, Environment and Sustainability | | Harvard system |
| Philosophical, Historical and International Studies | History | Footnotes |

| School/Centre | Department | Recommended Style |
|---|---|---|
| Philosophical, Historical and International Studies | Philosophy and Bioethics | No particular style recommended, check with tutor/supervisor and be consistent. |
| Philosophical, Historical and International Studies | Religious studies | Harvard preferred. May use footnote/endnote following guide for History students. |
| Philosophical, Historical and International Studies | Philosophy | Modified Harvard |
| Social Sciences | Anthropology | Harvard (author/date) |
| Social Sciences | Behavioural studies | Harvard |
| Social Sciences | Politics & international relations | Use footnote or endnote style consistently. Check with supervisor/lecturer. |
| Social Sciences | Sociology | Harvard (author/date) |
| Social Sciences | Women's and gender studies | APA |

## *Business and Economics*

| Department | Recommended style |
|---|---|
| Accounting & Finance | APA |
| Economics | |
| Econometrics & Business Statistics | |
| Marketing | |
| Management | |
| Business Law & Taxation | APA/AGLC |

## *Education*

| Recommended Style |
|---|
| APA |

## *Engineering*

| Department | Recommended Style |
|---|---|
| Chemical Engineering | Use any style consistently |
| Civil Engineering | Harvard |
| Electrical and Computer Systems Engineering | IEEE |
| Mechanical Engineering | Use any style consistently |
| Materials engineering | AIP |

### Information Technology

| School/Centre | Recommended Style |
|---|---|
| All Faculty of Information Technology masters course-work and undergraduate units should use the American Psychological Association (APA) Style Guide | APA |
| **Note**: Some unit lecturers may instead specify Institute of Electrical and Electronic Engineers (IEEE) Style Manual | IEEE |

### Law

| Recommended Style |
|---|
| Australian Guide to Legal Citation (AGLC3) (Melbourne University Law Review Association, 3rd ed., 2010) |

### Medicine, Nursing and Health Sciences

| School/Centre | Department | Recommended Style |
|---|---|---|
| School of Biomedical Science | Biochemistry and Molecular Biology | Vancouver style |
| School of Biomedical Science | Microbiology | Details provided to students by department |
| School of Medical Imaging and Radiographic Sciences | | Vancouver<br>Harvard |
| School of Nursing and Midwifery | | APA |
| School of Primary Health Care | | APA |
| • Occupational Therapy | | Harvard |
| • Physiotherapy | | Vancouver or APA |
| • Social Work | | Vancouver |
| • Community Emergency Health and Paramedic Practice | | |
| • General Practice | | |
| School of Psychology, Psychiatry and Psychological Medicine | Psychology | APA |
| Central Clinical School | | Vancouver |
| Department of Nutrition and Dietetics | | Vancouver |

### Pharmacy and Pharmaceutical Sciences

| Recommended Style |
|---|
| Pharmacy: APA, Vancouver<br>Pharmaceutical Sciences: APA, Vancouver |

*Science*

| *Applied Sciences and Engineering* | *Harvard* | *Citing and Referencing Library Guide – Harvard* |
|---|---|---|
| Biological Sciences | CSIRO style | Essay Writing Guidelines for the School of Biological Sciences |
| Chemistry | Use any style consistently | |
| Mathematical Sciences | Use any style consistently | |
| Physics | Harvard | Citing and Referencing library guide – Harvar |

## Rules of References as per APA Style

APA has a few formatting guidelines for the reference list.

- The reference list should start on a *separate page* at the end of your paper.
- Use one-inch margins and continue the *header* from the rest of your paper.
- Title the page *References*, centered at the top (no bold, italics, quotation marks, etc.).
- References should be in a *hanging indent* format, meaning that the first line of each reference is set flush left and subsequent lines are indented.
- *Double-space* the entire list.
- *Alphabetise* the list by each source's first author's *last name.* If there is no author, start with the first significant word in the title.
- In *titles, capitalise* only the *first word* of the *title* and *subtitle,* and *proper nouns.*

### *Examples of References as per APA Style*

### *Audio and Visual Media*

*Films and Video-recordings of Films*

| | |
|---|---|
| Format | Producer, A. A. (Role in the production) & Writer, B. B. (Role in the production). (year of release). *Title of film* [Format]. Place of Publication: Publisher. |
| Example | Scorsese, M. (Producer) & Lonergan, K. (Writer/Director). (2000). *You can count on me* [Motion picture]. Hollywood, CA: Paramount Pictures.<br>*Note:* Place of publication = Location of Film Studio. Publisher = Name of Film Studio. |

*DVDs and Video Recordings*

| | |
|---|---|
| Format | Producer, A. A. (Role in the production). (year of release). *Title of film* [Format]. Place of Publication: Publisher. |
| Example | American Psychological Association. (Producer). (2000). *Responding therapeutically to patient expressions of sexual attraction* [DVD]. Washington, DC: Author.<br>*Note:* The word 'Author' is used as the publisher when the author and publisher are the same. Place of publication = Location of Film Studio. Publisher = Name of Film Studio. |

*Video File (e.g.Youtube video)*

| | |
|---|---|
| Format | Author, A. A. (year, date of posting). *Title of video* [Format]. Retrieved from 'website address' |
| Example | markapsolon. (2011, September 9). *Real ghost girl caught on Video Tape 14* [Video file]. Retrieved from http://www.youtube.com/watch?v=6nyGCbxD848<br>*Note:* Use the screen name markapsolon as it appears online. If the user's real name is available list it first, followed by the screen name in brackets; for example: Smith, J. [markapsolon]. |

*Webstreaming Video*

| | |
|---|---|
| Format | Author, A. A. (year of posting). *Title of video* [Format]. Place of publication: Publisher. Retrieved from 'database name' |
| Example | Fukuyama, M. (2006). *At the corner of me and myself: Voices of multiple social identities* [Streaming video]. Hanover, MA: Microtraining Associates. Retrieved from Alexander Street Press database. |

*Television and Radio Programmes—Single Episode in a Series*

| | |
|---|---|
| Format | Author, A. A. (role in production). (year of release). Title of episode [Format]. In A. Author (role in production), *Title of series*. Place of publication: Publisher. |
| Example | Thomason, M., Rudd, P., & Fineri, W. (Writers/Directors). (2007). North West Passage [Television series episode]. In T. Wright (Supervising Producer), *Captain Cook: Obsession and discovery*. Melbourne, Vic: Film Australia.<br>Stem, J. D. (Writer), Weiss, D. (Writer), & Muzquiz, R. (Director). (1996). Chanukah [Television series episode]. In V. Coffey, G. Csupo, & A. Klasky (Executive producers), *Rugrats*. New York, NY: Nickelodeon. |

### Television and Radio Programmes—Series or Single Programme

| | |
|---|---|
| Format | Author, A. A. (role in production). (year of release). *Title of programme* [Format]. Place of publication: Publisher. |
| Example | Leonard, D. (Producer), & de Pieri, S. (Presenter). (2009). *A gondola on the Murray* [Television series]. Melbourne, Vic: ABC Television.<br>*Note:* A single programme is called a Television broadcast. Specify the broadcast date for a single programme. |

### Podcasts

| | |
|---|---|
| Format | Author, A. A. (role in production). (year, date of posting). *Title of podcast* [Format]. Retrieved from 'website address' |
| Example | Seega, B. (Producer), & Swan, N. (Presenter). (2005, November 28). ***Adult ADHD*** [Audio podcast]. Retrieved from http://www.abc.net.au/rn/talks/8.30/helthrpt<br>Holland, A. (Producer), & Harris, H. (Director). (2008, June 12). Bog man [Video podcast]. Retrieved from ABC: http://www.abc.net.au/catalyst/stories/2272392.htm |

### Images from the Web

| | |
|---|---|
| Format | Artist, A. (year). *Title of image* [format]. Retrieved from URL |
| Example | Monash University. (2011). *CORE body comp* [photograph]. Retrieved from https://imagelibrary.monash.edu |

### Music Recordings

| | |
|---|---|
| Format | Composer, A. A. (copyright year). Song title [Recorded by if Artist is different from the writer]. On *Title of CD* [Format]. Place of publication: Publisher. (date of recording) |
| Example | *In-text citation*<br>"The Last of the Pioneers" (Williamson, 2003, track 5)<br>*Note:* Include the side, band or track number in in-text citation<br>*End text reference*<br>Badnews, U. R. (1927). We only live twice [Recorded by P. Murray]. On *Resurrection* [CD]. Sandgate, Qld: Ibis Records. (1999)<br>*Note:* Include Artist in [ ] after song title if Artist is different from the Writer of the song. Place of publication can also be location of recording. Publisher can be the label the recording was published on. |

*Map or Chart—Electronic*

| | |
|---|---|
| Format | Author, A. A. (year of publication). Title of the map or chart [Format]. Retrieved from 'web address' |
| Example | Idaho Department of Commerce. (2010). Idaho Rivers [Map], Retrieved from http://www.visitidaho.org/mapsimages/maps.aspx |
| | *Note:* When scale is not known, use "Scale not known". |

*Map or Chart—Singular Sheets*

| | |
|---|---|
| Format | Author, A. A. (year of publication). *Title of map or chart* [Format]. (scale) Place of publication: Publisher. |
| Example | Metsker Maps. (1979). *Metsker's map of Island County, Washington* [Map]. (ca. 1:70,000.) Tacoma, WA: Metsker Maps. |
| | *Note:* When scale is not known, use "Scale not known". |

*Map or Chart—Book*

| | |
|---|---|
| Format | Author, A. A. (year of publication). Title of map or chart [Format]. scale. In B. B. Author, *Title of Publication.* Place of publication: Publisher. |
| Example | Magocsi, P. R. (2003). Population movements, 1944-1948 [Map]. 1:8 890 000. In P. R. Magocsi, *Historical atlas of central Europe.* (Rev. & ex. ed.) Seattle: University of Washington Press. |
| | *Note:* When scale is not known, use "Scale not known". |

*Works of Art (Paintings, Sculptures etc) in Physical form or Online*

| | |
|---|---|
| Format | Artist, A. A. (date of creation). *Title of art* [Format]. Place of publication: Publisher. |
| Example | Rodin, A. (1902). *The thinker* [Bronze and marble sculpture]. Paris, France: Musée Rodin.<br>Wyeth, A. (1948). *Christina's world* [Painting]. Retrieved from http://www.moma.org/explore/collection/index |
| | *Note:* For Place of location also consider using Geographic location of where piece is. For Publisher also consider using the name of the institute where piece is housed. |

***Books***

Elements of a book reference

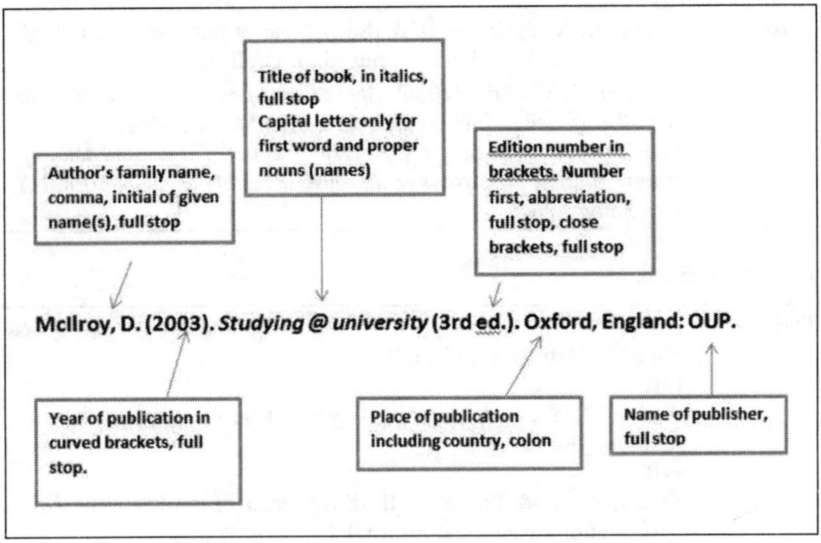


*Notes:*

*Editions:* No edition information is required for first editions.

*Publication location:* Publisher locations in the U.S.A. should include the city and the abbreviated version of the state (e.g. NY for New York); elsewhere in the world, include the city and country. Where more than one location is provided, use the first location listed.

### Print Book

| | |
|---|---|
| Format | Author, A. A., & Author, B. B. (year of publication). *Title of book.* Location of publication: Publisher.<br>Author, A. A., & Author, B. B. (year of publication). *Title of book* (edition). Location of publication: Publisher. |
| Example | Ibn Abdulaziz, T. (2004). *Classic experiments in psychology.* Westport, CT: Greenwood. |

### Edited Book

Use the author rules as listed above. Where there is an editor instead of an author, follow the author rules, but also include the abbreviation 'Ed.' or' Eds.' in parentheses following the editor names: e.g. Editor, A..A., & Editor, B. B.(Eds.).

| | |
|---|---|
| Format | Editor, A. A., & Editor, B. B. (Eds.). (year of publication). *Title of book* (edition). Location of publication: Publisher. |
| Example | Williams, J. M. (Ed.). (2006). *Applied sport psychology: Personal growth to peak performance* (5th ed.). Boston, MA: McGraw-Hill.<br>Lee-Chai, A. Y., & Bargh, J. A. (Eds.). (2001). *The use and abuse of power: Multiple perspectives on the causes of corruption.* New York, NY: Psychology Press. |

*Electronic Book*

| | |
|---|---|
| Format | Author, A. A., & Author, B. B. (year of publication). *Title of book* (edition). Retrieved from URL<br>OR<br>Author, A. A., & Author, B. B. (year of publication). *Title of book* (edition). doi:xxxx<br>OR<br>Editor, A. A., & Editor, B. B. (Eds.). (year of publication). *Title of book* (edition). Retrieved from URL<br>OR<br>Editor, A. A., & Editor, B. B. (Eds.). (year of publication). *Title of book* (edition). doi:xxxx |
| Example | Bennett, P. (2006). *Abnormal and clinical psychology: An introductory textbook* (2nd ed.). Retrieved from http://www.eblib.com/<br>Marlatt, G. A., & Witkiewitz, K. (Eds.). (2009). *Addictive behaviors: New readings on etiology, prevention, and treatment.* Retrieved from http://www.apa.org/pubs/databases/psycbooks/index.aspx |

*Chapter in a Print Book*

| | |
|---|---|
| Format | Author, A. A., & Author, B. B. (year of publication). Title of chapter. In A. Editor & B. Editor (Eds.), *Title of book* (pp. xxx-xxx). Location of publication: Publisher. |
| Example | Ramsey, J. K., & McGrew, W. C. (2005). Object play in great apes: Studies in nature and captivity. In A. D. Pellegrini & P. K. Smith (Eds.), *The nature of play: Great apes and humans* (pp. 89-112). New York, NY: Guilford Press. |

*Chapter in an Electronic Book*

| | |
|---|---|
| Format | Author, A. A., & Author, B. B. (year of publication). Title of chapter. In A. Editor & B. Editor (Eds.), *Title of book* (pp. xxx-xxx). Retrieved from URL<br>OR<br>Author, A. A., & Author, B. B. (year of publication). Title of chapter. In A. Editor & B. Editor (Eds.), *Title of book* (pp. xxx-xxx). doi:xxxx |

Example Branch, S., Ramsay, S., & Barker, M. (2008). The bullied boss: A conceptual exploration of upwards bullying. In A. Glendon, B. M. Thompson, & B. Myors (Eds.), *Advances in organisational psychology* (pp. 93-112). Retrieved from http://www.informit.com.au/humanities.html

### Conferences

#### Paper Presentation or Poster Session

This example is for un-published proceedings

Format Presenter, A. A. (Year, Month). *Title of paper or poster.* Paper or poster session presented at the meeting of Organisation Name, Location.

Example Jodel, F., Russell, F, Tepper, K., Todd, P. &Zahora, T. (2009, September). *Joined at the hip: Partnerships between librarians and learning skills advisers.* Poster session presented at the International Congress of Medical Librarianship, Brisbane.

#### Paper from Published Conference Proceedings Available Online

Format Contributor, A. B. & Contributor, C. (Year, Month). *Title of paper.* Paper presented at title of conference, location of conference. doi or location URL

Example MacIntyre, S. (2008, August). *Participation in the classroom, productivity in the workforce: Unfulfilled expectations.* Paper presented at the 13th Australian Council for Educational Research Conference, Brisbane Qld. Retrieved from research.acer.edu.au/research_conference_2008/8/

#### Paper from Published Conference Proceedings Available in Print

Format Contributor, A. B. & Contributor, C. (Year). Title of paper. In Editor, D & Editor, E (Eds.), *Title of conference*(pages). Location: Publisher.

Example Arem, G. L. (2006). The effects of teaching and playing experience on ability to diagnose a motor skill. In P. Brewer & Firmin, M. (Eds.), *Ethnographic and qualitative research in education: Proceedings of the seventeenth annual conference* (pp.1-20). Newcastle, UK: Cambridge Scholars Press.

### Data Files

Format Author, A. A., & Author, B. B. (year of publication). *Title of data file* [Data file]. Retrieved from URL
OR
Author, A. A., & Author, B. B. (year of publication). *Title of data file* [Data file]. doi:xxxx

| | |
|---|---|
| Example | Department of Planning and Community Development (Vic). (2013). *Projected population by age and sex: Vic RVic MSD 2006-2056* [Data file]. Retrieved from https://www.data.gov.au/dataset/<br>Koopman, B., &Zuccon, G. (2016). *A test collection for matching patient to clinical trials: V2* [Data file]. http://doi.org/10.4225/08/574CE878156EE |

### ***Reference Works (Dictionaries, Encyclopedias, Guides)***

#### *Entire Reference Work (Print)*

| | |
|---|---|
| Format with editor or author | Editor, A. A. (Ed.). (year of publication). *Title of work* (xx ed.). Location of publication: Publisher.<br>Editor, A. A., & Editor, B. B. (Eds.). (year of publication). *Title of work* (xx ed.). Location of publication: Publisher. |
| Format with no author or editor | *Title of work* (year of publication). (xx ed.) Location of publication: Publisher. |
| Reference List | Martin, E. A. (Ed.). (2007). *Concise colour medical dictionary* (4th ed.). Oxford, England: Oxford University Press.<br>*Merriam-Webster's medical desk dictionary.* (2005). (Rev. ed.). Springfield, MA: Merriam-Webster. |

#### *Entire Reference Work (Online)*

| | |
|---|---|
| Format with DOI<br>Format without DOI | Editor, A. A. (Ed.). (year of publication). *Title of work* (xx ed.). doi: DOI<br>Editor, A. A., & Editor, B. B. (Eds.). (year of publication). *Title of work* (xx ed.). doi: DOI |
| Format with no author or editor | *Title of work* (year of publication). (xx ed.) Retrieved from URL |
| Reference List | Martin, E. A. (Ed.). (2015). *Concise colour medical dictionary* (9th ed.). doi: 10.1093/acref/9780199687817.001.0001<br>*Merriam-Webster's online dictionary.* (2018). Retrieved from http://www.m-w.com/dictionary |

#### *Chapter in a Book or Entry in a Reference Work (Print)*

| | |
|---|---|
| Format | Author, A. A. (year of publication). Title of chapter or entry. In A. A. Editor (Ed.), *Title of work* (Vol. xx, pp.xxx-xxx). Location of publication: Publisher.<br>NOTE: For the reference work containing the chapter or entry being referenced, the author or editor's initials should *precede* the family name(s). |
| Format with no author or editor | Title of entry. (year of publication). In *Title of reference work* (pp. xxx-xxx). Location: Publisher. |

| | |
|---|---|
| Reference List | Dalleck, L. C. (2012). Balance training. In J. L. Longe (Ed.). *The Gale encyclopedia of fitness* (Vol. I, pp. 59–62). Farmington Hills, MI: Gale, Cengage Learning.<br>Fire. (1981). In *Penguin-Hellenews English-Greek dictionary* (pp. 313). Athens, Greece: Hellenews-Paidia. |

*Chapter in a Book or Entry in a Reference Work (Online)*

| | |
|---|---|
| Format with DOI | Article name. (year of publication). In *Title of work.* doi: DOI<br>Article name. (year of publication). In A. Editor (Ed.), *Title of work.* doi: DOI |
| Format without DOI | Article name. (year of publication). In *Title of work.* Retrieved from URL<br>Article name. (year of publication). In A. Editor (Ed.), *Title of work.* Retrieved from URL |
| Reference List | Gestational diabetes mellitus. (2012). In *Encyclopædia Britannica.* Retrieved from http://www.britannica.com/EBchecked/topic/232126/gestational-diabetes-mellitus<br>Fibromyalgia. (2015). In E. A. Martin (Ed.), *Concise medical dictionary* (9th ed.). doi: 10.1093/acref/9780199687817.001.0001 |

*Several Volumes in a Multivolume Work*

| | |
|---|---|
| Format | Editor, A. A., & Editor, B. B. (Eds.). (year of publication). *Title of work* (xx ed., Vols. xx-xx). Location of publication: Publisher.<br>NOTE: Use (xxxx-xxxx). as the format for a range of years of publication |
| Reference List | Olendorf, D., Jeryan, C., & Boyden, K. (Eds.). (1999). *The Gale encyclopedia of medicine* (Vols. 1–5). Farmington Hills, MI: Gale Research. |

## ***Scholarly Journals/Periodicals***

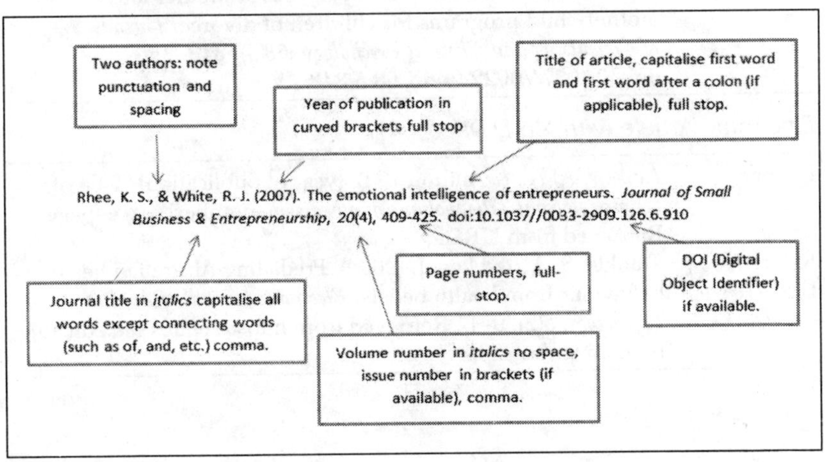

### *Journal Article with One Author*

| | |
|---|---|
| Format | Author, A. A. (year of publication). Title of article. *Journal Title, volume number* (issue number), page–page. doi:xxxx |
| Reference List | Matney, G. T. (2014). Early mathematics fluency with CCSSM. *Teaching Children Mathematics, 21*(1), 27-35. doi:10.5951/teacchilmath.21.1.0026 |

### *Two to Seven Authors*

| | |
|---|---|
| Format | Author, A. A., & Author, B. B. (year of publication). Title of article. *Journal Title, volume number*(issue number), page–page. doi:xxxx<br>When a reference has up to seven authors, spell out all authors' names in the reference list |
| Reference list | Hadgkiss, E. J., & Renzaho, A. M. (2014). The physical health status, service utilisation and barriers to accessing care for asylum seekers residing in the community: A systematic review of the literature. *Australian Health Review, 38*, 142-159. http://dx.doi.org/10.1071/AH13113 |

### *Eight or More Authors*

| | |
|---|---|
| Format | Author, A. A., Author, B. B., & Author, C. C. (year of publication). Title of article. *Journal Title, volume number*(issue number), page–page. doi:xxxx<br>When an article has more than eight or more authors, type the first six authors' names followed by an ellipsis (...) then the last author's name. |
| Reference | Wolchik, S. A., West, S. G., Sandler, I. N., Tein, J., Coatsworth, D., Lengua, L., ...Griffin, W. A. (2000). An experimental evaluation of theory-based mother and mother-child programs for children of divorce. *Journal of Consulting and Clinical Psychology, 68*(5), 843–856. doi:10.1037//0022-006X.68.5.843 |

### *Electronic Article with No DOI*

| | |
|---|---|
| Format | Author, A. A., & Author, B. B. (year of publication). Title of article. *Journal Title, volume number*(issue number), page–page. Retrieved from URL. |
| Reference List | Trankle, S. A., & Haw, J. (2009). Predicting Australian health behaviour from health beliefs. *Electronic Journal of Applied Psychology, 5*(2), 9–17. Retrieved from https://epubs.scu.edu.au/tourism_pubs/328/ |

### Electronic Article with No Issue or Page Numbers

| | |
|---|---|
| Format | Author, A. A., & Author, B. B. (year of publication). Title of article. *Journal Title, volume number*, document number (if available). doi:xxxx |
| Reference List | Forero, R., McDonnell, G., Gallego, B., McCarthy, S., Mohsin, M., Shanley, C., ...Hillman, K. (2012). A literature review on care at the end-of-life in the emergency department. *Emergency Medicine International, 2012*, 486516. doi:10.1155/2012/486516 |

### Print Article with no DOI

| | |
|---|---|
| Format | Author, A. A., & Author, B. B. (year of publication). Title of article. *Journal Title, volume number*(issue number), page–page. |
| Reference List | Crowden, A. (2008). Professional boundaries and the ethics of dual and multiple overlapping relationships in psychotherapy. *Monash Bioethics Review, 27*(4), 10–27. |

## Newspapers/Magazines

### Print Newspaper Article

| | |
|---|---|
| Format | Author, A. A. (year, month date of publication). Title of article. *Newspaper Title*, page–page. |
| Reference list | Packham, B. (2010, January 18). Bullies to show concern: Schools to try Euro method that lets thugs off the hook. *Herald Sun*. p. 6. |

### Online Newspaper Article

| | |
|---|---|
| Format | Author, A. A. (year, month, date of publication). Title of article. *Newspaper Title*. Retrieved from URL |
| Reference list | Gadher, D. (2007, September 2). Leap in gambling addiction forecast. *The Sunday Times*. Retrieved from http://www.timesonline.co.uk. |

### Online Magazine Article

| | |
|---|---|
| Format | Author, A. A. (year, month of publication). Title of article. *Magazine Title, volume number*(issue number), page–page. Retrieved from URL |
| Reference list | Novotney, A. (2010, January). Integrated care is nothing new for these psychologists. *Monitor on Psychology, 41*(1). Retrieved from www.apa.org/monitor |

### Print Magazine Article

| | |
|---|---|
| Format | Author, A. A. (year, month date of publication). Title of article. *Magazine Title, volume number*(issue number), page–page. |

| | |
|---|---|
| Reference list | Wilson, D. S., & Wilson, E. O. (2007, November 3). Survival of the selfless. *NewScientist, 196*(2628), 42–46. |

## Patents and Standards

### Patents

| | |
|---|---|
| Format | Author, A. A. (year). *Patent Identifier No. xxx.* Location: Source Name. |
| Example | U.S. Patent No. 66,991,798-B1 (2004)<br>OR<br>(U.S. Patent No. 66,991,798-B1, 2004)<br>*End text reference*<br>Lindsay, S. J. (2004). *U.S. Patent No. 66,991,798-B1.* Washington, DC: U.S. Patent and Trademark Office.<br>*Intext citation*<br>Australian Patent No. 2016101507 (2016)<br>OR<br>(Australian Patent No. 2016101507, 2016)<br>*Reference list entry*<br>Calaby, R. & Baker, N. (2016). *Australian Patent No. 2016101507.* Canberra: IP Australia. |

### Standards

| | |
|---|---|
| Format | Standards Organisation. (year of publication). *Title of standard* (Standard number). Retrieved from 'website address' |
| Example | Standards Australia. (2010). *Child restraint systems for use in motor vehicles* (AS/NZ 1754:2010). Retrieved from http://www.saiglobal.com<br>Note: Shorten the URL to main website |

## Doctoral Dissertations and Master's Theses

### Published Thesis

| | |
|---|---|
| Format | Author, A. A. (Year of publication). *Title of thesis or dissertation* (Doctoral dissertation or Master's thesis). Retrieved from Name of database. (Accession or Order no.) |
| Example | Bozeman, A. Jr. (2007). *Age of onset as predictor of cognitive performance in children with seizure disorders.* (Doctoral dissertation). Retrieved from Proquest Dissertations and Theses. (UMI 3259752) |

### *Unpublished Thesis*

| | |
|---|---|
| Format | Author, A. A. (Year of publication). ***Title of thesis or dissertation*** (Unpublished Doctoral dissertation or Master's thesis). Name of Institution, Location. |
| | Imber, A. (2003).***Applicant reactions to graduate recruitment and selection.*** (Unpublished Doctoral dissertation.) Monash University, Melbourne, Victoria, Australia. |

## ***University Course Materials***

### *Lecture Notes—Available on Moodle*

| | |
|---|---|
| Format | Author, A. A. (publication date). ***Title of lecture*** [Lecture notes]. Retrieved from 'website address' |
| Example | Cioe, J. (2012). ***The normal distribution*** [Lecture notes]. Retrieved from http://moodle.vle.monash.edu.au<br>Note: These are treated like books if they are published, but like personal communication if they are your own notes or unpublished. Lecture notes are considered published if they have been copied and distributed in print or on the web with the instructor's permission. |

### *Class Notes*

| | |
|---|---|
| Format | Note: Cite information from your own personal notes from a lecture as a personal communication and refer to it only in the body of your essay. |
| Example | Citation in text: In a lecture on August 10, 2012, to a BTW1110 class, Professor Smith said... |

### *Class Handouts*

| | |
|---|---|
| Format | Author, A. A. (publication date). ***Title of handout*** [Class handout]. Place of Publication: Publisher. |
| Example | Woodworth, M. (2006). ***Psychopaths*** [Class handout]. Kelowna, Canada: Department of Psychology, University of British Columbia: Okanagan. |

### *Class Handouts—Available on Moodle*

| | |
|---|---|
| Format | Author, A. A. (publication date). ***Title of handout*** [Class handout]. Retrieved from 'website address' |
| Example | Woodworth, M. (2006). ***Psychopaths*** [Class handout]. Retrieved from http://moodle.vle.monash.edu.au |

### *Powerpoint Presentation—Available on Moodle*

| | |
|---|---|
| Format | Author, A. A. (publication date). *Title of powerpoint* [PowerPoint slides]. Retrieved from 'website address' |
| Example | Cioe, J. (2012). *Biological foundations of sexuality* [PowerPoint slides]. Retrieved from https://moodle.vle.monash.edu.au |

### *MOOC—Massive Open Online Course*

| | |
|---|---|
| Format | Author, A. A. (Producer). (Year). *Title of course* [Format]. Retrieved from 'website address' |
| Example | Monash University (Producer). (2015). *The role of water in "cities of the future"* [MOOC]. Retrieved from https://futuerlearn.com/courses/liveable-cities/steps/23354/progress<br>Note: With regard to Monash University MOOCs produced through FutureLearn, Monash maintains the copyright. This might differ for other MOOCs and MOOC providers. Often MOOCs will provide a copyright statement at the bottom of each page. |

## ***Websites and Social Media***

### *Document on the Web*

| | |
|---|---|
| Format | Author, A. A. & Author, B. B. (Year of publication). *Title of work.* Retrieved from URL |
| Example | Huges, L., & McMichael, T. (2011). *The critcal decade: Climate change and health.* Retrieved from http://www.climatecouncil.org.au/uploads/1bb6887d6f8cacd5d844fc30b0857931.pdf<br>Mansai, G. (2014). *Dehydration (children): Oral rehydration solution* [Evidence summary]. Retrieved from http://joannabriggslibrary.org<br>Note: this example of the Joanna Briggs document could also be treated as an authored report from a non-government organisation if you wish to include more specific details of the source. |

### *Web Page*

| | |
|---|---|
| Format | Author, A. A. & Author, B. B. (Year of publication). Title of work. Retrieved from URL |
| Example | Anderson, L. (2012). Why communication in the nursing profession is important. Retrieved from http://www.nursetogether.com/why-communication-in-the-nursing-profession-is-important |

### *Web Page with No Author*

| | |
|---|---|
| Format | Name of organisation in full. (Year of publication). Title of work. Retrieved from URL<br>or<br>Title of page or document. (Year of publication). Retrieved from URL |

Examples Australian Psychological Society. (2010). Bushfire resources: Psychological preparedness and recovery. Retrieved from http://www.psychology.org.au/bushfires/

A pedagogy of listening. (2011). Retrieved from http://reggioaustralia.org.au/component/content/article/59

### *Image from the Web*

Format Artist last name, initial. (year). Title of work [Format]. Retrieved from URL

Example Sievers, W. (1966). Monash University [Photograph]. Retrieved from http://trove.nla.gov.au/work/15565401?q=monash&c=picture&versionId=18284000

### *Online Forum, Discussion Group, or Blog Post*

Format Author, A. A. (Year, Month Day). Title of post [description of form]. Retrieved from http://www.xxx

Example Chee, C. (2010, January 10). The most important psychology article of the 21st century: The U.S. isn't discovering how mental illness works, it's spreading it worldwide [Web blog post]. Retrieved from http//www.psychologytoday.com/blog/addiction-in-society/201001/the-most-important-sychology-article-the-21st-century

### *Twitter*

Format Username or Group Name. (Yr, Mth, Day). Post title [Page type]. Retrieved Month, Day, Year, from http://www.twitter.com/specificpageURL

Example BarackObama. (2009a, July 15). Launched American Graduation Initiative to help additional 5 mill. Americans graduate college by 2020: http://bit.ly/gcTX7 [Twitter post]. Retrieved July 15, 2009, from http://twitter.com/BarackObama/status/2651151366

### *Facebook*

Format Username or Group Name. (Yr, mth, day.). Update title [Page type]. Retrieved Month, Day, Year, from http://www.facebook.com/specificpageURL

Example Barack Obama. (2009, October 9). Humbled. http://my.barackobama.com/page/community/post/obamaforamerica/gGM45m [Facebook update]. Retrieved October 11, 2009, from http://www.facebook.com/posted.php? id=6815841748&share_id=154954250775&comments=1#s154954250775<./p>

### *Abbreviations Used in Citation and Referencing*

Standard abbreviations can be used in citations and references. Some of the more commonly used examples of abbreviations are listed below.

*And Others*

| | |
|---|---|
| Format | et al.<br>This means 'and others'. It is used in in-text citations where there are 3 or more authors. NOTE: full stop after 'al.' not after 'et' |
| Example | 3 to 5 authors<br>(Alberto, Jacobi & Keating, 1993) for the first citation and (Alberto et al., 1993) in subsequent citations.<br>6 or more authors<br>(Szerman et al., 2005) |

#### *Compiled or Custom Textbook*

| | |
|---|---|
| Format | Comp.<br>Compiled or custom textbooks are created to support specific units. |
| Example | Jones, T. S. (2012). Over the rainbow. In B. Smith (Comp.), Readings for ABC1001 (pp 10-20) |

#### *Edition*

| | |
|---|---|
| Format | ed.<br>For the edition of a book |
| Example | Ibn Abdulaziz, T. (2004). Drugs and life (4th ed.). |

#### *Editor(s)*

| | |
|---|---|
| Format | Ed. or Eds.<br>When a book includes editors rather than authors |
| Example | Robinson, D. N. (Ed.). (1992). |

#### *No Date*

| | |
|---|---|
| Format | n.d.<br>For sources that do not have a date of publication, substitute 'n.d.' (no date) after the name of the author. |
| Example | In-text citation<br>(Southey, n.d.)<br>End-text reference<br>Southey, R. (n.d.). The life of Nelson. London, England: Blackie. |

### *No Page Numbers*

| | |
|---|---|
| Format | n.p.<br>No page numbers |
| Example | Mathews' use of...(2010, n. p.). |
| Format | NOTE: For electronic sources without page numbers use:<br>approximate page number (p. 3 of 9); or<br>paragraph number for short text (para. 2); or<br>the heading given in the source for the particular section. |
| Example | The ABS (2004, p. 1 of 4) defines residents as 'economic entities (persons, organizations or enterprises) which have a closer association with the territory of Australia than with any other territory'.<br>OR<br>Flitton(2012, para. 1) reports 'Australia is about to confront the biting reality of US military decline'. |

### *Number*

| | |
|---|---|
| Format | No.<br>Use in your end text referencing when the resource incorporates a number that represents the accession, order, catalogue, etc. number |
| Example | Australian national accounts: National income, expenditure and product (Cat. No. 5206.0).<br>Dissertation Abstracts International. (University Microfilms No. 82-06, 181). |

### *Page(s)*

| | |
|---|---|
| Format | p. or pp.<br>These are included in the in-text citation. If one page number is being referred to, use the abbreviation p. for page. If there are multiple pages use pp. to represent pages. |
| Example | (Ezzy, 2002, p. 30)<br>According to Gibbs (2009, pp. 34-35) |

### *Paragraph*

| | |
|---|---|
| Format | para.<br>For electronic sources that do not provide page numbers, use the paragraph number and, if available, preceded by the abbreviation 'para.' |
| Example | (Clarkson, 2001, para. 2) |

### *Revised Edition*

| | |
|---|---|
| Format | Rev. ed.<br>Used in end-text referencing when item is identified as being a revised edition |
| Example | Referencing guide (14th Rev. ed.). |

### ***Translator(s)***

| | |
|---|---|
| Format | Trans.<br>Name the translator or editor only in the end-text reference, immediately following the title. In the case of translated works, cite the title in its translated form, not in its original form. |
| Example | In-text citation<br>(Genet, 1966, p. 61)<br>End-text reference<br>Genet, J. (1966). The balcony (B. Frechtman, Trans.). London, England: Faber. |

### *Volume(s)*

| | |
|---|---|
| Format | Vol. or Vols.<br>Include in end text referencing if books include volume information |
| Example | Robinson, A. (1994). The principals of genetics and heredity. In The new encyclopedia Britannica (Vol. 19, pp. 699-740). Chicago, IL: Encyclopedia Britannica. |

CHAPTER 8

# Quoting, Paraphrasing and Summarising

It is crucial to understand how to quote, paraphrase and summarise for academic writing. These skills will help support claims and add credibility to your work. In academic writing, it is essential that you incorporate the research from outside sources to support your arguments. This is done through quoting, paraphrasing and summarising the work of others. The majority of these citations should be paraphrased or summarised, with quotes used sparingly.

In all academic writing, it is essential to use information from outside sources (e.g., books, journals, magazines, and the Internet) to support your position. Quoting, paraphrasing and summarising are tools used to show important information, evidence, ideas and the work of others in your academic writing. They are important tools for reshaping information for use in any written assessment task. These must be incorporated into your academic writing to demonstrate your understanding and interpretation of a text, and to avoid plagiarism. To show the reader where you obtained your information quoting, paraphrasing and summarising are different ways of including the works of others in your assignments.

## Purpose of Quotations, Paraphrases and Summaries

Quotations, paraphrases and summaries serve many purposes. These may be used to:

- Provide support for claims or add credibility to the writing.
- Refer to work that leads up to the work you are now doing.
- Give examples of several points of view on a subject.
- Call attention to a position that you wish to agree or disagree with.
- Highlight a particularly striking phrase, sentence, or passage by quoting the original.
- Distance yourself from the original by quoting it in order to cue readers that the words are not your own.
- Expand the breadth or depth of the writing.

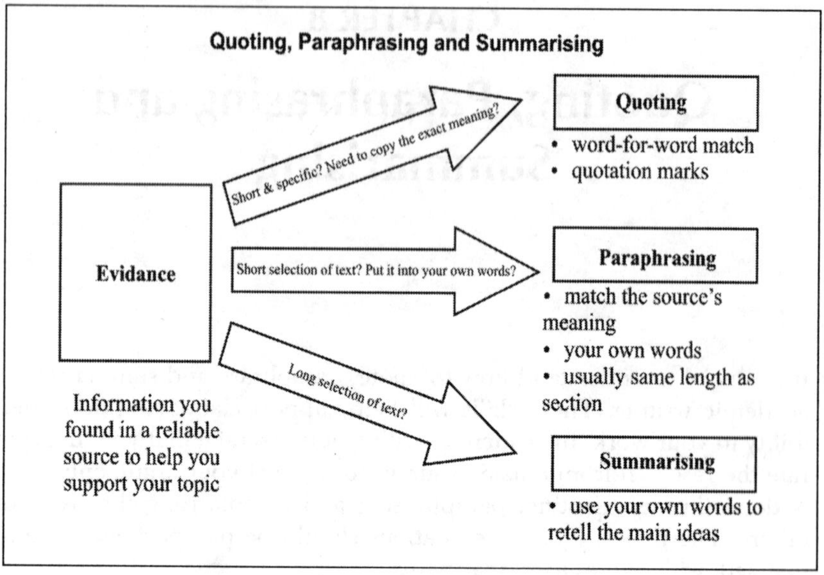


Figure 8.1: Quoting, Paraphrasing and Summarising

***When to Give Credit to a Source?***

Give credit to your source in all of the following situations:

- You directly quote a source.
- You borrow an idea from a source.
- You paraphrase or summarise a source.
- If you gain information from interviewing a person or from a class lecture.
- When you use diagrams, illustrations, or other images that you did not create yourself.
- Radio broadcasts, movies, podcasts.
- Things that are not common knowledge.

## QUOTING

The first skill to master is the ability to use quotations to support a main idea. This is when a writer uses word-for-word information from a source and gives credit to the original writer. A quotation has to be an exact match and be attributed to the original source author. For example, if you were beginning a paper on Martin Luther King, Jr., it might be impactful to start your paper with a direct quotation of his to help create a mood or set up your main idea. When the words of an expert, authority, or relevant individual are particularly clear or expressive, you may want to quote them.

**Original Text**

"....there are two ways to become wealthy: to create wealth or to take wealth away from others. The former adds to society. The latter typically subtracts from it, for in the process of taking it away, wealth gets destroyed. A monopolist who overcharges for his product takes away money from those whom he is overcharging and at the same time destroys value. To get his monopoly price, he has to restrict production."

Stiglitz, J. E. (2013). The Price of Inequality. London: Penguin.

**Quote**

Of the two ways to become wealthy creating wealth adds to society; whereas, taking wealth away from others, "typically subtracts from it, for in the process of taking it away, wealth gets destroyed" (Stiglitz, 2013: 40).

Figure 8.2: Example of Quoting

## When to Use Quoting?

Quotations are the exact words of an author, copied directly from a source, word for word. Quotations must appear with quotation marks, and they need to be cited with in-text citations and on the reference page.

Use quotations when:

- You want to add the power of an author's words to support your argument
- You want to use the author as an authoritative voice in your own writing
- You want to disagree with an author's argument
- You want to highlight particularly eloquent or powerful phrases or passages
- You are comparing and contrasting specific points of view
- You want to note the important research that precedes your own
- Language is particularly vivid or expressive
- Exact wording is needed for technical accuracy
- The words of an important authority lend weight to an argument
- You want to support claims in, or provide evidence for, your writing.

Table 8.1: How to Quote from the Original Source without Plagiarism

| *Original* | *Accurate Quoting* | *Plagiarism* |
|---|---|---|
| Because of their unique perspective, Americans fear globalization less than anyone else, and as a consequence they think about it less than anyone else. When Americans do think about globalization, they think of the global economy as an enlarged version of the American economy.<br><br>(*Source*: Thurow, L. (1993). Fortune Favors the Bold (p. 6). New York: Harper Collins.) | Economist Lester Thurow (1993) has asserted that the American reaction to globalization is different from that of the rest of the world in that "American's fear globalization less than anyone else, and as a consequence . . . think about it less than anyone else" (p. 6).<br><br>*Why is this accurate?*<br>• The writer has introduced the quotation with his/her own words.<br>• S/he has also named the source in an introduction phrase.<br>• S/he has indicated where exact words of the source begin and end by using quotation marks.<br><br>(Complete Thurow reference appears in bibliography) | The American view of globalization is unlike that of the rest of the world. **Because of their unique perspective, Americans fear globalization less than anyone else, and therefore think about it less than anyone else** (Thurow, 1993).<br><br>*Why is this plagiarism?*<br>• The writer has identified the source but has not put quotation marks around the words.<br>• Lack of quotation marks allows the reader to think the words are the writer's, not Thurow's. |

### How do I show what I am quoting?

- Name the source in an introductory phrase.
- Use quotation marks or indent long quotations.
- Cite the source appropriately.

If you fail to do this, it is plagiarism.

### Advantages of Quoting

When quotes are employed, they should be used to:

- Provide indisputable evidence of an incredible claim.
- Communicate an idea that is stated in a particularly striking or unique way.
- Serve as a passage for analysis.
- Provide direct evidence for or proof of an author's own claim.
- Support or clarify information you have already reported from a source.
- Provide a definition of a new or unfamiliar term or phrase.

## PARAPHRASING

Paraphrasing is a second skill that allows a writer to legitimately utilize a passage of text from a source. The writer has to restate the original material in their own words while still maintaining the main ideas. In order for paraphrasing to be done correctly, it also has to offer credit to the original writer. In writing papers, you will paraphrase more than you will quote. For a report or research paper, you may need to gather background information that is important to the paper but not worthy of direct quotation. Indeed, in technical writing direct quotation is rarely used.

A paraphrase is a restatement or rewording of a paragraph or text, in order to borrow, clarify, or expand on information without plagiarising. Paraphrasing is an important tool to use when writing research papers, essays, and pieces of journalism.

Paraphrasing means taking the words of another source and restating them, using your own vocabulary. In this way, you keep the meaning of the original text, but do not copy its exact wording.

### When to Use Paraphrasing?

Paraphrasing is stating an idea or passage in your own words. You must significantly change the wording, phrasing and sentence structure (not just a few words here and there) of the source. These also must be noted with *in-text citations* and the *reference page.*

**Original Text**

"....there are two ways to become wealthy: to create wealth or to take wealth away from others. The former adds to society. The latter typically subtracts from it, for in the process of taking it away, wealth gets destroyed. A monopolist who overcharges for his product takes away money from those whom he is overcharging and at the same time destroys value. To get his monopoly price, he has to restrict production."

Stiglitz, J. E. (2013). The Price of Inequality. London: Penguin.

**Paraphrase**

Creating wealth adds to society; whereas taking away the wealth of others detracts from it and destroys wealth in the process. For example a monopolist overcharging for a product takes money away from the customer, but also destroys value because in order to get the monopoly price, production has to be restricted (Stiglitz, 2013).

Figure 8.3: Example of Paraphrasing

Paraphrase when:

- You want to clarify a short passage from a text
- You want to avoid overusing quotations
- You want to explain a point when exact wording is not important
- You want to explain the main points of a passage
- You want to report numerical data or statistics (preferred in APA papers)
- You want as an alternative to a direct quotation
- You rewrite someone else's ideas without changing the meaning
- You want to express someone else's ideas in your own words
- You want to support claims in, or provide evidence for, your writing.

## How do I Paraphrase?

Whenever you paraphrase, remember these two points:

- You must provide a reference.
- The paraphrase must be in your own words. You must do more than merely substitute phrases here and there. You must also create your own sentence structures.

Table 8.2: How to Paraphrase from the Original Source without Plagiarism

| *Original* | *Paraphrasing* | *Plagiarism* |
|---|---|---|
| Because of their unique perspective, Americans fear globalization less than anyone else, and as a consequence they think about it less than anyone else. When Americans do think about globalization, they think of the global economy as an enlarged version of the American economy.<br><br>(Source: Thurow, L. (1993).Fortune Favors the Bold(p. 6). New York: Harper Collins.) | Lester Thurow (1993) maintains that because Americans see globalization simply as a bigger form of their own economy, they are less concerned about it than is the rest of the world.<br><br>*Why is this acceptable?*<br>The writer has kept the meaning of the original passage without copying words or structure. Words like globalization and Americans are generic terms (i.e., terms that are commonly used for the concept they illustrate - it is difficult to find synonyms for them). Thus you may use these words without placing them in quotation marks.<br><br>(Complete Thurow reference appears in bibliography) | According to Lester Thurow (1993) Americans fear globalization less than people from other countries and as a consequence spend less time thinking about it. Indeed, Americans see globalization as an enlarged version of their own economy.<br><br>*Why is this plagiarism?*<br>The writer has used Thurow's exact words without enclosing them in quotation marks. S/he has only substituted synonyms here and there. Even though Thurow is credited with a citation, this would be considered plagiarism. |

## Advantages of Paraphrasing

- Paraphrasing blends more easily with your own ideas and makes a piece of writing more coherent;
- Paraphrasing enables you to express another writer's ideas in a way which more closely supports your own argument;
- Paraphrasing enables you to express another's ideas and views more concisely;
- Paraphrasing creates the effect of a more impersonal, academic style;
- Paraphrasing eliminates less relevant information;
- Paraphrasing maintains the flow of the writing;
- Paraphrasing communicates relevant statistics and numerical data;
- Paraphrasing establishes the credibility of the author;
- Paraphrasing explains or simplifies a passage that may be difficult to understand.

## Types of Paraphrasing

1. *Change of Parts of Speech:* Parts of speech ranging from verbs and nouns to adjectives and adverbs are replaced with new parts of speech in this type of paraphrasing. Here is an example:
   Original Sentence:
   *The boy quickly ran across the finish line, seizing yet another victory.*
   Paraphrase:
   *The quick boy seized yet another victory when he ran across the finish line.*
   In this example, many parts of speech are changed: the adverb quickly becomes the adjective quick, and the verb phrase with the gerund seizing becomes the verb seized.
2. *Change of Structure:* This type of paraphrasing involves changing the sentence's structure, sometimes creating a passive voice from an active voice and vice versa. The change in structure can be used to reflect the writer's interpretation of the original quote. Here is an example of change of structure paraphrasing:
   Original Sentence:
   *Puppies were adopted by numerous kind souls at the puppy drive.*
   Paraphrase:
   *Many kind souls adopted puppies during the puppy drive.*
   In this example, the object of the sentence (kind souls) becomes the subject with an active voice (adopted) rather than a passive voice (were adopted).
3. *Reduction of Clauses:* Reduction of clauses paraphrases reduce the number of clauses in a sentence, which can be interruptive or

confusing, by incorporating the phrases into the sentence. Here is an example of reduction of clauses paraphrasing:
Original Sentence:
While I understand where you're coming from, and truly respect your opinion, I wish you would express yourself more clearly, like Clara does.
Paraphrase:
I understand where you're coming from and respect your opinion, but I wish you would be more like Clara and express yourself more clearly.

4. *Synonym Replacement:* Synonym replacement paraphrasing is one of the simplest forms of paraphrasing: replacing words with similar words, or synonyms. Here is an example:
Original Sentence:
*The older citizens were honoured with a parade for those once in the military.*
Paraphrase:
*Senior citizens were honoured with a march for veterans.*
In this example, many synonyms are used: older citizens are senior citizens, a parade becomes a march, and those once in the military refers to veterans.

### Strategies for Paraphrasing

- Use synonyms for all words that are not generic. Words like world, food, or science are so basic to our vocabulary that it is difficult to find a synonym.
- Change the structure of the sentence.
- Change the voice from active to passive and vice versa.
- Change clauses to phrases and vice versa.
- Change parts of speech.

## SUMMARISING

A summary is a synthesis of the key ideas of a piece of writing, restated in your own words – i.e., paraphrased. You may write a summary as a stand-alone assignment or as part of a longer paper. Whenever you summarise, you must be careful not to copy the exact wording of the original source.

### When to Use Summarising?

Summaries are significantly shorter than the original material and they take a broad overview of the source material as a whole. Summary must be cited with *in-text citations* and on your *reference page.*

**Original Text**

"....there are two ways to become wealthy: to create wealth or to take wealth away from others. The former adds to society. The latter typically subtracts from it, for in the process of taking it away, wealth gets destroyed. A monopolist who overcharges for his product takes away money from those whom he is overcharging and at the same time destroys value. To get his monopoly price, he has to restrict production."

Stiglitz, J. E. (2013). The Price of Inequality. London: Penguin.

**Summary**

Stiglitz (2013) suggests that creating wealth adds value to society, but that taking away the wealth of others detracts from it. He uses the example of a monopolist who overcharges for the product resulting in loss of wealth for the customer, but also loss of value as the monopolist has to restrict production in order to charge the higher price.

Figure 8.4: Example of Summary

Summarise when:

- You want to establish background or offer an overview of a topic;
- You want to describe knowledge (from several sources) about a topic;
- You want to determine the main ideas of a single source;
- You want to outline the main points of someone else's work in your own words, without the details or examples;
- You want to include an author's ideas using fewer words than the original text;
- You want to briefly give examples of several differing points of view on a topic;
- You want to support claims in, or provide evidence for, your writing.

### How do I Summarise?

A good summary:

- Identifies the writer of the original text.
- Synthesises the writer's key ideas.
- Presents the information neutrally.

Table 8.3: How to Summarise from the Original Source without Plagiarism

| Original | Summarising | Plagiarism |
|---|---|---|
| *Like many* anuran *species worldwide*, the *frogs and toads* of North Carolina *have a difficult road ahead.* Worldwide, *scientists have documented drastic declines in many frog and toad populations.* For many of these disappearances and declines, the exact causes are difficult to determine. In some parts of the United States, scientists have documented strange body malformations in some species. These alarming developments have prompted an increased interest in the threats facing amphibians. Many organizations have developed programs to monitor the status of frogs and toads throughout the world.<br><br>*In North Carolina, loss of quality habitat is one of the greatest threats* frogs and toads face. Habitat destruction and fragmentation threaten entire populations by:<br>• *Eliminating wetland* habitats necessary as breeding sites,<br>• *Removing forested* areas *and* other *upland habitats* where many species live most of the year, and<br>• *Creating barriers* between these two habitats that *prevent* individuals from *migrating* to and from breeding areas. | Environmental conditions in North Carolina pose a threat to frogs and toads. According to scientists, wetland destruction has already occurred on a massive scale. The destruction of wetlands, along with forests, uplands, and migration routes, could destroy vast numbers of these species. This is not only a concern in North Carolina, as frog and toad populations are declining around the world (Dorcas 8).<br><br>*Why is this acceptable?*<br>It is acceptable because here the main ideas have been written into author's own words. | *Like* most *species* in the *world, frogs and toads have* a hard *road ahead. Scientists have* recorded major *declines in many populations of frogs and toads. In North Carolina, loss of* good *habitat is one of the greatest* problems, caused by the *elimination* of *wetlands, removal* of *forestsand upland habitats, and creation* of *barriers* that *prevent migration* (Dorcas 8).<br><br>*Why is this plagiarism?*<br>The Italic bold text indicates how the wording and order have been directly copied from the original text above. Even though a citation has been provided in both cases, the example on the right side below is considered plagiarism. |

*(Table 8.3 Contd.)*

*(Table 8.3 Contd.)*

| Original | Summarising | Plagiarism |
|---|---|---|
| Scientists estimate that one-half of North Carolina's original wetlands have been lost due to urban development and conversion to cropland. Our state ranked sixth in the nation for total acres of land developed between 1992 and 1997.<br><br>(Source: Dorcas, Michael E., et al. The Frogs and Toads of North Carolina: Field Guide and Recorded Calls. Raleigh, NC: North Carolina Wildlife Resources Commission, 2007. Print.) | | |

Summaries can vary in length. Follow the directions given by your instructor for how long the summary should be.

## Advantages of Summarising

A good summary:

- contains only the most important information;
- is concise; it should always be shorter than the original;
- paraphrases any information taken from the source;
- refers directly to the original source;
- does not use exact wording (quotes) except for special word or words that cannot be expressed otherwise.

## Difference between Paraphrasing and Summarising

Summarising and paraphrasing are somewhat different. A paraphrase is about the same length as the original source, while a summary is much shorter. Nevertheless, when you summarise, you must be careful not to copy the exact wording of the original source. Follow the same rules as you would for paraphrase.

Paraphrasing Vs. Summarizing

| **Paraphrasing** | **Summarizing** |
|---|---|
| • Change the sentence structure of the original text.<br>• Change the vocabulary of the original text. | |
| • Use all the details in the original text.<br>• A paraphrase is often a similar length as the original. | • Use only the most important ideas in the original text.<br>• A summary is significantly shorter than the original. |

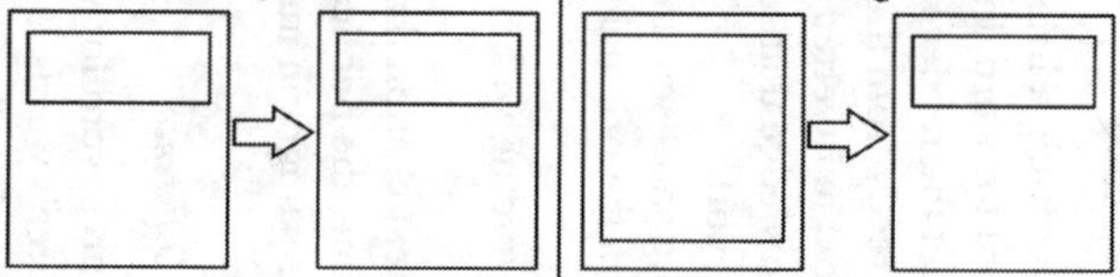

Figure 8.5: Difference between Paraphrasing and Summarising

The difference between quoting, paraphrasing and summarizing is given in the Table 8.4

Table 8.4: Difference between Quoting, Paraphrasing and Summarising

| Quoting | Paraphrasing | Summarising |
|---|---|---|
| *Meaning* | *Meaning* | *Meaning* |
| • Quoting involves using a brief segment of a source, word for word, in your essay or report. You let the reader know you have quoted directly from the source by enclosing the text in inverted commas. You must acknowledge that source in your essay or report.<br>• involves copying short sentences or passages from the original text word-for-word<br>• places copied wording within "quotation marks"<br>• includes an in-text citation that states the author's last name, the publication year, and the page or paragraph number: (Lee, 2016, p. 1). | • Paraphrasing involves putting information from a source into your own words, without changing the meaning of the source you used. You must then acknowledge that source in your essay or report.<br>• involves putting a section of a text into your own words<br>• changes the words and phrasing of the original text, but keeps the original meaning of the text<br>• includes an in-text citation that states the author's last name and the publication year: (Lee, 2016) | • Summarising involves putting the main idea(s) from a source into your own words, but including only the main point(s). You must then acknowledge the original source in your essay or report.<br>• involves stating the main ideas and findings of a text into your own words<br>• presents a general overview, so is usually much shorter than the original text<br>• includes an in-text citation that states the author's last name and the publication year: (Lee, 2016) |
| *Difference* | *Difference* | *Difference* |
| • Matches the source word for word.<br>• You use the source's words.<br>• Exactly same length as the source, unless you follow the rules for adding or deleting material from a quote. | • Matches the source in terms of meaning.<br>• You use your own words.<br>• Approximately the same length, though often shorter than the source. | • Sums up the central point of the source.<br>• You use your own words.<br>• Much shorter than the source. |

<table>
<tr>
<td>Purpose<br>• To provide credibility for what you are saying (you support your point by quoting an authority)<br>• To get someone's exact words (when HOW someone said something is as important as WHAT they said).</td>
<td>Purpose<br>• To get down the meaning of someone else's words when:<br>1. Their exact words are not important<br>2. Their exact words are not appropriate (style too dense or too simple for example) or useful (what they emphasise is different from what you want to emphasise)<br>• To show that you have command of the material (not a slave to the original author's word).<br>• To "shorten" a section from the source that is too long to quote.<br>• To demonstrate comprehension (independent assignment).</td>
<td>Purpose<br>• To get down the gist of someone else's work<br>• To avoid unnecessary details when the main point is all you need<br>• To show that you understand what the source is saying<br>• To refresh the reader's memory if they have read the source<br>• To give your audience a general introduction to the source.</td>
</tr>
<tr>
<td>How to<br>• Copy the source's words exactly.<br>• There are special rules for capitalisation and punctuation within quotes.<br>• Cite it according to whatever style you require (e.g. APA)</td>
<td>How to<br>• Carefully read the section of the source you are going to paraphrase. Put it away and write down in your own words what the source is saying. Then go back and check to see if you missed anything.<br>• Cite it just like a quote.<br>• Appears on works cited page.</td>
<td>How to<br>• Carefully read the section of the source you are going to paraphrase. Put it away and write down the main points of the source. Do not be a slave to the source's organisation – you decide what the main points are.<br>• First sentence: "(John Doe)'s essay ('Wild Gift') states that….."</td>
</tr>
</table>

# CHAPTER 9

# Citing, Quoting, Paraphrasing and Summarising Authors

## CITING AUTHORS

Quoting from outside sources is an important part of academic writing because it puts you into the scholarly conversation and makes your own ideas and your paper more credible. Using quotes is a great way for readers to "hear" the expert voices talking about your writing topic. One of the most important aspects of academic writing is making use of the ideas of other people. This is important as you need to show that you have understood the materials that you have studied and that you can use their ideas and findings in your own way. In fact, this is an essential skill for every student. Spack (1988, p. 42) has pointed out that the most important skill a student can engage in is *"the complex activity to write from other texts"*, which is *"a major part of their academic experience."* For this reason, any academic text you read or write will contain the voices of other writers as well as your own.

In your writing, however, the main voice should be your own and it should be clear what your point of view is in relation to the topic or essay question. The object of academic writing is for you to say something for yourself using the ideas of the subject, for you to present ideas you have learned in your own way. The emphasis should be on working with other people's ideas, rather than reproducing their words. If your view is not clear, you will be told you have not answered the question or something similar. It is essential, therefore, that it must always be clear whose voice is being spoken.

It will always be assumed that the words or ideas are your own if you do not say otherwise. When the words or ideas you are using are taken from another writer, you must make this clear. If you do not do this and use another person's words or ideas as if they were your own, this is plagiarism and plagiarism is regarded as a very serious offence.

The ideas and people that you refer to need to be made explicit by a system of citation. The object of this is to supply the information needed to allow a user to find a source. You need to acknowledge the source of an idea unless it is common knowledge in your subject area. In your academic writing, you have to support your points with concrete evidence taken from a variety of valid sources and name the author/source of your evidence in your writing.

### *Citing Authors*

Referencing is a very important academic convention that recognizes that academic writing builds on previous research. In nearly all academic assignments, writers are required to refer to the work of others. You must always explicitly acknowledge these sources as:

- an in-text reference in the body of your assignment
- an item in the list of references at the end of your work.

There are a number of referencing styles and writers must know the appropriate style for their work.

## APA Author-date Referencing Style

The APA Author-date referencing style uses in-text citations (integrating the names of authors in your paragraph) to credit information to the correct source. This format is the same for all types of references (e.g. print, multi-media, Internet). In-text references contain three items:

- the name/s of author/s
- year of publication
- page number or paragraph number (if no page number is available).

When you write up your reference list at the end of your assignment, each author mentioned in-text must be included in this reference list.

*Exercise 1: Author-date referencing*

Read this example and note the format for citing in-text authors:

*Placing the Author in Your Writing:* There are two techniques you can use to put the names of authors in your writing:

- *Strong Author Orientation:* Before you give the information, you use the surname/s of the author/s as part of your writing followed by the year, page in brackets.
  *Example: According to Elton (2009, pp. 106-109), students who show mastery in assignment writing …*
- *Weak Author Orientation:* After you have given the information, you place a bracket around the surname/s of the author/s year, page.
  *Example: Recent studies into student assignment writing show that … (Elton, 2009, pp. 106-109)*

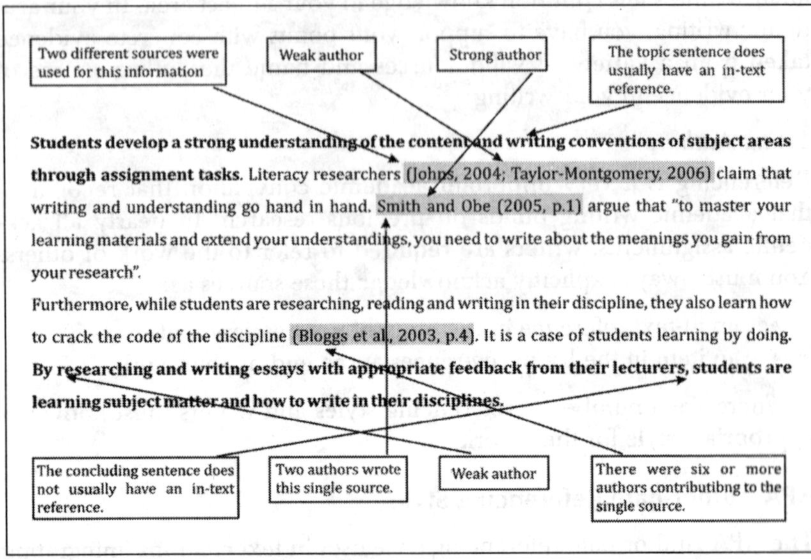


Figure 9.1: Author-date-referencing

*Exercise 2: Author Orientation*

Read this paragraph and identify the author orientation.

Students develop a strong understanding of the content and writing conventions of subject areas through assignment tasks. Literacy researchers **(Johns, 2004, pp. 199-208; Taylor, 2006, pp. 156-159)** claim that writing and understanding go hand in hand. **Smith and Brown (2005, p. 1)** argue that "to master your learning materials and extend your understandings, you need to write about the meanings you gain from your research". Furthermore, while students are researching, reading and writing in their discipline, they also learn how to "crack the code" of the discipline **(Bloggs et al., 2003, p. 44)**. It is a case of students learning by doing. By researching and writing essays with appropriate feedback from their lecturers, students are learning subject matter and how to write in their disciplines.

Figure 9.2: Author Orientation

## Reporting Words for Authors

There are many ways to bring your authorities (authors) into your writing. It is very important that you choose the correct words to match the meaning you are making in your writing. Following is a sample list of reporting words to help you make correct choices:

Table 9.1: Answer Key for Author Orientations

| *Author Orientation* | *Response* | *Answer* |
|---|---|---|
| (Johns, 2004, pp. 199-208; | Strong author | Incorrect |
| Taylor, 2006, pp. 156-159) | Weak author | Correct |
| Smith and Brown (2005, p. 1) | Strong author | Correct |
| | Weak author | Incorrect |
| (Bloggs et al., 2003, p. 44) | Strong author | Incorrect |
| | Weak author | Correct |

Table 9.2: Reporting Words for Incorporating Author Names

| *Alphabet(s)* | *Reporting Words* |
|---|---|
| A | acknowledges, adds, admits, affirms, agrees, argues, asserts, assumes, assures |
| C | challenges, claims, clarifies, comments, concedes, concludes |
| D | declares, demonstrates, denies, describes, disagrees, discusses, doubts |
| E | elaborates, emphasises, explains |
| I | implies, infers, informs |
| M-O | maintains, mention, notes, observes |
| P-Q | points out, presents, proves, questions |
| R | reasons, recognises, refutes, relates, remarks, reports, requests, responds, reveals |
| S | shows, states, suggests |
| T-W | thinks, urges, warns |

### *ICE Method for Citing Authors*

When quoting, focus on (a) introducing the quote, (b) explaining its relevance, and (c) citing the sources–both in your writing and in formal citations. This form is known as the ICE method.

When including outside sources in your writing, follow the ICE method:

- I: Introduce
- C: Cite
- E: Explain

Use this method when inserting direct quotations as well as when you are paraphrasing or summarizing the ideas of another.

*Introduce the Source:* Introduce the source by giving your reader any information that would be useful to know: Who said it? Where did this idea come from? When was it said? Here are some examples of how to introduce a source:

- In her essay, "The Crummy First Draft," Lekkerkerk (2014) argues that…
- Michandra Claire Jones (2015), celebrated poet and author, wrote that…
- In the textbook, Information Literacy, Mossler (2015) states…
- According to Michael Smith, "you should use the author's first and last name when you cite that author for the first time in your paper".
- As Smith explains, "you can introduce your quotes with a number of different phrases."
- Smith suggests that "if the introduction to your quote isn't a dependent clause, it doesn't need to be followed by a comma".
- Smith observes the following in his article: "When you use a colon to introduce a quote, you need a complete sentence preceding the colon."

After introducing the quote, be sure that you use a signal verb to indicate that the source's words are next. In the third example above, you can see that "states" has been used to signal the source's words. Other signal verbs include:

Table 9.3: Signal Verbs

| | | | | | | |
|---|---|---|---|---|---|---|
| acknowledges | advises | agrees | argue | analyses | Answers | asserts |
| assumes | believes | charges | claims | considers | criticises | declares |
| describes | disagrees | discusses | explains | emphasises | Expresses | holds |
| implies | interprets | leaves us with | lists | objects | Observes | offers |
| opposes | points to | presents | proposes | recognises | Regards | remarks |
| replies | reports | reports | reveals | says | States | suggests |
| supports | tells us | thinks | wants to | wishes | Wonders | |

*Cite the Source:* When citing outside sources, you are required to include: the author(s)' last name(s); the date of publication; and, for direct quotations, the page number on which the quoted passage appears. If there is no page number, use the paragraph number to indicate the location of the quotation.

There are two options for inserting the above information into the writing:

- The first is to include the full or last name(s) of the author(s) directly in a sentence and the year of publication in parentheses just following the name(s). If directly quoting, include at the end of your sentence the page number where the quotation can be found. Here are some examples:

> Johansson (2009) says he believes that scholars...
> OR
> Norman Johansson (2009) says, "Scholars should pursue PhDs" (p. 167).

- Your second option is to include all of the required information in parenthesis at the end of the sentence. Here are some examples:

> Research suggests that graphic warnings on cigarette packages promote smoking cessation (Smith, 2015).
> OR
> According to one research study, "In the year following the introduction of graphic warnings..." (Smith, 2015, p. 16).
> OR
> Marcus explains that smoking can be deterred by "carefully placed warnings with disturbing imagery included" (Tomlinson, 2008, p. 16).

Notice in the above examples that quotation marks always have a beginning and end, occurring immediately before the first word of the quotation and immediately after the last word. Periods are always placed after the end-of-sentence parentheses, as in (p. 132).

*Explain the Relevance:* Now, you will need to explain the significance of the quote. Some important questions related to this are:

- How might this author's idea relate to my thesis?
- How does this data add to what I am trying to prove in this paragraph?
- Why am I putting this quotation in my paper?
- What am I trying to show here?

Here is an example of an explanation that would be appropriate to accompany the Mack quotation above: Judge Mack viewed juveniles as children first. He envisioned a system that would protect and give treatment to these young offenders so that they could become productive adults and saw no place for criminal responsibility and punishment within this system.

Now, here is an example of the ICE method at work in a paragraph:

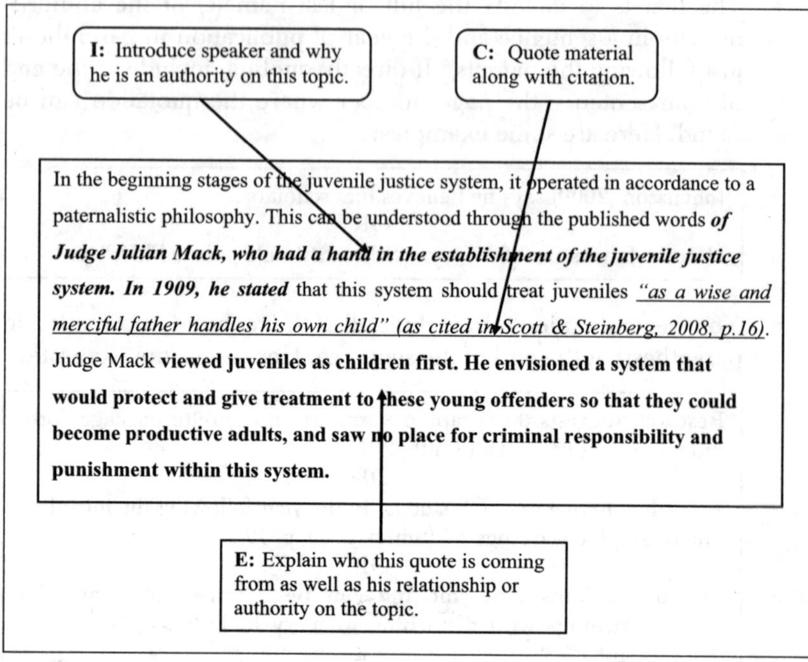


Figure 9.3: ICE Method for Citing Author

## Steps for Citing

- Choose your citation style;
- Create in-text citations;
- Determine the kind of source;
- Study your style's rules for bibliographic citations;
- Identify citation elements;
- Repeat the steps for creating an in-text citation and a bibliographic citation for each of your sources.

## QUOTING AUTHORS

One of the writer's jobs is to guide his/her reader through his/her text. Do not simply drop quotations into your paper and leave it to the reader to make connections. Integrating a quotation into your text usually involves two elements:

- *Signal:* A signal that a quotation is coming– generally the author's name and/or a reference to the work
- *Assertion:* An assertion that indicates the relationship of the quotation to your text.

Often both the signal and the assertion appear in a single introductory statement, as in the example below. Notice how a transitional phrase also serves to connect the quotation smoothly to the introductory statement.

*Ross (1993), in her study of poor and working-class mothers in London from 1870-1918 [signal], makes it clear that economic status to a large extent determined the meaning of motherhood [assertion]. Among this population [connection], "To mother was to work for and organize household subsistence" (p. 9).*

The signal can also come after the assertion, again with a connecting word or phrase:

*Illness was rarely a routine matter in the nineteenth century [assertion]. As [connection] Ross observes [signal], "Maternal thinking about children's health revolved around the possibility of a child's maiming or death" (p. 166).*

## Types of Quotations

Two types of quotations are discussed below:

### *Direct Quotation*

Direct quotation is a word-for-word reproduction of an expression or a section of a text. The quotation should be clearly separated from the rest of the text, so that the reader can see where the quotation begins and ends. You choose to use a direct quotation when it is important that the source's choice of words and tone is conveyed, but this technique should be used in moderation in a written assignment.

*Example:*
Students do not always see the importance of citing all sources in written work. *"Serious academic literature authors use sources, and they cite the sources they use" (Spangen, 2007, p. 9).* This is just as important when writing a semester assignment as when writing a scientific dissertation. When using direct quotations, you should always cite which page(s) you are referring to.

### *Indirect Quotation*

Indirect quotation is a reproduction of the meaning of an expression or a section from a source formulated in your own words. This way, you achieve better flow in your text. It is important that you choose your words so that you retain the original meaning. It is good practice to also provide page numbers when quoting indirectly.

*Example:*
Students do not always see the importance of citing all sources in written work. *All of the sources you use in written work must be provided if you are*

*to be perceived of as a serious academic author (Spangen, 2007, p. 9).* This is just as important when writing a semester assignment as when writing a scientific dissertation.

Occasionally, you may use direct quotes (the exact words of the author) as evidence in your writing. It is useful sometimes to use the original words of the author when those exact words carry special significance. Direct quoting should not, however, be the primary strategy for presenting evidence in your writing.

### About Direct Quotes

When you use a direct quote, you copy and reference the exact word/s of the author into your writing. A direct quote may be:

- One word
- A phrase or part of a sentence
- A sentence
- A group of sentences

*Exercise 1: Identifying Direct Quotes*
Read this paragraph and note the direct quotes:

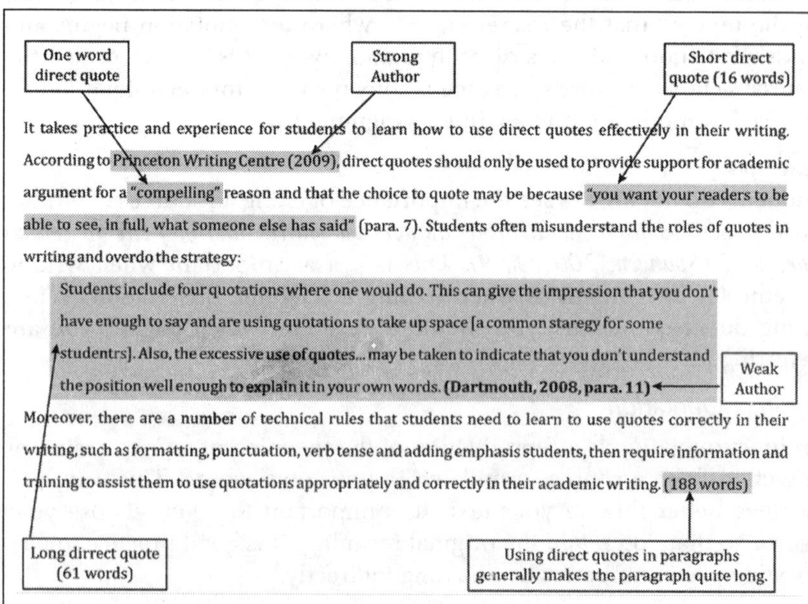


Figure 9.4: Types of Quotes

### *Rules for Short and Long Direct Quotes*

When you decide to use the exact words of an author in your writing, you will need to consider whether you want to use only a few words (short quote) or a longer chunk of text (long quote). There are different rules for using quotes according to the length of the quote.

*Short direct quotes (APA rules):* Short quotes are less than 40 words. Follow these conventions:

- use double quotation marks "…"
- include the quote in the text by using reporting words

> According to Princeton Writing Centre (2009, para. 7), direct quotes should only be used provide support for academic argument for a "compelling" (one word) reason and the choice to quote may be because "you want your readers to be able to see, in full, what someone else has said" (16 words) before you go on to analyze the statement.

Figure 9.5: Short Direct Quotes

*Long direct quotes (APA rules):* Long quotes are 40 words or more. Follow these conventions:

- leave no space above and below the long quote
- make the text size the same as the essay text size
- indent approximately one centimeter to the right
- do not use quotation marks

> Students often misunderstand the role of quotations in writing and overdo the strategy:
>
> Students include four quotations where one would do. This can give the impression that you don't have enough to say and are using quotations to take up space [a common strategy for some students]. Also, the excessive use of quotes … may be taken to indicate that you don't understand the position well enough to explain it in your own words. (Dartmouth, 2008, para. 11) (62 words)
>
> Moreover, there are a number of technical rules that students need to learn to use quotations correctly in their writing.

Figure 9.6: Long Direct Quotes

### *Rules for Punctuating Direct Quotes*

When you join your introductory words to your quote, use the following punctuation rules:

- No punctuation if the quote is fully integrated.
- A comma if you have used a reporting word or phrase.
- No comma if you've used a reporting word or phrase followed by 'that'.
- Punctuation mark goes after the end of the quote.
- A colon (:) OR a comma precedes (goes before) most long quotes (more than 40 words).

*Rules for Modifying Quotes*

*Exercise 2: Modifying Direct Quotes*

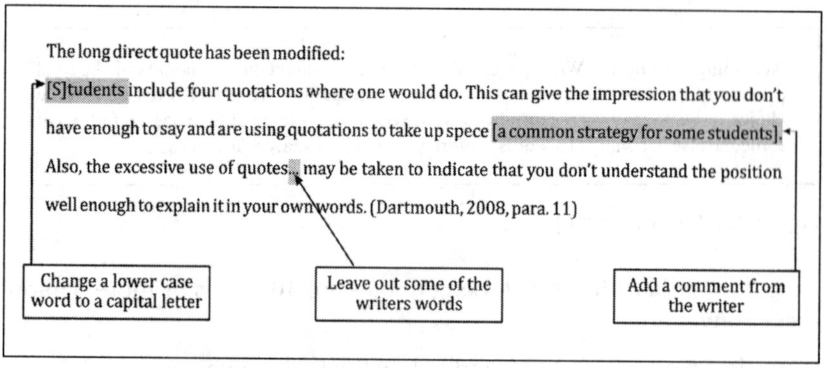


Figure 9.7: Modifying Direct Quotes

In the exercise above, see how the quotes have been modified

*Conventions for Modifying Direct Quotes*

The following table gives you a few of the most common rules for modifying the words of authors in a direct quote:

Table 9.4: Rules for Modifying the Words of Authors in a Direct Quote

| *Making a Change* | *Correct Convention* |
|---|---|
| Leaving out some words (because you may not need all of the words in the middle of the quote) | Use an ellipsis signal (three dots ...). Leave a space either side of the 3 dots |
| Changing the capitalization of a letter | Use square brackets [ ] around the letter |
| Adding words to the quote (without changing the meaning) | Use square brackets [ ] around the added words |

## *Signal Words related to Quotes and Paraphrases*

Words that introduce Quotes or Paraphrases are basically three keys verbs:

*Neutral Verbs:* When used to introduce a quote, the following verbs basically mean "says"

Table 9.5: Examples of Neutral Verbs

| | | | |
|---|---|---|---|
| The author says. | The author notes. | The author believes. | The author observes. |
| The author comments. | The author relates. | The author declares. | The author remarks. |
| The author discusses. | The author reports. | The author explains. | The author reveals. |
| The author expresses. | The author states. | The author mentions. | The author acknowledges. |
| The author suggests. | The author thinks. | The author points out. | The author responds. |
| The author shows. | The author confirms. | | |

*Stronger Verbs:* These verbs indicate that there is some kind of argument, and that the quote shows either support of or disagreement with one side of the argument.

### *Examples of Stronger Verbs*

Table 9.6: Examples of Stronger Verbs

| | | | |
|---|---|---|---|
| The author agrees . . . | The author rejects. | The author argues. | The author compares. (the two studies) |
| The author asserts. | The author admits. | The author cautions. | The author disputes. |
| The author emphasises. | The author contends. | The author insists. | The author denies. |
| The author denies. | The author refutes. | The author claims. | The author endorses. |

*Inference Verbs:* These verbs indicate that there is some kind of argument, and that the quote shows either support of or disagreement with one side of the argument.

Table 9.7: Examples of Inference Verbs

| | | |
|---|---|---|
| The author implies. | The author suggests. | The author thinks. |

### *Steps for Quoting*

- Start with an introduction to the quote saying who says it and giving the author's credentials.
- Give the quote. Do not forget to use an in-text citation and quotation marks.
- Tell what the quote means. Briefly give your explanation of the quote.

## PARAPHRASING AUTHORS

Paraphrasing is clearly restating in your own words the ideas or thoughts of another person. A paraphrase differs from a summary in scope. A summary usually conveys all of the main ideas of a text, while a paraphrase can convey the just main point or a small bit of the text, like a single paragraph or sentence.

Paraphrasing (writing information in your own words) is a highly acceptable way to include the ideas of other people in your writing. It is very important, however, to paraphrase correctly because there is a fine balance between acceptable paraphrasing and unacceptable paraphrasing (plagiarism).

*Paraphrasing Authors*

To paraphrase is to rewrite something 'in your own words'. Lecturers like to see you using paraphrasing in your writing because it demonstrates what you know and understand about their subject (because it is in your own words).

Most of your academic reading texts are made up of paraphrases. Any information in a paragraph that does not have quotation marks and is referenced is either a paraphrase or a summary.

*Exercise 1: Paraphrasing in Your Writing*

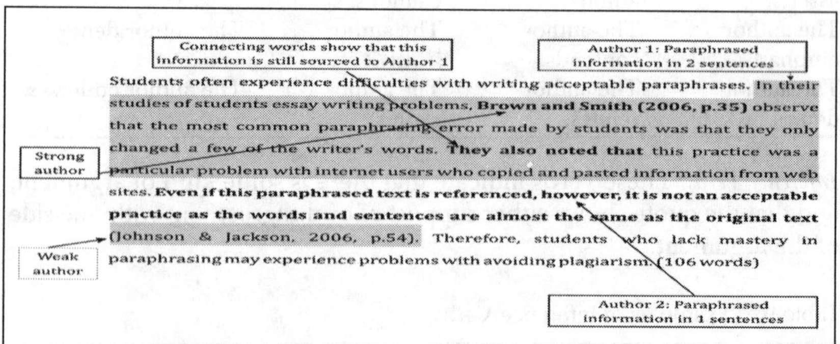


Figure 9.8: Paraphrasing in Writing

In the exercise above, see how paraphrasing works in academic paragraphs is done.

## Assessing your Paraphrase

It is critical that you assess every paraphrase of an author's work. Following are guidelines to help you to practise doing this activity accurately, so that you will avoid plagiarism problems.

*Exercise 2: Assessing a Paraphrase for Plagiarism*

Read the texts below and then answer the questions that follow:

**Original Text**

Traditionally, in oral and written discourses, the masculine pronoun 'he' was used as a pronoun to refer to a person whose gender was unknown or irrelevant to the context. Recently, this usage has come under criticism for supporting gender-based stereotypes and is increasingly considered inappropriate (reference).

*(adapted from Wikipedia)*

| *Paraphrase 1* | *Paraphrase 2* |
|---|---|
| If the gender of a person was not known or was unimportant to the meaning of oral or written discourses, it was customary to use the masculine form of 'he' when a pronoun was required. In modern usage, however, there has been growing concern about this practice because it appears to privilege stereotypes based on gender (reference). | In oral and written discourses, it has been traditional to use the masculine 'he' as a pronoun to refer to an individual whose gender was not known or irrelevant to the context. Increasingly, in recent times, this usage has been criticised for supporting gender-based stereotypes that are considered inappropriate (reference). |

Figure 9.9: Assessing a Paraphrase for Plagiarism

Compare paraphrases 1 and 2 to the original text. For a paraphrase to be acceptable, you need to be able to answer yes to the following:

1. The meaning is the same
2. Most of the words have been changed.
3. The sentences have been significantly restructured.
4. The information is referenced.
5. All the rules for paraphrasing have been followed.

Choose the appropriate response to these paraphrases:

Table 9.8: Answer Key for Assessing the Paraphrases for Plagiarism

| *Response* | *Answer* | *Reason* |
|---|---|---|
| Paraphrase 1 is acceptable | Correct | Only paraphrase 1 is acceptable. |
| Paraphrase 2 is acceptable | Incorrect. | Paraphrase 2 has mostly the same words and the sentence structure has only been changed in small ways. Paraphrase 2 would be considered plagiarized writing. |
| Paraphrases 1 & 2 are both acceptable | Incorrect. | Only paraphrase 1 is acceptable. Paraphrase 2 has mostly the same words and the sentence structure has only been changed in small ways. Paraphrase 2 would be considered plagiarized writing. |

*Example 3*

The paragraph below is a paraphrase written by a student. Its aim is to support one of the key contentions in their essay on learning motivation among older students studying off campus. Compare the student's paraphrase to the original text and answer the following question.

| *Original Source* | *The Student's Paraphrase* |
|---|---|
| Course design and content were critical influences on interest. For instance, courses that students chose to do, or that offered opportunities for choice of sub-topics or assessments, enabled them to follow their interests and therefore experience that positive spiral. On the other hand, compulsory courses and topics that did not interest the students often led to boredom and frustration. Boredom was consistently linked with lower behavioural and cognitive engagement. Bored students procrastinated more, studied less, and, importantly, found the learning more difficult. | In the research study undertaken by Kahu (2014), students struggled to learn material that did not interest them. However, they were highly motivated to learn, and more successful, when studying topics they chose themselves. Kahu concludes that student interest in learning is greatly influenced by the design and content of the curriculum.<br><br>*Why it is a good paraphrase?*<br>This is an example of good paraphrasing. The original text has been changed substantially in terms of vocabulary and sentence structure without changing the original meaning. The paraphrase has also been referenced correctly. |

*Example 4*

Below is an extract from a text which a student intends to use in an assignment, followed by two attempts at paraphrasing it. Read through these, then indicate which you think does a better job of paraphrasing.

*Assignment topic*

It is generally agreed that homelessness is increasing in Australia, yet there is no commonly accepted definition. What does it mean to be 'homeless', and why is it so hard for governments, charities and social commentators to agree on a definition?

| *Original Text* | *Paraphrasing - Example A* | *Paraphrasing - Example B* |
|---|---|---|
| Because of the complexity of homelessness from a social policy and service delivery perspective, there are a wide range of views on what constitutes homelessness. Definitions of homelessness are culturally and historically contingent. They range from limited objective measures which conflate homelessness with rooflessness to more subjective definitions founded on culturally and historically determined ideas of 'home'. | Homelessness is complicated from both policy-making and service delivery points of view. For this reason, there are many different opinions on what homelessness means. Characterisations of homelessness are linked to culture and history. They encompass both narrow objective views which define being homeless as being roofless, and more personal definitions based on cultural and historical understandings of 'home' (ABS, 2012).<br><br>*Why it is a bad paraphrase?*<br>This is too close to the original text. Rather than expressing his own understanding of the concept, this student has just replaced some words, or reordered the original sentences. | A multi-faceted concept, homelessness can be defined in a variety of ways, most simply as the basic lack of shelter. However, our understanding of what constitutes a 'home' is also informed by our culture and history. This complexity impacts the development of effective policy and services to address homelessness (ABS, 2012).<br><br>*Why it is a good paraphrase?*<br>This student has expressed the meaning of the original text in his own words without changing the author's meaning. |

### Steps for Paraphrasing

For successful paraphrasing, you can use a step-by-step approach. The order of each step is given below:

1. Read the text a number of times until you understand its meaning
2. Underline subject-specific words that you will keep in your paraphrase
3. Circle words that could be exchanged for synonyms (words of similar meaning)
4. Change sentences by re-ordering and combining sentences in new ways
5. Put your in-text reference/s to acknowledge the author/s
6. Revise your writing and compare it to the original.

## SUMMARISING AUTHORS

A summary is a brief account of the main ideas of an information source (or sources) that you write in your own words. It is a highly acceptable way to include the ideas of others in your writing. All summaries from information sources must be acknowledged in your writing with an in-text reference and in the reference list.

### What is a Summary?

A summary uses the writer's own words to concisely explain the main point(s) or major argument(s) of a source or passage. Key words and main ideas from the original text should be used to create a brief, accurate review of the source's original ideas. A summary does not include minor details, and therefore, should be significantly shorter than the original text. Summarised material should be integrated into the writer's work using a signal phrase, which informs the reader of the source's author(s), title, and/or origin.

### What is Summarising?

Summarising means briefly outlining the main points of a reading in your own words without adding your own ideas or changing the author's meaning. Summarised information must be accompanied by a citation.

*Summarising Authors*

'Summarising Authors' is a restatement of someone else's words in your own words. There are many different kinds of summaries, and they vary according to the degree to which you interpret or analyse the source. Some are pages long, while others are just one or two sentences. However, for all types of summary, the writer is responsible for generally stating, in his or her own words, the main information or argument of another writer.

Many assignments are accompanied by a compulsory and/or suggested reading list. No doubt you have often wondered how your 2000 or so word assignment could possibly incorporate all those resources that are meant to inform your writing. Summaries of material may be used to give an overview of the work of one or more authors. Because they are very brief outlines of arguments made, they are very useful when you want to indicate the support given for and/or against some position you are taking in your argument.

In your writing you may make a summary from:

- one or more paragraphs
- an entire article, chapter or complete work
- a combination of readings with similar ideas.

You can get an idea from your reading as to whether an author has used a direct quote, paraphrase or summary to support their argument.

*Example 1*

The following paragraph is a summary of the original source below written by a student as part of a report on the dietary habits of Australian adolescents. Compare the student's summary to the original text and see what makes a good summary.

| *Original Source* | *Student's Summary* |
|---|---|
| With respect to daily intakes of specific micronutrients, 40% of adolescent girls and 8% of adolescent boys were at risk for inadequate intakes of iron. While protein intakes were adequate in these subpopulations, the top two sources of iron were from plant-based, iron fortified sources (breakfast cereals and breads and bread rolls). With regard to higher iron bioavailability and density, animal-based protein sources may be another strategy to address iron intake, particularly among females, as it has been previously shown to be a less popular food choice among Australian children and adolescents and avoided by young female adults (Fayet-Moore et al., 2017). | Fayet-Moore et al. (2017) found that 40% of adolescent girls, compared to 8% of boys, are likely to have an inadequate amount of iron in their diets, in spite of a sufficient protein intake. They attribute this to a tendency to avoid foods derived from animals.<br><br>*Why it is a good summary?*<br>This is an example of good summarising. The student has summarised the main points in their own words without changing the meaning or adding any additional points not mentioned in the original text. It is also correctly referenced. |

| *Original Source* | *Summary-1* | *Summary-2* | *Summary-3* |
|---|---|---|---|
| Longitudinal studies have also confirmed the role of beliefs in teacher practice. The impact of previously held beliefs was found to be enduring when four school teachers were observed over a two-year period implementing a new and specific method of teaching reading (Stephens et al., 2000). Despite the teachers receiving special training, new practice was not comprehensively sustained, with one teacher reverting to practice based on prior-held beliefs at the end of the training period. Similar reliance on earlier beliefs has been observed in studies of pre-service teachers. In a two-year study on development of professional belief systems about reading instruction the teachers appeared to create fictive images of themselves as teachers consistent with their prior knowledge of teachers and reading, and the experiences they had on teaching practicum (Stoube, 2009). These factors seemed more important in forming these teachers' notions about teaching reading, than formal reading courses undertaken as part of teacher training. In a similar fashion, research with pre-service teachers at two American universities found that previous, personal experience and beliefs continued to influence content and instructional choices of these participants (Barnyak & Paquette, 2010). | Teachers' reluctance to implement new methods of teaching reading to adults is regrettable (McHardy & Chapman, 2016). By holding onto their old belief systems, they are not making the most of their training and thereby disadvantaging their students. Studies by Stephens et al. (2000), Stoube (2009) and Barnyak & Paquette (2010) all support this assertion.<br><br>*Why it is a bad Summary?*<br>This writer is expressing her/his own views which are not appropriate in a summary. McHardy and Chapman do not make any value judgements about teachers' behaviours. | McHardy and Chapman (2016) prove that teachers find it impossible to change their approach to teaching reading to adults despite being trained in alternative methods. They always return to the practices they believe are best. Their views are supported by at least three other studies.<br><br>*Why it is a bad Summary?*<br>This summary misinterprets the authors' analysis and overstates the case. Chapman & McHardy do not say change is impossible. | McHardy and Chapman (2016) discuss previous research into pre-service teachers (Stoube, 2009; Barnyak & Paquette, 2010) and experienced teachers (Stephens et al., 2000) and conclude that even when they have received training in methods of teaching reading that differ from their existing practices and beliefs, they often revert to the old ways after the training is completed.<br><br>*Why it is a good Summary?*<br>The student has condensed the McHardy & Chapman discussion using her own words. Because, the purpose of this paragraph is to summarise the article, she does not include her own opinions. |

*Example 2*

Read the original source of an article and three examples of summary based on it and see how bad and good summaries are of the original paragraph.

*Exercise 1: Identify Summaries in Academic Writing*

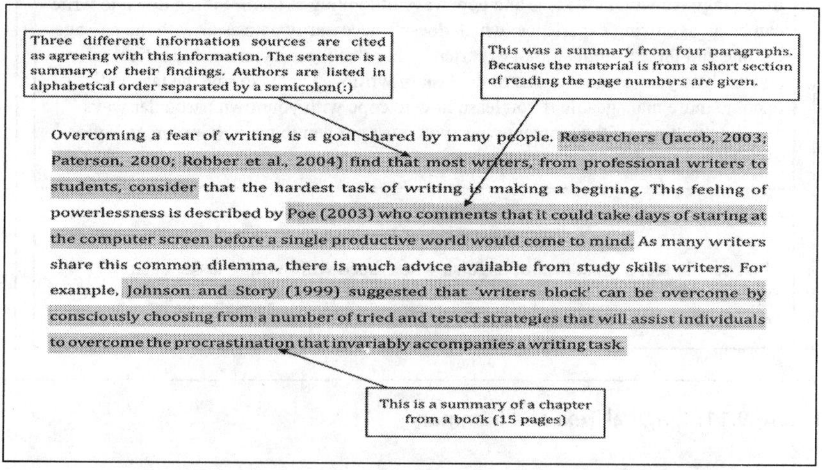


Figure 9.10: Summarising in Academic Writing

In the exercise above, see how summarising works in academic paragraphs.

## Assessing Your Summary

It is critical that you assess every summary you write. Following are guidelines to help you to practise doing this activity accurately, so that you will avoid plagiarism problems.

*Exercise 3: Write and Assess Your Summary*

Read the matter given in the figure below and then write one or two short sentences (less than 30 words) to summarise the key ideas identified in the figure.

*Check Your Summary*

Now, we can check the summary on the following criteria:

| *Summary Criteria* | *Answer (Yes/No)* |
|---|---|
| Is the meaning of the original writing maintained? | Yes |
| Does the summary keep the degree of certainty of the writer? | Yes |
| Is this a much shorter version of the original writing? | Yes |
| Is the source of the summary referenced? | Yes |

**Original**
**Direct quote from Gordon & Taylor (1989, p. 3)**

For most people, writing is an extremely difficult task if they are trying to grapple in their language with new ideas and new ways of looking at them. Sitting down to write can be an agonizing experience, which doesn't necessarily get easier with the passage of time and the accumulation of experience. For this reason you need to reflect upon and analyze your own reactions to the task of writing. That is to say, the task will become more manageable if you learn how to cope with your own particular ways avoiding putting off the moment when you must put pen to paper (Gordon & Taylor, 1989). (103 words)

**Summary of key ideas**

Most people feel a great deal of anguish when faced with writing tasks, even experienced writers. This response can be managed by recognising and coping with personal avoidance strategies (Gordon & Taylor, 1989). (29 words)

Figure 9.11: Original Text and Summary

A summary, as compared to a paraphrase, is always much shorter that the original text. When you write a summary, you limit yourself to giving your readers only the main idea/argument of an article or chapter of a book.

## Steps for Summarising

You can use a step-by-step approach for summarising. The steps for summarising are given below:

1. Skim read the text. Note sub-headings, the first and last paragraphs and topic sentences.
2. Read the text carefully using a dictionary.
3. Re-read a difficult text several times.
4. Write notes in point from using key words and ideas.
5. Put your text away and write your summary from your notes.
6. Refer back to the original to ensure your summary reflects the writer's ideas and opinion.

# CHAPTER 10

# Rhetorical Modes in Academic Writing

## *Arguing and Discussing*

The word argument is derived from the Latin word *"arguer"*, which means *"to make clear."* An essential aspect of academic writing is arguing and discussing. This involves proposing a claim and offering a rational reason with the help of evidence that strengthens an author's point of view. When presenting an argument, the possible counter-arguments should be taken into account. Thus, an academic argument can be called as an evidence-based defence of a complex issue.

### What is Rhetoric?

Rhetoric refers to the study and use of written, spoken and visual language. It investigates how language is used to organize and maintain social groups, construct meanings and identities, coordinate behaviour, mediate power, produce change, and create knowledge. Rhetoricians often assume that language is constitutive (we shape and are shaped by language), dialogic (it exists in the shared territory between self and other), closely connected to thought (mental activity as "inner speech") and integrated with social, cultural and economic practices.

### What is Mode?

Mode may be defined as:

- A manner, way or method of doing or acting
- A particular form, variety or manner: a mode of expression.

### What are Rhetorical Modes?

Good writing depends on factors such as purpose, type of writing and audience. That is why, knowledge of the major categories of the rhetorical modes is important. Rhetorical modes (also known as modes of discourse) describe the variety, conventions, and purposes of the major kinds of language-based communication, particularly writing and speaking. The term rhetorical modes refer to the different styles and techniques we use when we write.Four of the most common rhetorical modes and their purpose are: narration, description, exposition, and argumentation. The first codification of these rhetorical modes was by Samuel P. Newman in *"A Practical System of Rhetoric"* in 1827.

***Two Types of Writing***

There are two writing environments in which you will use rhetoric:

*Expository* writing; and *Creative* (or narrative) writing.

The difference lies in the purpose of the piece. An expository essay aims to inform and instruct, while a narrative essay is a story meant to entertain.

## Types of Rhetorical Modes

Here is a list of common rhetorical modes along with brief definitions:

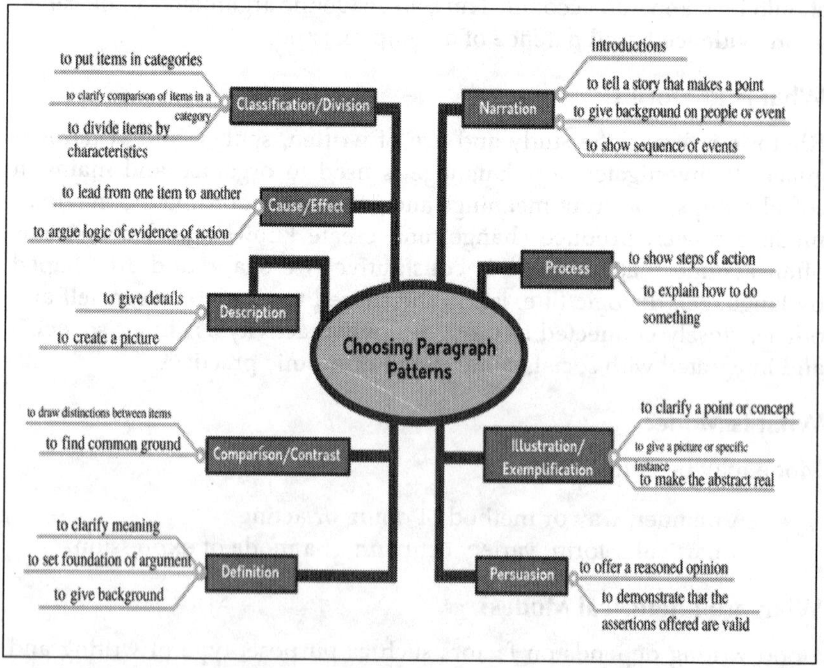


Figure 10.1: Types of Rhetorical Modes

*Argumentation and Persuasion:* It means making a case for your opinion or the perspective you wish your audience to take by offering supporting ideas or facts.

*Narrative:* The purpose of narration is to tell a story or relate an event. Narration is an especially useful tool for sequencing or putting details and information into some kind of logical order, usually chronological.

*Description:* The purpose of description is to recreate, invent, or visually present a person, place, event, or action so that the reader can picture that which is being described. It is heavily based on sensory details: what we experience through our five senses.There are two basic types of description, objective and subjective.

*Process Analysis:* The purpose of a process analysis essay is to explain how to do something or how something works. Analysing a process can also be thought of as *"how-to"* instruction. Academic writing can incorporate process analysis to show how an existing problem came to be, or how it might be solved, by following a clear series of steps.

*Illustration and Exemplification:* To illustrate means to show or demonstrate something clearly through the use of evidence. It is common to see examples used in all kinds of situations. An exemplification essay extends this idea even further: it carries one or more examples into great detail, in order to show the details of a complex problem in a way that is easy for readers to understand.

*Cause and Effect:* The purpose of the cause-and-effect essay is to determine how various phenomena relate in terms of origins and results. Cause/effect essays offer an explanation about why that sequence matters. Cause/effect writing is particularly powerful when the author can provide a cause/effect relationship that the reader was not expecting, and as a result see the situation in a new light.

*Comparison and Contrast:* Comparison in writing discusses elements that are similar, while contrast in writing discusses elements that are different. A compare-and-contrast essay, then, analyses two subjects by comparing them, contrasting them, or both. Comparison focuses on similarities between things, and contrast focuses on their differences. We innately make comparisons all the time, and they appear in many kinds of writings. The goal of comparison and contrast in academic essays is generally to show that one item is superior to another, based on a set of evaluations included as part of the writing.

*Definition:* The purpose of the definition essay is to simply define something. In academic speaking, it is often necessary to define your terms.

The rhetorical mode *"definition"* explains a term that may be contentious, controversial, or ambiguous so that the audience and writer develop a common understanding of the idea.

*Problem/Solution:* This type of academic writing has two equally important tasks: clearly identifying a problem, and then providing a logical, practical solution for that problem. Establishing that a particular situation IS a problem can sometimes be a challenge– many readers might assume that a given situation is "just the way it is", for instance.

*Division/Classification:* Classification takes one large concept and divides it into individual pieces. A nice result from this type of writing is that it helps the reader to understand a complex topic by focusing on its smaller parts. This is particularly useful when an author has a unique way of dividing up the concepts, to provide new insight into the ways it might be viewed.

## Argumentation and Persuasion

Argumentation and persuasion are rhetorical modes used to convince others of an opinion, belief, or the merits of a course of action.

### *Argumentation*

Argumentation uses logic and objective support to convince the audience of the veracity of an argument. Argumentation relies on logic and evidence to build a case for a specific claim. Argumentation de-emphasizes appeals to emotion.

According to the *Oxford Advanced Learner's Dictionary*:

- *"A conversation or discussion in which two or more people disagree, often angrily."*
- *"A reason or set of reasons that somebody uses to show that something is true or correct".*

### *Steps to Creating an Argument*

- Consider your topic.
- Research the topic.
- Choose the perspective you agree with.
- Go back to the literature to support your thesis statement.
- Identify each counter-argument, finding the most cogent resources for each, and make your best argument against these using the most applicable and reliable sources to support your perspective.
- Organise your paper in a way that will most effectively anticipate the reader's mental journey through the topic.

### *Persuasion*

Persuasion appeals to the emotions of the audience to convince them of the inherent value of a stance. Persuasion appeals to readers' emotions to make them believe something or take specific action. Persuasion can also use logic and evidence. Oxford Advanced Learner's Dictionary has defined persuasion as: *"The act of persuading somebody to do something or to believe something."*

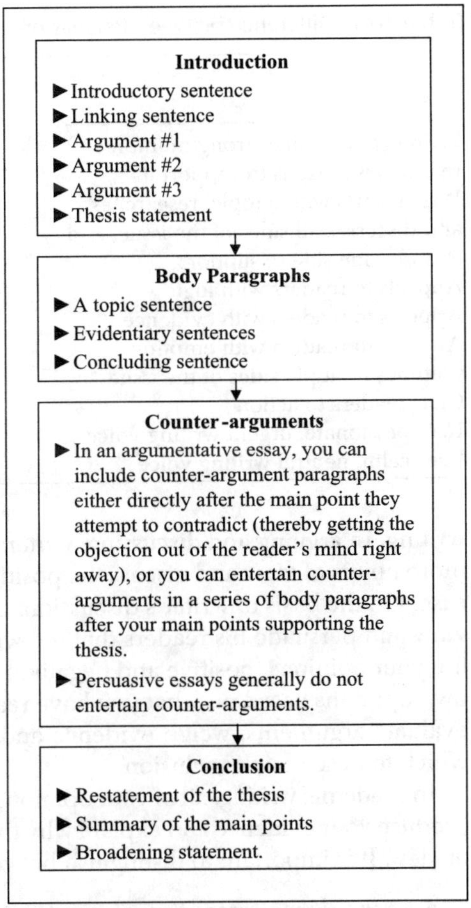


Figure 10.2: Structure of the Argumentative and Persuasive Essay

*Steps to Persuasion*

- Search your feelings for a response to the topic.
- Decide what you want to convince others about concerning this issue.
- Outline an argument based on what you believe and feel.
- Find or create stories and sensory imagery that will speak to the reader's emotions.
- Organise your paper in a way that puts increasing pressure on the reader's emotions.

### *Difference between Persuasion and Argumentation*

The table 10.1 will help you recognize the differences between persuasion and argumentation.

## Arguing and Discussing in Academic Writing

Arguing and discussing is the essential part of academic writing. In academic writing, arguing and discussing is often part of a larger piece of

Table 10.1: Difference between Persuasion and Argumentation

| | *Persuasive Writing* | *Argumentative Writing* |
|---|---|---|
| Writer starts with a strong opinion and researches reasons to support it | X | |
| Writer starts with a topic, researches and discusses all sides of the issue, and chooses one side to support | | X |
| Appeals to readers with logic | X | X |
| Appeals to readers with evidence | X | X |
| Appeals to readers with emotion | X | |
| Outlines multiple sides of the issue | | X |
| Calls readers to action | X | |
| Uses passionate, urgent writing voice | X | |
| Uses calm, neutral writing voice | | X |

writing. In arguing and discussing, writers are expected to present two or more points of view and discuss the positive and negative aspects of each case. On the basis of writer's discussion, he can then choose one point of view and persuade his readers that the writer is correct. This means giving your opinions (positive and negative) on the work of others and your own opinions based on what you have read and learned. Writers need to evaluate arguments, weigh evidence and develop a set of standards on which to base their conclusion.

In academic writing, all of your opinions must be supported. You should produce your evidence and explain why this evidence supports your point of view. It is important to distinguish between (*see* Toulmin, 1958):

- *your claim (proposition, thesis, point, position)*–your point of view, what you believe;
- *your reason(s) (explanations)*–why you believe what you do;
- *your evidence (support or grounds)*–the facts, data and examples that support your point of view; and
- *your argument (warrant)*–how the evidence you have provided leads to the claim, your are making.

*Example:* A simple example would be:

- *your claim* e.g. John is a good teacher;
- *your reasons* e.g. He gets on well with his students;
- *your evidence* e.g. I have seen him in class.
- *your argument:* Good rapport with students is essential for a good teacher.

## What is Argument?

An argument is a statement or set of statements that you use in order to try to convince people that your opinion about something is correct. In academic writing, an argument is usually a main idea, often called a *"claim"* or *"thesis statement"*, backed up with evidence that supports the idea. In the majority of research papers, you will need to make some sort of claim and use evidence to support it, and your ability to do this well will separate your papers from those of students who see assignments as mere accumulations of fact and detail.

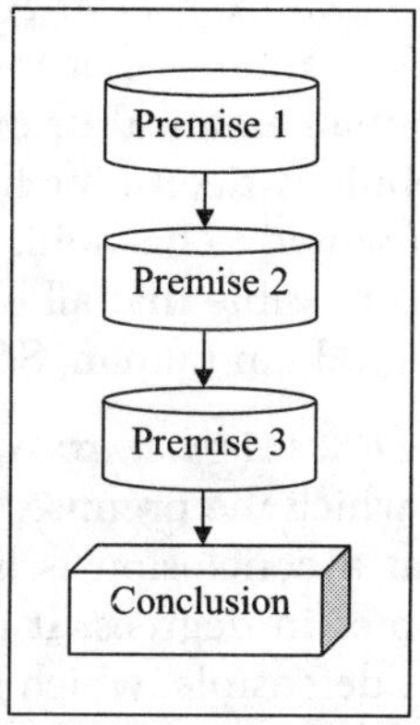


Figure 10.3: Visualisation of the Definition of Argument

## Definition of Argument

1. A coherent series of reasons, statements, or facts intended to support or establish a point of view.
2. Argument is series of sentences, statements, propositions where some are the premises and one is the conclusion and where the premises are intended to give a reason for the conclusion.

### *Academic Argument*

An academic argument is your stance, your claim, or your take on your topic. This stance, claim, or take is your contribution to the current conversation on your topic and provides your readers with a position, perspective, and/or point of view on your topic. An academic argument is also based in the research, what we often call *"evidence-based"*. This means you must support your argument with findings from sources you read.

### *Features of an Effective Argument*

- An effective argument is well grounded and supported by relevant date;
- Presenting an effective argument does not involve mere participation but also contribution to an existing argument or scholarship in the field;
- A fruitful academic argument defends against rational counter-arguments promoted by experts in defence of their perspective.

## Types of Argument

There are two types of arguments:

*Deductive Argument:* A deductive argument is one in which the premises guarantee that the conclusion is true. These occur when, perhaps by mathematical or definitional necessity, the truth of the premise will definitely determine the truth of the conclusion. It is an argument that is presented to be valid. Therefore, it cannot have a false conclusion when it is possible that all of its premises are true. *Example:* All humans have brain. I am human. So, I have brain.

*Inductive Arguments:* An inductive argument, on the other hand, is one in which the premises provide a sufficient reason for a reader to believe that a conclusion is likely to be true. It is an argument that strength comes in degrees. It is not supposed to be valid. Inductive arguments are defensible, which means they might be strong or weak, but not true or false.

Types of inductive arguments

- Statistical Generalisations
- Causal Reasoning
- Probability
- Inference to Best Explanation
- Arguments from Analogy.

## Parts of an Argument

The purpose of an argument, whether it is in a paper or a speech, is to convince or persuade. The parts of an argument include claims, counterclaims, reasons, evidence, warrant, acknowledgment and response.

*Claim/Thesis Statement:* Claims are not just opinions. A claim tells what you think is true about a topic based on your knowledge and your research. Claim is a statement that the reader is being asked to accept. This is the position the author is arguing for and the conclusion that they will ultimately reach. This is what they want to persuade their readers to believe as well. All of the other elements of the argument will be focused around this initial point.

Simply put, a claim is on what your argument is based upon. It is not a known and accepted argument, such as *"the sky is blue"*. Instead, it is a statement about which listeners or readers of a formal paper will want to know more and will want to hear your reasons for believing this claim to be true

*Counterclaims/Counter-arguments:* A counterclaim is just the opposite of a claim. Counterclaims are also provable and supportable by reasons and evidence. Counterclaims are rebuttals to a previous claim. Reasons support claims. Evidence backs up your reasons with statistics, facts based on published research and other concrete proof. Counter-arguments are ideas that are opposite to your ideas. In an academic discussion, you must show that you are familiar with both sides of the argument, and provide reasons to support your position. It is usual to deal with the counter-arguments first, before giving your view.

*Rebuttal:* One way to strengthen your argument and show that you have a deep understanding of the issue you are discussing is to anticipate and address counter-arguments or objections. The strongest arguments take opposing points of view, or counter-arguments, into account and discredit them. Counter-arguments can be rebutted immediately, when the argument is first introduced, or throughout the argument. A rebuttal is like a mini argument and can include several or all of the various elements.

*Warrant:* The warrant is the author's explanation of why the grounds are relevant to the claim. The warrant can be explicit (clearly expressed) or implicit (only implied, not stated outright), however, an implicit warrant can leave the argument open to questioning by the reader.A warrant is the general principle that connects your reasons to the claim and is generally known by the audience to whom you are presenting your argument.

*Reason:* A reason tells why. A reason makes someone care and tells the importance of the claim and the argument.

*Ground/Evidence:* Ground/Evidence tells your reader how your claim is proved. The grounds are the evidence that the author provides to support their claim. They can include data and hard facts, proof of the author's expertise, or just the basic premises on which the claim is built. It is important that the grounds be information which cannot be challenged, otherwise it can be seen as simply another claim, which would itself need to be based on a deeper level of evidence.

*Acknowledgment and Response:* Acknowledgment and response are when the reader or audience confronts you with counterclaims or support of the argument.

## Models of Argument

Scientific arguments can vary in complexity. Three models of argument are discussed below:

### *Classical Argument Model*

The study of rhetoric has existed for thousands of years, predating even Socrates, Plato and the other ancient Greek philosophers that we often credit as the founders of Western philosophy. The Classical or Aristotelian Model of argument is the most common type of argument. It was developed by a Greek philosopher and rhetorician, Aristotle. The goal of this model is to convince the reader about some particular point of view. In the classical model, both sides of an argument are analyzed and one side is proven right using clear evidence. This model efficiently utilizes Ethos (authenticity) + Pathos (emotion) + Logos (logic) to persuade an audience to a side of an argument.

Aristotle provides a crucial point of reference for ancient and modern scholars alike. Over 2000 years ago, Aristotle wrote the book on rhetoric. His text *Rhētorikḗ (On Rhetoric)* explores the techniques and purposes of persuasion in ancient Greece, laying the foundation for the study and implementation of rhetoric in future generations.

***The Rhetorical Appeals:*** To understand how argument works in *On Rhetoric*, you must first understand the major appeals associated with rhetoric. Aristotle identifies four major rhetorical appeals: *ethos (credibility), logos (logic), pathos (emotion)*, and *Kairos (time).*

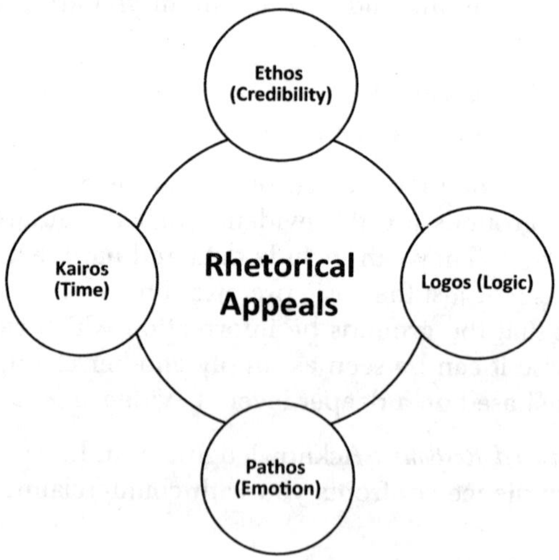


Figure 10.4: Rhetorical Appeals

- *Ethos* – an appeal to credibility. This is the way a speaker (or writer) presents herself to the audience. You can build credibility by citing professional sources, using content-specific language, and by showing evidence of your ethical, knowledgeable background.

- *Logos* – an appeal to logic. This is the way a speaker appeals to the audience through practicality and hard evidence. You can develop logos by presenting data and statistics, and by crafting a clear claim with a logically-sequenced argument.
- *Pathos* – an appeal to emotion. This is the way a speaker appeals to the audience through emotion, pity, or passions. The idea is usually to evoke and strengthen feelings already present within the audience. This can be achieved through story-telling, vivid imagery, and an impassioned voice.
- *Kairos* – an appeal made through the adept use of time. This is the way a speaker appeals to the audience through notions of time. It is also considered to be the appropriate or opportune time for a speaker to insert herself into a conversation or discourse, using the three appeals listed above. A Kairotic appeal can be made through calls to immediate action, presenting an opportunity as temporary, and by describing a specific moment as propitious or ideal.

***Components and Structure:*** The classical argument is made up of five components, which are most commonly composed in the following order:

- *Exordium* – The introduction, opening, or hook.
- *Narratio* – The context or background of the topic.
- *Proposito* and *Partitio* – The claim/stance and the argument.
- *Confirmatio* and/or *Refutatio* – positive proofs and negative proofs of support.
- *Peroratio* – The conclusion and call to action.

The classical model argumentative essay takes into account the following things:

- Introduces the main claim or the argument of the essay.
- Present the writer's perspective on the argument. The reasons something is not working and why something should be done.
- Take into account the other side of the argument. Explain them in detail and refute them with the help of evidence.
- Provide clear evidence that proves that your side of the claim is true.
- Provide the conclusion which states the benefits of accepting your claim.

***Structure of the Classical Argument Model in Academic Writing:*** The structure of the classical model in academic writing is as follows:

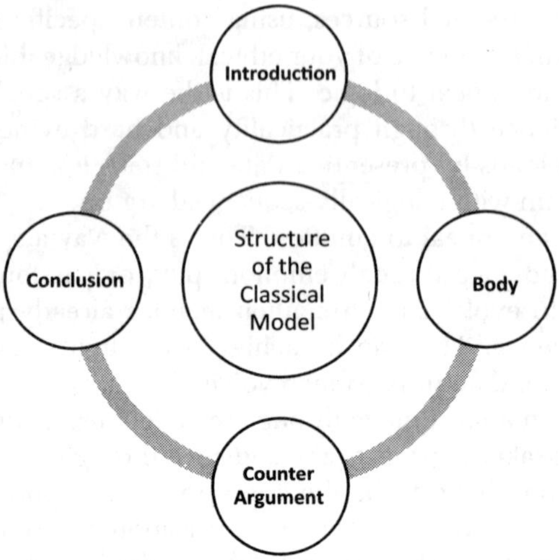


Figure 10.5: Structure of Classical Argument Model

- *Introduction* - hook statement, brief background, thesis statement
- *Body* - topic sentence, facts & evidence to prove the argument
- *Counter argument* - opposing arguments, evidence and reasons to refute the counter arguments
- *Conclusion* - restating the thesis statement, call to action and concluding remarks

### *Toulmin's Argument Model*

The Toulmin model (or system) is a six-part model of argument introduced by British philosopher Stephen Toulmin in his book *"The Uses of Argument"* (1958). The Toulmin model (or "system") can be used as a tool for developing, analysing and categorizing arguments. The Toulmin method suggests that claim, grounds and warrant are the three parts that are necessary to support a good argument. The grounds are the evidence used to prove a claim. The warrant is the assumption or principle that connects the grounds to the claim. All three parts are critical to achieving rhetorical analysis.

Stephen E. Toulmin identified elements of a persuasive argument. These give useful categories by which an argument may be analysed. The Toulmin method is a style of argumentation that breaks arguments down into six component parts: claim, ground, warrant, quantifier, rebuttal, and backing. In Toulmin's method, every argument begins with three fundamental parts: the claim, the ground, and the warrant.

### Elements of Toulmin's Argument Model

The six elements of Toulmin's Model are discussed below:

*Claim: A statement that something is so.*
A claim is the assertion that authors would like to prove to their audience. It is, in other words, the main argument. A claim is a statement that you are asking the other person to accept. This includes information you are asking them to accept as true or actions you want them to accept and enact. For example: *You should use a hearing aid.*

*Grounds: The backing for the claim.*
The grounds of an argument are the evidence and facts that help support the claim. The grounds (or data) is the basis of real persuasion and is made up of data and hard facts, plus the reasoning behind the claim. It is the *'truth'* on which the claim is based. Grounds may also include proof of expertise and the basic premises on which the rest of the argument is built. For example: *Over 70% of all people over 65 years have a hearing difficulty.*

*Warrant: The link between the claim and the grounds.*
Finally, the warrant, which is either implied or stated explicitly, is the assumption that links the grounds to the claim. A warrant links data and other grounds to a claim, legitimizing the claim by showing the grounds to be relevant. The warrant may be explicit or unspoken and implicit. It answers the question *'Why does that data mean your claim is true?'* 'For example: *A hearing aid helps most people to hear better.*

*Backing: Support for the warrant.*
Backing refers to any additional support of the warrant. In many cases, the warrant is implied, and therefore the backing provides support for the warrant by giving a specific example that justifies the warrant. The backing (or support) for an argument gives additional support to the warrant by answering different questions. For example: *Hearing aids are available locally.*

*Qualifier: The degree of certainty employed in offering the argument*
The qualifier shows that a claim may not be true in all circumstances. Words like *"presumably," "some,"* and *"many"* help your audience understand that you know there are instances where your claim may not be correct. The qualifier (or modal qualifier) indicates the strength of the leap from the data to the warrant and may limit how universally the claim applies. They include words such as 'most', 'usually', 'always' or 'sometimes'. For example: *Hearing aids help most people.*

*Rebuttal: Exceptions to the initial claim.*
The rebuttal is an acknowledgement of another valid view of the situation. Despite the careful construction of the argument, there may still

be counter-arguments that can be used. These may be rebutted either through a continued dialogue, or by pre-empting the counter-argument by giving the rebuttal during the initial presentation of the argument. For example: *There is a support desk that deals with technical problems.*

*Using the Toulmin System*

Use the seven-part Toulmin system to begin to develop an argument. Here is the Toulmin system:

1. Make your claim.
2. Restate or qualify your claim.
3. Present good reasons to support your claim.
4. Explain the underlying assumptions that connect your claim and your reasons. If an underlying assumption is controversial, provide backing for it.
5. Provide additional grounds to support your claim.
6. Acknowledge and respond to possible counter-arguments.
7. Draw a conclusion, stated as strongly as possible.

***Examples of Toulmin's Argument Model:*** In Toulmin's Argument Model, every argument begins with three fundamental parts: the *claim*, the *grounds*, and the *warrant*.

- A *claim* is the assertion that authors would like to prove to their audience. It is, in other words, the main argument.
- The *grounds* of an argument are the evidence and facts that help support the claim.
- Finally, the *warrant*, which is either implied or stated explicitly, is the assumption that links the grounds to the claim.

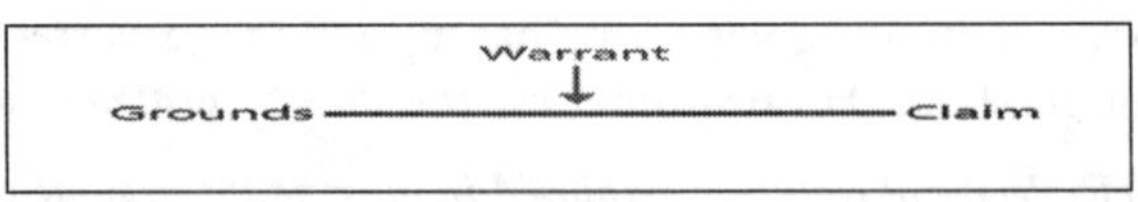


Figure 10.6: Claim, Grounds and Warrant

For example, if you argue that there are dogs nearby:

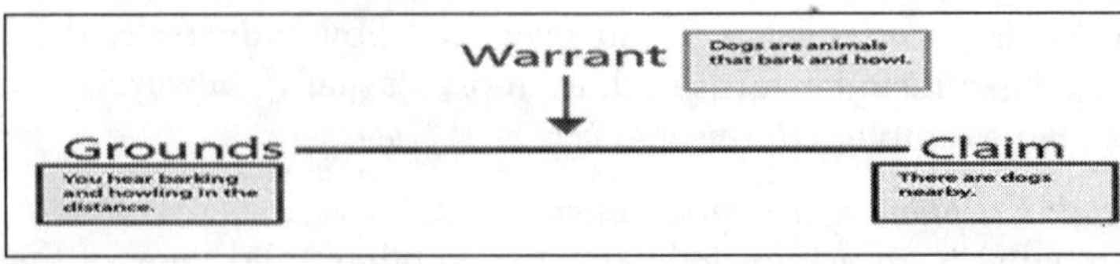


Figure 10.7: Example (1) of Toulmin's Argument Model

In the above example, in order to assert the *claim* that a dog is nearby, we provide evidence and specific facts or the *grounds* by acknowledging that we hear barking and howling. Since, we know that dogs bark and howl (i.e., since we have a *warrant*) we can assume that a dog is nearby.

Suppose that you are writing a paper on how more research needs to be done on the way that computer-mediated communication (CMC) influences online and offline relationships.

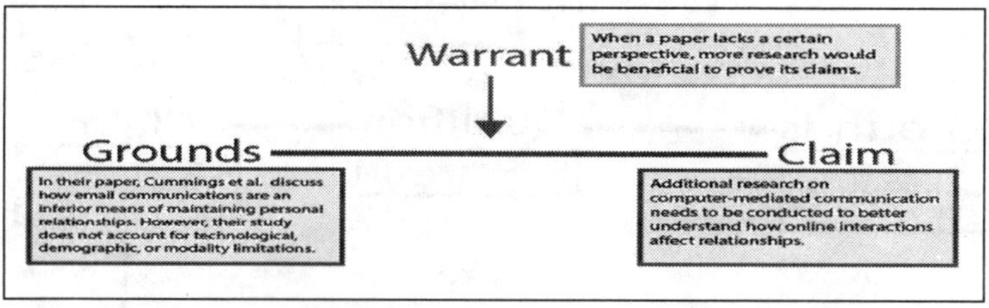


Figure 10.8: Figure 10.7: Example (2) of Toulmin's Argument Model

In this case, to assert the *claim* that additional research needs to be made on how online communication affects relationships, the author shows how the original article needs to account for technological, demographic, and modality limitations in the study. Since, we know that when a study lacks a perspective, it would be beneficial to do more research (i.e., we have a *warrant*), it would be safe to assume that more research should be conducted (i.e. the *claim*).

The other three elements are *backing*, *qualifier*, and *rebuttal* are not fundamental to a Toulmin argument, but may be added as necessary. Using these elements wisely can help writers construct full, nuanced arguments.

*Backing* refers to any additional support of the warrant. In many cases, the warrant is implied, and therefore the backing provides support for the warrant by giving a specific example that justifies the warrant.

The *qualifier* shows that a claim may not be true in all circumstances. Words like "presumably," "some," and "many" help your audience understand that you know there are instances where your claim may not be correct.

The *rebuttal* is an acknowledgement of another valid view of the situation.

Including a qualifier or a rebuttal in an argument helps build your ethos, or credibility. When you acknowledge that your view is not always true or when you provide multiple views of a situation, you build an image of a careful, unbiased thinker, rather than of someone blindly pushing for a single interpretation of the situation.

For example:

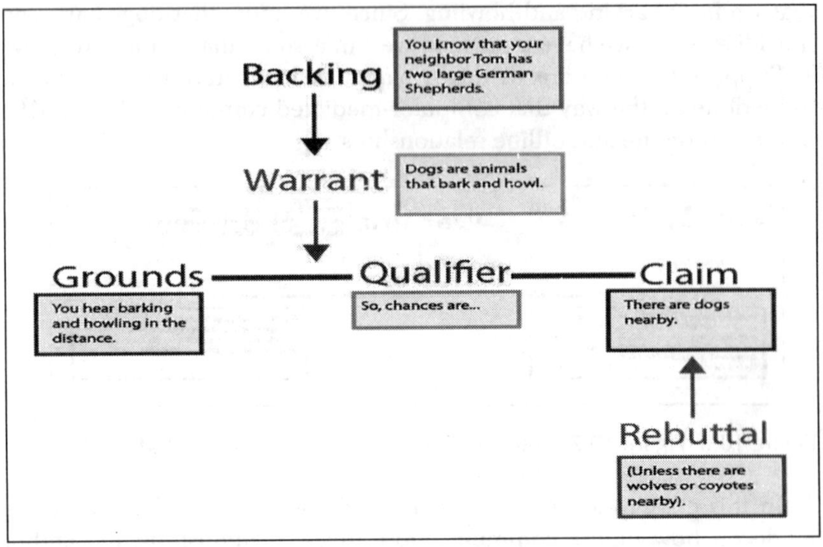


Figure 10.9: Figure 10.7: Example (3) of Toulmin's Argument Model

We can also add these components to our academic paper example:

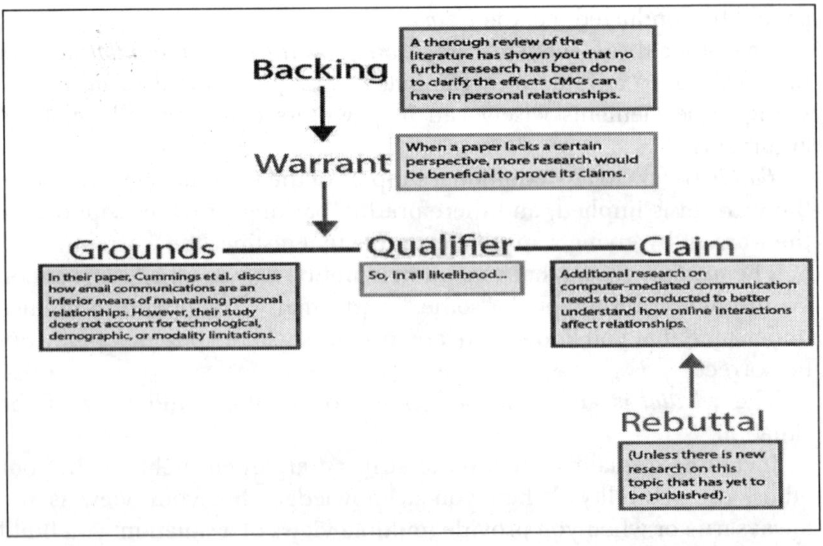


Figure 10.10: Figure 10.7: Example (4) of Toulmin's Argument Model

***Structure of the Toulmin Model in Academic Writing***

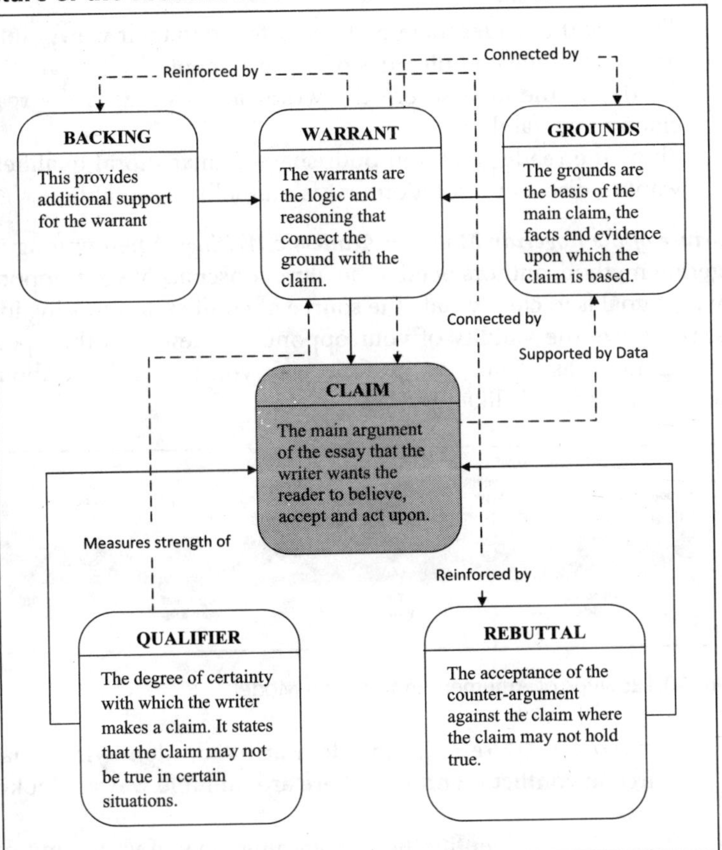


Figure 10.11: Six Components of Argument in Argumentative Academic Writing

The structure of the Toulmin model in academic writing is as follows:

- *Introduction* - thesis statement or the main claim
- *Body* - facts and evidence to support the argument
- *Conclusion* - rebuttal of counter arguments

## Rogerian Argument Model

The Rogerian of argument was developed by Carl R. Rogers to analyze an argument while providing a middle ground between opposing parties. This model works on collaboration and cooperation. It acknowledges that an argument can be looked at from different standpoints.

The objectives of the Rogerian model are:

- To show the reader that you have listened to their viewpoints and understood the complexities of the argument.
- To define the area where the writer acknowledges the reader's claim to be valid
- Show the reader that you both share similar moral qualities and want to discover a solution that is mutually acceptable.

***Structure of the Rogerian Model in Academic Writing:*** When writing in the Rogerian method, authors need to be ultra-conscious of your opponent's view; the goal is to clearly state the source of conflict or opposing ideologies, recognize the validity of your opponent's view, and then position your argument as equally valid. One way you might think about the order of your paper is like this:

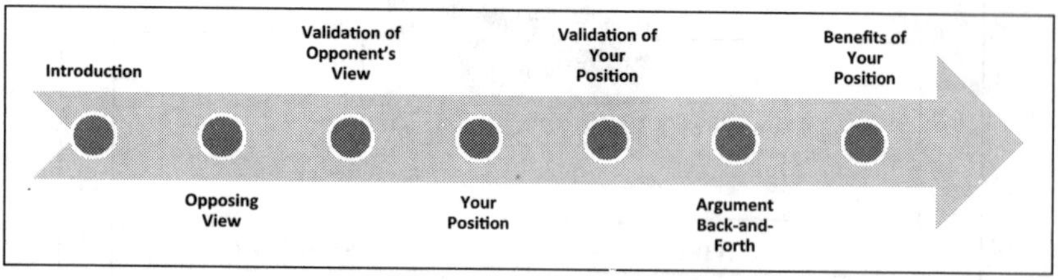


Figure 10.12: Steps of Argument in Rogerian Model

- *Introduction:* Address the problem at hand, identifying what the source in conflict is and why there are multiple ways of looking at the issue;
- *Opposing View:* Identify the overarching view of your component. If your opponent's view is complex, you may wish to just give a brief synopsis at this point, then clarify later. If your opponent's view is easily explained in two or three paragraphs, go ahead and describe it.
- *Validation of Opponent's View:* As a way to show respect an understanding, point out why your opponent's view is logical. State the view as you understand it and how you recognize why someone could feel or think the way they do.
- *Your Position:* After clarifying that you understand their perspective, shift politely to suggest what your view is on the matter. Again, if your view is complex, simply state the overarching point in 1 – 3 paragraphs.
- *Validation of Your Position:* Elaborate now on why your position also makes sense. Provide convincing evidence and sound

reasoning as to why your argument should also be considered. While you may be trying to persuade your reader that your idea is better than theirs, do not explicitly state that or you will often lose the respect and mutual understanding you are working towards.

- *Argument Back-and-Forth:* If the problem/issue at hand is sufficiently complex that it would help your reader to follow the argumentation by taking the argument in broken-down segments, move back and forth between their sub-arguments and your sub-arguments, always validating their point of view while showing convincing evidence as to why your point of view is also very strong.
- *Benefits of Your Position:* As you conclude, summarize your position, moving your reader towards knowing why that position is beneficial in some way.

## Approaches for Presenting an Argument

Two approaches for presenting an argument are discussed below:

*Balanced View:* In a balanced view approach, the argument is introduced to the reader with commentary on its relevance and contribution to the field. Next, reasons for and against the argument are presented with conclusive and convincing evidence. In the end, after summarizing and

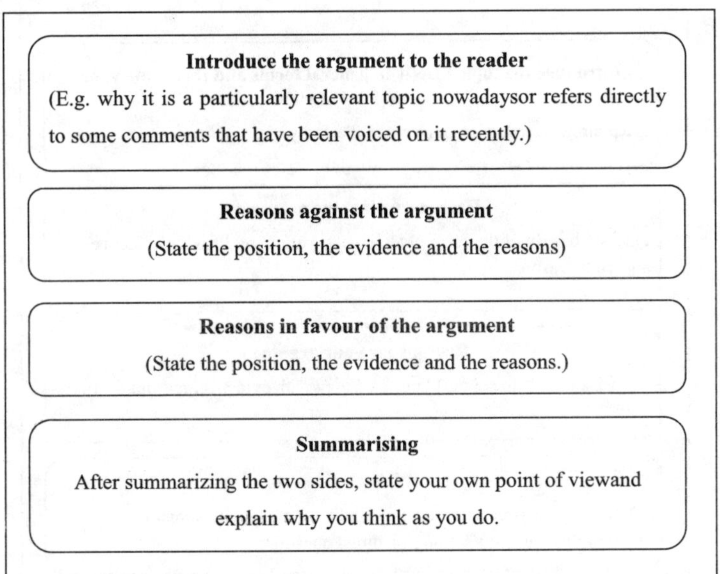


Figure 10.7: The Balanced View of Presenting Argument

considering a holistic and rational view of the argument, the author can present his own views with reasons and evidences supporting his claims.

In this case you present both sides of an argument, without necessarily committing yourself to any opinions, which should always be based on evidence, until the final paragraph.

At its simplest, your plan for writing will be as follows:

*Persuasive View:* The persuasive view involves a brief presentation of the argument and an immediate revelation of the author's perspective. Along with this, the author also reveals what they aim to prove in the manuscript. Next, reasons against the introduced argument are provided to the readers based on the evidence gathered. Counter-arguments are then presented in favour of the author's claim or perspective, leading up to a conclusive stance that convinces the reader to consider the author's point of view. In such argument structures, it is important to ensure that a degree of certainty dominates the manuscript (as opposed to the balanced view, which may often employ hedging).

This second type of argumentative writing involves stating your own point of view immediately, and then trying to convince the reader by reasoned argument that you are right. The form of the piece of writing will be, in outline, as follows:

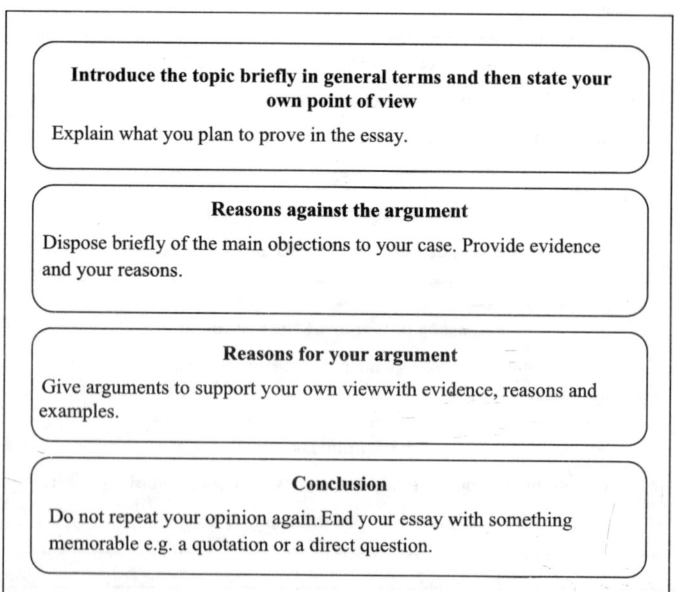


Figure 10.8: The Persuasive View of Presenting Argument

## Meaning of Discussion

The purpose of the discussion is to interpret and describe the significance of your findings in light of what was already known about the research problem being investigated, and to explain any new understanding or fresh insights about the problem after you have taken the findings into consideration.

*Language of Discussion*

When discussing common ideas avoid personal phrases such as in my opinion or personally, I think . . .

Use impersonal phrases instead, such as:

| | |
|---|---|
| It is generally accepted that | working from home saves commuting time . . . |
| It is widely agreed that | email and the internet reduce reliance on an office . . . |
| Most people appear | to need face-to-face contact with colleagues . . . |
| It is probable that | more companies will encourage working from home . . . |
| The evidence suggests that | certain people are better at self-management . . . |

These phrases suggest a minority viewpoint:

| | |
|---|---|
| It can be argued that | home-working encourages time-wasting |
| One view is that | home-workers become isolated |

When you are supporting your opinions with sources use phrases such as:

| | |
|---|---|
| According to Emerson (2003) | few companies have developed clear policies . . . |
| Poledna (2007) claims that | most employees benefit from flexible arrangements. |

## Comparison between Argument and Discussion

Comparison between argument and discussion is given in Table 14.2 given below:

Table 10.2: Comparison between Argument and Discussion

| | *Argument* | *Discussion* |
|---|---|---|
| Definition (Merriam-Webster) | • A statement or series of statements for or against something | • The act of talking about something with another person or a group of people: |

*(Table 10.2 Contd.)*

*(Table 10.2 Contd.)*

| | *Argument* | *Discussion* |
|---|---|---|
| | • A discussion in which people express different opinions about something<br>• An angry disagreement | a conversation about something<br>• A speech or piece of writing that gives information, ideas, opinions, etc., about something |
| Description | An argument is usually a loud conversation in which each person assumes they are right and they try to convince others of it. | A discussion is a conversation in which each party shares their views and points, and everyone discusses each other's views amicably. |
| Emotion | More emotional | Less emotional |
| Logic | Less logical | More logical |
| Purpose | To convince others that your view point is correct | To facilitate sharing of points and ideas in order to achieve growth. |

# CHAPTER 11
# Academic Integrity

The term *'Academic Integrity'* was coined by the late *Don McCabe*, who is considered to be the *"grandfather of academic integrity"*. This includes values such as avoidance of cheating or plagiarism; maintenance of academic standards; honesty and rigour in research and academic publishing. Academic integrity is essential to the foundation and ongoing viability of an academic community, including managers, researchers, teachers and students. It defines principles upheld by those in the community and which serve to guide the community in its work.

## Meaning of Academic Integrity

Academic integrity is the commitment to and demonstration of honest and moral behaviour in an academic setting. This is most relevant at the university level as it relates to providing credit to other people when using their ideas. In simplest terms, it requires acknowledging the contributions of other people. Failure to provide such acknowledgement is considered plagiarism.

'Integrity' relates to *'honesty'*, and academic integrity involves writing in an honest way, so that no one will think you are claiming that words or ideas from someone else are your own. This is very important in academic writing and if you do not do this you might be accused of plagiarism, which is a serious offence.

Academic integrity is the foundation of university success. Learning how to express original ideas, cite sources, work independently, and report results accurately and honestly are skills that carry students beyond their academic career. Academic dishonesty not only cheats the student of valuable learning experiences, but can result in a failing grade on assignments, a failing grade in a course, or even expulsion from the university for the student.

Academic integrity means putting those values into practice by being honest in the academic work a person does at University, being fair to others, and taking responsibility for his/her learning, and following the conventions of scholarship. It is your responsibility to ensure that you demonstrate academic integrity.

Academic Integrity is honest and responsible scholarship. As a member of an academic community, you are expected to submit original work and give credit to other peoples' ideas.

Academic integrity means conducting all aspects of your academic life in a professional manner. In a nutshell, academic integrity is about honest and responsible scholarship. As a student, and a scholar, we are expected to submit original work and give credit to other people's ideas.

## Definitions of Academic Integrity

1. According to Wikipedia, *"Academic integrity is the moral code or ethical policy of academia"*.
2. Academic Integrity is the practice of acting fairly, honestly and ethically in academic endeavour.
3. "Academic integrity is the pursuit of scholarly activity in an open, honest and responsible manner."

## Pillars of Academic Integrity

Academic integrity is the basis of the academic institution's goal to enable an exchange of ideas and develop new knowledge, and it requires that individual scholars work with and trust one another. Avoiding academically dishonest behaviour (plagiarism, fabrication, and falsification) is often cited as the way to promote academic integrity. But, when the focus is on negative behaviours, where integrity is absent, conversations about integrity are centered on suspicion rather than trust, respect, and growth.

The International Center for Academic Integrity (ICAI) has identified five pillars of academic integrity to generate positive conversations about integrity.

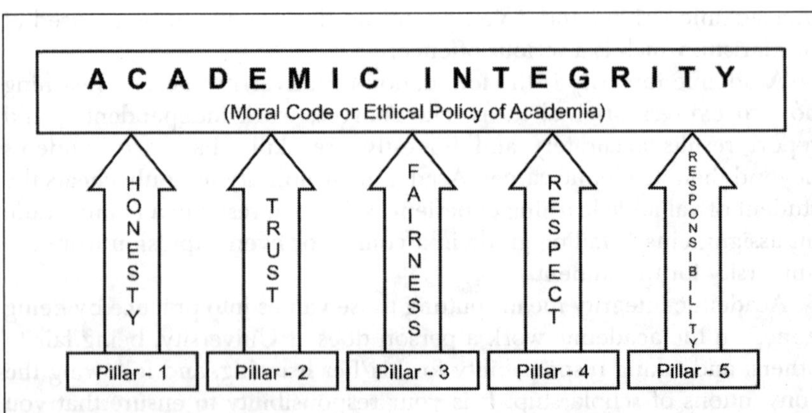


Figure 11.1: Pillars of Academic Integrity

*Pillar 1: Honesty:* Honesty is sincerity. All other pillars of academic integrity have some basis in honesty. Honest individuals take stock of individual abilities and represent their effort fairly.

*Pillar 2: Trust:* Trust in other people and in your community eases working relationships. Trust is established in a system where all members are doing their best work, where structures and policies are fair and all will be treated fairly.

*Pillar 3: Fairness:* Fairness goes hand in hand with trust. Every individual should believe that they will be treated fairly and judged by the same standard as all others in the community. For example, you can trust that your professors will evaluate all work fairly and not favour one person over another. The best work comes out of a fair system.

*Pillar 4: Respect:* Respect allows for individual points of view and opinions to be shared. Students show respect by "listening to other points of view, being prepared,...meeting... deadlines, and performing to the best of their ability." Teachers show respect by listening to students' ideas and "providing full and honest feedback".

*Pillar 5: Responsibility:* Responsibility means acknowledging your agency and accountability in daily actions and in your work. Everyone is personally interested in performing their work with integrity and encourages others to act with integrity too. Academic integrity starts with individuals and positively influences the entire community.

## Principles of Academic Integrity

Academic integrity is based upon a number of core principles. For a member of academic community, this means:

- Taking responsibility for their own work and studies;
- Respecting the opinions of others, even if they do not agree with them;
- Respecting the rights of others to work and study within the 'learning community';
- Acknowledging the work of others, where it has contributed to their own studies, research or publications;
- Ensuring that the individual's contribution to group work is represented honestly;
- Supporting others to behave with academic integrity;
- Following the ethical requirements and where appropriate professional standards appropriate to the discipline;
- Avoiding actions which would give an unfair advantage over others;

- Ensuring that the results of research or experimental data are represented honestly;
- Complying with the assessment requirements.

## How to Maintain Academic Integrity?

You can demonstrate academic integrity by:

- using information appropriately, according to copyright and privacy laws;
- not presenting other people's work as your own;
- conducting research ethically, in line with the University's regulations;
- reporting truthfully on your research;
- acting in an ethical manner in all your academic endeavours;
- creating and expressing your own ideas in course work;
- acknowledging all sources of information;
- completing assignments independently or acknowledging collaboration;
- accurately reporting results when conducting your own research or with respect to labs;
- honesty during examinations;
- taking responsibility for your own work;
- respecting the rights of other scholars;
- behaving with respect and courtesy when debating with others even when you do not agree with them;
- fully acknowledging the work of others wherever it has contributed to your own thereby avoiding plagiarism;
- ensuring that your own work is reported honestly;
- following accepted conventions, rules and laws when presenting your own work;
- ensuring that you follow the ethical conventions and requirements appropriate to your discipline;
- if you are studying on a professionally-recognised vocational programme, maintaining standards of conduct which are appropriate to a practitioner in that area;
- supporting others in their own efforts to behave with academic integrity;
- avoiding actions which seek to give you an unfair advantage over others;
- following the requirements of the University Ethics Policy;
- complying with and undertaking your research responsibly, following all necessary regulatory, legal and professional obligations.

## Strategies for Acting with Integrity

It is important that you:

- act honestly and fairly in all areas of your studies
- do your own work and do not seek an unfair advantage
- respect the work of others through proper acknowledgement
- always promote academic integrity.

## Promotion of Academic Integrity and Prevention of Plagiarism in Higher Educational Institutions—UGC Regulations, 2018

The UGC had constituted a committee to look into the issue of plagiarism and this committee framed a draft regulation known as the University Grants Commission (Promotion of Academic Integrity and Prevention of Plagiarism in Higher Education Institutions) Regulations, 2017, which was publicly notified by the UGC on 1st September 2017. On 20th March 2018, the regulations were approved by the UGC awaiting notification after the approval of the Ministry of Human Resource Development (MHRD).

### *Objectives of the Regulation*

The objectives have been given in Section 3 of the regulation as:

1. To create awareness about responsible conduct of research, thesis, dissertation, promotion of academic integrity and prevention of misconduct including plagiarism in academic writing among student, faculty, researcher and staff.
2. To establish institutional mechanism through education and training to facilitate responsible conduct of research, thesis, dissertation, promotion of academic integrity and deterrence from plagiarism.
3. To develop systems to detect plagiarism and to set up mechanisms to prevent plagiarism and punish a student, faculty, researcher or staff of HEI committing the act of plagiarism.

### *Plagiarism Defined*

1. The definition of plagiarism has been defined in Section 2 (k) of UGC Act, 1956, the regulation as, "…an act of academic dishonesty and a breach of ethics. It involves using someone else's work as one's own. It also includes data plagiarism and self-plagiarism."
2. The definition of plagiarism has been defined in section 2 (l) ofthe *UGC (Promotion of Academic Integrity and Prevention of Plagiarism in Higher Educational Institutions) Regulations 2018* as *"Plagiarism means the practice of taking someone else's work or idea and passing them as one's own."*

*Similarity Checks for Exclusion from Plagiarism*

The similarity checks for plagiarism shall exclude the following:

- All quoted work reproduced with all necessary permission and/or attribution.
- All references, bibliography, table of content, preface and acknowledgements.
- All generic terms, laws, standard symbols and standards equations.

### Levels of Plagiarism

Plagiarism in all areas but the core areas is tolerable to a certain extent. The various levels of plagiarism have been quantified and given below:

*Level 0:* Similarities up to 10% – Minor similarities, no penalty
*Level 1:* Similarities above 10% to 40%
*Level 2:* Similarities above 40% to 60%
*Level 3:* Similarities above 60%

Note: The research work carried out by the student, faculty, researcher and staff shall be based on original ideas, which shall include abstract, summary, hypothesis, observations, results, conclusions and recommendations only and shall not have any similarities. It shall exclude a common knowledge or coincidental terms, up to fourteen (14) consecutive words.

### Penalties for the Act of Plagiarism

Penalties in the cases of plagiarism shall be imposed on students pursuing studies at the level of Masters and Research programmes and on researcher, faculty and staff of the HEI only after academic misconduct on the part of the individual has been established without doubt, when all avenues of appeal have been exhausted and individual in question has been provided enough opportunity to defend himself or herself in a fair or transparent manner. The various penalties for plagiarism have been provided in Section 12 of the guidelines.

*Penalties for Students (Penalties in case of plagiarism in submission of thesis and dissertations):* Institutional Academic Integrity Panel (IAIP) shall impose penalty on the students considering the severity of the Plagiarism. The punishments given to students for plagiarism for different levels of severity are given below:

- *Level 0:* Similarities up to 10% – Minor Similarities, no penalty.
- *Level 1:* Similarities above 10% to 40% – Such student shall be asked to submit a revised script within a stipulated time period not exceeding 6 months.

- *Level 2:* Similarities above 40% to 60% – Such student shall be debarred from submitting a revised script for a period of one year.
- *Level 3:* Similarities above 60% – Such student's registration for that programme shall be cancelled.

*Penalties for Faculty, Staff or Researcher (Penalties in case of plagiarism in academic and research publications):* Penalties for faculty, staff or researcher of Higher Education Institutes will also be given according to the severity of plagiarism.

- *Level 0:* Similarities up to 10% – Minor similarities, no penalty.
- *Level 1:* Similarities above 10% to 40%
  - ➢ Shall be asked to withdraw manuscript.
- Level 2: Similarities above 40% to 60%
  - ➢ Shall be asked to withdraw manuscript.
  - ➢ Shall be denied a right to one annual increment.
  - ➢ Shall not be allowed to be a supervisor to any new Master's, M.Phil., Ph.D. Student/scholar for a period of two years.
- *Level 3:* Similarities above 60%
  - ➢ Shall be asked to withdraw manuscript.
  - ➢ Shall be denied a right to two successive annual increments.
  - ➢ Shall not be allowed to be a supervisor to any new Master's, M.Phil., Ph.D. Student/scholar for a period of three years.

## Academic Misconduct

Academic misconduct is any type of cheating that occurs in relation to a formal academic exercise. Academic misconduct is any action or attempted action that may result in creating an unfair academic advantage for oneself or an unfair academic advantage or disadvantage for any other member or members of the academic community. Academic Misconduct is a broad term that includes plagiarism, cheating, fabrication, and facilitation.

### *Examples of Academic Misconduct*

Examples of academic misconduct include:

1. Cheating, acting dishonestly or otherwise attempting to gain an unfair advantage in any assessment task or colluding with or assisting someone else to do so.
2. reusing or recycling an assessment task, in whole or in part which is previously produced without appropriate acknowledgement and without prior permission;
3. undertaking an assessment task, or part thereof, for or on behalf of another student;

4. fabricating, falsifying or misusing documents;
5. misrepresenting, fabricating or falsifying information, authorship or data;
6. taking in and/or using unauthorised equipment, material, texts or information in a supervised assessment task;
7. engaging in unauthorised communication of any form with any other person in an assessment task;
8. attempting to bribe or coerce a University Representative or a Student in order to gain an academic advantage;
9. claiming joint authorship with other authors without their permission;
10. interfering with any research-related property or material of another person;
11. failing to comply with reasonable instructions from an examination supervisor;
12. failing to comply with University rules, policies or codes of ethics;
13. copying another student's work during a test or examination;
14. submitting an answer to an examination question prepared outside the examination room without authorisation;
15. possessing unauthorised aids at an examination site, such as a dictionary or a calculator in an exam, unless one is given permission to do so;
16. having someone else take one's examinations;
17. altering one's work without permission after it has been assessed, i.e., for the purpose of contesting the original assessment;
18. knowingly allowing one's work to be copied during a test/examination or otherwise;
19. collaborating on take-home exams or other assignments without permission;
20. improperly obtaining through theft, bribery, collusion or otherwise an examination or test paper or other materials;
21. signing in another student on an attendance sheet;
22. submitting any work for evaluation that has previously been submitted in another course, without the faculty member's prior approval;
23. obtaining a copy of a test before the test is administered;
24. distributing, either for money or for free, a test before it is administered;
25. encouraging others to obtain a copy of a test before the test is administered;
26. changing grades in a grade book, on a computer, or on an assignment;
27. continuing to work on a test after time is called;

## Academic Dishonesty

Academic dishonesty refers to committing or contributing to dishonest acts by those engaged in teaching, learning, research, and related academic activities, and it applies not just to students, but to everyone in the academic environment

### *Types of Academic Dishonesty*

Academic dishonesty can take many forms, which can be broadly classified as follows:

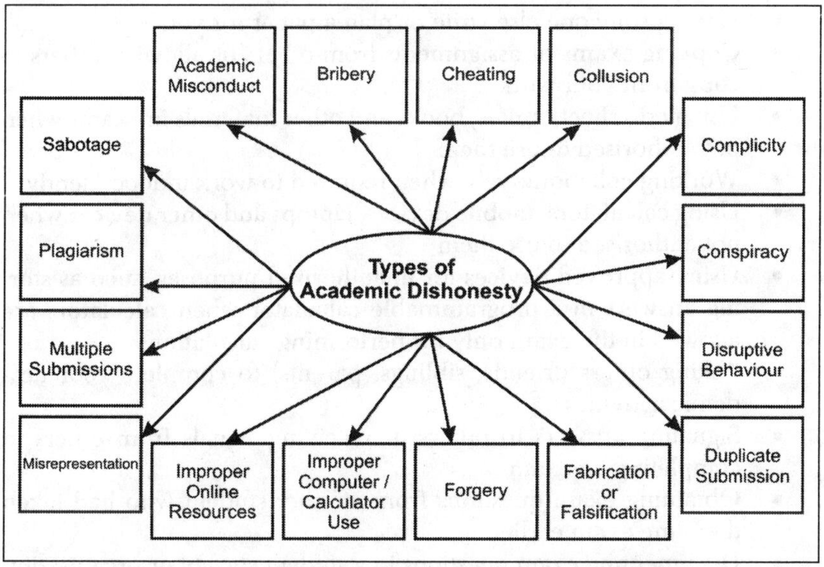


Figure 11.2: Types of Academic Dishonesty

*Bribery:* Bribery takes on two forms:

1. Bribing someone for an academic advantage, or accepting such a bribe (i.e. a student offers a professor money, goods, or services in exchange for a passing grade, or a professor accepts this bribe).
2. Using an academic advantage as a bribe (i.e. a professor offers a student a passing grade in exchange for money, goods, or services, or a student accepts this bribe).

*Cheating:* Cheating involves unauthorised use of information, materials, devices, sources or practices in completing academic activities. Cheating is intentionally using or attempting to use unauthorised materials, information, notes, study aids or other devices or materials in any academic exercise. Cheating is taking or giving any information or material which will be used to determine academic credit.

Examples of cheating include the following:

- Copying from another student's test or homework
- Allowing another student to copy from your test or homework
- Using materials such as textbooks, notes, or formula lists during a test without the professor's permission
- Collaborating on an in-class or take-home test without the professor's permission
- Having someone else write or plan a paper for you
- Copying exams or assignments from others or allowing others to copy from your work
- Using crib sheets, notes, books and other materials in exams when not authorised to use them
- Working collaboratively when required to work independently
- Using calculators, mobile devices, laptops and other devices when not authorised to use them
- Using approved devices for unauthorised purposes, such as storing answers in a programmable calculator when calculators are allowed in the exam only for performing calculations
- Asking others (friends, siblings, parents) to complete your academic activities
- Signaling answers to others or receiving signals from others in completing an exam
- Obtaining exam questions from another student who had taken the same exam earlier
- Documenting exam questions in a student society or organisation for others to obtain and cheat from in the future
- Purchasing answers or papers for assignments from the web and other sources
- Using unauthorised materials or procedures in completing experiments and other activities.

*Collusion:* Collusion is the act of two or more students working together on an individual assignment.

*Complicity:* Complicity is intentionally or knowingly helping or attempting to help another to commit an act of academic dishonesty.

*Conspiracy:* Conspiracy means working together with one or more persons to commit or attempt to commit academic dishonesty.

*Disruptive Behaviour:* Disruptive behaviour is any behaviour that interferes with the teaching/learning process. Disruptive behaviour includes:

- Disrespecting a professor or another student, in class or online.
- Talking, texting, or viewing material unrelated to the course during a lecture.
- Failing to silence one's cell phone during class.
- Posting inappropriate material or material unrelated to the course on discussion boards.

*Duplicate Submission:* A duplicate submission means a student submits the same paper for two different classes. If a student submits the same paper for two different classes within the same semester, the student must have the permission of both instructors. If a student submits the same paper for two different classes in different semesters, the student must have the permission of their current instructor.

*Fabrication or Falsification:* Fabrication or falsification involves unauthorised creation, alteration or reporting of information in an academic activity.

Examples of fabrication or falsification include the following:

- Artificially creating data when it should be collected from an actual experiment
- Unauthorised altering or falsification of data, documents, images, music, art or other work
- Unauthorised omission of data, information, or results in documents, reports and presentations
- Hiding data, results, or information using inappropriate scales, magnification and representation in charts, graphs and other forms of representation
- Falsifying information pertaining to the subjects participating in an experiment
- Falsely recruiting subjects for experiments without revealing the purpose of the experiments or receiving institutional approval for involving subjects in the experiment
- Fabricating sources of information
- Unauthorised impersonation of another person to complete an academic activity
- Unauthorised use of another individual's computer login ID and password
- Unapproved deviation from a predetermined experimental procedure.

*Forgery:* Forgery is defined as the act to imitate or counterfeit documents, signatures, and the like.

*Improper Computer/Calculator Use:* Improper computer/calculator use includes:

- Unauthorised use of computer or calculator programmes
- Selling or giving away information stored on a computer or calculator which will be submitted for a grade
- Sharing test or assignment answers on a calculator or computer.

*Improper Online Resources:* Improper online resources include:

- Accepting or providing outside help on online assignments or tests
- Obtaining test materials or questions before the test is administered.

*Misrepresentation:* Misrepresentation is any act or omission that is intended to deceive an instructor for academic advantage. Misrepresentation includes lying to an instructor in an attempt to increase your grade, or lying to an instructor when confronted with allegations of academic dishonesty.

*Multiple Submissions:* Multiple submissions is the submission of substantial portions of the same work (including oral reports) for credit more than once without authorisation from instructors of all classes for which the student submits the work.

*Plagiarism:* Plagiarism is the use of someone else's language, ideas, or other material without making the source(s) evident in situations where there is a legitimate expectation of original work. Plagiarism does not occur when efforts to promptly identify sources by making source use apparent to the audience of the submitted material are obvious. Plagiarism may not necessarily include mistakes in citation style.

Plagiarism means using someone else's words, ideas or diagrams without acknowledgement. When we write an essay, research paper, etc. we need to refer to other people's ideas. We have to acknowledge other people's work for the following reasons:

- To show respect for other people's ideas and work
- To clearly identify information coming from another source
- To distinguish an external source from your interpretation or your own findings
- To support your own arguments, thus giving yourself more credibility
- To show evidence of wide (and understood) reading.

*Sabotage:* Sabotage involves disrupting or destroying another person's work so that the other person cannot complete an academic activity successfully. For example, destroying another person's artwork, experiment or design is considered sabotage. Failure to contribute as required to a team project can also be considered academic sabotage.

Examples of sabotage include the following:

- Destroying another person's work (including documents, design, data, artwork, etc.)
- Not contributing to a collaborative effort adequately when required to do so
- Withholding information when it should be shared with others in a collaborative project
- Revealing confidential data about another person's project or procedures to others
- Disturbing the setup or calibration of equipment arranged by another person
- Colluding with others to falsely accuse others of academic dishonesty
- Installing viruses, spyware, or other damaging software in another person's computer
- Stealing another person's property, such as computers, experimental setups, data or designs, to prevent that person from completing his or her academic activities
- Destroying books and materials in the library, laboratory or similar places to prevent other students from completing their work successfully.

## Causes of Academic Dishonesty

Literature on academic dishonesty cites a number of factors that contribute to dishonest academic practices. Contributing factors include:

- Peer pressure
- Performance anxiety
- Excuse making
- Inability to manage the demands of student life
- Situations that encourage academic dishonesty
- Self-justification habits
- Unfamiliarity with what constitutes academic dishonesty
- Lack of understanding about consequences.

## How to Avoid Academic Dishonesty

- Cite your sources. If it is not your original words or ideas, give credit to the person whose words or ideas you are using

- Submit your own work on papers, reports, projects, and tests
- Do not share your assignments. If a classmate has a question, try to help, but do not "give" them the answer
- Do not use social media to communicate with classmates about assignments or exams
- Do not post your papers on websites that offer them to other students
- Do not use websites that offer pre-prepared papers for your own assignments
- Protect your computer files so that others cannot copy your work
- Clarify what is expected of you when you are working on a team project, in a study group or collaborative research project. Learn what you are able to submit as your own
- Be cautious about where you sit during exams. Distance yourself from others, including your friends, to reduce any temptation to cheat.

# CHAPTER 12

# Avoiding Plagiarism

*"To plagiarise"* comes from the Latin word *"plagiare"* which means, *"to kidnap"*. There are many ways to *"kidnap"* or steal ideas, both intentional and unintentional. As a member of an academic community that takes the sharing of ideas and information very seriously, it is important to avoid even the suspicion of plagiarism. To that end, it is your responsibility to learn how to cite your sources. It is also important to remember that understanding your materials is paramount to writing a good paper, and that plagiarising reveals a lack of confidence in your own understanding. If you are ever tempted to kidnap someone else's words or ideas – think again – and go to your professor for help.

## What is Plagiarism?

Many people think of plagiarism as copying another's work or borrowing someone else's original ideas. But terms like *"copying"* and *"borrowing"* can disguise the seriousness of the offense. In other words, plagiarism is an act of fraud. It involves both stealing someone else's work and lying about it afterward.

Simply, plagiarism is the use of another's original words or ideas as though they were your own. Plagiarism is using someone else's ideas, research, thoughts, words, graphics, tables, etc., either directly or indirectly, without properly acknowledging where the information is from. You plagiarise when you pass off someone else's work as your own by using their exact words or intellectual property (ideas). Whether you are trying to cheat or not, if you do not tell your readers where you found your ideas or words in your paper, you are plagiarising.

## Definitions of Plagiarism

1. According to Funk and Wagnalls' New Standard Dictionary (1921), *"Plagiarism is the act of appropriating the ideas, writings, or inventions of another without due acknowledgement; specifically, the stealing of passages either for word or in substance, from the writings of another and publishing them as one's own."*

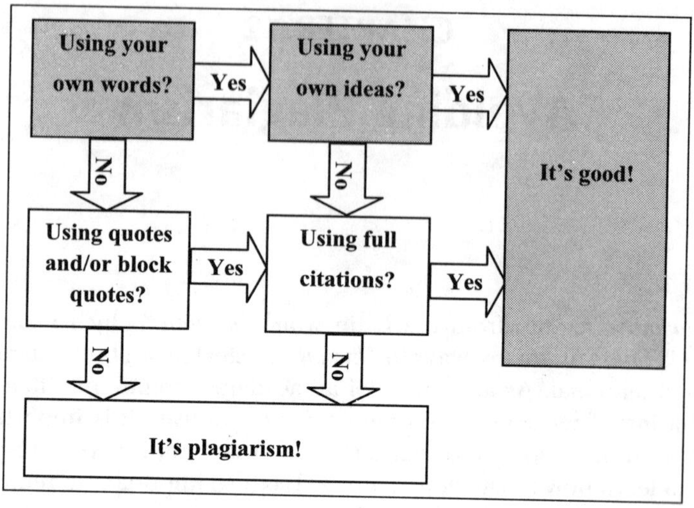


Figure 12.1: Is It Plagiarism?

2. Collin's Pocket English Dictionary (1987), *"Plagiarism is the taking of ideas, writings, etc. from another and passing them off as one's own."*
3. University of Hertfordshire, *"Plagiarism is the representation of another person's work as the student's own, either by extensive unacknowledged quotation, paraphrasing or direct copying."*
4. The Concise Oxford Dictionary (6th edition) (1976), *"Take and use another person's (thoughts, writings, inventions) as one's own."*
5. The Cambridge International Dictionary of English (1995), *"To use (another person's idea or part of their work) and pretend that it is your own."*
6. The Oxford Advanced Learner's Dictionary (5th edition) (1995), *"To take somebody else's ideas or words, and use them as if they were one's own."*
7. The Oxford Advanced Learner's Dictionary (6th edition) (2000), *"To copy another person's words or work and pretend that they are your own."*
8. MLA Handbook for Writers of Research Papers (1995), *"To use another person's ideas or expressions in your writing without acknowledging the source is to plagiarise."*
9. Stanford University sees plagiarism as the *"use, without giving reasonable and appropriate credit to or acknowledging the author or source, of another person's original work, whether such work is made up of code, formulas, ideas, language, research, strategies, writing or other form."*
10. Yale University views plagiarism as the *"... use of another's work, words, or ideas without attribution,"* which includes *"... using a source's*

*language without quoting, using information from a source without attribution, and paraphrasing a source in a form that stays too close to the original."*

11. Princeton University perceives plagiarism as the *"deliberate" use of "someone else's language, ideas, or other original (not common-knowledge) material without acknowledging its source."*
12. Oxford College of Emory University characterises plagiarism as the use of *"a writer's ideas or phraseology without giving due credit."*
13. Brown University defines plagiarism as *"... appropriating another person's ideas or words (spoken or written) without attributing those words or ideas to their true source."*
14. The U.S. Naval Academy defines plagiarism as *"the use of the words, information, insights, or ideas of another without crediting that person through proper citation."*
15. According to Bela Gipp (2014) academic plagiarism encompasses: *"The use of ideas, concepts, words, or structures without appropriately acknowledging the source to benefit in a setting where originality is expected."*
16. According to T. Fishman (2009), plagiarism occurs when someone:
    - uses words, ideas, or work products
    - attributable to another identifiable person or source
    - without attributing the work to the source from which it was obtained
    - in a situation in which there is a legitimate expectation of original authorship
    - in order to obtain some benefit, credit, or gain which need not be monetary.
17. According to the Merriam-Webster Online Dictionary, to "plagiarize" means:
    - to steal and pass off (the ideas or words of another) as one's own
    - to use (another's production) without crediting the source
    - to commit literary theft
    - to present as new and original an idea or product derived from an existing source.

## Examples of Plagiarism

Plagiarism is a form of Academic Misconduct and is the use of another person's work without appropriate acknowledgement and includes:

- turning in someone else's work as your own;
- copying words or ideas from someone else without giving credit;

- failing to put a quotation in quotation marks;
- giving incorrect information about the source of a quotation;
- changing words but copying the sentence structure of a source without giving credit;
- copying so many words or ideas from a source that it makes up the majority of your work, whether you give credit or not (*see* our section on "fair use" rules);
- the use of close paraphrasing of ideas, concepts, words, data or work of others without acknowledgement of sources;
- presenting extracts from sources without accurate and appropriate referencing;
- colluding with others to produce work that is presented misleadingly as the student's own work;
- failing to acknowledge work primarily produced by a collaborator;
- copying someone else's ideas and changing them into your own words and not citing the source;
- patch working (taking bits and pieces) from other sources so that it looks like your work and not citing the sources;
- copying and pasting information from the Internet and not citing the source;
- paraphrasing someone's writing so that it is only slightly different from the original writing even if you cite the source;
- copying and submitting part or whole of your own previously submitted and marked work;
- copying and submitting part of or the whole of another student's work (i.e. cheating);
- submitting work that has been written by another person as your own (i.e. cheating);
- Taking passages from their own previous work without adding citations;
- Re-writing someone's work without properly citing sources.;
- Using quotations, but not citing the source;
- Interweaving various sources together in the work without citing;
- Citing some, but not all passages that should be cited;
- Melding together cited and un-cited sections of the piece;
- Providing proper citations, but failing to change the structure and wording of the borrowed ideas enough;
- Inaccurately citing the source;
- Relying too heavily on other people's work. Failing to bring original thought into the text.

## Types of Plagiarism

The different types of plagiarism are given below:

1. *Direct Plagiarism or Verbatim Plagiarism:* If you copy language word for word from another source and use that language in your paper, you are plagiarising verbatim. Direct plagiarism is the word-for-word transcription of a section of someone else's work without attribution. Direct/Verbatim Plagiarism is the copying of another's words and works without providing proper attribution, indentation or quotation marks. This can take two forms. First, plagiarists may cite the source they borrowed from, but not indicate that it is a direct quote. In the second, no attribution at all is provided, essentially claiming the words of someone else to be their own.

   Even if you write down your own ideas in your own words and place them around text that you have drawn directly from a source, you must give credit to the author of the source material, either by placing the source material in quotation marks and providing a clear citation, or by paraphrasing the source material and providing a clear citation.

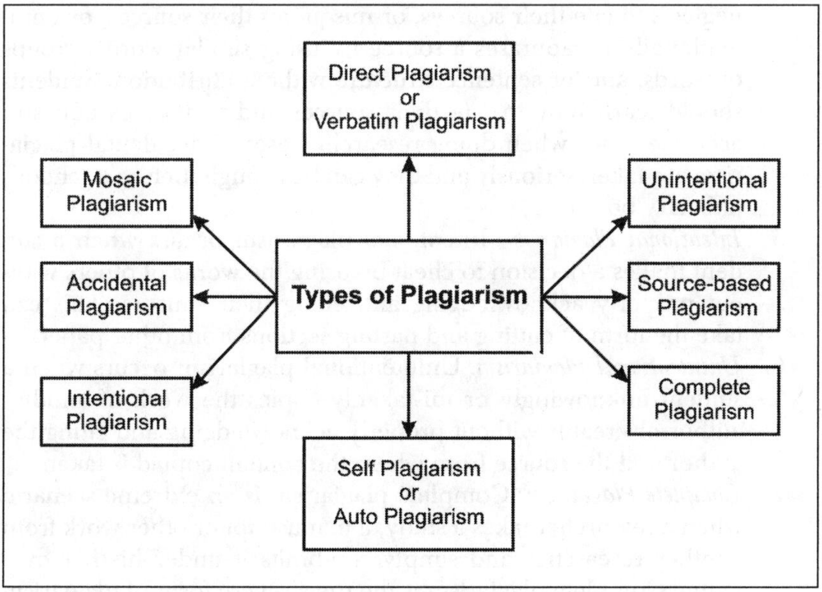


Figure 12.1: Is It Plagiarism?

2. *Self-Plagiarism or Auto Plagiarism:* Self-plagiarism is also known as auto plagiarism. It happens when an author reuses significant portions of his or her previously published work without attribution. Self-plagiarism occurs when an author recycles his or her own work, in part or in full. This means using the same work for multiple submissions. Self-plagiarism is considered academic misconduct because it does not contribute anything new to academic knowledge, but replicates work already completed. Repeatedly reusing material misleads readers and gives an author credit for more work than he or she has completed.
3. *Mosaic Plagiarism:* If you copy bits and pieces from a source (or several sources), changing a few words here and there without either adequately paraphrasing or quoting directly, the result is *mosaic plagiarism.* Mosaic Plagiarism occurs when a student borrows phrases from a source without using quotation marks or finds synonyms for the author's language while keeping to the same general structure and meaning of the original. Sometimes called *"patch writing"*, this kind of paraphrasing, whether intentional or not, is academically dishonesty.
4. *Accidental Plagiarism:* Accidental plagiarism occurs when a person neglects to cite their sources, or misquotes their sources, or unintentionally paraphrases a source by using similar words, groups of words, and/or sentence structure without attribution. Students should learn how to cite their sources and to take careful and accurate notes when doing research. Cases of accidental plagiarism are taken seriously and they can be brought before a school's judiciary board.
5. *Intentional Plagiarism:* Intentional plagiarism occurs when a student makes a decision to cheat by using the works of others without properly acknowledging and citing their sources. This can take the form of cutting and pasting sections from other papers.
6. *Unintentional Plagiarism:* Unintentional plagiarism occurs when a student unknowingly or mistakenly copies the work of another author or creator without properly acknowledging and citing the author and the source from where the content copied is taken.
7. *Complete Plagiarism:* Complete plagiarism is an extreme scenario when a researcher takes a study, a manuscript or other work from another researcher and simply resubmits it under his/her own name. Complete plagiarism is the most severe form of plagiarism where a researcher takes a manuscript or study that someone else created, and submits it under his or her name. It is tantamount to intellectual theft and stealing.

8. *Source-based Plagiarism:* Plagiarism may occur because of the different types of sources. For example, when a researcher references a source that is incorrect or does not exist, it is a misleading citation. Plagiarism also occurs when a researcher uses a secondary source of data or information, but only cites the primary source of information. Both these types lead to an increase in the number of references sources. This, in turn, increases the citation number of the references.

## To Reference or Not to Reference

When you write an academic text, you use information from three kinds of sources.

### *Self-generated Knowledge (no reference required)*

If you use your independent thoughts, experiences or experimental results and express these in your own writing and format, then you do not have to reference any of these (e.g. collecting data on your personal writing problems; setting your data on a graph and then writing a report on your findings).

### *Common Knowledge (no reference required)*

Common knowledge is usually information that is commonly known within the community or within a particular discipline and may be found in a wide range of sources (e.g. information such as an essay is a piece of writing expressing someone's opinion is widely known, common knowledge and would not require referencing). Determining whether information is common knowledge can be tricky (e.g. researching and writing essays stimulates student learning is an opinion. That is not common knowledge and would require referencing). However, if you use a direct quote, then you must always provide a citation.

### *Intellectual Property of others (reference required)*

Facts or ideas that belong to the research or thinking of other people require acknowledgment. These ideas are other people's independent thoughts and actions. The source can be any type of medium (e.g. a book, letter, an email, magazine, newspaper, film, speech, a lecture, interview, television programme, CD-ROM, YouTube, social media). You must acknowledge not only the ideas or facts themselves but also the language and format in which they are presented (e.g. if you use an image, table or diagram created by another writer, acknowledge it just as you would their ideas).

*Examples of Kinds of Knowledge*

| *Kinds of Knowledge* | *Example* |
|---|---|
| Intellectual Property | Researchers reveal that a fundamental cause of poor student writing is a lack of punctuation skills. |
| Self-generated Knowledge | My research into the writing problems of 300 students indicates that poor marks for essays correlates with difficulties with punctuation. |
| Common Knowledge | Punctuation codes are used in writing to ensure clarity of meaning. |

## Ways to Avoid Plagiarism

Following are the ways to avoid plagiarism:

*Paraphrase:* Suppose that you are writing a research paper and you have found some published information is perfect for your research paper then it is the right way to read the information carefully and write it into your own words. Keep in mind not to copy more than two words in a row from the text you have taken. If you are taking more than two words together then write it in quotation marks.

Paraphrasing means putting the ideas and information gained from other sources into your own words. Clearly, there may often be technical or discipline-specific words that you cannot replace; however, the sentence and paragraph structure must be your own. This is called paraphrasing, and the resulting piece of text is an indirect quote. Paraphrasing is easiest if you refer to your sources of information and try to draw out the main concepts or information. These then may be reorganised and words and word order changed so that the resulting text is in your voice. Try to avoid reliance on word-for-word paraphrasing that involves frequently resorting to a Thesaurus; the resulting writing will probably sound stilted and will not flow easily.

*Cite your Sources:* Citing is one of the effective ways to avoid plagiarism. If you are using the ideas of other researchers in your research, then give the proper in-text citation and reference list to avoid plagiarism. There are different citation and reference styles like– APA, MLA, Chicago, etc.

*Summarise:* A summary will also involve writing ideas or information from another source in your own words, but a summary will be shorter than the original. To summarise a longer piece of text, you will condense the main ideas into a shorter piece of text. When summarising, you need to consider the relationship between the length of the material in the original source and the importance of those ideas for the thesis

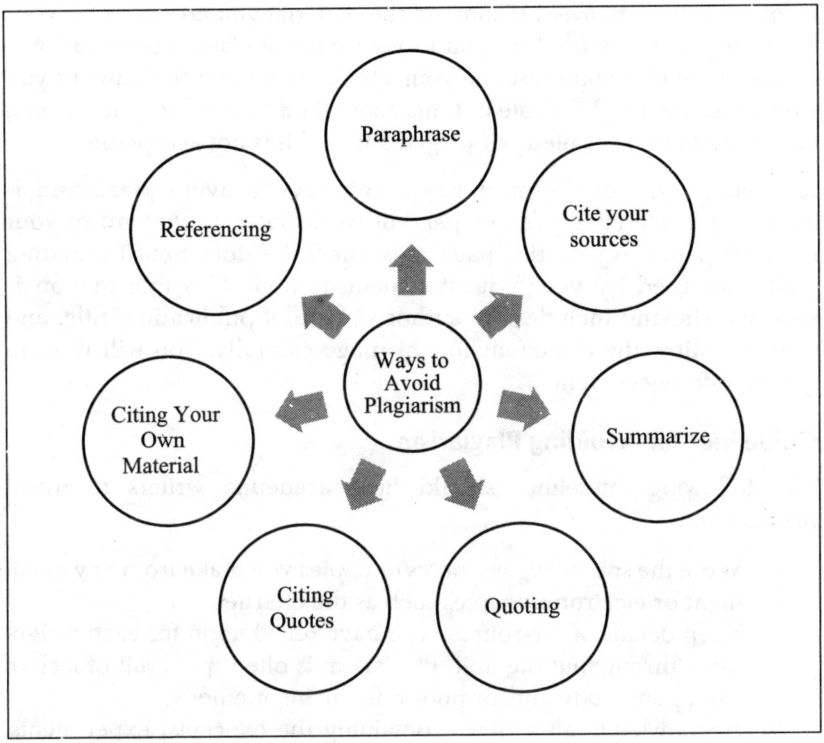


Figure 12.2: Ways to avoid Plagiarism

or paragraph topic in the essay. The approach to summarising will vary depending on this relationship. For example, do you want to summarise a paragraph from a source as a phrase or sentence in your essay? Do you want to summarise an entire article or book in several sentences in your essay? When writing summaries for an annotated bibliography, you will summarise each source as a paragraph.

*Quoting:* If you are taking the ideas of another researcher or author as it is or word-to-word from the original source, then it needs to be written in double quotes. Remember that the words in double quotes should not exceed more than 40. Try to avoid using quotes as much as possible and use paraphrasing for writing the ideas from other sources and proper citation to it wherever possible.

*Citing Quotes:* Citing a quote can be different than citing paraphrased material. This practice usually involves the addition of a page number, or a paragraph number in the case of web content.

*Citing Your Own Material:* If some of the material you are using for your research paper was used by you in your current class, a previous one, or anywhere else you must cite yourself. Treat the text the same as you would if someone else wrote it. It may sound odd but using material you have used before is called self-plagiarism, and it is not acceptable.

*Referencing:* One of the most important ways to avoid plagiarism is including a reference page or page of works cited at the end of your research paper. Again, this page must meet the document formatting guidelines used by your educational institution. This information is very specific and includes the author(s), date of publication, title, and source. Follow the directions for this page carefully. You will want to get the references right.

## Guidelines for Avoiding Plagiarism

The following guidelines should help academic writers to avoid plagiarism:

1. Write the source on any notes or copies you make from any document or electronic sources such as the internet;
2. Keep details of the sources you have relied upon for each assignment throughout the unit. Plagiarism is often the result of lack of care, poor study and/or poor referencing methods;
3. Acknowledge all sources containing the concepts, experiments, performances or results from which you have extracted or developed your ideas, even if you put those ideas into your own words;
4. Acknowledge the source of all images you include in your assignments;
5. Always use quotation marks or some other acceptable indicator of quotation when quoting directly from a work. It is not enough merely to acknowledge the source;
6. Avoid excessive paraphrasing and quoting, even where you acknowledge the source. Instead, read your sources then put them out of sight. Think about the meaning that is important and relevant to you and your task then write this in your own words;
7. Be familiar with the style of acknowledgment that is recommended for use in each of your academic assignment, including the referencing techniques required for information sourced from the internet;
8. Be aware of the rules regarding group work and collaboration. Collaboration (appropriately acknowledged) is permitted in the case of team or group projects. It is also permitted in the more

general case when the collaboration is limited to the discussion of general strategies or help of a general nature;

9. Understand that the distinction between what needs to be acknowledged and what is common knowledge is not always clear. As you gain experience you will learn the acceptable practices for acknowledgment in the disciplines in which you study, but while you are learning, always play safe and acknowledge;
10. Keep a printed (hard) copy and (where possible) an electronic copy of all of your submitted work to assist you in case you ever need to answer an allegation of plagiarism; and
11. Wherever possible, submit your assignment to Turnitin (or the equivalent text-matching software in your discipline) before you make the final submission, and look at the report produced on your assignment.

# CHAPTER 13
# Editing and Proofreading in Academic Writing

Editing and proofreading are two different stages of document preparation in academic writing:

Writing → Editing (multiple times) → Proofreading → Intended Use

## EDITING

Editing is a stage of the writing process in which a writer or editor strives to improve a draft by correcting errors and by making words and sentences clearer, more precise and more effective.Editing is the first task that should be undertaken after finishing the first draft of a piece of text. It involves checking the content of the text to ensure that the ideas are expressed clearly and logically and form a coherent and meaningful whole.

The process of editing involves adding, deleting, and rearranging words along with recasting sentences and cutting the clutter. Tightening our writing and mending faults can turn out to be a remarkably creative activity, leading us to clarify ideas, fashion fresh images, and even radically rethink the way we approach a topic.

### Definitions of Editing

According to Wikipedia, *"Editing is a stage of the writing process in which a writer or editor strives to improve a draft (and sometimes prepare it for publication) by correcting errors and by making words and sentences clearer, more precise, and more effective".*

### Goals of Editing

Editing requires focusing on the content of the text. The key goals of editing are to check that the text:

- flows logically
- is coherent and consistent
- forms a meaningful whole
- is clearly expressed
- is accurate in the information it provides
- has an appropriate tone
- is concise
- makes its purpose clear
- is targeted towards the reader.

## Criteria for Editing Text

Some key questions to ask you when editing a piece of text are:

1. Does the opening paragraph provide a clear indication of the purpose of the text and a broad outline of the content?
2. Does every part of the text contribute to the key idea in order to form a meaningful whole?
3. Does the purpose remain clear throughout the text?
4. Is every sentence relevant to the purpose of the text, with no digressions?
5. Is there a sentence (preferably the first) in each paragraph that summarises the key point of that paragraph?
6. Are the paragraphs unified, i.e. do they contain only one single idea each?
7. Has every idea been given sufficient weighting?
8. Does the text flow logically from one paragraph to the next?
9. Have transitional words or phrases (such as, for example, 'however', 'thus', 'therefore', 'as a result', 'in this way', 'furthermore', 'above all' and 'moreover') been used, but not overused, to help the reader to make connections between the ideas?
10. Are the sentence structure and vocabulary varied, without too much repetition?
11. Has the text been worded concisely?
12. Have irrelevant and unnecessary 'filler' words such as 'actually' or 'basically' been avoided?
13. Is the text free from colloquialisms, slang, jargon and clichés?
14. Has evidence been given to back up statements?
15. Has consistent terminology been used throughout, or if more than one term has been used to refer to something, is it clear that they are one and the same thing?
16. Is a positive and professional tone maintained throughout?
17. Is the tone appropriate for the reader?

18. Does the text meet the readers' needs?
19. Does the last paragraph neatly and concisely summarise and conclude?

If the answer to all of these questions is 'yes', the text is likely to be a well-written piece that will not require too many changes. However, if it seems that a lot of changes are needed, editing a piece of text to ensure that it forms a coherent and meaningful whole can sometimes involve making major changes or even rewriting. After the adjustments from the editing process have been made, the text is ready for proofreading.

## Benefits of Editing

The main benefits of editing a text are listed below:

- improves writing quality
- improves clarity, readability, organisation
- concise, cohesive, error-free text
- clearly communicates complex ideas
- clarifies scientific merit of research
- emphasises novelty and significance
- reduces stress of writing scientific publications
- reduces time spent on style, grammar
- increases favourable attitude of journal editors and reviewers
- reduces time and energy demanded of journal editors and reviewers
- increases likelihood of acceptance
- reduces demands for revision
- reduces time to publication
- publishes in journals with higher impact factors.

## Types of Editing

The types of editing are given below:

1. *Big Picture Editing:* This is also called *Developmental/Structural/Substantive/Content Editing.* This kind of editing involves moving large chunks of text around and possibly cutting some sections as well. It addresses the structure of a book. Substantive editing is a type of heavy editing that includes reviewing structure, style, grammar, spelling, and more. A substantive edit typically includes identifying/solving problems of clarity, reorganising sections/chapters to improve the order of your manuscript, and rewriting segments of the text to improve readability. Structural edits ensure your arguments are clear, your plot is developed, and your information is presented logically and accurately.

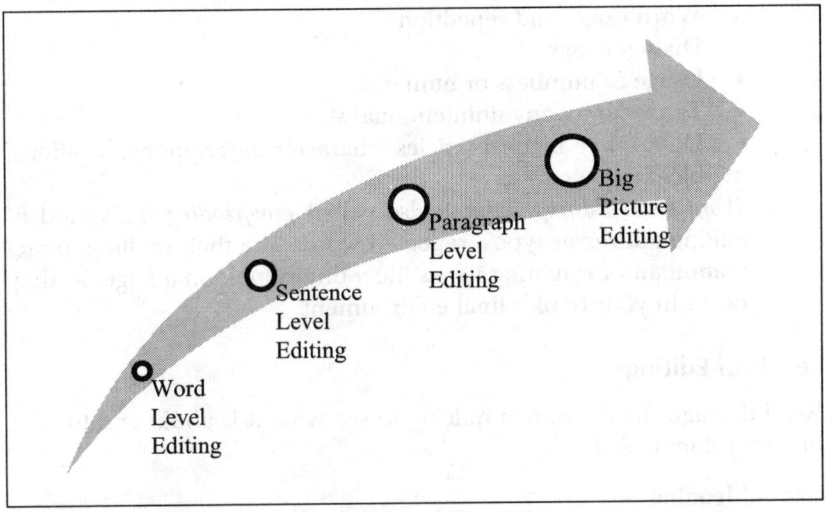


Figure 13.1: Ways to avoid Plagiarism

2. *Paragraph Level Editing:* This is also called *Stylistic/Line Editing.* This kind of editing involves recasting sentences for clarity and flow. It can also involve moving sentences around so that your meaning is clear. Stylistic editing always aims to preserve the author's voice, first and foremost. Suppose you have finished your manuscript, and everything is where it is supposed to be for best effect. What features of your finished book could indicate that it still might need a stylistic edit? Here are a few examples:
   - All your sentences are about the same length.
   - You use a lot of adjectives.
   - The vocabulary is not suited to the intended audience.
   - Your meaning is lost in too many big words or jargon.
   - Transitions from one paragraph to the next are awkward.
3. *Sentence Level Editing:* This is also called *Copy Editing.* This kind of editing addresses grammar, usage and consistency issues. Copy editing includes checking/correcting grammar, spelling, punctuation, syntax, and word usage while preserving the meaning and voice of your original text. It is entirely understandable that an author can lose track of many small details over the course of writing a book. A copy editor examines and corrects the following elements in the work:
   - Spelling
   - Grammar
   - Capitalisation

- Word usage and repetition
- Dialogue tags
- Usage of numbers or numerals
- Tense (to fix any unintentional shifts)
- Descriptive inconsistencies (character descriptions, locations, blocking, etc.).

4. *Word Level Editing:* This is also called *proofreading.* This kind of editing addresses typos, repeated words (the the), spelling, punctuation and formatting issues (how things look on a page) as they occur in your book's final environment.

## Levels of Editing

Read through the document quickly to see what it is about and to note major problems with

- Meaning
- Structure
- Content
- Words
- Grammar and spelling.

*Meaning*

- What is the manuscript as a whole trying to say?
- What is the overall message?
- What does each section or paragraph say?
  - ➢ Does each paragraph have a key sentence? Normally at the beginning or the end.
  - ➢ Consider writing run-in heads for each paragraph to focus its topic.

*Structure*

- Is it in the right order?
  - ➢ Does it flow logically?
  - ➢ Is it in the right order?
  - ➢ Does it follow logically from the previous text?
  - ➢ Use frequent headings.

*Content*

- Does it have the right information?
  - ➢ Is the information correct and complete?
  - ➢ Is it relevant?

*Words*

- Does it say it clearly?
  - ➢ Delete unnecessary words
  - ➢ Turn abstract nouns into verbs
  - ➢ Replace long words with short words
  - ➢ Get rid of jargon and abbreviations.

*Grammar and Spelling*

- Is the language correct?
  - ➢ Check for misspellings and poor grammar
  - ➢ Keep sentences short and varied.

## PROOFREADING

Proofreading is the final step in the editing process, and includes checking for any final errors and inconsistencies that may have slipped through during previous edits. This includes reading for typos, checking clarity, and reviewing basic grammar. Proofreading is a light edit and is meant to be a final clean up before publication.

Proofreading involves checking over the text in finer detail after the editing stage, to detect errors in spelling, punctuation, grammar and format. Proofreading is not merely casting a glance over what you have written: it requires concentration to disconnect your mind from the content of the text in order to focus on the language and layout. Errors can be difficult to spot, so it is essential to read the text word by word to ensure that you do not miss anything.

### Definitions of Proofreading

1. Proofreading is the process of finding and correcting mistakes in text before it is printed or put online.
2. It is the act of finding and correcting mistakes in copies of printed text before the final copies are printed.
3. Proofreading is the process of looking for and correcting errors in your work.
4. Proofreading is the process of finding and correcting spelling, grammar, punctuation and formatting errors.
5. Proofreading means examining your text carefully to find and correct typographical errors and mistakes in grammar, style, and spelling.

## Aims of Proofreading

The aim of proofreading is to spot and correct errors in:

- Inconsistencies in spelling, style and format
- Inconsistencies in layout and typography
- Grammar, punctuation and use of language
- Confusing or awkward page and word breaks
- Incorrect captioning on any illustrations and page numbers in the contents
- Anything missed at the editing stage.

## Common Mistakes with Grammar and Language Related to Proofreading

Here are some of the most common mistakes with grammar and language use that you should look out for when proofreading:

1. *Tense agreement:* mixing past and present tenses throughout a piece of text.
2. *Subject/verb agreement:* using plural verb conjugations with single subjects (e.g. 'one in ten people are ...' instead of 'one in ten people is ...').
3. *Pronoun/case agreement:* confusing the subject and object of the sentence (e.g. 'He sat between Bob and I' instead of 'He sat between Bob and me', or 'Me and John are working on that project' instead of 'John and I are working on that project').
4. Confusing similar words, such as the verbs 'imply' and 'infer', which describe different angles ('imply' is when the speaker/writer suggests something without explicitly stating it, and 'infer' is when the listener/reader logically deduces something from the information given by the speaker/writer).Another example is 'affect' and 'effect' ('affect' is normally used as a verb meaning 'to make a difference to', and 'effect' is used as both a noun and a verb – as a noun, it means 'a change that results from an action or cause', and as a verb it means 'to cause or bring about something').
5. Misuse of apostrophe before 's' at the end of a word, which is often incorrectly added before the 's' in plural words, e.g. 'The report's are finished' instead of 'The reports are finished' – an apostrophe should only be used before 's' to indicate possession (genitive case), e.g. 'The minister's cat is black' or 'My friend's desk is tidy'. However, in the case of the pronoun 'it', the possessive form is 'its'

without an apostrophe. Adding an apostrophe and 's' to 'it' indicates the abbreviated form of 'it is' or 'it has'. Look at the difference between 'The dog has lost its collar' (possessive form, i.e. the collar belongs to the dog) and 'Look over there – it's the dog without the collar' (it is). Apostrophes follow the added 's' when indicating possession by more than one person, e.g. Gents' toilet, the pupils' classroom.

6. Incorrect conjugation of modal verbs, such as 'should of' or 'would of' instead of 'should have' or 'would have'.
7. Words with similar spelling or pronunciation but different meanings, which cannot always be detected by automatic spelling and grammar checks, such as 'they're/'their'/'there', or 'where'/'were'/'we're'/'wear'.

## Common Errors related to Typography

Some other common errors relating to typography, style and format are:

- double spaces between characters, especially after a full stop
- wrong or missing headings or titles in a table, or captions
- misaligned columns or rows in a table
- misaligned margins
- incorrect text references
- inconsistent bullet formatting
- incorrect fonts/font sizes
- incorrect capitalisation
- footnotes or endnotes not matching references
- interchanging small words such as: of/off/on, and/an/as, or it/is/if
- incorrect use of trademarks
- missing numbers in a numbered sequence/list
- incorrect dates
- inconsistent use of abbreviations.

## Difference between Editing and Proofreading

The terms "proofreading" and "editing" are sometimes used interchangeably but there are significant differences between the two. Knowing which approach to utilize depends on what you need for a writing assignment. Are you looking for your content to improve in style and/or flow? Or do you need someone to purely remove spelling and grammatical errors? Refer to this chart to determine whether your writing needs editing or proofreading (or both):

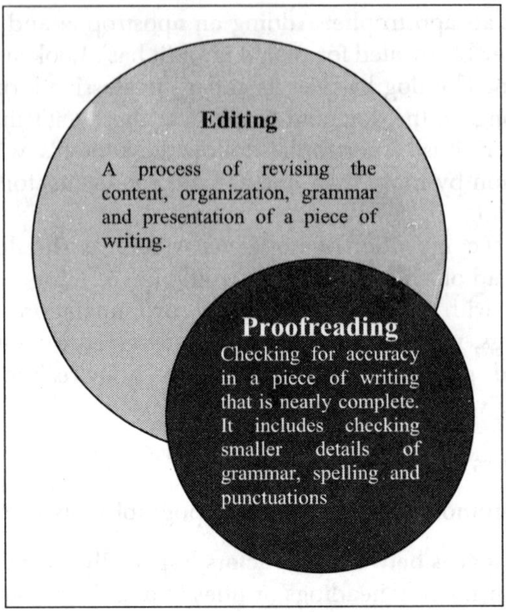


Figure 13.2: Proofreading is a part of editing but editing is much more than proofreading

Editing corrects issues at the core of writing like sentence construction and language clarity. A thorough editing will help improve the readability, clarity, and tone of the text. An editor will scrutinise and polish your writing for a smooth narration.

On the other hand, proofreading is a surface-level check. It is the final check performed on a document. A proof reader will look for misspellings, incorrect/missed punctuation, inconsistencies (textual and numerical), etc. The table below lists the main differences between proofreading and editing:

Table 13.1: Difference between Editing and Proofreading

| *Editing* | *Proofreading* |
|---|---|
| Primary goal is to ensure a written document makes total sense. | Primary goal is to create an error-free draft. |
| Reduces the word count of a document. | Only practiced once a document has been thoroughly edited. |
| Ensures the document is clear and easy to understand. | Reviews spelling and punctuation errors. |

*(Table 13.1 Contd.)*

| *Editing* | *Proofreading* |
|---|---|
| Reviews and changes text. | Ensures that English is used throughout. |
| Intends to change the overall flow of writing. | All grammatical errors are examined and corrected. |
| Improves the overall quality of writing. | Can be helpful when writer is not confident in their skills. |
| Entire sentences/paragraphs may be removed or rewritten. | Helpful when English is not the writer's first language. |
| Performed on the first draft of the document and continues till the draft is finalised. | Performed on the final draft of the document. |
| Addresses the core features of writing. | Addresses surface-level issues |
| Definition varies according to the scope of editing. | Universally accepted, consistent definition. |
| Enhances the language by making changes for clarity, readability, and smooth narration. | Eliminates misspellings, grammatical and punctuation errors, inconsistencies, formatting errors, etc. |
| Includes word reduction, if required. | Does not include word count reduction. |
| Overall quality of writing is improved. | Makes already good writing error-free. |
| Collaborative as it requires the editor to work with the author. | Does not require much collaboration with the author. |
| Slightly longer turnaround time (as the amount of work required is more). | Shorter turnaround time. |

# Annexture I

# Elements of Academic Writing

Writing in the academic style requires observing a certain set of rules and conventions. Academic writing is a well-structured product with careful considerations to the factors like audience, purpose, organisation, style, flow, and presentation and these factors are specific to who, why, and how questions.

*Who Question:* The audience, related to *who* question, is the reader or readers of the message of the writer. The selection of content, organisation, explanation, example supplied, and vocabulary in the writing are determined according to the nature of the audience.

*Why Question:* Similarly, the purpose is concerned with *why* question, and that guides the focus of writing. Purpose is the intention of the writing, or the main goal or message of the writer.

*How Question:* Finally, the *how* question is concerned with the aspects such as organisation, style, presentation, and flow of ideas. Dividing the writing text into three parts–introduction, body, and conclusion–helps make the writing well organized so that the readers feel comfortable in understanding the ideas or issues. Likewise, the style of writing needs to be clear and precise with formal grammar and formal vocabulary. Formal writing also needs avoidance of using the features like contraction, negation, weak endings, multi-word verbs, or redundancies. Similarly, good academic writing requires formal spelling, appropriate punctuation marks, and a good citation and referencing. It should have fluent flow in the presentation of ideas in such that it maintains cohesion (connectedness of the consecutive ideas using the techniques like repetition, substitution, and transition), and coherence (occurrence of the ideas contextually in orderly sequence).

The following are the most important elements which are responsible for good and purposeful academic writing:

- Types of Sentences
- Cohesion and Coherence
- Paragraph Structure
- Signposting Sentences
- Words, Phrases, Clauses and Sentences
- Common Expressions in Academic Writing
- Paragraph
- Transition Terms and Phrases in Academic Writing.

## Types of Sentences

*Defining Sentence?:* A sentence is a group of words that expresses a complete thought. Sentences are probably the most useful and important units of communication we have. Most of everything we say is in sentence form. Every sentence is a group of words but not every group of words is a sentence.

A complete sentence has:

- a *subject*–the person, place or thing the sentence is about.
- a *predicate*–tells what action the subject does.

Two examples of complete and simple sentences are as follows:

- Jack is under the tree.

Who or what the sentence is about? *Jack (subject)*
What is the subject doing in the sentence? *is under a tree (predicate)*

- The apple is very juicy.

Who or what the sentence is about? *The apple (subject)*
What does the sentence say about the subject? *is very juicy (predicate)*
Always remember that:

- A sentence must begin with a capital letter.
- A sentence must end with a punctuation mark (full stop, question mark, exclamation mark).

### *Types of Sentences (Function-wise)*

A combination of words which gives a complete meaning is called a sentence. There are various types of sentence depending upon its structure and function. On the basis of its function, a sentence has the following four kinds.

#### *Declarative/Assertive Sentence*

A sentence which declares or asserts a statement is called declarative/assertive sentence. It simply announces an idea. It has a plain statement. A declarative sentence ends with a full-stop mark or a period (.).
*Examples:*

- He bought a new laptop.
- They are playing football.
- He is going to college.
- I saw my friend in the street.
- He is studying a book.
- She is watching a movie.

#### *Interrogative Sentence*

A sentence that has a question is called Interrogative sentence. It is also called a question-sentence. An interrogative sentence ends with a question-mark (?).

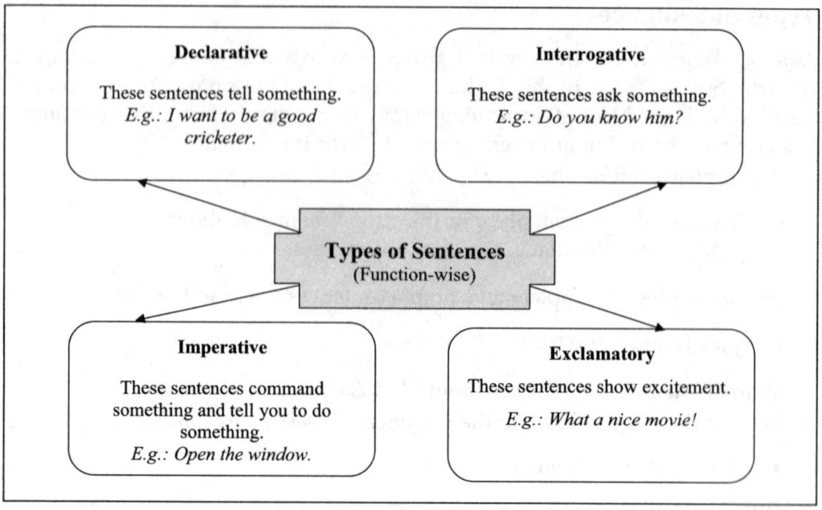


Figure I.1: Types of Sentences (Function-wise)

*Examples:*

- How are you?
- When will he come?
- Where are you going?
- What is your hobby?
- Will you help me?

## *Imperative Sentence*

A sentence which expresses a request, a command or an order is called imperative sentence. An imperative sentence mostly ends with a period (.). It can also sometimes ends with an exclamation mark (!) depending upon the emotion in the sentence.

*Examples:*

- Turn off the light. (command)
- Give me some food. (request)
- Please cooperate with me. (request)
- Don't smoke. (advice)
- Don't waste your time. (advice)
- Get out of the room. (command)

## *Exclamatory Sentence*

A sentence which expresses strong emotion or feeling is called an exclamatory sentence. It describes emotions or feelings of joy, anger, sorrow, surprise, excitement, frustration and appreciation. An exclamatory sentence ends with an exclamation mark (!).

*Examples:*

- Hurrah! We won the race! (emotions of joy)
- What a nice car! (emotions of surprise)
- Hurrah! I got selected for the job! (emotion of joy)
- How nicely they are dancing! (emotions of surprise)
- It's fantastic! (emotion of excitement)
- How intelligent you are! (emotions of surprise)

## *Types of Sentences (Structure-wise)*

A sentence can consist of one clause (independent clause) or more than one clause (independent and dependent clauses). The independent clause is also known as a main clause. The dependent clause is also known as a subordinate clause. Different sentences have different structures. There are four types of sentences depending upon on its structure or formation (the number of clauses in the sentence). Here we are explaining each type with examples so that you can understand the basic concept behind this.

### *Simple Sentence*

Simple sentences are also called independent clauses. They contain a subject, verb and a complete thought. This is the simplest form of sentences which is used in formal letters and essays. Let us see a few of its examples. The underlined part is subject and italic part is verb.

- I *love* my country.
- Imran *goes* to school and *studies* every day.
- Rahim and Malik *play* cricket.

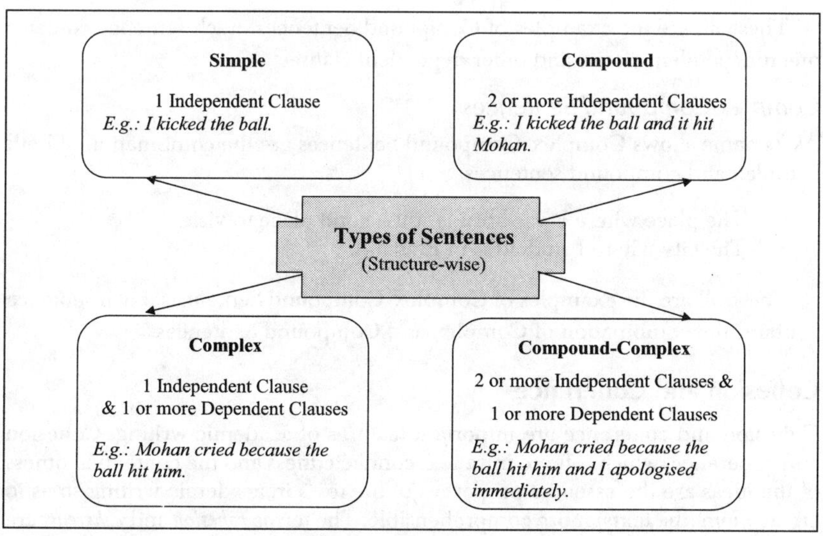


Figure I.2: Types of Sentences (Structure-wise)

These all are simple sentences. Note that sentence 2 contains compound verbs and sentence 3 contains compound subjects. So simple sentences may contain compound verbs and subjects.

### *Compound Sentences*

Compound Sentences contain two independent clauses which are joined by a coordinator. It is made up of two simple sentences which are not dependent on each other. Coordinators are for, and, but, or, so, yet. Let us see a few of its examples. The underlined part is subject, italic part is verb and bold italic part is coordinator.

- I *tried* to play football ***and*** my friend *tried* to play cricket.
- I *was playing* game, ***so*** Meena went to the market.
- Jasmine *was reading* ***but*** her mind was not there.

These all are compound sentences. Each sentence contains two independent clauses.

### *Complex Sentences*

Complex sentences have one independent clause and other dependent clauses. A complex sentence always have a subordinate such as although, after, when, since, because, who, whom and that.

Let us see a few of its examples:

- I returned my courier *after* I noticed the fault.
- John is studying hard *because* he has exam tomorrow.
- He is the owner of the mall *who* wants that shop.

These all are the examples of Compound Sentences. Each sentence contains one independent clause and other dependent clauses.

### *Complex-Compound Sentences*

As its name shows Complex-Compound Sentences are the combination of both complex and compound sentences.

- The place where I was born is still a good place to visit.
- The city where I studied is in England.

These all are the examples of Complex-Compound Sentences. Each sentence contains the combination of Complex and Compound Sentences.

## Cohesion and Coherence

Cohesion and coherence are important features of academic writing. Cohesion and coherence, which refer to intra-text connectedness and the contextual fitness of the ideas are the essential properties of the texts in academic writing so as to create them (the texts) more comprehensible. The terms *cohesion* and *coherence* are related to making the sense of language in the text/discourse analysis. Cohesion and coherence have significant role in the interpretation of message, and in the negotiation of meaning in the discourse. A good academic writing requires a good combination of cohesive ties and coherent features in the text.

Coherence means the connection of ideas at the idea level, and cohesion means the connection of ideas at the sentence level.

## *Cohesion*

Cohesion refers to the way texts use grammar and vocabulary to '*stick*' or '*glue*' ideas together. This is done through articles (a/an/the), pronouns (it/this/these/that/those/etc..), word families (analyse/ analysis) / summary nouns (approach/trend/issue) and synonyms (effect/consequence). In addition to these above key areas, relative clauses, ellipsis and connectors are also important. It is important for the parts of a written text to be connected together. Another word for this is cohesion. This word comes from the verb *cohere*, which means *'to stick together'*. Cohesion is therefore related to ensuring that the words and sentences you use stick together and make sense.

### *Methods of Cohesion*

Good cohesion is achieved through the following three main methods, each of which is described in more detail below:

1. *Repeated Words/Ideas:* One way to achieve cohesion is to repeat words, or to repeat ideas using different words (synonyms). Study the following example. Repeated words (or synonyms) are shown in bold.

   > *Cohesion is an important feature of academic writing. It can help ensure that your writing coheres or 'sticks together', which will make it easier for the reader to follow the main ideas in your essay or report. You can achieve good cohesion by paying attention to three important features. The first of these is repeated words. The second key feature is reference words. The final important aspect is transition signals.*

   In this example, the word *cohesion* is used several times, including as a verb (*coheres*). It is important, in academic writing, to avoid too much repetition, so using different word forms or synonyms is common. The word *writing* is also used several times, including the phrase *essay or report*, which is a synonym for *writing*. The words *important features* are also repeated, again using synonyms: *key feature, important aspect.*
2. *Reference Words:* Reference words are words which are used to refer to something which is mentioned elsewhere in the text, usually in a preceding sentence. The most common type is pronouns, such as 'it' or 'this' or 'these'. Study the previous example again. This time, the reference words are shown in bold.

> *Cohesion is an important feature of academic writing. It can help ensure that your writing coheres or 'sticks together', which will make it easier for the reader to follow the main ideas in your essay or report. You can achieve good cohesion by paying attention to three important features. The first of these is repeated words. The second key feature is reference words. The final important aspect is transition signals.*

The words *it* and *these* are reference words. The first of these, *it* refers to 'cohesion' used in the preceding sentence. The second *these* refer to 'three important features', also used in the sentences that precedes it.

3. *Transition Signals:* Transition signals, also called cohesive devices, are words which show the relationship between ideas. Some examples of transition signals are:
   - for example – used to give examples
   - in contrast – used to show a contrasting or opposite idea
   - first – used to show the first item in a list
   - as a result – used to show a result or effect.

   Study the previous example again. This time, the transition signals are shown in bold.

> *Cohesion is an important feature of academic writing. It can help ensure that your writing coheres or 'sticks together', which will make it easier for the reader to follow the main ideas in your essay or report. You can achieve good cohesion by paying attention to three important features. The first of these is repeated words. The second key feature is reference words. The final important aspect is transition signals.*

Here the transition signals simply give a list, relating to the *three* important features: *first, second,* and *final.*

4. *Substitution:* Substitution means using one or more words to replace (substitute) for one or more words used earlier in the text. Grammatically, it is similar to reference words, the main difference being that substitution is usually limited to the clause which follows the word(s) being substituted, whereas reference words can refer to something far back in the text. The most common words used for substitution are one, so, and auxiliary verbs such as do, have and be. The following is an example:

   Drinking alcohol before driving is illegal in many countries, since doing so can seriously impair one's ability to drive safely.

   In the above sentence, the phrase 'doing so' substitutes for the phrase 'drinking alcohol before driving' which appears at the beginning of the sentence.

5. *Ellipsis:* Ellipsis means leaving out one or more words, because the meaning is clear from the context. Ellipsis is sometimes called substitution by

zero, since essentially one or more words are substituted with no word taking their place.

Below is the example passage again. There is one example of ellipsis: the phrase 'The fourth is', which means 'The fourth (important feature) is', so the words 'important feature' have been omitted.

> Cohesion is an important feature of academic writing. It can help ensure that your writing coheres or 'sticks together', which will make it easier for the reader to follow the main ideas in your essay or report. You can achieve good cohesion by paying attention to five important features. The first of these is repeated words. The second key feature is reference words. The third one is transition signals. The fourth is substitution. The final important aspect is ellipsis.

## Coherence

Coherence is concerned with how a writer guides the reader through the argument using logical connectors. Basically, coherence refers to the "rhetorical" aspects of your writing, which include developing and supporting your argument (e.g. thesis statement development), synthesizing and integrating readings, organizing and clarifying ideas. It can be achieved by using signposting phrases. A signpost is a phrase that a writer or speaker uses to indicate different stages or parts of a written or spoken text.

*Example:* In contrast to the conclusion drawn by Smith (2004), Nguyen (2006) showed that the connection between the factors was not causal in most circumstances.

### *Cohesion vs. Coherence*

The words *'cohesion'* and *'coherence'* are often used together with a similar meaning, which relates to how an academic text sticks together to make a unified whole. Although they are similar, they are not the same. Cohesion relates to the micro level of the text, in other words, the words and sentences and how they cohere. Coherence, in contrast, relates to macro level features of a text which help it to stick together, such as topic sentences, thesis statement, the summary in the concluding paragraph (dealt with in the essay structure section), and other 'bigger' features including headings such as those used in reports.

## Paragraph Structure

A paragraph is an array of sentences prepared and related to a specific topic. The main structure of a paragraph is:

### *Topic Sentence(s)*

A paragraph consists of a main topic which is the main sentence or idea of a paragraph and tells its readers what the paragraph is going to talk about. It usually comes at the beginning of a paragraph, it is the first sentence of introduction that clearly states the main idea that is intended to progress. A topic sentence not only is the main sentence of a paragraph, it is the most common sentence in a written paragraph. Topic sentence is a preview for the reader, the kinds of info that the remaining paragraph is likely to contain. There are not many details in the sentence, but the sentence introduces an overall idea that is to be discussed later in the paragraph. Topic sentence functions as a thesis in a paragraph and further pushes the thesis of the essay and presents a debatable point.

### *Supporting Evidence/Analysis*

Supporting the evidence is to explicate the new idea and point that has been introduced. Elaboration may include investigation, illustration and persuasion etc. While writing a paragraph a student needs to find a sense of balance between evidence provided such as proofs, evidences, quotes, summary of actions/conspiracy, etc.and analysis which includes interpretation of evidence. The supporting sentences are the additional sentences in a paragraph. These sentence either:

- expand the main point
- describe key terms
- suggest explanations
- provide examples
- give added factors.

### *Concluding Sentence*

The last part of a paragraph is called the concluding sentence. A concluding sentence meets the requirements of the views expressed in order to connect the present paragraph to the subsequent paragraph. It is the summary of information that has been told so far. A concluding sentence is a good idea in case the paragraph is long which connects and draws connections of all the evidence stated. It is important that the claims you make in your conclusion are constant with the summary and body of the thesis.

### *Signposting Sentences*

Signposting sentences explain the logic of the writer's argument. They tell the reader what the writer is going to do at key points in his assignment. They are most useful when used in the following places:

- In the introduction
- At the beginning of a paragraph which develops a new idea
- At the beginning of a paragraph which expands on a previous idea
- At the beginning of a paragraph which offers a contrasting viewpoint
- At the end of a paragraph to sum up an idea
- In the conclusion.

### *Signposting Stems*

The following table should be used as a guide and as a way to get you thinking about how you present the thread of your argument. You may need to adapt certain words and phrases for your own purposes. You may also wish to add your own sentence stems to the list below:

Table I.1: Signposting Stems

| *Signposting stems for an introduction* |
|---|
| To understand the role of ... (your topic*) this essay aims to provide a discussion of ... (the ideas you will develop)<br>This essay seeks to investigate/evaluate/illustrate/discuss the impact of ... (your topic) in relation to ... (the ideas you will develop)<br>Firstly, this assignment examines ... (your topic) and its links with ... (your first idea) Next, it closely examines ... in relation to ... (your next idea) Finally, it focuses on ... and how this affects ...(your next idea). |
| *Signposting stems for a paragraph which introduces or develops a new idea* |
| One aspect which illustrates ... (your topic) can be identified as ... (the idea you want to develop)<br>The current debate about ... (your topic) identifies an interesting viewpoint on ...(the idea you want to develop)<br>This first/next/final section provides a general discussion of ...(the idea you want to develop). |
| *Signposting stems for a paragraph which expands upon a previous idea* |
| Building on from the idea that ... (mention previous idea), this section illustrates that ... (introduce your new idea).<br>To further understand the role of ...(your topic or your previous idea) this section explores the idea that ... (introduce your new idea)<br>Another line of thought on ... (your topic or your previous idea) demonstrates that ... (introduce your new idea). |
| *Signposting stems for a paragraph which offers a contrasting view* |
| However, another angle on this debate suggests that ... (introduce your contrasting idea)<br>In contrast to evidence which presents the view that ... (mention your previous idea) an alternative perspective illustrates that ... (introduce your contrasting idea)<br>However, not all research shows that ... (mention your previous idea). Some evidence agrees that ... (introduce your contrasting idea). |
| *Signposting stems to sum up an idea in a paragraph* |
| This evidence highlights that ... (sum up your idea)<br>There is general agreement that ... (sum up your idea)<br>The strength of such an approach is that ...(sum up your idea). |
| *Signposting stems for a conclusion* |
| Clearly, this essay has shown that the main factors which impact upon ... (your topic) are ...(summarise your main ideas)<br>The evidence presented in this assignment has shown that ... (mention the conclusions you have drawn)<br>To conclude, this assignment has addressed a number of significant issues which show that ... (mention the conclusions you have drawn). |

## Words, Phrases, Clauses and Sentences

Learning the basic rules of sentence construction will help you identify the parts of a sentence that make up the whole. This will help you to avoid punctuation errors like comma splices, as well as give you the knowledge to create more complicated sentence structures, which will improve the style of your writing.

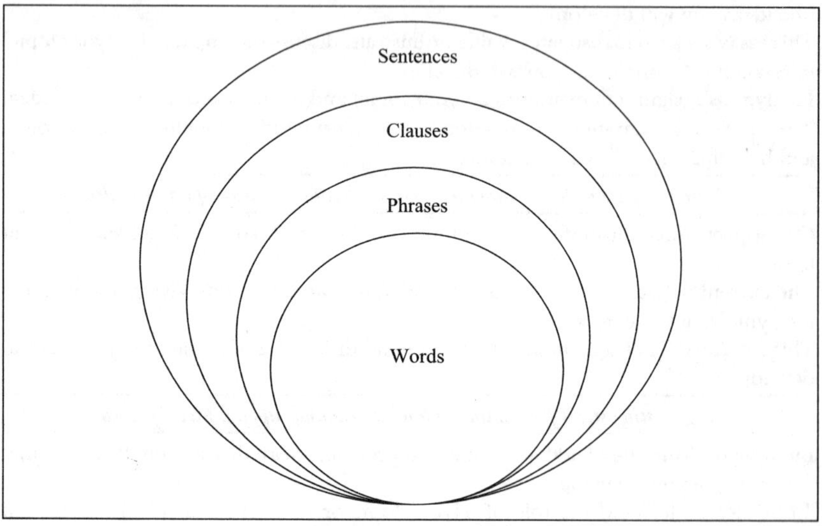


Figure I.3: Words, Phrases, Clauses and Sentences

### *Words*

Word is a letter or group of letters that has meaning when spoken or written. It is a unit of language, consisting of one or more spoken sounds or their written representation that functions as a principal carrier of meaning. Words are composed of one or more morphemes and are either the smallest units susceptible of independent use or consist of two or three such units combined under certain linking conditions. Words are usually separated by spaces in writing, and are distinguished phonologically, as by accent, in many languages.

### *Phrases*

A phrase is a group of words that form a single unit in a sentence, but does not include a subject, or a verb, or both. Since a phrase does not have a subject and/or verb, it does not form a complete idea or thought. Since a phrase does not contain a subject or verb, it cannot stand alone as a sentence and is considered a fragment.

Examples of Phrases

- closing the *door*
- under the *tree*

- because of his *illness*
- running past the *gate.*

In the above examples, you will see nouns (door, tree, illness, gate) and verbs or forms of a verb (closing, running), but the nouns are not functioning as the subject of a sentence and the verbs have no subject performing the action.

### Types of Phrases

1. *Noun:* his brand new bike; the stinky old cat
2. *Prepositional:* over the wall; in the bedroom
3. *Verb:* will be done; can swim
4. *Verbal:* There are 3 types of verbal phrases: participial, gerund, and infinitive.
    - *Participial:* The pond, *frozen over since early December*, is now safe for ice-skating.
    - *Gerund: Cramming for tests* is not a good study strategy.
    - *Infinitive:* My goal is *to be a teacher.*

## *Clauses*

According to the Oxford English Dictionary, a clause is *"a unit of grammatical organisation next below the sentence in rank and in traditional grammar said to consist of a subject and predicate."* A clause is a group of words that contain a subject and a predicate. A predicate is a word or phrase that describes the action or state of the subject. Predicates always include verbs.

### Types of Clauses

1. *Independent Clause:* Unlike a phrase, a clause can be a complete sentence, if it has a subject and a predicate. This type of clause is called an independent clause, as it can stand alone independently, with no other words or phrases needed to make it a complete sentence.

### Examples of independent clauses

- Fried green tomatoes are popular in the South.
- The door remained closed.
- The car sounded noisy.
- I stood on the shore.

2. *Dependent Clause:* Unlike an independent clause, a dependent clause cannot stand alone as a sentence, even though it has a subject and a verb. A dependent clause is dependent on an independent clause as part of either the subject or the predicate.

### Examples of Dependent Clauses

- while the wind was blowing.
- which I made by hand.
- although the room was cold.
- because the pool was deep.

These above examples begin with subordinate conjunctions– *while, which, although, because* – so do not form a complete thought. When we see subordinate conjunctions at the beginning of sentences, we expect extra information to complete the thought. These dependent clauses require other words to make a complete sentence.

### Sentences

According to the Oxford English Dictionary, a sentence is *"a set of words that is complete in itself, typically containing a subject and predicate, conveying a statement, question, exclamation, or command, and consisting of a main clause and sometimes one or more subordinate clauses."*A sentence is an independent clause that consists of a group of any number of words expressing a complete thought. It contains a subject and verb and can be a long sentence or as short as a one-word statement.

### Basic Elements of the Sentence

The sentence is made up of two basic parts: the subject and the predicate. The predicate may be simple, or it may be extremely complicated with its component parts.

| Sentence | = | Subject | + | Predicate |
|---|---|---|---|---|

- *The subject:* The simple subject is the noun or pronoun that identifies the person, place, or thing the sentence is about. The complete subject is the simple subject and all the words that modify it.
- *The predicate:* The predicate contains the verb that explains what the subject is or is doing. The simple predicate contains only the verb; the complete predicate contains the verb and all that follow, which can be direct object, indirect object, complement, modifier, prepositional phrase, or clause.

## Common Expressions in Academic Writing

Here is a list of key concepts, words, and phrases that academic writers may find useful if they are new to writing in educational context. It covers concepts and key words pertaining to the stages in the writing process, style, citation and reference, and other common expressions in academic writing.

*Account for:* Account for means that you provide an explanation for something. It is mostly used when you provide reasons for something.

*Analyse:* Analyse means that you examine a text in detail and discuss the components and parts of a text and talk about how they interact with each other.

*Argue:* Argue means that you say or write something in a way that you can convince or persuade your audience. In your argument, you will provide reasons or any explanation to support your argument. In some situations, you argue to prove your point.

*Assess:* Assess means that you evaluate or determine the value or quality of a given text. In an assessment, you will provide your own judgement of the value of a text and provide explanations and reasons for your evaluation.

*Characterise:* Characterise means that you describe the features and qualities of a concept or phenomenon. The features and qualities that you describe should be easily identifiable. When you characterise something, you make it different and distinguished from other things. For example, you could characterise one of the classes that you are taking as "interesting" or "boring".

*Classify:* Classify means that you organise information by categories or classes. In classification, you should be able to tell the difference between categories or classes that you use, and you should be able to explain why and how you classified the information.

*Comment:* Comment means that you say something about a text or a topic. When you comment on something, you make relevant remarks about a text or a topic and provide your ideas or opinions on the text or topic.

*Compare:* Compare means that you find some similarities or differences among two or more things and explain how they are similar or different. When you compare things, you will mostly focus on how you characterise or identify something by explaining similarities and differences.

*Consider:* Consider means that you think about something carefully. You will think about a variety of aspects of a certain topic to develop your ideas or opinions on the topic.

*Contrast:* Contrast means that you mainly find differences among two or more things and explain how different they are from each other. When you contrast things, it is important for you to explain how you identified differences among the things that you contrast.

*Criticise:* Criticise means that you find something that you disapprove of based on your evaluation of a given text or material. When you criticise certain texts, opinions, and ideas, you will make sure to find faults and explain why you disapprove of the things that you found. You will provide reasons and evidence to explain why you criticise certain ideas.

*Define:* Define means that you explain the meaning of certain words or concepts. While you are explaining the meaning, you will identify the main features and characteristics of certain words and concepts and explain what makes them different from other words or concepts.

*Demonstrate:* Demonstrate means that you prove something by showing explanations, illustrations, and supporting evidence.

*Describe:* Describe means that you explain and specify certain objects or ideas in a way that your audience can easily understand your point.

*Differentiate between:* When you differentiate between items it means that you make a distinction between two or more things. You will tell the difference between the things and explain how and why you differentiated them.

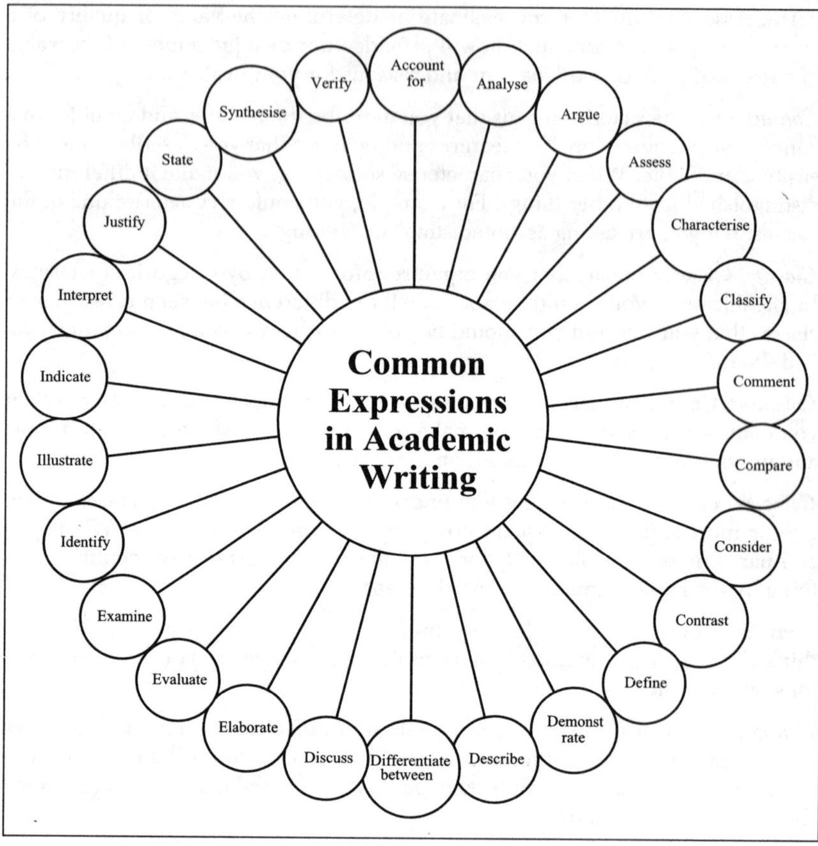


Figure I.4: Common Expressions in Academic Writing

*Discuss:* Discuss means that you think about certain aspects of a topic and explore them in detail in your text. You will often express your opinions or arguments based on the discussion.

*Elaborate:* Elaborate means that you explain something in more and at greater length. When you elaborate on something, you will illustrate an idea with rich description and explanations for it.

*Evaluate:* Evaluate means that you assess the value of certain texts or ideas based on your own judgement. In an evaluation of a text, you will see how well the ideas are developed according to certain contexts and audiences.

*Examine:* Examine means that you look at certain texts or ideas carefully and critically study them so you can make your own evaluation or arguments based on your judgement from the examination.

*Identify:* Identify means that you define certain concepts by providing identifying characteristics of them, or provide descriptions or explanations for certain concepts or words. For example, some assignments will ask you to "identify the meaning of concept A".

*Illustrate:* Illustrate means that you explain and describe certain characteristics or aspects of something. When you illustrate something in your text, you will provide relevant explanations and examples to make it clearer and understandable for your audiences.

*Indicate:* Indicate means that you point out or show something. Some assignments will ask you to indicate specific information about something, such as "indicate the name of the author, or book" and some assignments will ask you to "indicate the meaning of certain ideas."

*Interpret:* Interpret means that you explain your understanding of certain ideas in a more comprehensive way. Some assignments will ask you to write about your own interpretation of certain data or texts. You will provide your own judgement and evaluation of them and explain how and why you were able to interpret a given subject.

*Justify:* Justify means that you prove your point by explaining reasons for it. You will defend your ideas by providing logical explanation to justify your point.

*State:* State means that you clearly express something about certain topics. For example, some assignments will ask you to state your opinions.

*Synthesise:* Synthesise means that you combine information in a way that could coherently and effectively present your ideas or opinions. In some assignments, you will be required to synthesise sources or ideas. This means that you will combine the sources and ideas and organise them in a way that is appropriate and approachable to your readers.

*Verify:* Verify means that you prove something by showing evidence or information. It could also mean that you check and see to make sure certain information is correct and accurate.

## Paragraph

When we write essays, research papers, books, etc., we need to write paragraphs. A paragraph is a unit of writing in a larger body of work. A paragraph expresses a particular topic or theme. A paragraph is a group of sentences about one topic. It contains a topic sentence, supporting details and a concluding sentence. The sentences follow one another from the beginning to the end of the paragraph. A paragraph is usually part of a longer piece of writing, such as a letter or essay. Paragraphs are the building blocks of papers.

The purpose of a paragraph is to express a speaker's thoughts on a particular point in a clear way that is unique and specific to that paragraph. In other words, paragraphs should not be mixing thoughts or ideas. When a new idea is introduced, generally, a writer will introduce a new paragraph.

## Definitions of Paragraph

1. A paragraph is defined as *"a group of sentences or a single sentence that forms a unit"*.

### Parts of a Paragraph

A paragraph has three main parts: (1) a topic sentence (main idea), (2) supporting sentences (body), and (3) a concluding sentence (conclusion).

*The Topic Sentence:* The topic sentence is usually the first sentence of the paragraph. It states the main idea of the paragraph. A good topic sentence tells the reader exactly what the rest of the paragraph will be about.

*The Supporting Sentences:* The supporting sentences are the middle sentences of the paragraph. They provide details such as explanations or examples that expand on or support the topic sentence. Supporting sentences are sometimes connected by transition words or phrases.

*The Concluding Sentence:* A concluding sentence is sometimes used in longer paragraphs to sum up the ideas presented. It expresses the same idea as the topic sentence but in different words. It can start with a transition such as clearly or in conclusion.

## Types of Paragraphs

The type of paragraph we write will depend on a number of factors given below:

- The kind of writing we are producing. For example, paragraphs in a report tend to have a different purpose than paragraphs in an essay.

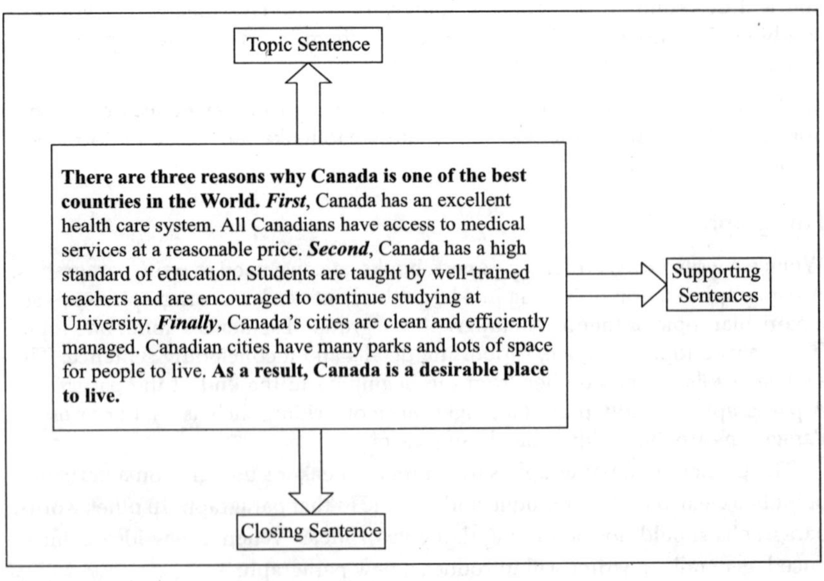


Figure I.5: Topic Sentence, Supporting Sentence and Closing Sentence

- The position of the paragraph in a longer piece of writing. A body paragraph in an essay has a different purpose to an introduction or conclusion.
- The logical order of the ideas and information in our writing. We may be presenting an argument, organising facts, comparing and contrasting ideas, defining a key concept, explaining the steps in a process, giving an example or recounting a series of events.

### *Argument Paragraph*

An argument paragraph presents a point of view, and provides evidence to support the position taken by the writer. Evidence to support the position can include reasons, personal experience, statistics, confirmed facts and expert research.

---

**ARGUE**

A paragraph can be used to argue for or against a point of view. Each paragraph should focus on developing one main point for/or against the position.

*Topic Sentence*
Introduce the argument and position for/or against.
*Supporting Sentences*
Develop the reasons for your position and present facts and examples to support this; address any counter-arguments.
*Conclusion*
restate position.

*Useful transitional words and phrases*

- *For giving reasons:* first, second, third, another, next, last, finally, because, since, for
- *For counter-argument:* but, however, of course, nevertheless, although, despite
- *For concluding:* therefore, as a result, in conclusion, thus

---

### *Classification Paragraph*

In this type of paragraph, separate items are grouped together according to shared characteristics.

---

**COMPARE or CONTRAST**

This paragraph structure can be used to organise information, items or ideas into categories. The organisation of information will depend on your purpose and subject area.

*Topic Sentence*
Introduce the items being classified and/or the categories for classification.
*Supporting Sentences*
Provide more information about the items and how their characteristics fit into a particular category.
*Conclusion*
Repeat what classification the item or category belongs to.

*Useful transitional words and phrases*
Can be divided, Can be classified, Can be categorised, The first/second/third

---

### Compare or Contrast Paragraph

A compare and/or contrast paragraph is required if you are asked to examine similarities and/or differences. Compare focuses on similarities. Contrast focuses on differences.

---

**CLASSIFY**

Use this paragraph structure if you need to examine similarities and differences. This paragraph structure is useful for literature reviews and reports.

*Topic Sentence*
Introduce the items to be compared or contrasted, no similarity or difference.
*Supporting Sentences*
Identify, describe, and discuss any similarities or differences.
*Conclusion*
Summarise and interpret the similarities and differences discussed.

*Useful transitional words and phrases*

- *For comparison:* similar to, similarly, in the same way, like, equally, again, also, too
- *For Contrast:* in contrast, on the other hand, different from, whereas, while, unlike, but, although, however, conversely, yet, unlike.

---

### Definition Paragraph

The starting point for a definition paragraph is a simple definition in the first sentence (the topic sentence). Support sentences then give more information such as examples, description and explanation.

---

**DEFINE**

Use this paragraph structure when you need to define a concept and demonstrate an understanding of how it relates to a particular context or discipline.

*Topic Sentence*
Provide a simple definition of a concept.
*Supporting Sentences*
Provide more information through description, explanation and examples; makes links between the concept and how it applies to a particular context or field.
*Conclusion*
Not necessary; can transition to the next paragraph if related to the concept.

*Useful transitional words and phrases*
For example, for instance, an illustration of this, another example, firstly, the first step, secondly, the second step, finally, the final step.

---

### Description Paragraph

A description paragraph is used to write about how something looks, sounds, tastes, smells or feels. It includes specific details of the most important features

**DESCRIBE**

Use this paragraph structure if you are asked to provide information about something.

*Topic Sentence*
Introduce the item to be described.
*Supporting Sentences*
Provide specific and detailed information about the item's characteristics and functions.
*Conclusion*
Not necessary; can transition to the next paragraph if related to the item described.

*Useful transitional words and phrases*
In the foreground, in the middle distance, in the background, in the far distance, next to, near, up, down, between, beneath, above, below, on top of, left/right, centre, front, back, middle, in the interior, on the exterior, on the inside, on the outside, surrounding.

### *Explanation Paragraph*

An explanation paragraph is required if you are asked to describe how something works, or how something happens.

**EXPLAIN**

Use this paragraph structure if you need to explain how something works or the steps in a process.

*Topic Sentence*
Introduce what will be explained.
*Supporting Sentences*
Explain each of the steps involved in the process, in order that the steps are to be performed. Includes information about how something happens and why.
*Conclusion*
Provide a brief summary of the process.

*Useful transitional words and phrases*
At first, initially, the first step, while, at the same time, the second/third/next step, after, next, finally, eventually, the final/last step.

### *Illustration Paragraph*

In an illustration paragraph, specific examples are used to clarify and support a general statement.

**ILLUSTRATE**

Use this paragraph structure when you need to clarify a particular idea by offering specific examples and showing how they relate to your main point.

*Topic Sentence*
State a general idea.
*Supporting Sentences*
Introduce examples to support the idea.
*Conclusion*
Make a link between the examples and the general idea.

*Useful transitional words and phrases*
For example, for instance, an illustration of this, another example.

### *Principles of Good Paragraphs*

The following are the principles of good paragraph:

- A good paragraph should have variety and order.
- Good paragraph benefits students organise their ideas into a consistent paragraph.
- Begin a paragraph with a topic sentence and end it in conformity with the beginning.
- A descriptive paragraph uses precise details creating a clear impression of person, place, object and time.
- An example paragraph illustrates a point with examples.
- It helps show the structure of conceptions and idea.
- It validates in a actual way how evidence is connected.
- A paragraph will have a single sentence that visibly speaks its point.
- A comparison paragraph expresses similarities between two or more items.
- A process paragraph portrays or clarifies a method using chronology.
- A classification paragraph clusters items into classifications.
- A narrative paragraph uses a story or part of a story to develop ideas.

## Transition Terms and Phrases in Academic Writing

### *Meaning of Transitions*

A transition is a change from one idea to another idea in writing or speaking and can be achieved using transition terms or phrases. These are most often placed at the beginning of sentences, independent clauses, and paragraphs and thus establish a specific relationship between ideas or groups of ideas. Transitions are used to create "flow" in paper and make its logical development clearer to readers.

### *Meaning of Transition Terms/Words and Phrases*

As a "part of speech" transition terms/words and phrases are used to link words, phrases or sentences. They help the reader to progress from one idea (expressed by the author) to the next idea. Thus, they help to build up coherent relationships within the text.

### *Advantages of Transition Words and Phrases*

- Transition words and phrases are used in order to organise the thoughts and ideas in a particular text.
- A transition word can serve as a bridge that takes the readers from one idea to another and will help improve the overall coherence of the write-up.
- They provide a signal to the reader about what is coming next in the writing.

### *Categories of Transition Terms and Phrases*

Transition terms and phrases accomplish many different objectives. We can divide all transitions into four basic categories:

Table I.2: Important Additive Transition Terms and Phrases

| *Purpose* | *Common Additive Transition Terms/Words* | *Common Additive Transition Phrases* | *Examples of Additive Transitions in Academic Writing* |
|---|---|---|---|
| Adding Information | Also; Additionally; Furthermore; Moreover | In addition to; As well as; In fact; Not only…but also; As a matter of fact | "Furthermore, the data shows that X is a significant factor." "In addition to the above-mentioned study, Rogers also presents…" |
| Introducing/ Highlighting | Particularly; Notably; Especially | For example/instance; To illustrate; In particular; One example (of this is) | "Notably, only two species of this fish survive." "One example of thisphenomenon is X." |
| Referencing | Considering (this); Concerning (this); Regarding (this) | As for (this); The fact that; With regards to (this); On the subject of (this); Looking at (this information) | "Considering the amount of research in this area, little evidence has been found." "With regards to the Blue Whale, its teeth are also the largest of any mammal." |
| Showing Similarity | Similarly; Likewise; Equally | By the same token; In the same way; In a similar way | "Likewise, the algorithm was applied to Y." "By the same token, this principle can be applied to Z." |
| Clarifying/ Identifying Important Information | Specifically; Namely | That is (to say); In other words; (To) put (it) another way; What this means is; This means (that) | "There are two factors: namely, X and Y." "In other words, the fall of the Empire was caused by over-expansion." |

*Additive Transitions:* These terms signal that new information is being added (between both sentences and paragraphs); introduce or highlight information; refer to something that was just mentioned; add similar situation; or identify certain information as important.

*Adversative Transitions:* These terms and phrases distinguish facts, arguments, and other information, whether by contrasting and showing differences; by conceding points or making counter-arguments; by dismissing the importance of a fact or argument; or replacing and suggesting alternatives.

*Causal Transitions:* These terms and phrases signal the reasons, conditions, purposes, circumstances, and cause-and-effect relationships. These transitions often come after an important point in the paper has been established or to explore hypothetical relationships or circumstances.

*Sequential Transitions:*These transition terms and phrases organise your paper by numerical sequence; by showing continuation in thought or action; by referring to previously-mentioned information; by indicating digressions; and, finally, by concluding and summing up your paper. Sequential transitions are essential to creating structure and helping the reader understand the logical development through your paper's methods, results, and analysis.

## *List of Transition Words*

The list shown below provides a wide variety of transition words and phrases that you can use depending on the kind of relationship that you want to convey.

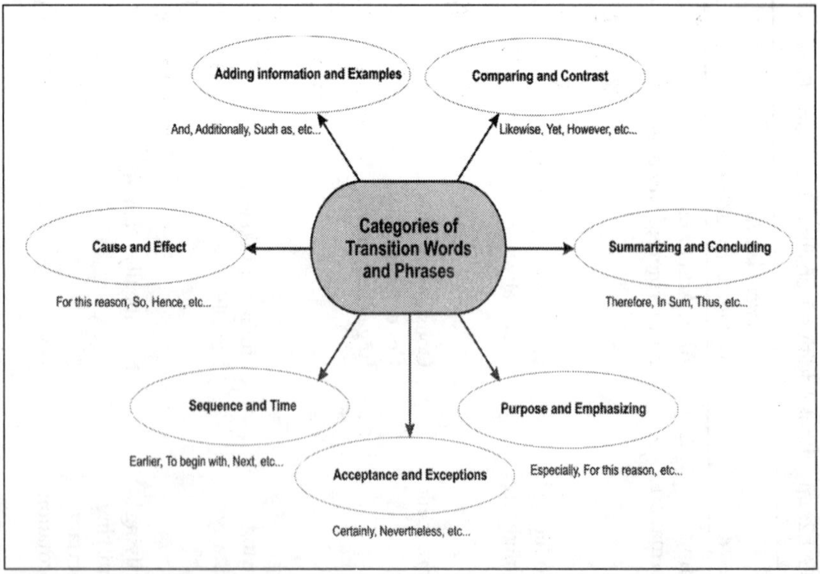


Figure I.6: Categories of Transition Words and Phrases

Table I.3: Important Adversative Transition Terms and Phrases

| *Purpose* | *Common Adversative Transitions Terms* | *Common Adversative Transitions Phrases* | *Examples of Adversative Transitions in Academic Writing* |
|---|---|---|---|
| Contrasting/ Showing conflict | But;<br>Still;<br>However;<br>While;<br>Whereas;<br>Conversely;<br>(and) yet | In contrast;<br>On the contrary;<br>On the other hand;<br>…when in fact;<br>By way of contrast | "However, there is still more research needed."<br>"On the other hand, the 1997 study does not recognise these outcomes." |
| Distinguishing/ Emphasising | Indeed;<br>Besides;<br>Significantly;<br>Primarily | Even more;<br>Above all;<br>More/Most importantly | "Indeed, a placebo is essential to any pharmaceutical study."<br>"Most importantly, the X enzyme increased." |
| Conceding a point | Nevertheless;<br>Nonetheless;<br>Although;<br>Despite (this);<br>However;<br>Regardless (of this);<br>Admittedly | Even so;<br>Even though;<br>In spite of (this);<br>Notwithstanding (this);<br>Be that as it may | "Nevertheless, X is still an important factor."<br>"In spite of this fact, New York still has a high standard of living."<br>"Although this may be true, there are still other factors to consider." |
| Dismissing an argument or assertion | Regardless (of) | Either way;<br>In any case;<br>In any event;<br>Whatever happens;<br>All the same;<br>At any rate<br>(or) at least | "Regardless of the result, this fact is true."<br>"Either way, the effect is the same."<br>"In any event, this will not change the public's view." |
| Replacing/ Indicating an Alternative | Instead (of);<br>(or) rather; | | "Instead of using X, the scientists used Z."<br>"Or rather, why not implement a brand new policy?" |

Table I.4: Important Causal Transition Terms and Phrases

| *Purpose* | *Common Causal Transition Terms* | *Common Causal Transition Phrases* | *Examples of Causal Transitions in Academic Writing* |
|---|---|---|---|
| Showing Cause or Reason | Since;<br>For;<br>As;<br>Because (of the fact that) | Due to (the fact that);<br>For the reason that;<br>Owing to (the fact); | "Since the original sample group was too small, researchers called for more participants."<br>"Due to budgetary demands, funding will be cut in half." |
| Explaining the Conditions | If…then;<br>Unless;<br>Granting (that);<br>Granted (that);<br>Provided (that) | In the event that;<br>As/So long as;<br>Only if | "Unless these conditions change, more will need to be done."<br>"As long as there is oxygen, there will be oxygenation." |
| Showing the Effects/Results | Consequently;<br>Therefore;<br>Thus;<br>Accordingly;<br>Because (of this) | As a result (of this);<br>For this reason;<br>As a consequence;<br>So much (so) that | "Therefore, we can conclude that this was an asymmetric catalysis."<br>"As a consequence, many consumers began to demand safer products." |
| Showing the Purpose | | For the purpose(s) of;<br>With (this fact) in mind;<br>In the hope that;<br>In order that/to;<br>So as to | "For the purpose of following standards, X rule was observed."<br>"With the current state of pandas in mind, this study focused on preservation." |
| Highlighting the Importance of Circumstances | Otherwise | Under those circumstances;<br>That being the case;<br>In that case;<br>If so;<br>All else being equal | "Otherwise, this effect will continue into the future."<br>"All else being equal, the economic impact of this law seems positive." |

Table I.5: Important Sequential Transition Terms and Phrases

| *Purpose* | *Common Sequential Transition Terms* | *Common Sequential Transition Phrases* | *Examples of Sequential Transitions in Academic Writing* |
|---|---|---|---|
| Organising by Number | Initially; Secondly; Thirdly; (First/Second/Third); Last | First of all; To start with; In the (first/second/third) place | "Initially, subjects were asked to write their names." "First of all, dolphins are the smartest creatures in the sea." |
| Showing Continuation | Subsequently; Previously; Afterwards; Eventually; Next; After (this) | | "Subsequently, subjects were taken to their rooms." "Afterwards, they were asked about their experiences." |
| Summarising/ Repeating Information | (Once) again; Summarising (this) | To repeat; As (was) stated before; As (was) mentioned earlier/above | "Summarising this data, it becomes evident that there is a pattern." "As mentioned earlier, pollution has become an increasing problem." |
| Digression/ Resumption | Incidentally; Coincidentally; Anyway | By the way; To resume; Returning to the subject; At any rate | "Coincidentally, the methods used in the two studies were similar." "Returning to the subject, this section will analyse the results." |
| Concluding/ Summarising | Thus; Hence; Ultimately; Finally; Therefore; Altogether; Overall; Consequently | To conclude; As a final point; In conclusion; Given these points; In summary; To sum up | "Ultimately, these results will be valuable to the study of X." "In conclusion, there are three things to keep in mind–A, B, and C." |

Table I.6: Categories of Transition Words and Phrases

| *Transition Words Used for Adding Information* | *Transition Words Used to Show Contrast* | *Transition Words Used in Giving Examples* | *Transition Words Used in Summarising or Concluding* | *Transition Words Used to Show Sequence* | *Transition Words Used to Indicate Purpose* |
|---|---|---|---|---|---|
| and | but | for example | to sum up | after that | so that |
| additionally | although | in other words | therefore | in the second place | to this end |
| afterward | conversely | an analogy | accordingly | following that | for this purpose |
| equally important | Though this may be | to show | to summarise | second/secondly | for that reason |
| moreover | despite | for one thing | as has been noted | immediately | because of this |
| after | however | consider | in short | following | |
| again | in contrast | to bring to light | as I have said | on the next occasion | |
| also | inspite of | take the case of | in brief | later on | |
| first | counter to | as an example | as I have shown | in turn | |
| at last | instead | consider as an illustration | on the whole | next | |
| thus | otherwise | in one example | summing up | at the beginning | |
| at the same time | namely | for instance | to conclude | at the onset | |
| besides | regardless | in this situation | it follows | commencing with | |
| embracing | but another | on this occasion | as a consequence | from this point | |
| initially | a clear difference | to illuminate | as a result | in the first place | |
| concurrently | nonetheless | to illustrate | consequently | to begin with | |
| as mentioned earlier | a distinct difference | that is | hence | initially | |
| furthermore | rather | such as | to sum up | at first | |
| eventually | a strong distinction | suppose that | in conclusion | once upon a time | |
| at length | at the same time | specifically | therefore | starting with | |
| extending | conversely | to be exact | in sum | | |
| further | nevertheless | to exemplify | so | | |
| in addition | not withstanding | in particular | then | | |
| and then | on the other hand | to demonstrate | thus | | |
| in conclusion | indeed | as an illustration | | | |
| too | still | | | | |
| other | though | | | | |

| *Transition Words Used for Adding Information* | *Transition Words Used to Show Contrast* | *Transition Words Used in Giving Examples* | *Transition Words Used in Summarising or Concluding* | *Transition Words Used to Show Sequence* | *Transition Words Used to Indicate Purpose* |
|---|---|---|---|---|---|
| finally | yet | | | | |
| including | the reverse of | | | | |
| another | to oppose | | | | |
| encompassing | to differentiate | | | | |
| later | even though | | | | |
| likewise | on the contrary | | | | |
| meanwhile | for all that | | | | |
| as was previously stated | and yet | | | | |
| next | despite the fact that | | | | |
| overall | contrarily | | | | |
| presently | while | | | | |
| previously | or | | | | |
| second | although this may be true | | | | |
| consequently | even so | | | | |
| what is more | by contrast | | | | |
| since | up against | | | | |
| soon | in opposition to | | | | |
| subsequently | an opposing view | | | | |
| supplementing | balanced against | | | | |
| then | against | | | | |
| simultaneously | alternatively | | | | |
| now | | | | | |
| following this | | | | | |
| so too | | | | | |
| to begin with | | | | | |
| while | | | | | |
| a further nor | | | | | |
| moreover | | | | | |
| last | | | | | |

Table I.7: Categories of Transition Words and Phrases

| *Transition Words Used to Show Concession/ Acceptance of an Idea* | *Transition Words Used to Indicate Time Order* | *Transition Words Used to Show Cause and Effect* | *Transition Words Used to Emphasise* | *Transition Words Used in Comparing* | *Transition Words Used to State an Exception* |
|---|---|---|---|---|---|
| although this may be | earlier | therefore | most important of all | correspondingly | sometimes |
| true | formerly | thus | certainly | however | in spite of |
| although it is true that | yesterday | in view of | moreover | in contrast | yet |
| admittedly | recently | it follows that | decidedly | in like manner | nevertheless |
| naturally | previously | so | in fact | equal | despite |
| granted | of late | on subsequently | definitely | equally important | once in a while |
| of course | not long ago | account of | especially | equivalent | however |
| certainly | at present | otherwise | of great concern | of little difference | still |
| it is true that | in the past | owing to | furthermore | in the same way | of course. |
| true. | preceding | the end result | more emphatically | identical | |
| | at the same time | the outcome | increasingly | nevertheless | |
| | immediately | then | important | in a similar | |
| | right away | for this purpose | indeed | fashion | |
| | at this moment | henceforth | equally important | in comparison | |
| | until now | due to | most of all | likewise | |
| | simultaneously | by reason of | of major concern | as well as | |
| | currently | furthermore | certainly | balanced against | |
| | by now | consequently | above all | compared to | |
| | concurrently | hence | after all | correlate | |
| | after a short while | caused by | decidedly | consistent with | |
| | hereafter | because of this | especially | along the same lines | |
| | thereafter | for this reason. | actually | correspondingly | |
| | soon after | | definitely | comparable. | |
| | in the future | | as a matter of fact. | | |
| | afterward | | | | |
| | later on | | | | |
| | while | | | | |
| | right after. | | | | |

# Annexture II

# Language Accuracy in Academic Writing

Academic writing is linear, which means it has one central point or theme with every part contributing to the main line of argument, without digressions or repetitions. Its objective is to inform rather than entertain. As well as it is in the standard written form of the language. Academic writing is to some extent: complex, formal, objective, explicit, hedged and responsible. It uses language precisely and accurately. It should be well organised and planned.

Academic writing requires precise clear structure so the reader can follow the argument as clearly as possible. Accuracy in academic writing refers to how the writer uses the correct language system. It includes correct use of grammar, pronunciation and vocabulary. Academic writing should be accurate. Academic writers use a lot of technical language in their discipline and they must make sure that they do not use the wrong terms. Writing should be accurate. In academic writing you need to be accurate in your use of vocabulary. The following are the most important elements of writing which are responsible for good and purposeful academic writing:

- Sentence Structure
- Parts of Speech
- Punctuation
- Tenses
- Articles
- Modifiers
- Determiners
- Capitalisation.

## Sentence Structure

In grammar, a sentence is the basic grammatical unit. It contains a group of words and expresses a complete thought. A sentence is a self-contained unit of meaning. A sentence is a collection of words that convey sense or meaning and is formed according to the logic of grammar. Clear, short sentences are preferable and more effective, than long, complex ones.

Writing is constructed by putting sentences in sequence, one after another and, if a single sentence is read aloud, it should be understandable. Meaning should flow from one sentence to the next, carrying the argument or point of view forward in a clear and concise manner.

Sentence structure is the way a sentence is arranged, grammatically. The sentence structure of writing includes where the *noun* and *verb* fall within an individual sentence. Every word in a sentence serves a specific purpose within the structure of that particular sentence. According to rules of grammar, sentence structure can sometimes be quite complicated. For the sake of simplicity, however, the basic parts of a sentence are discussed here:

### *Parts of Sentences*

The parts of a sentence are discussed below:

(A) *Subject:* Subject is a noun or a pronoun used in a sentence. It is an agent in the sentence which does some action in the sentence. The *subject* of a sentence is the person, place, or thing that is performing the action of the sentence. The subject represents what or whom the sentence is about. The simple subject usually contains a noun or pronoun and can include modifying words, phrases, or clauses.

Read the following examples.

- *He* is writing a poem.
- *She* is laughing.
- *They* are playing football.
- *David* works in a factory.

It can be seen in the above examples, that the subjects (he, she, they, David) are performing certain action.

(B) *Predicate:* Predicate is the part of a sentence which says something about the subject of the sentence. Predicate is usually a large part of the sentence. The part of sentence, other than the subject, is called predicate of the sentence. The *predicate* expresses action or being within the sentence. The simple predicate contains the verb and can also contain modifying words, phrases, or clauses.

The underlined part in the examples given below is the predicate of each sentence.

- He *is writing a poem.*
- She *is laughing.*
- They *are playing football.*
- David *works in a factory.*

It can be seen in the above examples, that underlined part of each sentence is predicate part of the same sentence as it is telling something about the subject.

The subject and predicate make up the two basic structural parts of any complete sentence. In addition, there are other elements, contained within the subject or predicate that adds meaning or detail. These elements include the *Object* (*direct object* and, *indirect object)*, and *subject complement.* All of these elements can

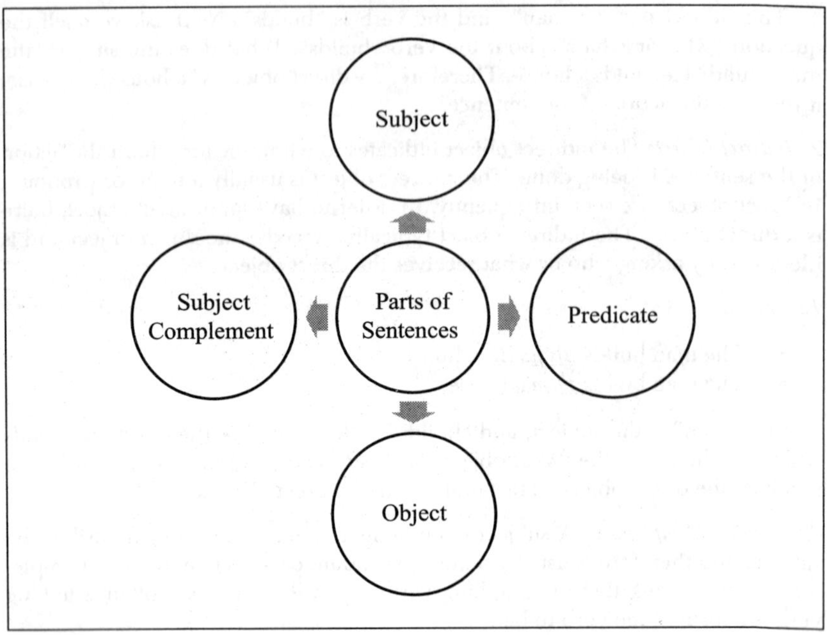


Figure II.1: Parts of Sentences

be expanded and further combined into simple, compound, complex, or compound/complex sentences.

(C) *Object:* Unlike the subject who acts, an object is a noun or a pronoun in a sentence which is acted upon. The subject is the actor of the sentence who acts upon the object. The object is a noun or a pronoun that is acted upon by the subject. The object is the person or a thing upon whom or upon which the action of the verb is carried out. In simple words, an object is the receiver of the verb.

*Example:* 'The teacher is teaching the ***students***.' The one who is taught is the object (receiving the action), hence students is the object.

1. *Direct Object:* The direct object receives the action of the sentence. The direct object is usually a noun, pronoun, clause or phrase that follows transitive verbs (action verbs that require something or someone to receive the action). You can identify the direct object by using this simple formula: *Subject + verb + who? or what? = Direct Object*

*Examples:*

- The man builds *a house*.
- The man builds *it*.

The subject is "The man", and the verb is "builds". Next ask yourself the question "who or what?" about the verb "builds". What does the subject, the man, build? He builds a house. Therefore, the direct object is "a house", because, it receives the action of the sentence.

2. *Indirect Object:* The indirect object indicates to whom or for whom the action of the sentence is being done. The indirect object is usually a noun or pronoun. Indirect objects are seen infrequently. In order to have an indirect object, there is a direct object. The indirect object typically precedes the direct object and is identified by asking who or what receives the direct object.

*Examples:*

- The man builds ***his family*** a house.
- The man builds ***them*** a house.

"The man" is the subject, and "builds" is the verb. Ask the question "builds what?" "A house" is the direct object. To determine the indirect object, ask who received the direct object. "His family" is the indirect object.

(D) *Subject Complement:* A subject complement either renames or describes the subject, and therefore is usually a noun, pronoun, or adjective. Subject complements occur when there is a linking verb within the sentence (often a linking verb is a form of the verb to be).

*Example:* 'Brandon is a gifted *athlete*.'

*Here:* Brandon = subject; is = linking verb; athlete = noun as subject complement.

## Parts of Speech

Words are used and arranged grammatically to construct a sentence. The ways in which words can be arranged to form a sentence are limitless. Words are categorised into parts of speech. To write a sentence, one has to be familiar with the parts of speech which are noun, pronoun, verb, adjective, adverb, preposition, conjunction and interjection. There are eight of them. Sometimes, determiner is added as a part of speech to bring the total to nine. A word can belong to more than one part of speech. Part of speech indicates how the word functions in meaning in a sentence.

It is important to be able to recognise and identify the different types of words in English, so that you can understand grammar explanations and use the right word form in the right place. Here is a brief explanation of what the parts of speech are:

### Noun

Noun is an important part of speech which is used a lot in written as well as in spoken English. A noun is a word that names a place, a person, a thing, an animal or an idea.

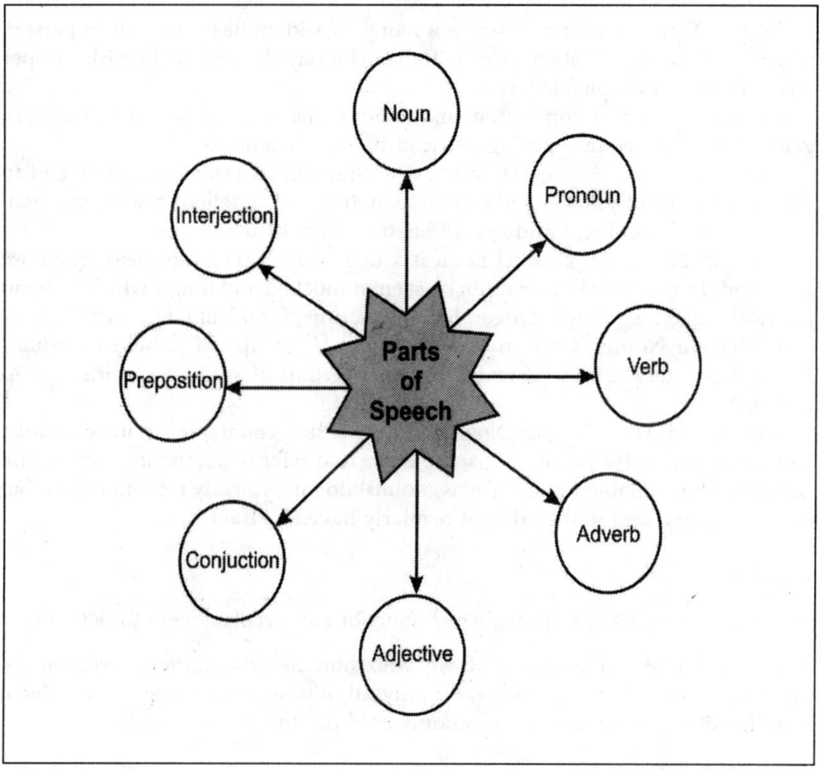


Figure II.2: Parts of Speech

*Examples:* 'table, chair, New York, book, cup, boy, computer, Newton, hospital, garden, room, Paris, man, doctor, engineer, glass, dog, cat, rabbit, hen' are all nouns because each of them is a name of a person, a place, a thing or an animal.

A noun can also be a name of an abstract feeling or an idea such as 'love, anger, happiness etc'.

*Examples of Noun in Sentences:*

- I have two *computers.*
- They were playing in a *garden.*
- *David* will come today.
- He is riding a *horse.*
- Never go against the *law.*

## Types of Noun

There are different types of nouns as follows:

Proper Noun: A proper noun is a name that identifies a particular person, place, or thing, e.g. Mohan, Africa, India, Monday. In written English, proper nouns begin with capital letters.

Common Noun: A common noun is a noun that refers to people or things in general, e.g. boy, country, bridge, city, birth, day, happiness.

Concrete Noun: A concrete noun is a noun which refers to people and to things that exist physically and can be seen, touched, smelled, heard, or tasted. Examples include dog, building, coffee, tree, rain, beach, tune.

Abstract Noun: An abstract noun is a noun which refers to ideas, qualities, and conditions – things that cannot be seen or touched and things which have no physical reality, e.g. truth, danger, happiness, time, friendship, humour.

Collective Nouns: Collective nouns refer to groups of people or things. Example: faculty (group of teachers), class (group of students), pride (group of lions).

Count and Mass Nouns: Nouns can be either countable or uncountable. Countable nouns (or count nouns) are those that refer to something that can be counted. Uncountable nouns(or mass nouns) do not typically refer to things that can be counted and so they do not regularly have a plural form.

## Pronoun

A pronoun is a part of a speech which functions as a replacement for a noun.

*Examples:* 'He, she, it, they, you, I, we, who, him, her, them, me, us, whom, his, its, their, your, mine, our and whose, myself, himself, herself, yourself, which, this, that these, those' are the commonly used pronouns.

*Examples of pronoun in sentences:*

1. The largest slice is *mine.*
2. *We* are number one.
3. *They* are dancing in the room.
4. *They* are singing songs.
5. *I* asked her why *she* was crying.
6. *She* ate the food and became happy.

### *Types of Pronouns*

The pronouns are of following six types:

1. *Personal Pronouns:* e.g. I, you, he, she, it, they, who, me, him, her, them, whom
2. *Possessive Pronouns:* e.g. yours, mine, his, hers, ours, theirs
3. *Reflexive Pronouns:* e.g. myself, himself, herself, itself, yourself, ourselves, themselves
4. *Reciprocal Pronouns:* e.g. each other, one another
5. *Relative Pronouns:* e.g. who, whom, whose, which, that
6. *Demonstrative Pronouns:* e.g. this, these, that, those.

## Adjective

This part of a speech is used to describe a noun or a pronoun. Adjectives can specify the quality, the size, and the number of nouns or pronouns.

*Examples:*

- Red, white, black, purple, green, yellow, and brown' are some adjectives because they tells us about the colour of a noun.
- 'Thin, fat, short, tall, beautiful, and ugly' are some adjectives telling about the physical characteristics of the nouns or the pronouns.
- 'Brave, intelligent, courageous, exuberant, diligent, and determined' are some adjectives telling about personal trait of the nouns or the pronouns.

*Examples of adjectives in sentences: hot* tea, *old* man, *beautiful* girl, *white* shirt, *intelligent* student, *interesting* story, *handsome* boy, *huge* room.

A sentence can have one adjective as well as more than one adjective.

- A handsome boy won the competition. (one adjective)
- A handsome and intelligent boy won the competition. (two adjectives)
- A handsome, tall and intelligent boy won the competition. (three adjectives)
- A handsome, tall, smart and intelligent boy won the competition.(four adjectives)

### *Using Adjectives in a Sentence*

Adjectives are used at two places in the sentence on the basis the structure of the sentence.

1. *Use of adjectives before a noun*

Adjectives are mostly used before a noun the sentences.

*Examples:*

- He bought an *expensive* car.
- He gifted me a *nice* shirt.
- She gave me a *red* rose.
- A *beautiful* girl is dancing in the room.
- They gave us *delicious* food.

2. *Use of adjectives after a verb (stative verbs)*

An adjective is also used after a stative verb (seem, consist, is, have, feel, possess) or verbs used as a stative verb in the sentence. Unlike a dynamic verb which expresses an action (e.g. eat, write, go), the stative verb is a verb that expresses a state of something (e.g. seem, consist, is, feel, possess)

*Examples:*

- The movie is *interesting.*
- The soldier is *brave.*
- His problems seem *complicated.*

## Verb

This is the most important part of a speech, for without a verb, a sentence would not exist. Simply put, this is a word that shows an action (physical or mental) or state of being of the subject in a sentence.

Examples: am, is, was, are, were, go, write, come, run, play, eat, weep, read, catch, clean, drink, walk, speak, cut, hold.

*Example of verb in sentence:* She is *driving* a car. In the above sentence, the word *'drive'* is a verb because it tells about an action being done by the subject (she) of the sentence. It tells what is being done – the action.

### *Types of Verbs*

Most of the verbs express the action of something but a few verbs also express a state of something.

1. *Dynamic Verb:* The verbs which tell about the action of something are called dynamic verb. e.g. go, come, play, run, eat, drink, etc.

*Examples*

- She is *singing* a song. (expresses an action)
- He is *laughing* at a joker. (expresses an action)
- The kids are *making* a noise. (expresses an action)

2. *Stative Verb:* On the other hand, those verbs which tells about a state of something, are called stative verbs. e.g. seem, resemble, consist of, belong to, be, impress, surprise.

*Examples*

- He *seems* a nice man. (expresses a state)
- She *resembles* her sister. (expresses a state)
- She *belongs* to a noble family. (expresses a state)

3. A few verbs can be used both as dynamic as well as a stative verb.

*Example*

- He looks very handsome. ('look' used as stative verb)
- He looked at the door. ('look' used as dynamic verb)

### *Forms of Verbs*

There are three forms of verbs depending upon its usage in sentence according to the tense.

- Base Form (1st Form)
- Past Simple (2nd Form)
- Past Participle (3rd Form)

| *Base Form* | *Past Simple* | *Past Participle* |
|---|---|---|
| Write | Wrote | Written |
| Go | Went | Gone |

### *Formation of Past Simple and Past Participle Forms*

Verbs are divided into following two types depending on formation of its 2nd and 3rd forms.

1. *Regular Verbs:* A verb whose past-simple and past-participle are formed simply by adding *'-ed'* to it, is called a regular verb.

| *Verb* | *Base Form* | *Past Simple* | *Past Participle* |
|---|---|---|---|
| To work | Work | Worked | Worked |
| To look | Look | Looked | Looked |
| To dry | Dry | Dried | Dried |
| To help | Help | Helped | Helped |
| To move | Move | Moved | Moved |

2. *Irregular Verbs:* A verb whose past-simple and past-participle are formed in different ways (not by adding *'-ed'*) is called an irregular verb.

| *Verb* | *Base Form* | *Past Simple* | *Past Participle* |
|---|---|---|---|
| To Send | Send | Sent | Sent |
| To buy | Buy | Bought | Bought |
| To teach | Teach | Taught | Taught |
| To do | Do | Did | Done |
| To fly | Fly | Flew | Flown |

3. A few verb remains the same in all three forms (base, past-simple and past-participle).

| *Verb* | *Base Form* | *Past Simple* | *Past Participle* |
|---|---|---|---|
| To shut | shut | shut | shut |
| To cut | cut | cut | cut |
| To spread | spread | spread | spread |
| To read | read | read | read |

## Adverb

An adverb is a word that modifies (gives us more information about) a verb in a sentence.

*Example:*
She is singing a song *loudly.*

The adverb *"loudly"* in the sentence modifies the verb *"sing"* by giving us more information that the song is sung with a loud voice. Such a word is called an adverb.

Adverbs modify a verb by giving us information about the following aspects of a verb.

- How an action occurs
- Where an action occurs
- When an action occurs
- How often an action occurs.

Depending on the above aspects of modification, the adverbs have following four types.

### Types of Adverbs

The different types of adverbs are:

*Adverb of Manner*: This refers to how something happens or how an action is done.

*Example:* Sita danced *gracefully*. The word *"gracefully"* tells how Sita danced.

Other examples of Adverb of Manner are:

- They are living *happily*.
- She completed her work *nicely*.
- He was behaving *angrily*.
- She treats the kids *sympathetically*.
- Sara is driving *carelessly*.
- Students were listening to lecture *carefully*.

*Adverb of Time:* It states "when" something happens or "when" it is done. E.g. soon, late, today, tonight, early, tomorrow, yesterday, then, now, etc.

*Example:* She came *yesterday*. The italicised word *"yesterday"* tells when she "came."

Other examples of Adverb of Time are:

- He will go to school *tomorrow*.
- I am *still* waiting for my friend.
- He will come *soon*.
- Please call him *now*.
- I met him *yesterday*.

*Adverb of Place:* This tells something about "where" something happens or "where" something is done. E.g. here, there, near, outside, inside, bottom, top, ahead, somewhere, beneath, etc.

*Example:* Of course, I looked *everywhere!* The adverb "everywhere" tells where I "looked".

Other examples of Adverb of Place are:

- He went *downstairs.*
- Kids are playing near the *house.*
- They live *somewhere* in Paris.
- Please come *inside.*
- They were coming *here.*
- Someone is talking *outside.*

*Adverb of Degree/Frequency:* This states the intensity or the degree to which a specific thing happens or is done. E.g. daily, weekly, seldom, frequently, usually, sometimes, most of the times, again and again, often, etc.

*Example:* The child is *very* talented. The italicised adverb answers the question, "To what degree is the child talented?"

Other examples of Adverb of Frequency are:

- They *always* helped me.
- They come here *too often.*
- She is calling me *again and again.*
- The failed student was *frequently* thinking about his failure in exam.
- I meet him *daily.*
- He *usually* sleeps in the day.

## Preposition

A preposition is a word which expresses relationship of a noun or a pronoun to other words of the sentence. A preposition is used before a noun or pronoun to show the relationship of the same noun or pronoun to other words of the sentence.

*Example:* 'in, of, to, at, by, for, with, under, above, into, onto, upon, about, behind, beside, before, after, towards, inside, outside, below, around' are commonly used examples of prepositions.

*Examples of prepositions in sentences:*

| *Words of the sentence (i.e. subject, verb)* | *Preposition* | *Noun or Pronoun* |
|---|---|---|
| He was sitting | on | a table. |
| She is going | to | college. |
| There is a cat | under | the bed. |
| They are dancing | in | the room. |
| He was drawing a picture | on | a wall. |
| His family lives | in | America. |
| She was knocking | at | the door. |
| She is throwing stones | into | a river. |
| The students were discussing | about | the exam. |

| | | |
|---|---|---|
| The meeting was held | on | 25th December. |
| They will come here | in | July. |
| The party will start | at | 8 P.M. |
| He goes to factory | by | bus. |
| The lock cannot be opened | with | the key. |
| This book has been written | by | John Keats. |
| The guests were invited | by | her. |

In the above examples, all the prepositions express relationship of a noun or a pronoun to the other words of the sentence.

### *Types of Prepositions*

Different preposition are used for time, place, direction, agent, device and so on. Some of the examples are follows:

- *Preposition for time* e.g. in, on, at, etc.
- *Preposition for place* e.g. in, on, at, etc.
- *Preposition for direction* e.g. to, towards, into, through etc.
- *Preposition for agent* e.g. by
- *Preposition for device, instrument or machines* e.g. on, by, with, etc.

### *What is a Prepositional Phrase?*

A preposition phrase, in a sentence, is a group of words consisting of a preposition and a noun. It is a group of a preposition, a noun and other linked word within a sentence. The noun in a prepositional phrase is called object of the preposition.

*Example:* on a table, on a paper, in a room, at the door, into a river.

### *Examples of Prepositional Phrases*

In the following examples, the underlined words are prepositional phrases:

- He is throwing ball *into the river.*
- Someone is knocking *at the door.*
- He was sitting *on a table.*
- She is writing *on a paper.*
- Kids were dancing *in a room.*

## Conjunction

Conjunction is a word that joins words, phrases, clauses or sentences.

*Example:* but, and, yet, or, because, nor, although, since, unless, while, where, etc.
*Example of conjunction in sentences:*

- She bought a shirt *and* a book.
- You can write your paper with a pen *or* a pencil.

- I sent him a letter *but* he did not respond.
- She laughed *and* entered into the room.
- He sings songs *because* he wants to become a singer.
- You cannot succeed *unless* you work sincerely.
- I saw him *while* I was driving my car.
- I went to a market *where* I saw a joker.

A conjunction can be a single word or a group of words

- *Single-word conjunctions:* e.g. and, but, yet, because etc.
- *Compound conjunctions:* e.g. as long as, as far as, as well as, in order to, even if, so that etc.

*Examples of compound conjunctions:*

- You live a happy life *as long as* you think optimistically.
- I will not tell him the secret *even if* he insists a lot.
- He bought a laptop *as well as* a bag for it.
- Always speak the truth *in order to* avoid problems in life.
- He *as well as* I had gone to cinema.
- He came here *so that* you can meet him.

### *Types of Conjunctions*

There are three types of conjunctions:

- Coordinating Conjunctions
- Subordinating Conjunctions
- Correlative Conjunctions.

## Interjection

This part of a speech refers to words which express emotions. Since interjections are commonly used to convey strong emotions, they are usually followed by an exclamation point. *Examples:* Ouch!. Oh!, Wow!, No!, Oops!

*Example of interjection in sentences:*

- *Ouch!* That must have hurt.
- *Hurray*, we won!
- *Hey!* I said enough!

The bold italic words attached to the main sentences above are some examples of interjections.

## Punctuation

The most essential skill in academic writing is the ability to use suitable punctuation. Punctuationis used to create clarity and stress in the sentences. One should use punctuation marks to organise his writing. The main purpose of punctuation in sentences is to shape words so that it helps the reader understand what is clearly said or written.

### *Punctuation Marks*

Punctuation is the use of symbols that we generally use to separate written sentences and parts of sentences, and to make their meaning clearer and more flawless. Each symbol is called a "punctuation mark". Punctuation helps to create the logic of the written word. Without the use of punctuation, writing would become open to multiple interpretations. When writing, we must use punctuation in order to specify places of emphasis.

(.) Full Stop/Period: The period is possibly the simplest and easiest punctuation mark to master. You use it like a knife to cut the sentences to the desired length. Normally, while writing one can break up the sentences using the full stop at the end of a logical and complete thought that looks and sounds right.

(') Comma: The comma indicates a pause that would occur if the sentence were spoken aloud at other times; the comma separates grammatical components of the sentence. We use commas inside sentences. Commas separate parts of a sentence into logical elements. Even though we are often taught that commas are used to help us add 'breathing spaces' to sentences they are, in fact, more precisely used to organise chunks of thought or reasonable groupings.

(;) Semicolon: Semicolons can be used to join phrases and sentences or to separate sentences that are grammatically independent but that have closely connected meaning without having to use a conjunction. Semicolons can also be used instead of commas to separate the items in a list when the items themselves already contain commas. The semicolon is sometimes described as stronger than a comma but weaker than a period.

(:) Colon: The job of the colon is simple: to introduce. The colon expands on the sentence that precedes it, often introducing a list that demonstrates or elaborates whatever was previously stated. The colon is also used to divide the hour from the minutes in writing a time in English.

(-) Hyphen: A hyphen joins two or more words together and is not separated by spaces. It is a very short horizontal line between words.

(–) 'm' Dash: The 'n' dash (–) is slightly wider than the hyphen (-) but narrower than the 'm' dash (–). 'n' Dash separates words into parenthetical statements. It has a space on either side. 'm' Dashes can be used to create emphasis in a sentence. Use a 'm' dash to show a pause or break in meaning in the middle of a sentence or an afterthought. Dash can be used like a colon to introduce a list or to show that letters or words are missing.

(?) Question Mark: The question mark is used at the end of a direct question. The main function of a question mark is to indicate a question or query.

Table II.1: Punctuation Marks

| *Punctuation Mark* | *Name* | *Usage* | *Example* |
|---|---|---|---|
| . | *Full Stop* (in British English) or *Period* | It is used *at the end of a sentence or at the end of the short form of a word* | • I like flowers.<br>• I like football. |
| ‘ | Comma | It is used to *separate parts of a sentence showing a slight pause, or to separate the single things in a list.* | • I like roses, jasmine and sunflower.<br>• I want to eat meat, bread and tomatoes. |
| ; | Semicolon | It is used *between two parts of a sentence, usually when each of the two parts could form grammatical sentences on their own* | • I do not often go jogging; I prefer to play tennis. |
| : | Colon | It is used especially to *introduce a list of things or a sentence or phrase taken from somewhere else.* | • You have two choices: finish the work today or lose your job.<br>• We have two choices: work hard or fail. |
| – | Hyphen | It is used to*join words together to indicate that they have a combined meaning or to show that a word has been divided into parts.* | • This is a rather out-of-date magazine.<br>• well–to–do<br>• rock–forming minerals,<br>• pick–me–up. |
| – | Dash (m) | It is used to *separate parts of a sentence.* | • In each town–Paris, UK and Rome–we stayed in youth accommodations.<br>• We saw two movies at the theatre today–I did not really like either of them. |
| ? | Question Mark | It is used *at the end of a phrase or sentence to show that it is a question.* | • Where is the Bahama islands located?<br>• Where is the bank? |
| ! | Exclamation Mark | It is used immediately *after an exclamation.* | • “Help!” she cried.<br>• “I can’t walk!”<br>• What an exceptional child this is! |
| / | Slash, Forward Slash, Oblique | It is used in writing to *separate letters, numbers, or words.* | • Please press your browser’s Refresh/Reload button.<br>• and/or<br>• 05/10 (October 5)<br>• 2/3 = two-thirds |

*(Table II.1 Contd.)*

*(Table II.1 Contd.)*

| *Punctuation Mark* | *Name* | *Usage* | *Example* |
|---|---|---|---|
| \ | Backward Slash | It is mainly used in computing. | • C:\Files\mo.doc |
| " " | Double Quotation Marks | Quotation Marks ("") are a pair of punctuation marks used primarily to mark the beginning and end of a passage attributed to another and repeated word for word. They are also used to indicate meanings and to indicate the unusual or dubious status of a word. | • "I love you too," she said. |
| ' | Single Quotation Marks | Single quotation marks (' ') are used most frequently for quotes within quotes. | • 'I love you too,' she said. |
| ' | Apostrophe | It is used to *show when a letter or a number has been left out, as in I'm (=I am), or that is used before or after "s" to show possession, as in Sarah's house.* | • This is Ali's car.<br>• This is Steven's car. We're ready |
| **<u>English</u>** | Underline | It is used to especially *emphasise.* | • The meeting will start at <u>10:00 am</u>. |
| _ | Underscore | It is used to *draw a line under.* | turn_around@dance.com<br>d_k@yah.com |
| ( ) | Round Brackets (in British English) or Parentheses | It is used to *add extra information to a sentence.* | • I went to Singapore (my favourite city) and stayed there for three weeks.<br>• Lisa (8 years-old) is a little girl. |
| [ ] | Square Brackets | It is used to *enclose words added by someone other than the original writer or speaker, typically in order to clarify the situation.* | • The newspaper reported that the hostages [most of them Irish] had been released.<br>• "It [electricity] is really just organised lightning. |
| ... | Ellipsis Mark | It is used in writing to *show where one or more words have been intentionally left out* | • One happy customer wrote: "This is the best lunch...that I have ever had."<br>• You went to the restaurant. And**...**? |

(!) Exclamation Mark: The exclamation mark is used to express strong feeling, such as surprise, anger or joy, exasperation, astonishment, or to emphasise a comment or short, sharp phrase. An exclamation mark is usually used in writing quoted speech.

(/) (\) Forward Slash and Backslash: A slash is often used to indicate "or". It is also known as: forward slash, stroke, oblique. The backslash is a typographical mark used mainly in computing. It is called a "backslash" because it is the reverse of the slash (/) or forward slash.

(" ") (' ') Quotation Marks (double, single): We use quotation marks to show (or mark) the beginning and end of a word or phrase that is somehow special or comes from outside the text that is written. Use quotation marks to cite something someone said exactly.

(') Apostrophe: The apostrophe ( ' ) has three uses:

- *Contractions*– cannot → can't, they have → they've, I would (or I had) → I'd
- *Plurals*– four A's and two B's, yes's than no's
- *Possessives*– New York's nightmare scenario, the moon's phases

Examples:

| | | | | | | | |
|---|---|---|---|---|---|---|---|
| isn't | wouldn't | he's | Germany's | You'll | I'd | They'd | You're |
| hasn't | can't | it's | who's | She'll | You'd | I've | They're |
| hadn't | she's | Martin's | I'm | We'll | He'd | You've | We're |
| didn't | there's | Jonna's | I'll | They'll | We'd | We've | They've |

( _ ) Underline: An underline is a horizontal line immediately below a piece of writing. In handwriting, we traditionally use underlining to indicate emphasis.

( _ ) Underscore: The underscore ( _ ) is also known as an understrike or underbar and is a character that was originally on a typewriter keyboard and was used simply to underline words or numbers for emphasis. Today, the character is used to create visual spacing in a sequence of words where whitespace is not permitted. The most common instance of this is in computer file names and titles, email addresses, and Internet URLs. Some computer programming automatically underlines a word or sentence that begins with an underscore or ends with an underscore.

( ) [ ] Brackets and Parentheses: Parentheses refers to round brackets () and brackets to square brackets []. Round brackets are basically used to add extra information to a sentence. We typically use square brackets when we want to modify another person's words.

(...) Ellipsis Mark: The ellipsis mark is also called a "suspension point" or "dot dot dot". The ellipsis mark consists of three dots (periods). It is used in place of missing words. If we deliberately omit one or more words from an original text, we replace them with an ellipsis mark.

## Tenses

### *Definition of Tenses*

Tense is a grammatical term that refers to how a verb shows the time of happening in the sentence.

### *Tenses in English*

Grammar tenses refer to the state of the verb. The state, or tense, of the verb explains the time of the action. There are three major tenses in English. These include past, present, and future. Each of these tenses can explain an event that occurred in the past, an event that occurs in the present, or an event that will occur in the future.

### *Types of Tenses*

Tenses can be broadly classified into three broad categories:

- Past Tense
- Present Tense
- Future Tense

*Past Tense:* This tense is used to refer to something that happened in the past. Sometimes, past tense is also called as 'simple past tense'. Example: We stayed in a hotel.

- *Past Indefinite Tense:* In the past indefinite tense, verb shows the past time, telling the completion of action in the past. In this tense we should use verbs in past tense.

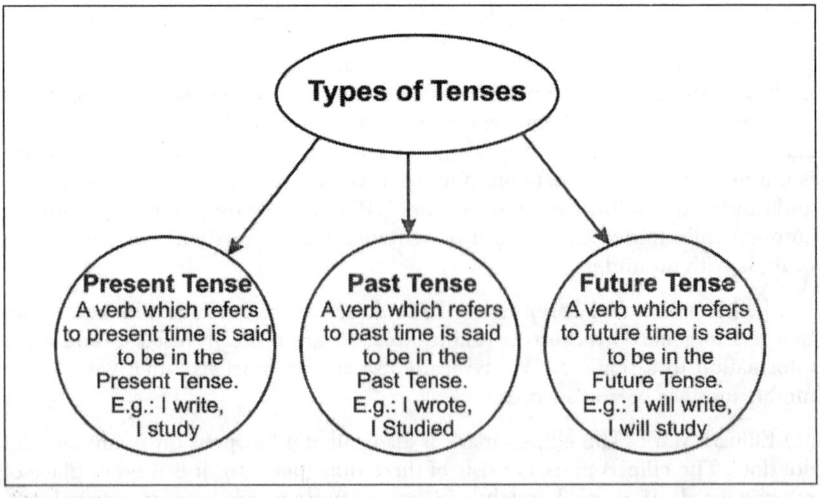


Figure II.3: Types of Tenses

- *Past continuous tense:* This type of past tense is used to describe an event or occurrence that was ongoing or continuing in the past.
- *Past Perfect Tense:* This type of tense is used to describe an event in the past that has been completed.
- *Past Perfect Continuous Tense:* This type of past tense verb is used to indicate an event, action or occurrence that started before another event, action or occurrence in the past and had not stopped till that time. We can say that one action or event interrupted another.

*Present Tense:* This tense is used to refer or indicate to something that occurs in the present. Example: The dogs bark.

1. *Present Indefinite Tense:* The present indefinite tense is used to describe an action, event, or condition that is occurring in the present while being spoken about or written.
2. *Present Continuous Tense:* This tense indicates the continuous nature of an act or event in the present and has not been completed. The activity has begun in the past and will be completed in the future.
3. *Present Perfect Tense:* This tense is used to describe an action that had begun in the past, continues into the present and has just been completed. The time of occurrence of the action is generally not mentioned. This tense is also used to describe an action happened in the past before another action took place.
4. *Present Perfect Continuous Tense:* This tense is used to describe an action, event or occurrence that has begun in the past and continues into the present. It is also used for an action that began and just finished in the past or in cases where there is no mention of time.

*Future Tense:* This tense is used to refer to or indicate something that has not happened at the time of speaking or writing. 'Simple Future Tense' commonly formed with the use of words 'will' and 'shall'. Example: We shall be there by noon.

1. *Future Indefinite Tense:* In future indefinite tense, verb shows the future time telling the action to take place. In these sentences, 'shall' is used with first person of singular number and plural number. 'Will' is used with second person and third person singular number and plural number.
2. *Future Continuous Tense:* This tense is used to describe actions that are ongoing or continuing in the future. It is commonly used in sentences by using the simple future tense of the verb with the present participle i.e. 'ing'.
3. *Future Perfect Tense:* This tense is used to refer or describe an event that will be completed sometime in the future before another action takes place. It is written by using the past participle of the verb with the simple future tense of the verb.
4. *Future Perfect Continuous Tense:* This tense is used to describe an action that is continuing into the future and will be completed at a specified time in

the future. This tense is written using the future perfect tense of the verb with the present participle.

*Examples of Tenses*

- *Past Tense*
  1. Past Indefinite (Example: "I played tennis.")
  2. Past Continuous (Example: "I was playing tennis.")
  3. Past Perfect (Example: "I had played tennis.")
  4. Past Perfect Continuous (Example: "I had been playing tennis.")
- *Present Tense*
  5. Present Indefinite (Example: "I play tennis.")
  6. Present Continuous (Example: "I am playing tennis.")
  7. Present Perfect (Example: "I have played tennis.")
  8. Present Perfect Continuous (Example: "I have been playing tennis.")
- *Future Tense*
  9. Future Indefinite (Example: "I will play tennis.")
  10. Future Continuous (Example: "I will be playing tennis.")
  11. Future Perfect (Example: "I will have played tennis.")
  12. Future Perfect Continuous (Example: "I will have been playing tennis.")

## Articles

Articles are words which are used to point out or refer a noun. According to *Oxford Dictionary*, Article is a part of speech that indicates, specifies and limits a noun. It particularises the grammatical definiteness of the noun. It is always followed by a noun/noun phrase.

There are three articles in English i.e. 'a', 'an' and 'the'. In fact, there are certain situations where no article is needed. We have to follow certain guidelines in order to decide which article to use before a noun in the sentence.

## Examples of Articles

- He is _a_ doctor.
- He is _the_ doctor who treated me.
- This is _an_ apple.

### *Types of Articles*

Article is categorised into two parts i.e. the Definite Article and Indefinite Article.

*Definite Article:* Definite articles are used to tell about specific person, place or thing.

*Example of Definite Article:*

- 'He is _the_ doctor who treated me'. In this example, 'He' is the specific doctor who treated me, so we use 'the'.

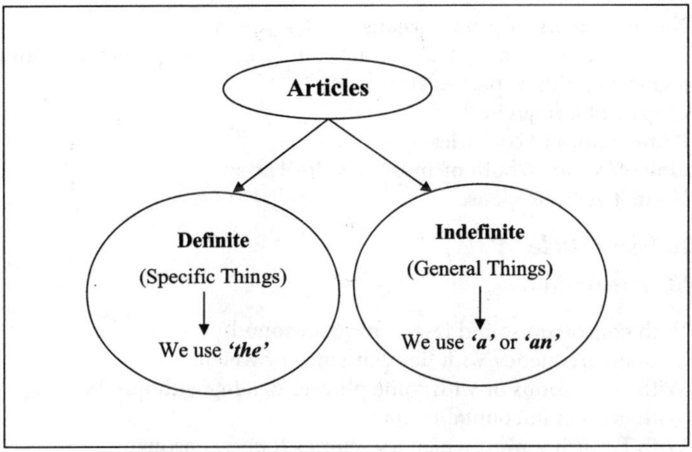


Figure II.4: Types of Articles

- '*The* cow was of black colour'. In this example, we are talking about a specific cow of black colour, so, 'the' is a definite article.

*Indefinite Article:* They are used to tell about something general.

*Example of Indefinite Article:*

- 'He is *a* doctor'. In this example, 'He' is one of many, so we use 'a'.
- 'I saw *a* cow'. In this example, we are talking about any one, not a specific cow, so, 'a' is an indefinite article.

### *When to Use Article 'The'*

Article 'The' is used with:

- Superlative degree of adjective
- Parallel comparatives
- The nouns which are repeated
- Religious groups and their holy books
- Heavenly bodies, i.e. planets, asteroids etc.
- Musical instruments
- The name of newspaper
- The name of inventions and discoveries
- Ordinal numbers
- Historical buildings or to denote parts of the house
- Mountain ranges, group of islands, deserts, canals etc.
- Name of directions and physical positions
- 'The +noun + relative clause'
- Daybreaks, period of history, decades and historical events
- Hotels, theatres, special meals, museums and libraries

- Name of rivers, seas and oceans
- Nationalities, races, social groups, different job posts and positions, names of political parties etc.
- Organs of human body
- Plural names of countries
- One of/some of/both of/most of + the +nouns
- Noun + definite clause.

### *When to Use Article 'A'*

Article 'A' is used with:

- With consonant sound (a + consonant sound)
- To show frequency with time, distance or weight
- With expressions or with some phrases dealing with number
- With units of uncountable noun
- With English vowels which sometimes sound consonant
- After words like: what, quite, many, such etc.
- With collective expressions.

### *When to Use Article 'An'*

Article 'An' is used:

- With a vowel sound
- Before abbreviation which begins with consonant letter but has vowel sound
- With singular countable noun starting with consonant letter but has vowel sound
- With some expressions and phrases.

### *Where Articles should not be Used?*

There are many cases where the uses of articles are discouraged. Articles should not be used:

- before proper nouns, plural nouns, etc.
- before clothing items, religious institutions, etc.
- before mountains, languages, games, etc.

## Modifiers

Modifiers are words or group of words that qualify or describe other words in a sentence. A modifier can be a single word, a phrase, or a clause.

## Examples of Modifiers

Read the sentences below to get an idea on modifiers. The modifiers are underlined and the words that each modifier describes are italicised:

- The famous *architect* lived in an old-fashioned house.
- Robert Frost was *born* in San Francisco.

- The duck *waddled* warily, beginning to suspect danger.
- Steve became *furious* when he learned the truth.

### *Types of Modifiers*

Modifiers bring sentences to life by providing vivid description about things and actions. Regardless of length or form (words, phrases, or clauses), modifiers fall into two categories. They function as adjective if they describe people, places, things, or ideas; they function as adverb if they describe verbs, adjectives, or other adverbs.

1. *Adjectives:* The words that modify nouns and pronouns are called adjectives. An adjective modifies a word by telling:

- *What kind?* Example: big, easy, exciting...
- *Which one?* Example: that, last, middle ...
- *How much/many?* Example: less, many...

*(A)* Adjective as Modifier*:* An adjective may come after or before the word it modifies.

*Example:* "The conference on improving water resources was attended by several activists."

Here:
several = adjective
activists = noun

*(B)* Adjective Phrase as Modifier: An adjective phrase is a prepositional phrase that modifies a noun or a pronoun.

*Example:* "Have you read the novel by Margaret Atwood?"

Here:
novel = noun
by Margaret Atwood = adjective phrase
In the sentence above, the adjective phrase 'by Margaret Atwood' answers the question 'which one'. It modifies the noun 'novel'.

*(C)* Adjective Clause as Modifier*:* An adjective clause is a dependent clause that modifies a noun or a pronoun. An adjective clause begins with the relative pronouns such as who, whom, whose, that, and which.

Example: "We must find a person who will help to restore consumer confidence."

Here:
person = noun
who will help to restore consumer confidence = adjective phrase
The adjective clause 'who will help to restore consumer confidence' modifies the noun 'person' and gives information on 'what kind of person'.

2. *Adverbs:* An adverb modifies a verb, an adjective, or another adverb by making its meaning more specific. An adverb tells when, where, why, how, or to what extent the action occurs.

*(A)* Adverb Modifying Verb: Example*:* "I voluntarily offered help to an old man to cross the road."

Here:
voluntarily = adverb
offered = verb
In this sentence, the adverb 'voluntarily' modifies the verb 'offered', telling how the action is done.

*(B)* Adverb Modifying Adjective*:* Example: "We would be extremely grateful if you could have a word with Mark."

Here:
extremely = adverb
grateful = adjective
The adverb 'extremely' modifies the adjective 'grateful', telling to what extent.

*(C)* Adverb Modifying another Adverb*:* Example: "Ramesh fell and hurt his leg rather badly."

Here:
rather = adverb
badly = adverb
The adverb 'rather' modifies another adverb 'badly', which modifies the verb 'hurt'.

*(C)* Adverb Phrase as Modifier*:* An adverb phrase is a prepositional phrase that modifies a verb, an adjective, or an adverb.

*Example:* "When I was at the podium, I was surprised to see all my friends seated in the front row."

Here:
seated = verb
in the front row = prepositional phrase (adverb)
In this sentence, the prepositional phrase 'in the front row' functions as an adverb modifying the verb 'seated.'

*Adverb Clause as Modifier:* An adverb clause is a subordinate clause that modifies a verb, an adjective, or an adverb in the main clause. Adverb clauses are introduced by subordinating conjunctions such as after, although, as, because, before, if, since, than, though, unless, until, when, and where.

*Example:* "When Robert Frost was about eleven years old, his father died."

Here:
when Robert Frost was about eleven years old = adverb clause
died = verb
The adverb clause modifies the verb 'died,' telling when Frost's father died.

## Determiners

Determiners are those words which function in a noun phrase to identify it as general or specific without explaining or modifying it. Determiners are used to modify and clarify nouns and are used before nouns. We can say that, determiners are used to refer and quantify nouns.

## Examples of Determiners

This, that, the, a, an, my, our, a few, a lot of, any, enough, all, each, every, such, rather, quite, one, two, twenty, both, less, least, which, whose, his, her, its, several, their, many, more.

Determiners are often considered as same groups of words as Adjectives. However, we should understand that they are different and should not be put into the same category. Determiners are generally obligatory in sentences unlike Adjectives. Determiners also cannot form degrees unlike Adjectives.

### *Categories of Determiners*

Determiners can be divided into two main groups:

*Specific Determiners:* Specific Determiners are those determiners which we use when we know exactly what we are referring to. Specific Determiners are as follows:

- Definite Article: the
- Interrogatives: which
- Possessives: my, his, her, our, your, their
- Demonstratives: this, that, those, these.

## Examples of Specific Determiners in Sentences

- Thank you for *the* dress.
- *Whose* pen is this?
- Look at *these* books.
- Can you pass *her* pizza?
- *Our* house is beautiful.

*General Determiners:* General Determiners are those determiners which we use when we are not sure of what exactly we are referring to. General determiners are: what, another, any, a, an, other, another, several, neither.

## Examples of General Determiners in Sentences

- Give me *another* cup of coffee.
- You can wear *any* dress of mine.
- *What* is his profession?
- I need *a* pretty pair of shoes.
- I can't help you. Why don't you ask *other* friends?

### *Types of Determiners*

Determiners are also categorised in the following way:

1. *Articles:* A/an (Indefinite),The (Definite)
   *Use in sentences*
   - The man is a doctor.
   - She is a murderer.
2. *Quantifiers:* little, few, much, more, most, some, several, any, each.
   *Use in sentences*
   - Some people are really very selfish.
   - More teenagers are smoking these days.
3. *Numbers:* one, two, five, eight, eleven, thirteen, fifteen.
   *Use in sentences*
   - I only have eleven dollars.
   - Can you give me two apples?
4. *Demonstratives:* This, that, those, these
   *Use in sentences*
   - This book is mine.
   - That house is new.
   - These people are nasty.
   - Those children are orphans.
5. *Possessives:* my, our, his, her, your, its, their, Harry's, Elizabeth's, etc.
   *Use in sentences*
   - This is my car.
   - Your work is rough.
6. *Interrogative Determiners:* what, which
   *Use in sentences*
   - What is her name?
   - Which laptop is that?

## Capitalisation

Capitalisation is a very important concept in standard grammar in the written form of the English language. Capitalisation is the writing of a word with its first letter in uppercase and the remaining letters in lowercase. The practice of using capital letters in writing or printing is called capitalization.

### *Rules of Capitalisation*

The following are the important rules of capitalisation:

1. Capitalise the first word in a sentence.
2. Capitalise proper nouns and adjectives.
3. Capitalise brand names, company names, and organisational names.
4. Capitalise the names of continents, countries, nationalities and languages.
5. Capitalise the names of ethnic, tribal and religious groups.
6. Capitalise the given and family names of people.

7. Capitalise the names of the days of the week and months of the year.
8. Capitalise the names of government bodies and documents.
9. Capitalise the names of historical eras.
10. Capitalise the names of holidays.
11. Capitalise the names of specific geographic places.
12. Capitalise the names of man-made structures.
13. Capitalise the names of planets and constellations.
14. Capitalise the names of sports teams.
15. Capitalise the names of street names.
16. Capitalise the names of religions, their followers and their books.
17. Capitalise the names of special events.
18. Capitalise job titles when used as part of a name.
19. Capitalise royalty titles and honorary titles attached to a person's name.
20. Capitalise the letters in an acronym.

# Bibliography

Adams, W. R. (1986). *Think, Read, React, Plan, Write, Rewrite.* New York: Holt Rinehart and Winston.

American Psychological Association (1983). *Publication Manual of the American Psychological Association* (3rd Ed.). Washington, DC: American Psychological Association.

—— (1994). *Publication Manual of the American Psychological Association* (4th ed.). Washington, DC: American Psychological Association.

—— (1999). Electronic Reference Formats recommended by the American Psychological Association. From: http://www.apa.org/journals/webref.html.

—— (2001). Publication Manual of the American Psychological Association (5th ed.). Washington: American Psychological Association. Buehring, G. C. Bacon, Inc.

—— (2001). Publication Manual of the American Psychological Association (5th Ed.). Washington, DC: American Psychological Association.

—— (2010). Publication Manual of the American Psychological Association (6th Ed.). Washington, DC: American Psychological Association.

Arnaudet, M. L. and Barrett, M. E. (1984). *Approaches to Academic Reading & Writing.* Englewood Cliffs, NJ: Prentice Hall Regents.

Arnold, J. & Harmer, J. (1978). *Advanced Writing Skills.* Harlow: Longman.

Badenhorst, C. (2007). *Research Writing.* Pretoria: Van Schaik Publishers.

Bailey, S. (2006). *Academic Writing: A Handbook for International Students* (2nd ed). London: Routledge.

—— (2011). *Academic Writing: A Handbook for International Students.* Routledge.

—— (2011a). *Academic Writing: A handbook for International Students* (3rd Ed). London: Routledge.

—— (2011b). *Academic Writing for International Business Students.* London: Routledge.

Bayley, L. & Eldredge, J. E. (2003). The Structured Abstract: An Essential Tool for Researchers. *Hypothesis,* 17(1), 1 and 11–15. http://research.mlanet.org/structured_ abstract.html.

Borg, E. (2008). Understanding the Nature, Possibilities and Challenges of Academic Writing in S. Moore (ed.) *Supporting Academic Writing among Students and Academics.* London: Staff and Educational Development Association. (pp. 9–14).

Buehring, J. E. & Gerard, P. D. (2007). Lost in Citation: Vanishing Visibility of Senior Authors. *Scientometrics,* 72(3), 459–68.

Chandler, D. (1995). *The Act of Writing: A Media Theory Approach.* Aberystwyth: University of Wales.

Chris Thaiss and Terry Myers Zawacki (2006). *Engaged Writers and Dynamic Disciplines: Research on the Academic Writing Life*, Portsmouth: Boynton/Cook.

Coffin, C., Curry, M., Goodman, S., Hewings, A., Lillis, T. & Swann, J. (2003). *Teaching Academic Writing*: A Toolkit for Higher Education. London: Routledge.

Coulthard, M. (2004). Author Identification, Idiolect and Linguistic Uniqueness. *Applied Linguistics*, 25(4), 431–47.

Craig, J.L. (2013). *Integrating Writing Strategies in EFL/ESL University Contexts.* New York: Routledge.

Cramer, S. (2001). Choosing a Topic. In *Guide to Library Research* (Part 1). http://www.lib.duke/edu /libguide/choosing.htm.

Craswell, G. (2005). *Writing for Academic Success: A Postgraduate Guide.* Sage Publications.

Creme, P., & Lea, (2003). *Writing at University.* Maidenhead: Open University Press.

Day, R. A. (1983). *How to Write and Publish a Scientific Paper.* 2nd ed. Philadelphia: ISI Press.

—— (1992). *Scientific English: A Guide for Scientists and other Professionals.* Phoenix, AZ: Oryx Press.

Dr. George, Jacob, Dr. Anwar Sadath (2017). Writing for Academic and Professional Success, Calicut University Edition.

Elbow, P. (1988). *Writing Without Teachers* (2nd Ed.) New York: Oxford University Press.

—— (1998). *Writing with Power* (2nd Ed.). New York: Oxford University Press.

—— (2000). *Everyone Can Write.* New York: Oxford University Press.

—— & Belanoff, P. (2003). *Being a Writer.* Boston: Mc Graw Hill Higher Education.

Etherington, S. (2008). Academic Writing and the Disciplines. In Friedrich, P. (Ed.), *Teaching Academic Writing* (pp. 26-58). London: Continuum.

Friedrich, P. (2008). (Ed.). *Teaching Academic Writing.* New York: Continuum International Publishing.

Ghiselin, B. (Ed.). (1980). *The Creative Process: A Symposium.* Berkeley, CA: University of California Press.

Giltrow, Janet and Michele Valiquette. (1994). Genres and Knowledge: Students Writing in the Disciplines. In Freedman, Aviva; Peter Medway (Eds.), *Learning and Teaching Genre.* Portsmouth, NH: Boynton/Cook (pp. 47-62).

Glasman-Deal, H. (2010). Science Research Writing for Non-native Speakers of English. Imperial College Press. https://www.goodreads.com/book/show/7934951-science-research-writing-for-non-native-speakers-of-english.

Goodall, H. Lloyd, Jr. (2000). *Writing Qualitative Inquiry: Self, Stories, and Academic Life* (Walnut Creek, CA: Left Coast Press)

Goodson, P. (2012). *Becoming an Academic Writer: 50 Exercises for Paced, Productive, and Powerful Writing.* Sage Publications. https://www.goodreads.com/book/show/14554574-becoming-an-academic-writer.

Gopen, G. D. & Swan, J.A. (1990). The Science of Scientific Writing. *American Scientist.* 78:550-558.

Graetz, N. (1985). Teaching EFL Students to Extract Structural Information from Abstracts. In Ulign J. M and Pugh A. K. (eds) *Reading for Professional Purposes: Methods and Materials in Teaching Languages*, Leuven: Acco, pp. 123–135

Groom, N. (2000). Attribution and Averral Revisited: Three Perspectives on Manifest Intertextuality in Academic Writing. In P. Thompson (ed.) *Patterns and Perspectives: Insights into EAP writing practice. Reading*: CALS, 14–25.

Hamid, S. (2004). Writing a Research Paper. http://owl.english.purdue.edu/ workshops /hypertext/researchw/index.html.

Hart, C. (1998). *Doing a Literature Review: Releasing the Social Science Research Imagination*. Sage Publications.

Hartley, J. (1994). Three Ways to Improve the Clarity of Abstracts. *British Journal of Educational Psychology*, 64(2), 331–43.

—— (2008). *Academic Writing and Publishing*. London: Routledge.

—— Pennebaker, J. W. & Fox, C. (2003). Abstracts, Introductions and Discussions: How far do they differ in Style? *Scientometrics*, 57(3), 389–98.

——, Sotto, E. & Fox, C. (2004). Clarity Across the Disciplines: An Analysis of Texts in the Sciences, Social sciences, and Arts and Humanities. *Science Communication*, 26(2), 188–210.

——, Trueman, M. & Meadows, A. J. (1988). Readability and Prestige in Scientific Journals. *Journal of Information Science*, 14(1), 69–75.

Hayes, J. R. (2006). New Directions in Writing Research. In C.A. MacArthur, S. Graham & J. Fitzgerald (Eds.), *Handbook of Writing Research* (pp. 28–40). New York: Guilford Press.

Hayot, Eric (2014). The Elements of Academic Style: Writing for the Humanities. Columbia University Press.

Hirvela, A. & Du, Q. (2013). 'Why am I Paraphrasing?': Undergraduate ESL Writers' Engagement with Source-based Academic Writing and Reading. *Journal of English for Academic Purposes* 12, 87–98.

Howard, R. M. (1995). Plagiarisms, Authorships, and the Academic Death Penalty. *College English*, 57(7), 788–806.

Huff, A. S. (1999). *Writing for Scholarly Publication*. Thousand Oaks, CA: Sage Publications.

Hunston, S. (2000). Evaluation and the Planes of Discourse: Status and Value in Persuasive Texts. In S. Hunston & G. Thompson (eds.) *Evaluation in Text: Authorial Stance and the Construction of Discourse*. Oxford: Oxford University Press, 176–207.

Hyland, K. (1999). Academic Attribution: Citation and the Construction of Disciplinary Knowledge. 20(3), 341–367.

—— (2004). *Disciplinary Discourses: Social Interactions in Academic Writing*. Ann Arbor: University of Michigan Press.

—— (2009). *Academic Discourse: English in a Global Context*. London: Continuum.

Ilakovac, V., Fister, K., Marusic, M. & Marusic, A. (2007). Reliability of Disclosure Forms of Authors' Contributions. *Canadian Medical Association Journal*, 176(1), 41–6.

International Reading Association. (ERIC Document Reproduction Service No. ED462715).

Jalalian M, Mahboobi H. (2014). Hijacked Journals and Predatory Publishers: Is there a Need to Re-think How to Assess the Quality of Academic Research. *Walailak Journal Science and Technology.* 11(5):389-94. http://wjst.wu.ac.th/index.php/wjst/article/view/1004/385 .

Jalalian M. (2014). Hijacked Journals are attacking the Reliability and Validity of Medical Research. *Electron Physician.*; 6(4):925-6.

John Langan (2008). *College Writing Skills with Reading.* (7th Ed.) Boston: McGraw Hill Higher Education.

Johns, Ann M. (1997). Text, Role and Context: Developing Academic Literacies (Cambridge: Cambridge University Press)

Johnson, Samuel. "Abstract (noun)." *A Dictionary of the English Language*: A Digital Edition of the 1755 Classic by Samuel Johnson. Edited by Brandi Besalke.

Jordan, R. R. (1999). *Academic Writing Course: Study Skills in English* (3rd Ed.). Harlow, MA: Pearson Education.

Kamler, B., & Thomson, P. (2006). Helping Doctoral Students Write: Pedagogies for Supervision. London: Routledge.

Kantz, Margaret. (1990). Helping Students Use Textual Sources Persuasively. *College English,* 52.1: 74-91.

Kanvaria, Vinod Kumar (2018). *Academic Writing, Anti Plagiarism and Citations.* Delhi: Shipra Publications

Keck, C. (2006). The Use of Paraphrase in Summary Writing: A Comparison of L1 and L2 Writers. *Journal of Second Language Writing.* 15(4), 261–278.

—— (2014). Copying, Paraphrasing, and Academic Writing Development: A Re-examination of L1 and L2 Summarization Practices. *Journal of Second Language Writing.* 25(1), 4–22.

Kitchin, R. & Fuller, D. (2005). The Academic's Guide to Publishing. London, UK: Sage Publications.

Klausmeier, H.J. (2001). *Research Writing in Education and Psychology–from Planning to Publication.* Springfield, IL: Charles C. Thomas Publisher.

Klingner, J. K., Scanlon, D., & Pressley, M. (2005). How to Publish in Scholarly Journals. *Educational Researcher* 34(8), 14-20.

Lee, M. (2011). Finding Voice: Appreciating Audience in T. S. Rocco, & T. Hatcher (eds.), *The Handbook of Scholarly Writing and Publishing.* San Francisco: Jossey Bass.

Leki (1998). *Academic Writing: Exploring Processes and Strategies.* (2nd Ed.) New York: Cambridge.

Lester, J. D. (1996). *Writing Research Papers: The City University Style Manual* (8th Ed.). New York, NY: Harper Collins.

—— (1999). *Writing Research Papers: A Complete Guide* (9th Ed.). New York, NY: Addison-Wesley Educational Publishers.

Levin, P. (2004). *Write Great Essays: Reading and Essay Writing for Undergraduates.* London, New York, Open University Press.

Lillis, T. (1997). Essay Writing. In S. Drew & R. Bingham (Eds.). *The Student Skills Guide* (pp. 53-76 & 195-221). Aldershot: Gower.

—— (2003). Student Writing as ‹Academic Literacies›: Drawing on Bakhtin to move from critique to design. *Language and Education,* 17, 192-207.

—— & Curry, M. J. (2010). *Academic Writing in a Global Context: The Politics and Practices of Publishing in English.* London: Routledge.

Lillis, T. & Scott, M. (2007). Defining Academic Literacies Research: Issues of Epistemology, Ideology and Strategy. *Journal of Applied Linguistics*, 4, 5-32.

Lores, Rosa (2004) On RA Abstracts: From Rhetorical Structure to Thematic Organization. *English for Academic Purposes*, 23: 280–302.

Maton, K. (2013). Making Semantic Waves: A Key to Cumulative Knowledge-building. *Linguistics and Education*, 24(1), 8–22. http://dx.doi.org/10.1016/j.linged.2012.11.005

McMillan, J. H. & Schumacher, S. (2000). *Research in Education: A Conceptual Introduction* (5th ed). Addison-Wesley Educational Publishers.

Markham, R., Markham, P., & Waddell, M. (2001). *10 Steps in Writing the Research Paper* (6th Ed.). Happauge, NY: Barron's.

Martin, J. R. (1992). *English Texts: System and Structure.* Amsterdam: John Benjamins.

—— (1993). Genre and Literacy: Modelling Context in Educational Linguistics. *Annual Review of Applied Linguistics*, 13, 141-171

Matthews, J. R., Bowen, J. M. & Matthews, R. W. (2000). *Successful Scientific Writing.* Cambridge: Cambridge University Press.

Mauch, J. E. & Birch, J. W. (1993). *Guide to the Successful Thesis and Dissertation: A Handbook for Students and Faculty.* 3rd Ed. New York: Marcel Dekker.

Medawar, P. (1964). Is the Scientific Paper a Fraud? http://bioq.weblog.com/pt/arquivo/medawar.pdf.

Menasche, L. (1997). *Writing a Research Paper* (Rev. ed.). Ann Arbor: University of Michigan Press.

Mouton, J. (2001). How to Succeed in Your Master›s and Doctoral Studies, Pretoria: Van Schaik.

Moxley, J.M. (1992). *Publish, do not Perish: The Scholars Guide to Academic Writing and Publishing.* Westport, Connecticut: Greenwood Press.

—— & Taylor, T. (1997). *Writing and Publishing for Academic Authors.* Lanham, Maryland: Rowman & Littlefield Publishers, Inc.

Mulvanney, M. K. & Joliffe, D. A. (2005). *Academic Writing: Genres, Samples and Resources.* New York: Pearson Longman.

Murray, R. & Moore, S. (2006). *The Handbook of Academic Writing: A Fresh Approach.* Maidenhead: Open University Press.

Nesi, H. & Gardner, S. (2006). Variation in Disciplinary Culture: University Tutors' Views on Assessed Writing Tasks. In Keily, R., Clibbon, G., Rea-Dickins, P. & Woodfield, H. (Eds.), *Language, Culture, and Identity in Applied Linguistics* (British Studies in Applied Linguistics, Vol. 21). London: Equinox Publishing.

Neville, C. (2010). *The Complete Guide to Referencing and Avoiding Plagiarism.* 2nd Ed. Berkshire: Mc Graw Hill, Open University Press.

Olsen, G.A. (1997). Publishing Scholarship in Humanistic Disciplines: Joining the Conversation. In J.M Moxley & T. Taylor (Eds.), *Writing and Publishing for Academic Authors* (pp. 53–69). Lanham, MD: Rowman and Littlefield Publishers.

Pecorari, D. (2003). Good and Original: Plagiarism and Patchwriting in Academic Second-language Writing. *Journal of Second Language Writing.* 12(4), 317–345.

Pelias, Ronald J. (1999). *Writing Performance: Poeticizing the Researcher's Body* (Carbondale, IL: Southern Illinois University Press)

Pennebaker, J. W., Francis, M. E. & Booth, R. J. (2001). Linguistic Inquiry and Word Count: LIWC. Mahwah, NJ: Erlbaum.

Phyllis, Creme; Mary, Lea (2008). *Writing at University: A Guide for Students.* McGraw-Hill Education (UK).

Porter, James. (1986). Intertextuality and the Discourse Community. *Rhetoric Review.* 5.1: 34-47.

Ramage, J. D., Bean, J. C., & Johnson, J. (2003). *The Allyn and Bacon Guide to Writing*: Concise edition. New York, NY: Longman Publishers.

Reid, J. M. (2000). *The Process of Composition* (3rd Ed.). New York, NY: Prentice Hall Regents.

Reinking, J., Hart, A., & Von Der Osten, R. (1996). *Strategies for Successful Writing.* 4th Ed. New Jersey: Prentice Hall.

Richards, J. C. & Millers, S. K. (2005). *Doing Academic Writing in Education: Connecting the Personal to the Professional.* Mahwah, NJ: Lawrence Erlbaum Associates, Publishers.

Ridley, D. (2008). *The Literature Review: A Step-by-Step Guide for Students.* Sage.

Riebschleger, J. (2001). Writing a Dissertation: Lessons Learned. *Families in Society: The Journal of Contemporary Human Services,* 82(6), 579-82.

Rolls, N. & Wignell, P. (2013). *Communicating at University: Skills for Success.* Darwin Australia, Charles Darwin University Press.

Roozen, Kevin. (2015). Texts Get Their Meaning from Other Texts. Naming What We Know: Threshold Concepts in Writing Studies, Adler-Kassner & Wardle, eds. Logan: Utah State UP.

Samuels, Boba and Garbati, Jordana (2018). *Mastering Academic Writing.* SAGE.

Sansanwal, D. N. (2020). *Research Methodology and Applied Statistics.* Delhi: Shipra Publications.

Schriver, K. A. (1989). Evaluating Text Quality. *IEEE Transactions on Professional Communication,* 32(4), 238–55.

Sharples, M. (1999). *How We Write.* London: Routledge.

Smyth, T. R. (1996). *Writing in Psychology: A Student Guide.* New York: Wiley.

—— (2004). *The Principles of Writing in Psychology*: London: Palgrave Macmillan.

Stephen C. and Christopher Ireland. Developing Writing Skills for International Students: Adopting a critical pragmatic approach. ResearchGate.

Swales, J (1990). *The Concept of Discourse Community. Genre Analysis: English in Academic and Research Settings.* Boston: Cambridge University Press.

—— (1990). *Genre Analysis – English in Academic and Research Settings.* Cambridge: Cambridge University Press.

—— (2004). *Research Genres - Explorations and Applications.* Cambridge: Cambridge University Press.

—— and Feak, C. (1994). *Academic Writing for Graduate Students – A Course for Nonnative Speakers of English.* Ann Arbor: The University of Michigan Press.

Tardy. C. M. & Courtney, J. (2008). Assignments and Activities in Teaching Academic Writing in P. Friedrich (ed.), *Teaching Academic Writing.* New York: Contunuum.

Thomas, G. V. & Robinson, E. J. (1994). The Writing Strategies of Graduate Researchers in the Social Sciences. *Higher Education*, 27, 379–92.

Thompson, P. & Kamler, B. (2013). *Writing for Peer Reviewed Journals.* London: Routledge.

Thyer, B. (1994). *Successful Publishing in Scholarly Journals.* Thousand Oaks, CA: Sage Publications.

Turabian, K. (1996). *A Manual for Writers of Research Papers, Theses and Dissertations.* 6th ed. Revised by Grossman, J. & Bennet, A. Chicago: University of Chicago Press.

University of Birmingham (2015). A Short Guide to Referencing Figures and Tables for Postgraduate Taught Students. https://intranet.birmingham.ac.uk/as/libraryservices/library/skills/asc/documents/public/pgtreferencingtables.pdf.

University of Leeds (2019). Academic Writing: What is Academic Writing? https://library.leeds.ac.uk/info/14011/writing/106/academic_writing.

University of Manchester (2019). Academic Phrasebook: Being Critical. http://www.phrasebank.manchester.ac.uk/being-critical/.

University of Toronto (2019). Engineering Communication Program: Revising, Editing and Proofreading. https://ecp.engineering.utoronto.ca/resources/online-handbook/thewriting-process/revising-editing-and-proofreading/.

Van Til, W. (1986). Writing for Professional Publication. Boston, Massachusetts: Allyn and

Verheijen, L. (2015). The Language of Quoting in Academic Writing. *Dutch Journal of Applied Linguistics.* 4(1), 101–121.

Vintzileos, A. M., & Ananth, C. V. (2010). How to Write and Publish an Original Research Article. *American Journal of Obstetrics and Gynecology*, 202(344), e1–6.

Visser, N. (1992). *Handbook for Writers of Essays and Theses.* 2nd Ed. Cape Town: Maskew Miller Longman.

Wallace, M. & Gray, A. (2006). *Critical Reading and Writing for Postgraduates.* Los Angeles: Sage.

Walliman, N. (2001). *Your Research Project: A Step-by-Step Guide for the First-time Researcher.* London, England: Sage Publications.

Wellington, J. (2003). *Getting Published.* London: Routledge Falmer.

—— & Torgerson, C. J. (2005). Writing for Publication: What Counts as a 'high status, eminent academic journal'. *Journal of Further and High Education*, 29(1), 35-48.

Wilbers, S. (2000). *Keys to Great Writing.* Cincinnati, OH: Writer's Digest Books.

Wilcox, B. L. (2002). *Thinking and Writing for Publication: A Guide for Teachers.* Newark, DE.

Yates, C. St. J. (1988). *English for Academic Purposes - Earth Sciences.* London: Prentice Hall.

—— (1992a). *English for Academic Purposes - Agriculture.* London: Prentice Hall.

—— (1992b). *English for Academic Purposes - Economics.* London: Prentice Hall.

Zemach, D. E. & Rumisek, L. A. (2005). *Academic Writing: From Paragraph to Essay.* Oxford: Macmillan.